American Foreign Relations

Recent titles in
Contributions in American History

Series Editor: Jon L. Wakelyn

Farmers Without Farms: Agricultural Tenancy in Nineteenth-Century Iowa
Donald L. Winters

The Half-Opened Door: Discrimination and Admission at Harvard, Yale, and Princeton, 1900-1970
Marcia Graham Synnott

The Tarnished Dream: The Basis of American Anti-Semitism
Michael N. Dobkowski

Sobering Up: From Temperance to Prohibition in Antebellum America, 1800-1860
Ian R. Tyrrell

Alcohol, Reform, and Society: The Liquor Issue in Social Context
Jack S. Blocker, Jr.

War and Welfare: Social Engineering in America, 1890–1925
John F. McClymer

The Divided Metropolis: Social and Spatial Dimensions of Philadelphia, 1800–1975
William W. Cutler, III, and Howard Gillette, Jr.

The Southern Common People: Studies in Nineteenth-Century Social History
Edward Magdol and Jon L. Wakelyn

Northern Schools, Southern Blacks, and Reconstruction: Freedmen's Education, 1862–1875
Ronald E. Butchart

John Eliot's Indian Dialogues: A Study in Cultural Interaction
Henry W. Bowden and James P. Ronda

The XYZ Affair
William Stinchcombe

American Foreign Relations

A HISTORIOGRAPHICAL REVIEW

Edited by Gerald K. Haines
and J. Samuel Walker

Contributions in American History, Number 90

GREENWOOD PRESS WESTPORT, CONNECTICUT

Library of Congress Cataloging in Publication Data
Main entry under title:

American foreign relations, a historiographical review

(Contributions in American history; no. 90
ISSN 0084-9219)
Bibliography: p.
Includes index.
1. United States—Foreign relations—Addresses, essays, lectures. I. Haines, Gerald K., 1943–
II. Walker, J. Samuel.
E183.7.A56 327.73'009 80-545
ISBN 0-313-21061-6 (lib. bdg.)

Library of Congress Catalog Card Number: 80-545
ISBN: 0-313-21061-6
ISSN: 0084-9219

First published in 1981

Greenwood Press
A division of Congressional Information Service, Inc.
88 Post Road West, Westport, Connecticut 06881

Printed in the United States of America

10 9 8 7 6 5 4 3 2 1

To my mother and father
—J.S.W.

To Joanne
—G.K.H.

Contents

Acknowledgments

The editors gratefully acknowledge the efforts of scholars who reviewed individual essays at the request of their authors. John A. DeNovo, Milton O. Gustafson, Lawrence S. Kaplan, Arthur S. Link, Keith W. Olson, Aaron D. Miller, Thomas G. Paterson, David S. Patterson, Ronald E. Swerczek, and Thomas Zoumaras each criticized one essay; Wayne S. Cole and David F. Trask commented on more than one. George T. Mazuzan served as a perceptive critic, experienced counselor, and procurement specialist. Sara Strom of the National Archives Library provided valuable assistance by tracking down copies of scarce publications. We have also benefitted from the patience and encouragement of our wives, Pat Walker and Joanne Haines. We feel particularly indebted to our contributors, who responded to our unreasonable deadlines and irascible criticisms with remarkable promptness and good cheer.

Introduction

American diplomatic history has undergone a major reassessment in the past several years. During the late 1960s and early 1970s, revisionist interpretations of many aspects of the history of United States foreign relations stirred contentious debates and helped inspire an imposing body of monographs and articles on the course of American diplomacy. The growing volume of writings and the reexamination of a wide range of questions made it difficult even for specialists to keep abreast of all the developments and controversies. The essays in this volume are intended to illuminate the current status of United States diplomatic history by reviewing the relevant literature and by delineating past and present historiographical trends in the field.

The articles in this book provide a comprehensive review of the most significant literature in American diplomatic history. We have chosen topics to span the field as fully as possible, though some worthy subjects are omitted or receive more cursory treatment than they deserve. As a rule, the essays discuss historical writing on subjects through the 1940s; sources after that time are still limited and most work on the 1950s and 1960s is too recent for historiographical trends to emerge clearly. The various articles are also selective rather than exhaustive in their coverage. Some of them build on previously published historiographical surveys while others that lack adequate foundations start from naught. Neither the general subject classification nor the individual essays attempt to include all relevant writing. The forthcoming, updated edition of Samuel Flagg Bemis's and Grace Gardner Griffin's *Guide to the Diplomatic History of the United States* will feature a comprehensive listing of titles, but these essays seek to identify major works and seminal interpretations and place them in a historiographical framework.

Some readers may be disturbed by the lack of a uniform format in this book. Our initial impulse was to prescribe a standard structure; we soon decided, however, that since each topic was significantly different, imposing a rigid organizational scheme might sacrifice creativity for a contrived consistency. Therefore, we allowed the authors a great deal of leeway in determining the content, structure, and emphasis of their articles. To be sure, the reader will encounter the same basic interpretations: those of orthodox or traditional observers who defend, if not apologize for, American diplomatists; realist critics who deplore excessive moralism and legalism in United States foreign policy; and new left writers who condemn American overseas economic expansion. But the reader will also discover a wide variety of schools of thought (moderates, conservatives, anti-interventionists, neorealists, Beardians, and structuralists, for example) that are prominent in some topics but not in others. The identification of those groups emphasizes nuances of interpretation that could be lost by insistence on a standard format. To avoid confusion and ambiguity, we have asked that authors clearly explain their terminology.

The articles in this book, again by design, lack ideological consistency. We have not attempted to balance ideological approaches in selecting authors for this volume nor have we requested that they write from a single perspective. Most contributors have chosen a neutral tone, though some make their own points of view quite evident. In any case, the ideological inclinations of the authors were not a factor in their selection or the editorial process. Instead, our primary concern was that they write a thorough, fair-minded, and original essay.

Each of the articles is an independent contribution and can be considered apart from the other essays. Taken as a whole, however, the essays reveal broad trends and suggest opportunities for further research in United States diplomatic history. They make clear that the heated debates of the late 1960s and early 1970s have largely given way to the process of digesting, refining, and synthesizing. Although the disputes of that era have not been fully resolved, their tone has become more restrained and their divisions less sharp. In recent years, many studies have appeared that critically examine conflicting arguments and provide new syntheses. New left interpretations, though seldom accepted without qualification, have made a significant impact. Yet despite their influence, new left scholars have overlooked or given inadequate attention to some important subjects, particularly on topics before the Civil War.

The articles also indicate that new sources of information will continue to reshape and refocus United States diplomatic history. This is readily apparent on subjects covering the post-1945 period. Surprisingly, it is also true for the eighteenth and early nineteenth centuries and the World War I era because of the notable contributions of editorial projects that ferret out, compile, and publish the papers of key policymakers.

The essays indicate many areas that merit fuller investigation. Writings in diplomatic history have tended to focus on certain subjects while leaving others relatively untouched. Little has been published in recent years about American foreign policy in the eighteenth and first half of the nineteenth centuries and in many parts of the Third World. Although those topics have lacked the urgency and appeal of studies of United States policies during the World War I, World War II, and cold war eras, they deserve careful examination both because of their intrinsic importance and because of the insight they provide into the overall conduct of American foreign relations. Opportunities for fruitful research abound in a rich variety of other subjects as well.

Many of the contributors to this book stress the need to view international relations as contacts between cultures rather than simply between leaders or foreign offices. Concentration on formal diplomatic conferences and messages, though obviously important, too often produces narrow and one-dimensional studies of international exchanges. A fuller assessment of American foreign policy requires careful scrutiny of the societies, cultures, and traditions of the countries with which the United States interacted. In a similar manner, an understanding of how United States diplomacy is conducted will remain incomplete until the full range of influences on it are thoroughly explored. A wide variety of intellectual, political, economic, societal, bureaucratic, and personal factors enter into the formulation of United States foreign policy, though, of course, with varying importance in different situations. By fully considering the impact and the complexities of the dynamic forces that result in a certain course of action, diplomatic historians can help ensure that their writings will be as absorbing and meaningful as the events they seek to explain.

American Foreign Relations

1 ______ American Foreign Relations Before the Constitution: A Historiographical Wasteland

JONATHAN R. DULL

How exciting a prospect for historians: a period whose current histories soon will become little used, a period calling for a new generation of scholars. In general the historiography of American foreign relations before the ratification of the Constitution is not a battleground of conflicting interpretations but a wasteland of outdated scholarship. If a tendency toward hagiography has been partially responsible for this state of affairs, a more fundamental cause has been the use of inadequate sources. The most exciting development in the period does not come from new monographs or interpretations but from the appearance of adequately edited (or catalogued) primary sources. This development is so recent that only a few scholars have yet tapped the new material. Within the next few years this largely dormant period in diplomatic history may well provide some of the most vibrant opportunities for scholarly research. This is not a denigration of past historians but is, rather, a recognition that any historian is only as good as his sources. Edward Corwin, for example, was an excellent diplomatic historian—thorough, imaginative, sophisticated, supple. His work, however, is seriously flawed by his lack of access to necessary evidence, a problem his successors need no longer face.[1]

The initial problem in studying American foreign relations is to fix their beginnings. Historians have considered America's place in the British Empire[2] and shown the relationship of American diplomacy to its colonial origins[3] and to such preexisting conditions as America's geographical isolation. Although one cannot date precisely the origins of America as a major object of European diplomacy,[4] clearly the middle of the 18th century was a time of critical quickening. By the 1750s American colonial affairs assumed new importance to the British government and American territorial disputes increasingly concerned British and other European diplomats. America no longer was merely the unwilling beneficiary of Europeans' enthusiasm for killing one another. In the collision with the French near the Ohio River, Virginians enjoyed for the first time the honor of helping to start their own war.[5]

Searching questions need to be asked about the origins of this war, but perhaps even more important is a change of perspective. The Great War for the Empire was not a glorious triumph for the cause of human freedom but a tragic and at least postponable conflict between two peoples with much in common. W. J. Eccles's *France in America* is enormously useful in pointing out the similarities between New France and the British colonies, which until the 1750s had managed to limit their hostilities.[6] The conquest of New France was a disaster for the conquerors as well as for the conquered because it undermined the basis of British usefulness to America. This point has been acknowledged by Lawrence Henry Gipson, a proconquest chronicler of the war,[7] but a less romantic view of the war is needed—one which will question its necessity and fully recognize its destructiveness. One model for such an assessment is John Shy's superb *Toward Lexington*, which shows the deleterious effects on colonial relations of the introduction of a large standing army into America.[8] Diplomatic historians have yet to show the disastrous effects of the war on British diplomacy.[9] Indeed there is no general survey of British diplomacy between 1763 and 1775, nor, in spite of numerous dissertations and monographs on the duc de Choiseul, of French diplomacy. Perhaps the best introduction to France's English and American policy after 1763 is still the opening chapters of Corwin's book.[10]

With the disappearance of the French threat America entered a brief period in which foreign relations declined to insignificance.[11] Relations with the mother country are part of American political history rather than diplomatic history; in spite of some resemblances to diplomats, colonial agents were chiefly lobbyists and political liaisons.[12] Even during his mysterious and complex negotiations with the British cabinet in the winter of 1774-1775 Benjamin Franklin claimed no power to speak for the Continental Congress.[13] The origins of American diplomacy date from well after Lexington and Concord. The delegates to the second Continental Congress had to confront the same ambiguity which underlies all of American colonial history. From the founding of Jamestown the American experience differed from that of Britain, yet the inhabitants of the

American colonies were participants in a British political and cultural heritage few wished to repudiate. Economically, Americans shared in an empire which conveyed benefits, even if distributed unevenly; if Americans saw in British society dangers to be avoided, they also perceived themselves as the heirs of more virtuous generations of Britons. At least through the end of 1775 it is apparent most leaders of British America saw themselves as both Britons and Americans; only the course of the war itself with its accumulation of bitterness caused for American "patriots" the final divorce (a divorce which many other Americans, the "loyalists," were unable to accept).

The records of the Continental Congress itself perhaps are the best source of information for the development of American independence in foreign relations. These papers still need much study, partly because until now they have not been fully indexed. The appearance of this index greatly facilitates research.[14] Scholars long have had easier access to the official proceedings of the Continental Congress,[15] but because these do not include debates they must be supplemented by the diaries and letters of individual delegates. The 8-volume edition of *Letters of Members of the Continental Congress*, published more than 40 years ago, is now being replaced by a vastly expanded edition.[16] The most detailed study of congressional proceedings is still Edmund Cody Burnett's *The Continental Congress*, published in 1941.[17]

The use of new materials and techniques has permitted a far more sophisticated understanding of congressional politics. Historians differ on the meaning of the data. Jack N. Rakove has found a high degree of congressional consensus, H. James Henderson, the beginning of party divisions.[18] Jackson Turner Main has used roll-call analysis to study the origins of political parties on the state level. His study, unlike those of Rakove and Henderson, unfortunately has little to say about the effect of political attitudes on foreign affairs.[19] Of exceptional importance to students of foreign affairs are the superbly researched books of E. James Ferguson on the financing of the American Revolution and of William C. Stinchcombe on public and congressional opinions of the French alliance.[20] These studies show the ever-increasing dependence of America on France for financial and military support after 1778. A striking example of the importance of using new materials is James H. Hutson's careful analysis of the prevailing attitudes on foreign policy in 1776.[21] Using materials assembled for *Letters of Delegates to Congress*, he has found neither isolationism nor an idealistic internationalism, but rather a sweeping consensus that American independence was dependent on balancing Britain against France. The consensus lasted until the 1790s. Hutson persuasively refutes the major thesis of Felix Gilbert, who argued that American attitudes were grounded in the isolationism of British Whigs and the internationalism of French philosophes.[22]

Few diplomatic historians as yet have produced comparable breakthroughs. In many respects the best survey of American wartime diplomacy is still Samuel Flagg Bemis's *The Diplomacy of the American Revolution*, first published in 1935 and almost entirely dependent on published sources.[23] Richard W. Van Alstyne's *Empire and Independence* is based largely on Tory pamphlets with predictably strange results.[24] The most important recent study of American diplomacy is Richard Morris's account of the peace negotiations of 1782-1783, *The Peacemakers*.[25] Morris has done extensive archival research and unearthed valuable information but his book is badly flawed by anti-French bias, an almost total ignorance of the military background to the negotiations and an obsessive preoccupation with tracing the movements of secret agents.

Any new survey may be premature, however. The standard collections of diplomatic documents are inadequate,[26] but given the lack of a central directing authority behind American diplomacy, the first necessity is detailed study of the leading individual American diplomats and statesmen. Such works are dependent on adequate source materials. Scholars already have access through microfilm to the papers of statesmen like John Adams (Massachusetts Historical Society) and Henry Laurens (South Carolina Historical Society). These unedited collections, however, are not equivalent to modern scholarly editions, which provide not only a complete documentary record but also detailed discussion of the documents and identification of the people and events mentioned. The publication of new editions of the papers of Benjamin Franklin, John Adams, John Jay, Robert Morris, Henry Laurens, George Washington, Alexander Hamilton, James Madison, Thomas Jefferson, and others represent numerous years of research. They should further greatly the more balanced appraisal of the founding fathers needed for a modern diplomatic history of the Revolution.

Franklin has attracted an enormous number of biographers and yet there is no adequate study of his mission to France. Future scholars will find useful Gerald Stourzh's perceptive work on Franklin's ideas on foreign policy and Claude-Anne Lopez's work on his private life in France,[27] but the best general biography of Franklin was written almost forty years ago by Carl Van Doren.[28] In preparation now, however, is volume twenty-two of *The Papers of Benjamin Franklin*, covering his eighteen months in Congress, and subsequent volumes will follow him to France.[29] Members of the staff of the Franklin Papers have already produced a number of articles on his French mission.[30] A new picture is emerging of Franklin not as a mythic embodiment of America but as a dedicated and professional diplomat laboring with such problems as the relief and exchange of war prisoners and the sending of supplies to the American army.

We are even closer perhaps to a more realistic appraisal of John Adams. James Hutson has published a major work on Adams's diplomacy; in addition, a biography by Peter Shaw makes imaginative use of psychoanalytical techniques.[31] Shaw is weakest on Adams as a practicing diplomat, but Hutson gives a detailed assessment as will the coming volumes of *The Adams Papers*. The *Adams Family Correspondence* is complete through September 1782 and work is in progress on volumes five and six of *The Papers of John Adams*, extending to October 1778.[32]

Of great use are the two published volumes of *The Papers of John Jay*.[33] Although comparable in scholarship to the other modern papers projects, it is only a selective edition that will not totally replace an earlier work.[34] There is no adequate biography of Jay, although Morris's *The Peacemakers* gives a great deal of information about his mission to Spain and participation in the peace negotiations.[35]

Because of the close connection between economics and diplomacy, historians should find enormously useful the superb edition of *The Papers of Robert Morris*.[36] Morris's importance can hardly be overestimated and opportunities for historians still await. (The next volume of *The Papers of Benjamin Franklin*, for example, will reveal something of the frequently ignored close political connection between Morris and Franklin).

Students of Laurens and Washington will have to be more patient. The splendid edition of *The Henry Laurens Papers* has not yet reached the Revolution,[37] and although six volumes of Washington's diaries have appeared, we are still awaiting the beginning of publication of his correspondence.[38] The Madison, Hamilton, and Jefferson papers are complete for the period of the Revolution.[39]

A full understanding of the diplomacy of the American Revolution also will be dependent on adequate study of lesser figures such as Robert Livingston, Richard Henry Lee, William Lee, Arthur Lee, Silas Deane, Francis Dana, William Bingham, Ralph Izard, William Carmichael, and C. W. F. Dumas.[40] While some recent work on them has appeared, much remains to be done. Some good work also has appeared using a thematic approach (particularly in studying some subjects such as international law),[41] but there is a particular danger in studying individual negotiations in isolation. Studies of the alliance negotiations or the Hussey-Cumberland negotiations, for example, now seem particularly antiquated.[42] A major difficulty in the study of negotiations has been the lack of reliable monographs on French, British, Spanish, and Dutch diplomacy. Much of the weakness of Corwin and Bemis's work has been its dependence on published sources.[43] By contrast my book, *The French Navy and American Independence*, based on research in both French diplomatic and naval archives, uses primary evidence to downplay the significance to French diplomacy of events in America (such as the battles of Long Island and Saratoga) and to emphasize European balance-of-power considerations and the indispensability of the Spanish military contribution.[44]

Other work is currently in progress on the French participation in the Revolution. Brian Morton and Orville T. Murphy, the authors of splendid articles on Caron de Beaumarchais and the Comte de Vergennes,[45] are nearing completion of books. Morton is also preparing a new edition of the correspondence of Beaumarchais, and Stanley Idzerda a selected edition of the papers of the Marquis de Lafayette.[46] For French public opinion there is the fine work of Durand Echeverria and for the French military presence in America a magnificent collection of memoirs and Lee Kennett's prize-winning monograph.[47] Somewhat older but still useful is John J. Meng's edition of the correspondence of Conrad-Alexandre Gérard and William E. O'Donnell's biography of the Chevalier de La Luzerne.[48]

British diplomacy by comparison has been neglected, perhaps because of the heavy concentration on political history by British historians. Studies currently available include: a masterpiece, Isabel de Madariaga's incomparable discussion of Sir James Harris's mission to St. Petersburg; a rather pedestrian account of Sir Joseph Yorke's mission to the Hague; and a scholarly if rather turgid analysis of Shelburne's diplomacy.[49] For the postwar period there are John Ehrman's magisterial studies of Pitt's government and the opening chapters of Charles R. Ritcheson's book on British-American relations.[50] Still lacking are significant studies of Secretaries of State Stormont, Suffolk, Weymouth, Hillsborough or Grantham. Fox can use further debunking (in spite of Madariaga's fine efforts) and Shelburne and North deserve more attention. The picture is even worse for the other belligerents in the war. Because Simon Schama's monumental study of Dutch politics in the period neglects diplomacy, Dutch historians are dependent on outdated work.[51] Spanish diplomacy remains virtually unexplored.[52] The research opportunities for eighteenth-century European diplomatic historians still are almost unlimited.

Unlike 1763, Americans at the end of the Revolution could not simply forget foreign affairs. They still had to face such major problems as British trade discrimination, British refusal to evacuate frontier posts, and Spanish restrictions on American use of the Mississippi. The effectiveness of Confederation government long has been the subject of debate.[53] Defenders of the Confederation have tended to minimize the significance of such problems,[54] while critics of the Confederation have assigned them more importance. One critic, Frederick W. Marks, holds that America's inability to resolve foreign policy problems was a major factor in the adoption of the Constitution,[55] a view seconded by Henderson's book on party politics.[56] Other than general treatments of Confederation foreign policy, the best work on the period has been done on Jefferson's mission to Paris, the subject of eight volumes of Boyd's edition of *The Papers of Thomas Jefferson*, a volume of Malone's great biography of Jefferson and of several articles.[57] Comparable work on Adams's and Franklin's missions probably will have to await the far-distant publication of the relevant volumes of the Franklin and Adams papers.

The initial period of American diplomatic history has not brought out the best in diplomatic historians. Perhaps it is the stature of the founding fathers that has produced in historians the tendency toward either hero worship or shallow cynicism.[58] The massive editorial projects in progress will permit historians to enter into the daily lives of the fathers. The resulting detailed work can hardly help but be more balanced and realistic.[59] More, however, will be needed. It is particularly unfortunate that this period of American history has been relatively neglected by new left historians; the businessmen and statesmen of the period were no less expansionist than their successors but new left historians seem less comfortable with the sources.[60] Certainly no period stands in greater need of lively and informed debate. There have been few historians like James Hutson to ask fundamental questions about the foundations of American diplomacy. The Revolution itself partakes of the simultaneous American traditions of aggressive and violent outward-turning and parochial inward-turning, yet one also can find in it a concern for the rule of law and for peaceful intercourse between nations. Unless the potential revolution in revolutionary historiography prompts a reexamination of the fundamental contradictions within American diplomacy it cannot be counted fully a success.

Notes

1. Edward S. Corwin, *French Policy and the American Alliance of 1778* (Princeton: Princeton University Press, 1916).

2. *See* Robert L. Middlekauff, "The American Continental Colonies in the Empire," in Frank Otto Gatell and Allen Weinstein, eds., *American Themes: Essays in Historiography* (New York: Oxford University Press, 1968), pp. 3-25.

3. Max Savelle, "Colonial Origins of American Diplomatic Principles," *Pacific Historical Review* 3 (September 1934): 334-50.

4. Max Savelle, *The Origins of American Diplomacy: The International History of Angloamerica, 1492-1763* (New York: Macmillan Co., 1967) treats this subject.

5. Excluded from discussion because they are outside the scope of this article are the repeated wars of extermination against native Americans and the diplomatic histories of New France, the various Caribbean colonies, Spanish America, and Canada.

6. W. J. Eccles, *France in America* (New York: Harper & Row, 1972). *See also* Patrice Louis-René Higonnet, "The Origin of the Seven Years War," *Journal of Modern History* 40 (March 1968): 57-90.

7. Lawrence Henry Gipson, *The British Empire before the American Revolution*, 15 vols. (Caldwell, Idaho: Caxton Printers [vols. 1-3] and New York: Alfred A. Knopf [vols. 4-15], 1936-1970).

8. John Shy, *Toward Lexington: The Role of the British Army in the Coming of the American Revolution* (Princeton: Princeton University Press, 1965).

9. The most recent studies of Pitt are Stanley Ayling, *The Elder Pitt, Earl of Chatham* (London: Collins, 1976) and Peter Douglas Brown, *William Pitt, Earl of Chatham* (Boston: George Allen & Unwin, 1978).

10. Corwin, *French Policy*, pp. 1-53.

11. Max Savelle, "The Appearance of an American Attitude toward External Affairs," *American Historical Review* 52 (July 1947): 655-66, notes that between 1763 and 1774 Americans gave little thought to Anglo-French relations.

12. The best introduction to the colonial agents is in the collective biography and analysis by Michael G. Kammen, *A Rope of Sand: The Colonial Agents, British Politics and the American Revolution* (Ithaca: Cornell University Press, 1968). More traditional in approach is Jack M. Sosin, *Agents and Merchants: British Colonial Policy and the Origins of the American Revolution* (Lincoln: University of Nebraska Press, 1965).

13. For these negotiations *see* William B. Wilcox, ed., *The Papers of Benjamin Franklin*, vol. 21, *January 1, 1774 through March 22, 1775* (New Haven: Yale University Press, 1978).

14. John P. Butler, comp., *The Papers of the Continental Congress: Index*, 5 vols. (Washington: Government Printing Office, 1978). The papers themselves are available in 204 rolls of microfilm from the National Archives, Washington, D.C.

15. Worthington Chauncy Ford et al., eds., *Journals of the Continental Congress*, 35 vols. (Washington, D.C.: Library of Congress, 1904-1976).

16. Edmund Cody Burnett, ed., *Letters of Members of the Continental Congress*, 8 vols. (Washington, D.C.: Carnegie Institution, 1921-1936), now being replaced by Paul H. Smith, ed., *Letters of Delegates to Congress, 1774-1789*, 6 vols. to date (Washington, D.C.: Library of Congress, 1976-).

17. Edmund Cody Burnett, *The Continental Congress* (New York: Macmillan Co., 1941).

18. Jack N. Rakove, *The Beginnings of National Politics: An Interpretive History of the Continental Congress* (New York: Alfred A. Knopf, 1979); H. James Henderson, *Party Politics in the Continental Congress* (New York: McGraw-Hill, 1974).

19. Jackson Turner Main, *Political Parties before the Constitution* (Chapel Hill: University of North Carolina Press, 1973).

20. E. James Ferguson, *The Power of the Purse: A History of American Public Finance, 1776-1790* (Chapel Hill: University of North Carolina Press, 1961); William C. Stinchcombe, *The American Revolution and the French Alliance* (Syracuse: Syracuse University Press, 1969). Also useful for congressional handling of diplomacy is Irving Brant, *James Madison: The Nationalist, 1780-1787* (Indianapolis: Bobbs-Merrill Co., 1948).

21. James H. Hutson, "Intellectual Foundations of Early American Diplomacy," *Diplomatic History* 1 (Winter 1977): 1-19.

22. Felix Gilbert, *To the Farewell Address: Ideas of Early American Foreign Policy* (Princeton: Princeton University Press, 1961). Also provocative is Edmund Morgan, "The Puritan Ethic and the American Revolution," *William and Mary Quarterly*, 3d ser. 24 (January 1967): 3-43.

23. Samuel Flagg Bemis, *The Diplomacy of the American Revolution*, rev. ed. (Bloomington: Indiana University Press, 1957).

24. Richard W. Van Alstyne, *Empire and Independence: The International History of the American Revolution* (New York: John Wiley & Sons, 1965).

25. Richard B. Morris, *The Peacemakers: The Great Powers and American Independence* (New York: Harper & Row, 1965). *See also* Morris, "The Treaty of Paris of 1783" in *Fundamental Testaments of the American Revolution* (Washington, D.C.: Library of Congress, 1973), pp. 82-107.

26. The standard collection of wartime diplomatic source materials is Francis Wharton, ed., *The Revolutionary Diplomatic Correspondence of the United States*, 6 vols. (Washington, D.C.: Government Printing Office, 1889). In spite of its inaccuracies and incompleteness Wharton is far superior to the collection of documents for the postwar period, *The Diplomatic Correspondence of the United States from the Signing of the Definitive Treaty of Peace, 10th September 1783, to the Adoption of the Constitution, March 4, 1789,* 7 vols. (Washington, D.C.: Francis Preston Blair, 1833-1834).

27. Gerald Stourzh, *Benjamin Franklin and American Foreign Policy*, rev. ed. (Chicago: University of Chicago Press, 1969); Claude-Anne Lopez, *Mon Cher Papa: Franklin and the Ladies of Paris* (New Haven: Yale University Press, 1966); Claude-Anne Lopez and Eugenia W. Herbert, *The Private Franklin: The Man and His Family* (New York: W. W. Norton & Co., 1975).

28. Carl Van Doren, *Benjamin Franklin* (New York: Garden City Publishing Co., 1941). David Schoenbrun, *Triumph in Paris: The Exploits of Benjamin Franklin* (New York: Harper & Row, 1976) is heavily dependent on Van Doren and adds little. Cecil B. Currey, *Code Number 72/Benjamin Franklin: Patriot or Spy* (Englewood Cliffs, N.J.: Prentice-Hall, 1972) is based on surmise and on documents quoted out of context. Still of some use for understanding Franklin's activities in France are two books by William Bell Clark, *Lambert Wickes, Sea Raider and Diplomat: The Story of a Naval Captain of the Revolution* (New Haven: Yale University Press, 1932) and *Ben Franklin's Privateers: A Naval Epic of the American Revolution* (Baton Rouge: Louisiana State University Press, 1956).

29. Leonard W. Labaree and William B. Willcox, eds., *The Papers of Benjamin Franklin*, 21 vols. to date (New Haven: Yale University Press, 1959-). Until the Yale edition reaches Franklin's mission to France, historians will be dependent on older editions, the best of which is Albert Henry Smyth, *The Writings of Benjamin Franklin*, 10 vols. (New York: Macmillan Co., 1907).

30. These articles include Claude-Anne Lopez, "Benjamin Franklin, Lafayette, and the *Lafayette*," *Proceedings of the American Philosophical Society* 108 (1964): 181-223; Catherine M. Prelinger, "Benjamin Franklin and the American Prisoners of War in England during the American Revolution," *William and Mary Quarterly*, 3d ser., 32 (April 1975): 263-94; and "Less Lucky than Lafayette: A Note on the French Applicants to Benjamin Franklin for Commissions in the American Army, 1776-1785," *Proceedings of the Fourth Annual Meeting of the Western Society for French History* (1976): 263-70.

31. James H. Hutson, *John Adams and the Diplomacy of the American Revolution* (Lexington: University Press of Kentucky, 1980); Peter Shaw, *The Character of John Adams* (Chapel Hill: University of North Carolina Press, 1976).

32. L. H. Butterfield and Marc Friedlander, eds., *Adams Family Correspondence*, 4 vols. to date (Cambridge, Mass.: Harvard University Press, Belknap Press, 1963-); Robert J. Taylor, ed., *Papers of John Adams*, 4 vols. to date (Cambridge, Mass.:

Harvard University Press, Belknap Press, 1977-). Already complete are L. H. Butterfield, ed., *Diary and Autobiography of John Adams*, 4 vols. (Cambridge, Mass.: Harvard University Press, Belknap Press, 1961).

33. The first two of the four projected volumes have been published as Richard Morris, ed., *John Jay: The Making of a Revolutionary; Unpublished Papers, 1745-1780* (New York: Harper & Row, 1975) and *John Jay: The Winning of the Peace; Unpublished Papers, 1780-1784* (New York: Harper & Row, 1980).

34. Herbert P. Johnston, ed., *The Correspondence and Public Papers of John Jay*, 4 vols. (New York: G. P. Putnam's Sons, 1890-1893).

35. The current standard biography is Frank Monaghan, *John Jay, Defender of Liberty* (New York: Bobbs-Merrill Co., 1935).

36. E. James Ferguson, ed., *The Papers of Robert Morris, 1781-1784*, 5 vols. to date (Pittsburgh: University of Pittsburgh Press, 1973-). Inferior to Ferguson's *Power of the Purse* but still useful is Clarence L. Ver Steeg, *Robert Morris, Revolutionary Financier* (Philadelphia: University of Pennsylvania Press, 1954).

37. Philip M. Hamer et al., eds., *The Henry Laurens Papers*, 7 vols. to date (Columbia, S.C.: University of South Carolina Press, 1968-). For a biography of Laurens *see* David Duncan Wallace, *The Life of Henry Laurens* (New York: G. P. Putnam's Sons, 1915).

38. Donald Jackson, ed., *The Diaries of George Washington*, 6 vols. to date (Charlottesville, Va.: University Press of Virginia, 1976-1979).

39. Also of importance for diplomatic historians is William Bell Clark and William James Morgan, eds., *Naval Documents of the American Revolution*, 8 vols. to date (Washington, D.C.: Government Printing Office, 1964-).

40. Collections of correspondence for these men are: Paul P. Hoffman, ed., *Lee Family Papers, 1742-1795* (8 rolls of microfilm, Curator of Manuscripts, Charlottesville, Va., University of Virginia Library, 1966); James Curtis Ballagh, ed., *The Letters of Richard Henry Lee*, 2 vols. (New York: Macmillan Co., 1911-1914); Worthington Chauncy Ford, ed., *Letters of William Lee*, 3 vols. (Brooklyn: Historical Printing Club, 1891); Richard Henry Lee, ed., *Life of Arthur Lee, LL.D.*, 2 vols. (Boston: Wells and Lilly, 1829); Charles Isham, ed., *The Deane Papers*, 5 vols. (New York: Collections of the New York Historical Society, [vols. 19-23] 1897-1891), and *The Deane Papers: Correspondence between Silas Deane, His Brothers and Their Business and Political Associates, 1771-1795* (Hartford, Conn.: Collections of the Connecticut Historical Society, [vol. 23] 1930). Biographical studies (varying enormously in quality) include George Dangerfield, *Chancellor Robert R. Livingston of New York, 1746-1813* (New York: Harcourt, Brace & Co., 1960); Oliver Perry Chitwood, *Richard Henry Lee: Statesman of the Revolution* (Morgantown, W.Va.: West Virginia University Library, 1967); Coy Hilton James, *Silas Deane—Patriot or Traitor?* (East Lansing: Michigan State University Press, 1975); David M. Griffiths, "American Commercial Diplomacy in Russia, 1780-1783," *William and Mary Quarterly*, 3d ser. 27 (July 1970): 379-410 [on Dana's mission]; Robert C. Alberts, *The Golden Voyage: The Life and Times of William Bingham, 1752-1804* (Boston: Houghton Mifflin Co., 1969); Samuel Gwynn Coe, "The Mission of William Carmichael to Spain," (Ph.D. diss., Johns Hopkins University, 1926); J. W. Schulte Nordholte, "Dumas, the First American Diplomat," *New Edinburgh Review* 35-36 (1976): 17-24.

41. A fine example is Gregg L. Lint, "The Law of Nations and the American Revolution," pp. 111-33 in Lawrence S. Kaplan, ed., *The American Revolution and "A Candid World"* (Kent, Ohio: Kent State University Press, 1977). Older works using a thematic approach include George C. Wood, "Congressional Control of Foreign Relations during the American Revolution" (Ph.D. diss., New York University, 1919); Vernon G. Setser, "Did Americans Invent the Conditional Most-Favored-Nation Clause?", *Journal of Modern History* 5 (September 1933): 319-23; Gaillard Hunt, *The Department of State of the United States: Its History and Functions* (New Haven: Yale University Press, 1914).

42. Examples of the dangers of studying individual negotiations out of context are: Samuel Flagg Bemis, *The Hussey-Cumberland Mission and American Independence* (Princeton: Princeton University Press, 1931); Claude H. Van Tyne, "Influences Which Determined the French Government to Make the Treaty with America, 1778," *American Historical Review* 21 (April 1916): 528-41; and Morris's *The Peacemakers.*

43. This is particularly dangerous for French historians because the published sources are extremely biased: Henri Doniol, ed., *Histoire de la participation de la France à l'etablissement des Etats-Unis d'Amérique*, 6 vols. (Paris: Imprimerie Nationale, 1885-1892). Other published collections of sources for foreign diplomacy include Benjamin Franklin Stevens, *Facsimiles of Manuscripts in European Archives relating to America, 1775-1783*, 25 vols. (London: privately printed, 1889-1898); L. G. Wickham Legg, *British Diplomatic Instructions, 1689-1789* (London: Royal Historical Society, 1934), 7, *France, pt. 4, 1745-1789*; Sir John Fortescue, *The Correspondence of King George the Third from 1760 to December 1783*, 6 vols. (London: Macmillan & Co. 1927-1928); Juan F. Yela Utrilla, *España ante la independencia de los Estados Unidos*, 2 vols. (Lérida: Mariana, 1925); Marvin L. Brown, *American Independence through Prussian Eyes: A Neutral View of the Peace Negotiations of 1782-1783; Selections from the Prussian Diplomatic Correspondence* (Durham: Duke University Press, 1959); Sir Francis Piggot and G. W. T. Omond, *Documentary History of the Armed Neutralities, 1780 and 1800* (London: University of London Press, 1919).

44. Jonathan R. Dull, *The French Navy and American Independence: A Study of Arms and Diplomacy, 1774-1787* (Princeton: Princeton University Press, 1975). For a conflicting view of French diplomacy also based on extensive archival research *see* Robert R. Crout, "The Diplomacy of Trade: The Influence of Commercial Considerations on French Involvement in the Anglo-American War of Independence, 1775-78" (Ph.D. diss., University of Georgia, 1977).

45. Brian N. Morton, "Beaumarchais, Francy, Steuben, and Lafayette: An Unpublished Correspondence or 'Feux de joye' at Valley Forge," *French Review* 49 (May 1976): 943-59; and " 'Roderigue Hortalez' to the Secret Committee: An Unpublished French Policy Statement of 1777," *French Review* 50 (May 1977): 875-90; Orville T. Murphy, "The Comte de Vergennes, the Newfoundland Fisheries and the Peace Negotiations of 1782: A Reappraisal," *Canadian Historical Review* 46 (March 1965): 32-46; and "Charles Gravier de Vergennes: Portrait of an Old Régime Diplomat," *Political Science Quarterly* 83 (September 1968): 400-418.

46. Brian N. Morton and Donald C. Spinelli, eds. *Beaumarchais Correspondence*, 4 vols. to date (Paris: A. G. Nizet, 1969-); Stanley J. Idzerda, ed., *Lafayette in the*

Age of the American Revolution: Selected Letters and Papers, 1776-1790, 2 vols. to date (Ithaca: Cornell University Press, 1977-).

47. Durand Echeverria, *Mirage in the West: A History of the French Image of American Society to 1815* (Princeton: Princeton University Press, 1957); Howard C. Rice, Jr., and Anne S. K. Brown, *The American Campaigns of Rochambeau's Army, 1780, 1781, 1782, 1783*, 2 vols. (Princeton: Princeton University Press, 1972); Lee Kennett, *The French Forces in America, 1730-1783* (Westport, Conn.: Greenwood Press, 1977). A worthy companion to Echeverria's book is Horst Dippel, *Germany and the American Revolution, 1770-1800: A Sociohistorical Investigation of Late Eighteenth-Century Political Thinking* (Chapel Hill: University of North Carolina Press, 1977). The pioneering work for the study of the American Revolution's impact on Europe was Robert R. Palmer, *The Age of the Democratic Revolution: A Political History of Europe and America, 1760-1800*, 2 vols. (Princeton: Princeton University Press, 1959-1964).

48. John J. Meng, ed., *Despatches and Instructions of Conrad Alexandre Gérard, 1778-1780* (Baltimore: Johns Hopkins Press, 1939); William E. O'Donnell, *The Chevalier de la Luzerne, French Minister to the United States, 1779-1784* (Bruges: Desclée de Brouwer, 1938).

49. Isabel de Madariaga, *Britain, Russia, and the Armed Neutrality of 1780: Sir James Harris's Mission to St. Petersburg during the American Revolution* (New Haven: Yale University Press, 1962); Daniel A. Miller, *Sir Joseph Yorke and Anglo-Dutch Relations, 1774-1780* (The Hague: Mouton, 1970); Vincent T. Harlow, *The Founding of the Second British Empire* (London: Longmans, Green and Co., 1952). vol. 1, *Discovery and Revolution*. There also are studies of Anglo-American negotiations such as Weldon A. Brown, *Empire or Independence: A Study in the Failure of Reconciliation, 1774-1783* (Baton Rouge: Louisiana State University Press, 1941) and Charles R. Ritcheson, *British Politics and the American Revolution* (Norman: University of Oklahoma Press, 1954). The best military history of the war, Piers Mackesy, *The War for America, 1775-1783* (Cambridge, Mass.: Harvard University Press, 1965) contains some discussion of diplomacy.

50. John Ehrman, *The British Government and Commercial Negotiations with Europe, 1783-1793* (Cambridge: At the University Press, 1962); John Ehrman, *The Younger Pitt* (London: Constable and Company, 1969), vol. 1, *The Years of Acclaim*; Charles R. Ritcheson, *Aftermath of Revolution: British Policy toward the United States, 1783-1795* (Dallas: Southern Methodist University Press, 1969).

51. Simon Schama, *Patriots and Liberators: Revolution in the Netherlands, 1780-1813* (New York: Alfred A. Knopf, 1977). Older works include Friedrich Edler, *The Dutch Republic and the American Revolution* (Baltimore: Johns Hopkins Press, 1911) and Francis P. Renaut, *Les Provinces-Unis et la guerre d'Amérique (1775-1884): De la neutralité à la belligérance (1775-1780)* (Paris: Graouli, 1931).

52. Among the few works dealing with Spanish diplomacy are: Richard Konetze, *Die Politik des Grafen Aranda* (Berlin: Emil Ebering, 1929); Manuel Danvila y Collado, *Reinado de Carlos III* (Madrid: El Progreso Editorial, 1896), vol. 5, and Mario Rodriguez, *La Revolucion Americana de 1776 y El Mundo Hispanico: Essayos y Documentos* (Madrid: Editorial Tecnos, 1976). For Russian diplomacy, see Nikolai N. Bolkhovitinov, *The Beginnings of Russian-American Relations 1775-1815*, trans. Elena Levin (Cambridge, Mass.: Harvard University Press, 1975).

53. For an introduction to this debate *see* Richard B. Morris, "The Confederation Period and the American Historian," in Gatell and Weinstein, *American Themes*, pp. 81-99.

54. *See* particularly Merrill Jensen, *The New Nation: A History of the United States during the Confederation* (New York: Alfred A. Knopf, 1950).

55. Frederick W. Marks, III, *Independence on Trial: Foreign Affairs and the Making of the Constitution* (Baton Rouge: Louisiana State University Press, 1973), is the only full-length analysis of foreign relations between 1783 and 1787. *See also* Samuel Flagg Bemis, *Pinckney's Treaty: A Study of America's Advantage from Europe's Distress, 1783-1800* (Baltimore: Johns Hopkins Press, 1926).

56. Henderson, *Party Politics*, pp. 383-429.

57. Julian Boyd, ed., *The Papers of Thomas Jefferson*, 19 vols. to date (Princeton: Princeton University Press, 1950-); Dumas Malone, *Jefferson and the Rights of Man* (Boston: Little, Brown & Co., 1951); Julian Boyd, "Two Diplomats between Revolutions, John Jay and Thomas Jefferson," *Virginia Magazine of History and Biography* 66 (April 1958): 131-46; Merrill Peterson, "Thomas Jefferson and Commercial Policy, 1783-1793," *William and Mary Quarterly*, 3d ser. 22 (October 1965): 584-610; Robert R. Palmer, "The Dubious Democrat: Thomas Jefferson in Bourbon France," *Political Science Quarterly* 72 (September 1957): 388-404. Those interested in Jefferson should not miss Howard C. Rice's delightful *Thomas Jefferson's Paris* (Princeton: Princeton University Press, 1976).

58. Unfortunate examples of personal attacks based on surmise are: Currey's accusations of Franklin in *Code Number 72/Benjamin Franklin*; the besmirching of Silas Deane by Julian Boyd, "Silas Deane: Death by a Kindly Teacher of Treason?", *William and Mary Quarterly*, 3d ser., 16 (April, July, October, 1959): 165-87, 319-42, 515-50; Thomas Perkins Abernethy, "Commercial Activities of Silas Deane in France," *American Historical Review* 39 (April 1934): 477-85 and "The Origin of the Franklin-Lee Imbroglio," *North Carolina Historical Review* 15 (January 1938): 41-52.

59. For a summary of recent work appearing in bicentennial symposia *see* Lawrence Kaplan, "The American Revolution in an International Perspective: Views from Bicentennial Symposia," *International History Review* 1 (July 1979): 408-26. Kaplan is author of the best introductory survey of eighteenth-century American diplomacy, *Colonies into Nation: American Diplomacy, 1763-1801* (New York: Macmillan Co., 1972).

60. Perhaps the best single article from a new left perspective is William Appleman Williams, "The Age of Mercantilism: An Interpretation of the American Political Economy, 1763 to 1828," *William and Mary Quarterly*, 3d ser. 15 (October 1958): 419-37. An example of a new left approach marred by insufficient familiarity with the sources is Walter LaFeber, "Foreign Policies of a New Nation: Franklin, Madison, and the 'Dream of a New Land to Fulfill with People in Self-Control,' 1750-1804," pp. 9-38 in William Appleman Williams, ed., *From Colony to Empire: Essays in the History of American Foreign Relations* (New York: John Wiley & Sons, 1972).

2 The Early National Period, 1789-1815: The Need for Redefinition

RONALD L. HATZENBUEHLER

The early national period, spanning the years 1789 to 1815, at first glance appears to be a useful demarcation in the study of United States diplomatic history. The adoption of the Constitution and the creation of a stronger central government inaugurated a new era in the conduct of the nation's foreign affairs, and the War of 1812 ushered in one hundred years of isolation from European politics. Both these occurrences are watersheds in the American past, and the period between is filled with important events. The Nootka Sound controversy, the Neutrality Proclamation, Jay's Treaty, Washington's Farewell Address, the XYZ Affair, the Quasi-War, the Convention of Mortefontaine, the Louisiana Purchase, the Embargo, and the War of 1812—each is the subject of numerous monographs and review articles tracing changing scholarly interpretations of its importance in American history.[1]

In the past three decades, despite the acknowledged significance of the period, most students of United States diplomatic history have viewed it either from the perspective of later events or as continuing prior trends or themes. Janus-like, contemporary scholars have interpreted the early national period either in terms of "lessons" learned from the cold war of the twentieth century or in terms of the legacies of the American Revolution.

The influence of the cold war is seen in two ways: 1) the development of a realist school of diplomatic historians and of its antagonist, the new left or expansionist school, and 2) the emphasis on consensus among the founding fathers in contrast to progressive historians' conflict interpretations. Criticisms in the early 1950s of idealism and moralism-legalism in United States foreign relations by Hans J. Morgenthau and George F. Kennan spurred a search for realism in the diplomacy of the founding fathers.[2] Paul A. Varg's inquiry into the period 1774-1812 concluded that a "determination to approach foreign relations in terms of the ideal rather than in terms of existing realities predominated during the Revolution, lost much of its hold during the Washington administrations, and regained prominence with the election of Thomas Jefferson."[3] Alexander Hamilton is portrayed as the main realist of the period who based his plans upon "a calculation of available power" whereas Jefferson and James Madison "began by rejecting existing realities and sought to implement an ideal." In the end, however, the War of 1812 convinced Jefferson and Madison of the wisdom of Hamilton's "foreign policy [of] national self-interest" and established a national legacy of reconciling an "appeal to justice and energetic defense of the national interest."[4]

Contemporaneous with Varg's research, Felix Gilbert also contrasted feelings of idealism-internationalism in the revolutionary era with the realism of the Federalists in 1789. Hamilton, for Gilbert as for Varg, threw "cold water on all those idealistic ideas which had been so popular in the first years of independence;" but Gilbert argued that John Jay, John Adams, George Washington, and even James Madison also saw the importance of power politics in 1789.[5] Indeed, Gilbert concluded that Washington's Farewell Address, much of which was authored by Hamilton, "reaches beyond any period in time and reveals the basic issue of the American attitude toward foreign policy: the tension between Idealism and Realism."[6]

Although they disagreed on many specifics, Varg and Gilbert each emphasized that antecedents for cold war realism—willingness to deal with power realities and to base foreign policy on the national interest—could be found in the early national period. Other scholars have likewise seen similarities between the two periods, especially in the policies of Alexander Hamilton. Gilbert L. Lycan portrayed Hamilton as the supreme realist whose consistency separates him from all other prominent early American leaders. "It is amazing to discover on how many issues he saw the correct answers when few others of the time could see them."[7] Ian Mugridge questioned Hamilton's clandestine British connections but, as did Lycan, concluded that Hamilton's contribution to the formation of foreign policy "remains basic to an understanding of the critical period of the 1790s—and, one may suggest, for the 1970s as well."[8] James H. Hutson linked the two periods even more tightly: "The foreign policy which the United States has pursued since the end of the Second World War, based on the creation of a balance of power in Europe and on a sufficiency of military power in the nation's hands, is identical to that followed by the statesmen of the Revolutionary era."[9]

For these scholars, therefore, the study of the early national period was didactic—insights into current foreign policy problems could be gained through a careful inspection of the founding fathers' motives. Ironically, new left historians have denied the validity of the realist approach but have arrived at similar conclusions regarding the relevance of the nation's early foreign policy to the problems of cold war America. With expansionism as the major thrust of U.S. history, the early national period was subsumed within "The Age of Mercantilism, 1740-1828," as William Appleman Williams first defined it. The early republic does figure prominently in this mercantilistic era as the time when "the feeble colonial confederation" was transformed "into a mighty republican empire," but the period is important not for what it was but for what it became. Trapped in an ideology "that wealth and welfare hinged upon expansion," and "unwilling . . . to make a fuller commitment to social property in the name of a corporate commonwealth," the founding fathers laid the groundwork for the Age of Laissez-Nous-Faire (1819-1896) and, finally, Corporate Capitalism (after 1882).[10] In short, as with the realists, the contours of American diplomacy were best seen from the present backwards.

This view of expansionism that emphasizes the essential unity of U.S. history is the central thesis of Alexander DeConde's book, *This Affair of Louisiana*. Arguing that "Federalist reactions" to the Louisiana procurement have created the view that the acquisition of Louisiana was "an accident of fate" or a "diplomatic miracle," DeConde traces the antecedents of the purchase to "the rise of Western nationalism and imperialism." English imperialists, in other words, molded the expansionist ideology; Puritans and other colonial settlers shaped it into an American motif; and the founding fathers—in the revolutionary period and later in the national years—pursued expansionist ventures in the name of national interest. Not only does DeConde argue that the Louisiana Purchase continued expansionist precedents, but he also portrays "this affair" as facing the future: "It fitted comfortably within the nationalistic and expansionist ideology of America's political leaders, regardless of party affiliation, and met the desires of the many Americans who felt that sooner or later the entire North American continent must be theirs. With minor variations it gave form to the idea of Manifest Destiny and served as a model for future expansion." The influence of new left perspectives on DeConde's thesis is substantial, especially the view that the fabric of the American experience is seamless with regard to the theme of expansionism. When Jefferson acted, he did so based upon an ideological commitment to expansion shared by his peers and not as a result of circumstances peculiar to his first administration.[11]

Realist and new left writers also focus on consensus among the founding fathers regarding foreign affairs. In contrast to progressive historians' interpretations that policy rifts occurred between Hamilton and Jefferson as representatives of competing commercial and agrarian interest groups, post-World War II historians have seen more unity of thought among the nation's early leaders. For the realists, Hamilton was *primus inter pares* not *prima donna*. From the Revolution through the writing of the Constitution, James H. Hutson has contended, all of the nation's leaders based foreign policy ideas on their perception of power politics in Europe and regarded a balance-of-power situation as in the nation's best interests.[12] Thomas Jefferson was a realist? Unquestionably, Lawrence S. Kaplan has argued. Jefferson's idealism was "tempered by a pragmatic regard for political realities." The Sage of Monticello effectively "blended the moralistic yearnings of the young Republic for a new international order with the practical pursuit of national self-interest." Far from being a Francophile who was so enamored with the ideas of the French Revolution that he refused to see the reality of French expansionism, Kaplan's Jefferson wooed French economic support to break the nation's dependence on British markets and credit. In using France as a counterweight to British influence in America, Jefferson was following different tactics than Hamilton and couching his policies in moral terms; but his morality was always based on the national interest.[13] Even after 1793 Hamilton and Jefferson (as well as the parties they headed) saw in the Constitution an opportunity to "extract vital concessions from Europe which had been unattainable in the past, from the relocating of boundary lines to the expansion of trade." On the ends of government they agreed. In extracting these concessions, however, the two men and their followers clashed sharply.[14]

Jerald A. Combs has provided an especially clear statement on the consensus of 1789 and its demise in formulating government priorities. Whereas Hamilton would "avoid war with England, protect American credit, and seek his goals of glory not by balancing superior power, but by joining it," Jefferson and Madison sought to use France as a lever for breaking United States dependence on Britain.[15] For Hamilton, the nation's foreign policy would form the basis of national greatness. Jefferson and Madison, however, reversed Hamilton's theory and saw foreign policy as flowing from the domestic pursuit of the "essentials of happiness—liberty, justice, and domestic tranquillity." Neither view was more realistic than the other, and each was the result of a quarrel over "proper goals and the extent of power necessary to implement them."[16]

Surprisingly, the new left has also emphasized that the founding fathers shared an ideology, although a different one from that depicted by the realists. James Madison, rather than Alexander Hamilton, was prime mover and apostle of mercantilism, not realism, but among the leaders of the early republic—north and south—consensus reigned.[17] Indeed, in the struggle to write and ratify the Constitution, wrote William A. Williams, "mercantilists [were jarred] into the stark realization that they had to compromise in order to build the kind of society that they wanted. . . . [The Constitution movement] was a well-organized campaign by a coalition of America's upper-class leadership determined to establish the institutions appropriate to an American mercantilist empire." Later, Hamilton's pro-British commercial attachments very nearly wrecked the mercantilistic dreams of the founding fathers, but Madison was able after 1800 to "put together a coalition of mechanics, planters, yeomen, and manufacturers that ruled the country for 30 years . . . under the *Weltanschauung* of mercantilism."[18]

The differences in interpretation between realist and new left historians, therefore, have obscured important similarities in their treatments of the diplomacy of the early national period. Intense concerns over post-World War II foreign policy triggered interest in the antecedents of today's problems. Viewed backwards, therefore, the early national period provides at least partial validation for theories explaining recent events. In the process, however, distinctive features of the early republic are obscured.

Historians other than cold war specialists also contributed to the demise of the early national period. Looking forward from the American Revolution and emphasizing the essential agreement among the founding fathers on foreign-policy questions from 1776 through the 1780s, some historians have emphasized that the process of founding the republic was not completed until 1815. The research of Cecilia M. Kenyon, Richard Buel, Jr., Bernard Bailyn, Gordon S. Wood, and John R. Howe, Jr., has shown that the revolutionary generation, drawing upon their reading of English opposition writers, believed liberty to be endangered by English politics and established the American republic to safeguard public and private virtue. This "pervasive ideological attachment to the concept" of republicanism formed the basis of the consensus motivating the founding fathers.[19] Unfortunately, however, this consensus "promoted discord rather than harmony" among the leaders of the early republic. Shared assumptions concerning the establishment and maintenance of republicanism—chief of which was the "widespread belief in the essential frailty and impermanence of republican government"—were greatly intensified by fears of disruptive factions in the new nation. Hence, both Federalists and Republicans overreacted to every potential external or internal threat to the nation. "Every decision they made loomed as fundamentally important. Their opportunity, they firmly believed, could not be recovered," John Howe has noted.[20]

Most illustrative of this view of early America are scholarly studies on the origins of the War of 1812. Beginning in the 1950s, research on the war's origins shifted emphasis from impressment, economic dislocations in the south and west, Indians on the frontier, and defense of neutral rights to focus on domestic causes of the war.[21] National honor, according to Norman K. Risjord and Bradford Perkins, was the only issue that could have united Republicans from all sections of the country to support a war against Great Britain.[22] Then, in 1964, Roger H. Brown established that shared feelings among the majority party concerning the future of the republican experiment was the main factor in the war decision. Brown traced the ideological origins of this concern for protecting republicanism backwards from 1812, through the drafting of the Constitution and the American Revolution to John Winthrop's dream of building "a Citty upon a Hill." More importantly, Brown viewed his book as a chronological extension of the work of Kenyon and Bailyn in the revolutionary period. He believed that "these studies [would] reinforce one another and cumulatively form a coherent pattern of new interpretation in the history of the Revolutionary and early national periods."[23]

This prophecy has been fulfilled with the publication of two books that link the republican synthesis of Kenyon, Bailyn, Wood, and Howe with that of Brown's research. Richard Buel, Jr., has demonstrated that Republican opposition to Federalist policies of the 1790s developed "as the only way to ensure that the nation would remain independent and [that] the promise of the Revolution would be fulfilled."[24] Concentrating on Jefferson's opposition to the Federalists during Adams's administration and his policies as president, Lance Banning has argued persuasively that Jefferson helped "to create a party that would call itself Republican and rest to a remarkable degree on a revival and Americanization of British opposition thought." During his presidency Jefferson implemented his party's policies which were born in the 1790s but traced their ideological and political heritage back to 1642. Jefferson established British "country" politics by overturning the Hamiltonian "court" faction.[25]

In summary, instances of political violence in the early national period should not be overemphasized, according to the republican synthesists. Consensus reigned among the founding fathers and finally triumphed with Federalist acceptance of Jeffersonian electioneering tactics and Republican employment of "Jeffersonian means to achieve classic Federalist ends." With the conclusion of the War of 1812, according to John Howe, "Americans could finally believe that the basic task of founding had been completed . . . [and] one of the major chapters in America's historical development came to a close."[26] As with the realists and the new left, therefore, the republican synthesists have concluded that the early national period cannot stand on its own. Rather, these groups have argued, it exists only as an island of realism in an ocean of idealism and moralism-legalism; as the seedtime of modern corporate capitalism; or as a continuation of revolutionary republicanism. The remainder of this essay will argue the opposite point of view, suggesting how the era can be seen as forming a unique chapter in the nation's past.

During the years 1789-1815, events that had their genesis in different time frames were suddenly joined together. What becomes important, therefore, is not to identify the causes of the events of the period but rather to understand how the events combined with one another to produce what Robert Berkofer, Jr., terms "the specific sequence of additive mixture."[27] One example of what can be done by following such a method already exists: Richard H. Kohn's *Eagle and Sword.* Kohn, a member of the republican synthesis group, argues that Federalists created the military establishment in order to save the republic from Republican antifederalism. What makes the study unique, however, is the emphasis placed on the importance of the sequence of events leading to the creation of the standing army and navy. British opposition writers such as John Trenchard viewed standing armies with horror, and these ideas were adopted by the revolutionary generation (Bailyn, Wood, and Banning make the same point). The experience of the American Revolution reinforced later Federalists' dispositions toward "order, tradition, the natural distinctions among men, and social harmony" and created a strong desire for a standing army by 1783. Following the Newburgh conspiracy, however, Federalists did not argue for a standing army until they were in power. Then, Indian wars, the Whiskey Rebellion, and Republican opposition in the late 1790s caused the Federalists to develop the beginnings of our contemporary military organization. In Kohn's book, therefore, tracing the development of the idea of a standing army is far less important than interrelating the events that gave it life.[28]

Most scholars of the era would agree that the interplay between politics and diplomacy in the early republic deserves further attention. Two factors have stymied research in recent years. First, the impressive work of Alexander DeConde and Bradford Perkins that integrated political and diplomatic history for the period 1790-1815 undoubtedly caused diplomatic historians to shift attention elsewhere, just as techniques of the new political history were being perfected. A second interpretive obstacle had to be overcome before new studies could systematically probe relationships between foreign policy and domestic problems: the consensus among political historians that the first party system began at the national level, in the Congress, in response to Hamilton's financial policies and the wars of the French Revolution. The parties were new groupings stemming from the breakup of the Federalist consensus of 1789 and have more in common with their modern descendants than with the factional politics of the colonial period, historians have traditionally argued.[29]

The first party system is currently under attack from two directions. Ronald P. Formisano faults research that views the early parties as forerunners of the parties of today. "Partisan behavior was certainly present [in the first party system], and some men even advocated party as a positive good.

But . . . the early republican era is best viewed as a deferential-participant phase somewhere between traditional forms and mass party politics, having some features of both." Formisano's attack is based in large part on the lack of institutionalization among the Federalists and Republicans—a crucial factor in distinguishing premodern from modern parties. He concludes that "fully developed parties" did not exist before about 1840.[30] Equally provocative is the contention of scholars working at the state level that the partisan divisions of the early republic were continuations of factional groupings of colonial times and stemmed from local rather than national issues. In Kentucky, for example, the same family-oriented political groups that existed in 1785 were present in 1792 at the time of statehood and formed the nucleus of the Federalist and Republican parties after 1793.[31] Similarly, Jackson Turner Main has argued that "localist and cosmopolitan cultural outlooks" in most of the colonial assemblies are directly linked with Anti-Federalists and Federalists in the 1780s and with Republicans and Federalists in the 1790s. During the party-building of the 1790s "the national parties adapted to and modified . . . state blocs" rather than the reverse.[32]

If the political parties of the 1790s were as much, if not more, concerned with local matters as with national ones—even foreign-policy problems—other fundamental assumptions are also endangered. The substantial increase in popular participation in politics—both in terms of voting and of holding office—begun during the Revolution but reaching its apex in Madison's administration indicates to some historians that public opinion was influencing the nation's affairs during the period.[33] David H. Fischer and Richard P. McCormick have argued that it was the competition between two well-organized, popularly oriented parties at the local level that created the surge in voter participation.[34] The issues of the period and their effect on the voters have yet to be tested systematically at the local, state, or national level. By and large, state studies have focused on newspaper articles and other traditional sources rather than on the votes and what they can tell regarding public opinion.[35] Even less informative are studies of national elections, especially the critical election of 1800.[36] Norman K. Risjord put his finger directly on the issue of public opinion and the election of 1800: "Reflecting on the preoccupation of the times with the durability of the republic, [Jefferson] felt that the Republican victory had saved the nation from tyranny and incipient monarchy. Yet if the issues were really that clearly drawn, the public did not seem particularly aware of the situation."[37] In support of Risjord's conclusions, David A. Bohmer has argued (in what will, it is hoped, serve as a model for future studies) that for Maryland at least the election of 1800 produced few changes in partisan behavior, was marked by little if any "noticeable response to the major issues of the campaign," and primarily "perpetuated a voting alignment . . . already present . . . that would persist for almost another twenty years. In this sense, stability, not change, was the central theme of the 1800 presidential election in Maryland.''[38] At the least, Bohmer's study casts impressive doubts on traditional interpretations linking the rise of democracy with Jefferson's victory in 1800 and should cause diplomatic historians to probe the exact relationship between politics and foreign policy in the early national period.

Important to this reconstruction of relationships between the development of political parties and foreign policy issues at the local level would seem to be a consideration of social turmoil in the early republic. Bernard Bailyn has noted that the 1780s and 1790s ''cannot be understood in essentially ideological terms'' but rather must be considered as a ''product of a complicated interplay between the maturing of Revolutionary ideas and ideals and the involvements of everyday life—in politics, in business, and in the whole range of social activities.''[39] One avenue of fruitful research would probe how pro-French and pro-British attitudes were formed. For example, Sanford W. Higginbotham has noted that in Pennsylvania from 1808-1815 Republican and Federalist positions on certain issues were drastically altered or even reversed. Economic questions and the debate over national power or state rights which had been significant factors in the party warfare of the 1790s no longer divided men along the same political lines. With respect to foreign affairs, however, traditional divisions over British or French attachments continued to arouse traditional partisan loyalties.[40] It is possible that even these foreign prejudices had local or personal roots and did not reflect a very deep knowledge of international relations. Work is at present being focused on the social changes that occurred in early national America. Local studies are needed that will test relationships among these social disjunctures and partisan attachments.[41] Perhaps the most promising area of social research involves what William Gribbin has termed the ''nexus between religion and politics'' accompanying the War of 1812. Using techniques of the new political history, studies are needed to detail the nature of denominational support for the Republican party on the local level. ''For among the very churches that supported the war effort were those who soon grew into the country's largest denominations, and the melding of their faith and patriotism was essential to the forging of American nationalism.''[42] One method for testing the full import of Gribbin's assertion would be to see whether rhetorical changes during the revivalism of the early nineteenth century influenced political matters in the same manner as following the Great Awakening.[43] Republican congressmen did change their rhetoric between the Embargo and the war session of the twelfth Congress, and a comparison of their statements with the language religious leaders used to build support for the war might prove valuable.[44]

A second possibility for research that will ask how the events came together as they did, rather than what antecedents triggered the events of the period, concerns the major events of Jefferson's and Madison's presidencies. Ever since Henry Adams vindicated his great-grandfather's administration by showing how Jefferson and Madison by 1816 had adopted the bulk of the Federalist program, historians have wrestled with the differences between Republican ideology in 1798 and the program they implemented while in power.[45] Crucial to future research should be a description of the process by which Republicans abandoned Jefferson's ideals expressed in his first inaugural address rather than a discussion which traces the ideological precedents for economic coercion. For example, instead of continuing the controversy over whether the Embargo was Jefferson's creation or Madison's or Gallatin's, more attention should be given to the events directly related to the Embargo's implementation.[46] Relations with the Congress, Republican factionalism in Pennsylvania and other states, and even the Burr trial are only a few examples of important matters Jefferson was considering in the summer and fall of 1807 following the attack on the *Chesapeake*.

Similarly, a situational approach to Madison's decision to ask Congress for a declaration of war promises new insights into that oft-studied topic and an escape from the swamp of multiple causes in which investigations of the origins of the War of 1812 have become mired. As J. C. A. Stagg observed, the usual list of causal factors bears little relation to the actual timing of the war's declaration; and the thesis of war hawk pressure on the president as an explanation for the June decision for war simply will not stand up under close scrutiny. "The role of Congress in the coming of the War of 1812 was . . . far less decisive than most historians have believed, while the role of the president was far more important." Madison reacted in terms of "the many diplomatic and political pressures which were brought to bear on him," not the least of which was the factionalism within his own party that came to a head as the first session of the twelfth Congress opened. Perhaps the fact that Stagg's article was recognized by the Society for Historians of American Foreign Relations as the best for 1976 indicates that diplomatic historians will take up his challenge to make intelligible the "dynamics behind the movement to war."[47]

A final example of the possibilities for future research following Kohn's method concerns the issue of economic and territorial expansion. Arguments over whether the War of 1812 was a classic war for trade and territory or if Washington's Farewell Address was realistic, isolationist, or expansionistic are not very productive of insight into the diplomacy of the early national period.[48] More substantive contributions will come from studies that isolate the components of a decision which resulted in the addition of territory or the expansion of markets, or that show how policies changed from administration to administration or from year to year in response to events. Stagg's current research on Madison's economic coercion of Great Britain is a good example of the first type of study. As Stagg has argued, Madison as congressman, secretary of state, and president thought a great deal about the possibilities of coercing England to protect American mercantile interests. These thoughts revolved not around the ideology of mercantilism or expansionism but rather were sharply focused on the British need to supply her West Indies colonies with staples. So long as the United States was the principal supplier, Madison felt economic coercion would force the English, however grudgingly, to respect American rights. But when he saw during his presidency that Canada had begun to replace the United States in the minds of policymakers in England, the future of economic coercion was thrown into jeopardy. Hence, the practical necessity of coping with the very threatening set of circumstances with regard to Canada may have influenced Madison's war decision far more than did his economic theories.[49]

Of equal importance, however, are studies that inquire into how the leaders of the early republic sought to protect the nation's mercantile interests. Gregg L. Lint's investigation of United States policy toward creating a "universal recognition of the law of nations" provides a good base on which to build future studies. According to Lint, it was self-interest "as reflected in the desire for free trade and the need to protect and maintain the nation's sovereignty" that stimulated interest in "the law of nations." Similarly, the concept "free ships make free goods" had little if any relation to theories of international law but rather represented American attempts to expand trade possibilities. What policymakers sought, in other words, was not a new international order but rather an "American law of nations." What needs to be done is to see how the changing situations each president faced altered the implementation of this idea.[50]

Studies that concentrate on the situational components of decision-making in the early republic will be aided by some of the forthcoming editions of the papers of the founding fathers and hindered by others. Because publication of *The Papers of Thomas Jefferson* has been stalled for some years now at 1791, scholars will for some time to come be forced to rely on earlier editions of his letters and manuscript collections.[51] By contrast, publication of *The Papers of James Madison* is already up to 1789 and will make a significant contribution to revisionist studies of Madison's role in the events of the early national period.[52] *The Adams Papers*, unfortunately, are a good example of how compartmentalization of the lives of these men can backfire. The most recent series dealing with Adams's political writings is divorced from his family letters and, in James H. Hutson's opinion, "give the impression of disembodied intellectualism, of ideas wrenched from their social context."[53] *The Papers of John Marshall*, however, have reached the critical years 1796-1798 and will stimulate renewed interest in the XYZ affair in both its national and international contexts.[54]

As diplomatic historians continue to study the foreign policy of the early republic they should give attention to how foreign affairs mixed with partisan politics, social change, and events at the local level during the period 1789-1815 to make the early national period distinctive from other eras. Leaders of the early republic saw themselves as continuing the republican experiment and as setting precedents for the conduct of foreign policy in later years. But they were also reacting to their own, unique sets of circumstances and trying to figure out how and why the events came together as they did. If we are to gain a better understanding of how the founding fathers made sense out of their nation's affairs, we must do likewise.

Notes

1. A recent bibliography of writings on the Washington and Adams administrations is Ian Mugridge, *U.S. Foreign Policy under Washington and Adams* (New York: Garland Publishing Co., 1979).

2. Hans J. Morgenthau, *In Defense of the National Interest: A Critical Examination of American Foreign Policy* (New York: Alfred A. Knopf, 1952), pp. 13-29; George F. Kennan, *American Diplomacy, 1900-1950* (Chicago: University of Chicago Press, 1951), pp. 11-12, 83-89. Morgenthau distinguishes three periods in U.S. foreign policy: realistic (1789-1801); ideological (the nineteenth century); and moralistic (Woodrow Wilson's diplomacy). Kennan does not specifically refer to the era of the founding fathers, but his appeals for a foreign policy based upon the national interest have influenced scholars of the early republic.

3. Paul A. Varg, *Foreign Policies of the Founding Fathers* (East Lansing: Michigan State University Press, 1963), p. 4.

4. Ibid., pp. 145-46, 304.

5. Felix Gilbert, *To the Farewell Address: Ideas of Early American Foreign Policy* (Princeton: Princeton University Press, 1961), pp. 111-12, 86-104.

6. Ibid., p. 136.

7. Gilbert L. Lycan, *Alexander Hamilton and American Foreign Policy* (Norman: University of Oklahoma Press, 1970), pp. ix-x.

8. Ian Mugridge, "Alexander Hamilton and the Diplomacy of Influence" in Frank J. Merli and Theodore A. Wilson, eds., *Makers of American Diplomacy* (New York: Charles Scribner's Sons, 1974), p. 50. *See also* Charles R. Ritcheson, *Aftermath of Revolution: British Policy Toward the United States, 1783-1795* (Dallas: Southern Methodist University Press, 1969) and Helene Johnson Looze, *Alexander Hamilton and the British Orientation of American Foreign Policy, 1783-1803* (The Hague: Mouton, 1969).

9. James H. Hutson, "Early American Diplomacy: A Reappraisal," pp. 56-62 in Lawrence S. Kaplan, ed., *The American Revolution and "A Candid World"* (Kent, Ohio: Kent State University Press, 1978); and "Intellectual Foundations of Early American Diplomacy," *Diplomatic History*, 1 (Winter 1977): 1-19. Hutson argues

that Varg continues the progressive distinctions between Hamilton and Jefferson, but I think his point is overdrawn based upon Varg's statements (see note 3). Those who think my analysis overemphasizes consensus both among the founding fathers and post-World War II historians should consult Charles S. Campbell, *From Revolution to Rapprochement: The United States and Great Britain, 1783-1900* (New York: John Wiley & Sons, 1974), esp. pp. 10-22.

10. William Appleman Williams, *The Contours of American History* (Chicago: Quadrangle Books, 1966), pp. 73, 272-73. *See also* Lloyd C. Gardner et al., *Creation of the American Empire: U.S. Diplomatic History* (Chicago: Rand McNally and Co., 1973), and Walter LaFeber, "Foreign Policies of a New Nation: Franklin, Madison, and the 'Dream of a New Land to Fulfill with People in Self-Control,' " in William A. Williams, ed., *From Colony to Empire: Essays in the History of American Foreign Relations* (New York: John Wiley & Sons, 1972).

11. Alexander DeConde, *This Affair of Louisiana* (New York: Charles Scribner's Sons, 1976), pp. 227-55.

12. Hutson, "Early American Diplomacy."

13. Lawrence S. Kaplan, "Thomas Jefferson: The Idealist as Realist," pp. 53-78 in Merli and Wilson, eds., *Makers of American Diplomacy. See also* his *Jefferson and France: An Essay in Politics and Political Ideas* (New Haven: Yale University Press, 1967).

14. Lawrence S. Kaplan, *Colonies into Nation: American Diplomacy, 1763-1801* (New York: Macmillan Co., 1972), pp. 182-243. In pursuing this line of thought, I have chosen only representative scholars. On the consensus to profit from Europe's distress, *see also* John C. Miller, *The Federalist Era: 1789-1801* (New York: Harper & Row, 1960), p. 128.

15. Jerald A. Combs, *The Jay Treaty: Political Battleground of the Founding Fathers* (Berkeley: University of California Press, 1970).

16. Ibid., pp. 33-69, 83-86. *See also* Albert Hall Bowman, *The Struggle for Neutrality: Franco-American Diplomacy During the Federalist Era* (Knoxville: University of Tennessee Press, 1974). Bowman presents the Jay Treaty controversy as a conflict between Federalist views of the nation's weaknesses and Republican views of the nation's strengths.

17. Williams, *Contours*, pp. 139-62.

18. Ibid., pp. 137, 148, 177.

19. Robert E. Shalhope, "Toward a Republican Synthesis: The Emergence of an Understanding of Republicanism in American Historiography," *William and Mary Quarterly*, 3d ser. 29 (January 1972): 49-80. *See also* John R. Howe, Jr., *From the Revolution Through the Age of Jackson: Innocence and Empire in the Young Republic* (Englewood Cliffs, N.J.: Prentice-Hall, 1973).

20. John R. Howe, Jr., "Republican Thought and the Political Violence of the 1790s," *American Quarterly* 19 (July 1967): 147-65.

21. *See* Warren H. Goodman, "The Origins of the War of 1812: A Survey of Changing Interpretations," *Mississippi Valley Historical Review* 28 (September 1941): 171-86, and Clifford L. Egan, "The Origins of the War of 1812: Three Decades of Historical Writing," *Military Affairs* 38 (April 1974): 72-75.

22. Norman K. Risjord, "1812: Conservatives, War Hawks, and the Nation's Honor," *William and Mary Quarterly*, 3d ser. 18 (April 1961): 196-210 and *The Old*

Republicans: Southern Conservatism in the Age of Jefferson (New York: Columbia University Press, 1965); Bradford Perkins, *Prologue to War: England and the United States, 1805-1812* (Berkeley: University of California Press, 1961).

23. Roger H. Brown, *The Republic in Peril: 1812* (New York: Columbia University Press, 1964).

24. Richard Buel, Jr., *Securing the Revolution: Ideology in American Politics, 1789-1815* (Ithaca, N.Y.: Cornell University Press, 1972).

25. Lance Banning, *The Jeffersonian Persuasion: Evolution of a Party Ideology* (Ithaca, N.Y.: Cornell University Press, 1978), pp. 15-18, 75-93, 273-302, esp. chap. 5. An alternative view is presented in Daniel M. Sisson, *The Revolution of 1800* (New York: Alfred A. Knopf, 1974). Sisson argues that Jefferson's election in 1800 was tantamount to a second American Revolution and saved the republic from monarchism (as Jefferson himself argued). Clearly outside the "republican synthesis," Sisson's book rests on conjectures and twisted logic. According to Noble E. Cunningham, Jr., "The book lacks both original research and reflection." Reviewed in the *Journal of American History* 60 (September 1975): 383-85.

26. Howe, *From the Revolution Through the Age of Jackson*, pp. 86-87, 90. With regard to the Federalists, the works of David H. Fischer, Gerald Stourzh, Linda K. Kerber, and James M. Banner, Jr., have established the Republican basis of Federalist policies even after 1801. Using different language from the Republicans and casting their ideas in a different rhetoric, Federalists nevertheless believed they were helping to save the republic from Jacobinism. Much as Jefferson and Madison had done in John Adams's administration, Federalist leaders after 1801 argued that Republican policies would destroy the nation. The Hartford Convention, therefore, was far from a separatist movement. Rather, the gathering of Federalists was necessary to rescue the nation from Republican degeneracy. David H. Fischer, *The Revolution of American Conservatism: The Federalist Party in the Era of Jeffersonian Democracy* (New York: Harper & Row, 1965); Gerald Stourzh, *Alexander Hamilton and the Idea of Republican Government* (Stanford, Calif.: Stanford University Press, 1970); Linda K. Kerber, *Federalists in Dissent: Imagery and Ideology in Jeffersonian America* (Ithaca, N.Y.: Cornell University Press, 1970); James M. Banner, Jr., *The Federalists and the Origins of Party Politics in Massachusetts, 1789-1815* (New York: Alfred A. Knopf, 1970).

27. Robert Berkhofer, Jr., *A Behavioral Approach to Historical Analysis* (New York: Free Press, 1969), p. 303.

28. Richard Kohn, *Eagle and Sword: The Federalists and the Creation of the Military Establishment, 1783-1802* (New York: Free Press, 1975).

29. Alexander DeConde, *Entangling Alliance: Politics and Diplomacy under George Washington* (Durham, N.C.: Duke University Press, 1958); and *The Quasi-War: The Politics and Diplomacy of the Undeclared War with France, 1797-1801* (New York: Charles Scribner's Sons, 1966); Bradford Perkins, *The First Rapprochement: England and the United States, 1795-1805* (Philadelphia: University of Pennsylvania Press, 1955) and *Prologue to War*. For the classic statement of the development of political parties, *see* Joseph Charles, *The Origins of the American Party System: Three Essays* (New York: Harper & Row, 1961).

30. Ronald P. Formisano, "Deferential-Participant Politics: The Early Republic's Political Culture, 1789-1840," *American Political Science Review* 68 (June 1974):

473-87. This article reviews writings on the first party system and may be consulted for earlier books and articles. For an alternative view *see* Harry W. Fritz, "The Case for Political Party in the Age of Jefferson" (Paper presented in Atlanta, Georgia, on April 7, 1977, at the Annual Meeting of the Organization of American Historians).

31. Patricia Watlington, *The Partisan Spirit: Kentucky Politics, 1779-1792* (New York: Atheneum, 1972).

32. Jackson Turner Main, *Political Parties Before the Constitution* (Chapel Hill: University of North Carolina Press, 1973).

33. *See* Buel, *Securing the Revolution*, esp. p. 51 and Roger Brown's review of Buel's book in the *Journal of Interdisciplinary History* 5 (Summer 1974): 163-67.

34. Fischer, *Revolution of American Conservatism*, p. 90; Richard P. McCormick, "New Perspectives on Jacksonian Politics," *American Historical Review* 66 (January 1960): 288-301.

35. *See* Formisano, "Deferential-Participant Politics," for a review of state studies for the period.

36. For a standard account of the election of 1800 *see* Noble E. Cunningham, Jr., "Election of 1800" in Arthur M. Schlesinger, Jr., et al., eds., *History of American Presidential Elections, 1789-1968*, 4 vols. (New York: Chelsea House Publishers, 1971), 1: 101-34.

37. Norman K. Risjord, *Forging the American Republic, 1760-1815* (Reading, Mass.: Addison-Wesley Publishing Co., 1973).

38. David A. Bohmer, "Stability and Change in Early National Politics: The Maryland Voter and the Election of 1800," *William and Mary Quarterly*, 3d ser. 36 (January 1979): 27-50 and "The Maryland Electorate and the Concept of a Party System in the Early National Period," in Joel Silbey, et al., eds., *The History of American Electoral Behavior* (Princeton: Princeton University Press, 1978).

39. Bernard Bailyn, "The Central Themes of the American Revolution: An Interpretation" in Stephen G. Kurtz and James H. Hutson, eds., *Essays on the American Revolution* (Chapel Hill: University of North Carolina Press, 1973).

40. Sanford W. Higginbotham, *The Keystone of the Democratic Arch: Pennsylvania Politics, 1800-1816* (Harrisburg: Pennsylvania Historical and Museum Commission, 1952).

41. A good example of how *not* to conceive such a study is Victor A. Sapio, *Pennsylvania and the War of 1812* (Lexington: University of Kentucky Press, 1970). Sapio relies exclusively on theories presented by other scholars and does not offer an original analysis.

42. William Gribbin, *The Churches Militant: The War of 1812 and American Religion* (New Haven: Yale University Press, 1973).

43. Harry S. Stout, "Religion, Communications, and the Ideological Origins of the American Revolution," *William and Mary Quarterly*, 3d ser. 34 (October 1977): 519-41.

44. Ronald L. Hatzenbuehler and Robert L. Ivie, "Justifying the War of 1812: Patterns of Congressional Behavior " (Paper presented in San Francisco on August 19, 1978, at the meeting of the Pacific Coast Branch of the American Historical Association, forthcoming in *Social Science History*).

45. Henry Adams, *A History of the United States During the Administrations of*

Jefferson and Madison, 9 vols. (New York: Charles Scribner and Sons, 1889-1891). For a most provocative account of Adams's volumes, *see* Peter Shaw, "The War of 1812 Could Not Take Place," *Yale Review* 62 (Summer 1973): 544-56.

46. *See* Drew R. McCoy, "Republicanism and American Foreign Policy: James Madison and the Political Economy of Commercial Discrimination, 1789 to 1794," *William and Mary Quarterly*, 3d ser. 31 (October 1974): 633-46, and Burton Spivak, *Jefferson and the Embargo* (Charlottesville, Va.: University Press of Virginia, 1979).

47. J. C. A. Stagg, "James Madison and the 'Malcontents': The Political Origins of the War of 1812," *William and Mary Quarterly*, 3d ser. 33 (October 1976): 557-58. On the war hawk controversy, *see* Ronald L. Hatzenbuehler, "The War Hawks and the Question of Congressional Leadership in 1812," *Pacific Historical Review* 45 (February 1976): 1-22.

48. *See* Arthur A. Markowitz, "Washington's Farewell and the Historians: A Critical Review," *Pennsylvania Magazine of History and Biography* 94 (April 1970): 173-91.

49. J. C. A. Stagg, "James Madison and the Coercion of Great Britain: Canada, the West Indies, and the War of 1812" (forthcoming in the *William and Mary Quarterly*). I am grateful to Professor Stagg for allowing me to see this important essay in manuscript.

50. Gregg L. Lint, "The Law of Nations and the American Revolution," in Kaplan, ed., *The American Revolution and "A Candid World."*

51. Julian P. Boyd, ed., *The Papers of Thomas Jefferson* (Princeton: Princeton University Press, 1950-). Volume eighteen, published in 1971, covers the period 4 November 1790-24 January 1791.

52. Robert A. Rutland and Charles F. Hobson, eds., *The Papers of James Madison* (Charlottesville, Va.: University Press of Virginia, 1979-).

53. Robert J. Taylor, ed., *The Adams Papers. Series 3: General Correspondence and Other Papers of the Adams Statesmen. Papers of John Adams.* (Cambridge, Mass.: Harvard University Press, Belknap Press, 1977), vol. 1, September 1755-October 1773; vol. 2, December 1773-April 1775. *See* James H. Hutson's review in the *William and Mary Quarterly*, 3d ser. 35 (October 1978): 752.

54. The March 1, 1979, issue of the *Newsletter* of the Institute of Early American History and Culture announces: Volume three of *The Papers of John Marshall* is "presently at the University of North Carolina Press . . . slated for publication in the near future. . . . William C. Stinchcombe, diplomatic editor for the project, has not only annotated the documents and supplied editorial essays on the mission, but has deciphered anew all of the decoded material relating to the period." *See* Stinchcombe, "The Diplomacy of the WXYZ Affair," *William and Mary Quarterly*, 3d ser. 34 (October 1977): 590-617.

3 ______ American Foreign Policy in an Age of Nationalism, 1812-1840

LESTER D. LANGLEY

The United States entered the War of 1812 bitterly divided and emerged with its territory barely intact and sectional animosities heightened. But the wartime experience induced nationalistic sentiment that left a profound mark on the political generation of the postwar period. The political leaders of this era—James Monroe, John Quincy Adams, Andrew Jackson, Henry Clay, and John C. Calhoun—held strong views about America's republican identity in a monarchical world. If the thirty years after the Revolution may be thought of as the formative era of American diplomacy, the three decades after the War of 1812 may be described as an age of nationalism. In the early years of the republic the great debate over the nation's political, economic, and cultural ties with Europe had disrupted politics, inspired several lofty statements on the nature of a republic's foreign policy (the most notable of which was Washington's Farewell Address), and ultimately precipitated the second war for independence in 1812. In the years after Ghent a postwar generation attempted to sharpen, if not redefine, the fundamental diplomatic truths of a New World society. The age's great contribution to diplomatic philosophy was the Monroe Doctrine; its architect of republican statecraft, John Quincy Adams.

The nationalistic age of American foreign relations is well-suited to an integrated narrative analyzing diplomatic issues from 1812 to about 1840, but no truly satisfactory study has appeared. The best works are biographical, such as Samuel Flagg Bemis's prize-winning study of America's premier diplomatist, *John Quincy Adams and the Foundations of American Foreign Policy.*[1] Adams, Bemis persuasively argued, was the quintessential

American diplomat. Reared a Federalist, Adams ultimately embraced Jeffersonian philosophies of American diplomacy in the great neutrality debate of 1801-1812. An archcontinentalist, Adams approved the Louisiana Purchase, which die-hard Federalists condemned, and, later, as secretary of state, justified Andrew Jackson's Florida rampage as evidence of Spain's inability to govern the colony and the right of the United States to annex it. In 1823, the most critical year for American diplomacy in the 1812-1840 era, Adams held steadfast against his colleagues in the Monroe cabinet in his contention for a unilateral declaration of American policy in the Western Hemisphere.[2]

In perhaps no other era of American diplomacy does the individual shaper of policy loom so large in the historiography or become so important in explaining the evolution of policy. Biographies of John Quincy Adams serve as examples, but others could be readily listed: among British scholars, Charles Webster's biography of Lord Castlereagh and Harold Temperley's study of George Canning's foreign policy; or, among American authors, W. P. Cresson's older study of Monroe, now supplanted by the prodigious biography of the fifth president by Harry Ammon, and, finally, Robert Remini's initial volume in a new biography of Jackson which identifies American frontier expansion with the thoughts and deeds of the most influential unofficial shaper of policy in that era. Even George Dangerfield's *The Era of Good Feelings*, which says a great deal about foreign relations, explains diplomacy through the biographical medium.[3]

This is not to suggest, of course, that the primacy of biography is unique to the historiography of this era in American diplomacy. But anyone seeking the larger theories, grand designs, or overarching themes must necessarily pursue them through myriad biographical studies of important persons—Adams, Monroe, Jackson, Clay, Canning, Castlereagh, Bolívar, to name a few, a point aptly illustrated by Walter LaFeber's edited work, *John Quincy Adams and American Continental Empire*.[4] Several studies offer a broad view of the important diplomatic issues of the day. Bradford Perkins's *Castlereagh and Adams*, the last volume in a trilogy on Anglo-American relations from Jay's Treaty to the Monroe Doctrine, goes beyond a mere chronicle of the thoughts and deeds of the two policymakers or diplomatic disputes between two governments. He assesses the impact of one culture on another, of the adjustment between former mother country and former colony, of the relationship between Old World power and New World Republic.[5]

Despite the richness of materials and the possibilities for broad interpretive studies of the 1812-1840 period, the major interpretive work is Arthur Whitaker's *The United States and the Independence of Latin America*. Published shortly before World War II, his book is still fresh in tone and timely in its judgments.[6] Influenced by the frontier studies of Frederick

Jackson Turner, Whitaker embarked in the mid-1920s on a multivolume study of the American frontier and its confrontation with the Spanish empire. In *The Spanish-American Frontier, 1783-1795*, he argued that frontier pressures, as much as European jealousies, dictated Spanish concessions to the United States in the Federalist era. A few years later *The Mississippi Question, 1795-1803*, dealt with the final years of the long American struggle to gain control over a river and city vital to its economic and military security.[7] Where the first and second volumes in Whitaker's study of Hispanic-American relations focused on frontier issues, his third volume, *The United States and Latin America*, represented a work much broader in scope and more daring in execution: a venture into cultural history in an age in which the United States was not only shaping a policy toward the hemisphere but, in the realm of trade and culture, getting to know the Hispanic culture with which it shared the Western Hemisphere. Whitaker began with those Jeffersonians who "encountered" Spanish America at the turn of the century and ended with Jefferson's successors, who eschewed a Pan-American alliance but who fashioned a hemispheric policy for the ages. It is lamentable that this volume is remembered more for its questionable argument that Monroe's message was really aimed at France than for its more substantial contribution to the history of American foreign relations: that diplomatic history is more than the record of intergovernmental relations; it is the history of contact between cultures.

The salient issues of American diplomacy in the years 1812-1840 with which historians have been most concerned are the diplomacy of the War of 1812, the Anglo-American relationship, the Florida question, the Latin-American independence movement, the Texas question, and, of course, the Monroe Doctrine. Diplomatic historians have spent much more time with the various aspects of the Monroe Doctrine than with other topics germane to the era. Indeed, scholarly attention to each of these issues has apparently followed closely the popular impressions of American triumphs of the age. The Monroe Doctrine, then, has drawn much more interest than the diplomacy of the War of 1812, not only because the doctrine occupies such a lofty place in the popular imagination but, in part, because the Ghent negotiations are remembered, if at all, for the idiosyncrasies and personality confrontations of the American delegates.

Historians have been more fascinated with the origins of the War of 1812 and its military aspects than with the often tortuous diplomatic wrangling that finally ended with the peace of Christmas Eve 1814. Generally, American historians agree that the United States achieved virtually none of the goals for which it fought (though Madison's biographer, Irving Brant, argues forcefully, in an effort to rehabilitate a president whose reputation Henry Adams had maligned, that the Americans won the war). Interpretations of wartime diplomacy have changed little since F. A. Updyke published in 1915 his Albert Shaw lectures, *The Diplomacy of the War of 1812*. Fred Engleman's more modern account of the Ghent negotiations credits the American delegation with tenacity and stubbornness in holding out against British demands. As is true of other issues of the age of nationalism, one's interpretation of events can depend heavily on which biography one is reading. Bemis credits Adams for American success at Ghent. Albert Gallatin's role as supreme peacemaker amidst the fractious American delegation has been considerably enhanced by Raymond Walters' biography. The British delegation at Ghent has traditionally been looked upon as second-rate, reflecting the presumably secondary importance of that conference to the more portentous negotiations of the Congress of Vienna. But Perkins, in *Castlereagh and Adams*, convincingly argued that Ghent was not always overshadowed by Vienna and that Castlereagh, the architect of British policy, considered the United States an important power that must be dealt with seriously.[8]

Of more interest to diplomatic historians than the problems of wartime diplomacy has been the Anglo-American relationship from about 1815 until the final solution of the Oregon question some three decades later. In the long span of Anglo-American affairs, the years from Ghent to the Oregon settlement occupy a place only slightly less important than another critical era in Anglo-American adjustment from 1895 to 1914. Bradford Perkins moved from *Castlereagh and Adams* to a study of the pre-World War I Anglo-American relationship, and was preeminently concerned with the resolution of troublesome issues between two societies that have formed in the twentieth century what has been aptly called a "natural alliance."[9] Some of this historiographic fascination with Anglo-American relations in the Monroe era, which has never been matched in intensity by works on Franco-American relations, is explained by the role played by British statesmen, notably George Canning, in the formulation of the Monroe Doctrine.[10] In the twentieth-century's recounting of the doctrine's origin, Canning's influence seemed almost preordained to bring about Anglo-American agreement. Had he not uttered the prophetic words about calling in the "New World to redress the balance of the Old"?

The high tide of such sentiment appeared in the World War II tract, *U.S. Foreign Policy: Shield of the Republic*, in which Walter Lippmann argued, in an unabashedly martial spirit of wartime unity, that the Monroe Doctrine derived logically from Canning's proposal of a joint statement on Latin America and thus constituted an unwritten Anglo-American alliance! This venture into historical illusion, though reassuring to the prophets of the Grand Alliance, was not supported by hard evidence, as Bemis wrote in his devastating review of Lippmann's work.[11] Yet, surprisingly, the myth of Anglo-American harmony in the Monroe era has survived in modern accounts. Richard Rush's autobiography of his ministry at the Court of St.

James (from 1817 until 1825), during which Canning made his famous overture about a joint statement on Latin America, has reinforced this view.[12] What has been overlooked is that Rush's book appeared during a time of agitation over the Oregon question in the 1840s, when tensions between Washington and London were high, and was, by the author's admission, designed to mitigate the anglophobic sentiment. As British scholars of this era, especially Charles K. Webster and Harold Temperley, have made clear, Britain's departure from the ways of continental diplomacy after Vienna in no way signified acceptance of American objectives. True, Castlereagh had some consideration for the United States and its role in Western Hemispheric affairs, and Canning often uttered sentiments which conjured up visions of Anglo-American agreement, but both operated on principles of practicality and self-interest.[13]

Much has been written on the Florida purchase but in a piecemeal fashion, reflecting, doubtless, the piecemeal manner by which Florida was originally acquired. The west Florida imbroglio, thus, has inspired a special historiography, beginning with Jefferson's crafty negotiating with France to compel its Spanish ally to cede to the United States the territory between the Perdido and the Mississippi. In these accounts Jefferson is less the statesman than the intriguer. I. J. Cox's monumental 1918 work virtually exhausts the topic and demonstrates, by the author's attention to local issues, the powerful role of the frontier in the settlement of territorial disputes in nineteenth-century American diplomacy.[14] East Florida, by contrast, has received less attention from historians.

The historiography of the Florida question has been characterized by the relatively large attention paid to the attitudes and actions of personalities—in this instance, to Adams and Jackson. While it is unquestionable that the Florida treaty owed much to the almost bullheaded negotiating of Adams and the reckless adventuring of Jackson, as the biographies by Bemis, Remini, and Marquis James attest, such emphasis obscures other explanations for the demise of Spanish Florida. Few works on this topic—Charles C. Griffin's and Philip C. Brooks's are notable exceptions—focus on the Florida question as part of a larger issue, the disintegration of the New World empire of an Old World power.[15]

The dominance of biography is evident also in the historiography of the United States response to the Latin American revolutions. This issue posed two fundamental considerations: the official American posture toward these upheavals and the commercial and cultural interchange between Hispanic America and the United States in an age of revolution. The period of Latin American revolutions was a long one, from 1808 until 1824, or from 1800 until 1830 if one begins with Jefferson, who displayed an unusual interest in Hispanic America, and concludes with the death of the Liberator, Simón Bolívar, in 1830. Whitaker has handled both the official and unofficial relationship, beginning with the intense commercial activity in New Orleans at the turn of the century and concluding with the Panama Congress of 1826. Other, less well-known, books explore the cultural exchanges between Anglo- and Hispanic-American peoples.[16]

Surprisingly, the scholarship in Spanish on this topic has not been fully integrated into the literature of American diplomacy. In part, of course, this omission can be explained by the often-lamented neglect of foreign-language sources by American diplomatic historians. And it can be explained partly by the historical fact that a profound debate ensued in the United States as to the posture the nation should adopt toward the rebellions. That is, scholars have demonstrated less interest in the myriad ways Americans related to the Latin American revolutions than in the intensity of the great debate on recognition between John Quincy Adams and Henry Clay. American hesitation in extending recognition to the new republics, explained by Adams's expedient maneuvering in the Florida negotiations and the secretary of state's predictable assessment of Latin Americans' capacity for self-government, left a legacy of bitterness in hemispheric relations and in the writings of Latin-American students of this era.[17]

American interpretations of the wars of independence remain heavily dependent on a rich documentary record: the unpublished reports of several South American commissions dispatched to study revolutionary situations; records of activities of naval vessels stationed in Latin American waters; and a truly monumental compilation of diplomatic correspondence by William R. Manning. Manning not only selected and edited documents reflecting American policy toward the revolutions and the new republics but in a perhaps unintentional way shaped subsequent scholarship on inter-American relations because he possessed an encompassing knowledge of the official record for this era. No other scholar of the period serving in an editorial role, with the possible exception of Charles K. Webster, who performed a similar role in editing British documents on the same topic, has equaled Manning's knowledge of the official record.[18]

There is nothing really comparable to the Manning or Webster collections, either in scope or importance, for any of the Latin American republics. Most have preserved few of the nineteenth-century official records. The result is a scholarship that is sometimes multiarchival but never truly multinational and almost always one-dimensional, focusing on the revolutions and the early independence periods from the view of the United States, or Britain, or France. Occasionally, comparative works, such as that by J. Fred Rippy, have appeared, but, like so many others of this genre, the comparison is limited to Anglo-American policies. The latest integrated history of the Spanish-American revolutions by John Lynch, a distinguished British scholar, portrays the United States as a sympathetic but alien power whose impact on the outcome of the revolutions was marginal.[19]

In the era 1812-1840 the most significant event in American diplomacy was, of course, the promulgation of what came to be known as the Monroe Doctrine.

The Monroe Doctrine has had, in reality, two histories. One refers to the changing interpretation of the doctrine in its evolution since 1823; stated weakly and ineffectually in the 1820s and 1830s, revived by an expansionist generation in the 1840s and 1850s, confirmed though not formally invoked in the 1860s, exploited in the early decades of the twentieth century as justification for intervention in the internal affairs of Caribbean republics, and presumably, Pan-Americanized in modern times. When the Russian premier, Nikita Khrushchev, declared the doctrine dead in the early 1960s, the Department of State and Congress, two institutions that have historically tried to define the doctrine, angrily denounced him. The other history of the doctrine refers to the scholarly debate over the origins and meaning of Monroe's famous message of 1823.

The most important statement on the Monroe Doctrine, a multivolume "biography" by Dexter Perkins, traces the origins and evolution of Monroe's message from 1823 to 1907, and noticeably reflects the impact that the twentieth century has made on what was originally a presidential comment on a nineteenth-century problem. Perkins began his study of the doctrine as a dissertation at Harvard in 1914, three years before America plunged into the European war under the leadership of a president imploring his people to embark on a new international mission. His first book on the subject did not appear until 1927, however, years after the Wilsonian infection had run its course, and the tone seemed to reflect more the nationalist sentiment of Theodore Roosevelt than the ringing phrases of internationalism sounded by Wilson. Monroe's message, Perkins concluded, advanced two great principles—noncolonization and nonintervention. The first, nourished by the fertile mind of the secretary of state, John Quincy Adams, emanated from the Russian threat on the northwest coast; the second was precipitated by the unjustified fear of European intervention to restore Spanish sovereignty over her former colonies. This fear was unrealistic, Perkins argued, after exhaustively searching the European archives, because British actions would have forestalled any European action, but Adams, always the nationalist, dared not let the opportunity pass without an American declaration.[20]

In a subsequent volume Perkins went so far as to describe the doctrine as an "obsolete shibboleth," a phrase used by Hiram Bingham, the famous discoverer of Machu Picchu, who had written, at the high tide of American intervention in the Caribbean, a stinging criticism of the misuses of the doctrine. But in the aftermath of World War I, which imbued in a generation of historians deep feelings of nationalism, Bingham reversed himself, declaring that the German peril in the Caribbean made the doctrine relevant. Still later, in the spirit of hemispheric unity in the face of European fascism, when the United States once more feared German encroachment in the New World, Perkins published a brisk survey of the doctrine with the defiant title, *Hands Off*. In 1940, when the United States joined with the other hemispheric republics at Havana in supporting a resolution forbidding transfer of hemispheric territory from one European power to another, the Monroe Doctrine was neither obsolete nor a shibboleth.[21]

The vicissitudes of twentieth-century inter-Americanism reveal a great deal about the tone of Monroe Doctrine historiography. In the twentieth century the official interpretation, which has dramatically influenced scholarly writing on the doctrine, has changed considerably. Secretary of State Richard Olney's 1895 statement on the Venezuelan boundary dispute declared the United States and its policies virtually sovereign in the hemisphere. In a private letter written a few years later, Olney stated that he had in fact limited the scope of the doctrine. And in 1914 Elihu Root, who, as secretary of war and of state had been closely identified with the application of Theodore Roosevelt's "police power" in the Caribbean, felt constrained to point out, in a speech to the American Society of International Law, that the "real" Monroe Doctrine was a policy of the American government, not a statute of international law. If America intervened in the affairs of its sister republics, it did so without recourse to the doctrine but to its rights of self-protection under the law of nations. In 1929, when anti-American sentiment in Latin America was running strong because of the Nicaraguan intervention, the solicitor of the State Department, J. Reuben Clark, offered a similar analysis. Perhaps the sternest official definition of the doctrine, however, had been delivered by Secretary of State Charles Evans Hughes, in a speech commemorating the centennial of Monroe's message. In an address before the American Bar Association, Hughes unashamedly declared that the United States had a right to intervene in Latin America to safeguard its security, but the Monroe Doctrine did *not* infringe upon the sovereignty of the hemispheric republics, nor did it impose any obstacle to Pan-Americanism.[22]

It may be true, as someone once said, that hypocrisy is the tribute vice pays to virtue. Certainly the discrepancy between profession and performance convinced a generation of Latin Americans that such utterances were patent deceptions. In Latin-American accounts of the doctrine, then, the general view is that an expansionist United States has distorted the true meaning of the original doctrine as justification for intervention. Not surprisingly, the most strident condemnation of the Monroe Doctrine appeared in the heyday of American imperialism in the Caribbean. Many of the great social and political thinkers of Latin America of this generation, such as the Argentine sociologist José Ingenieros, Manuel Ugarte, also an Argentinian and author of the brilliant anti-American manifesto *The Destiny of a Continent*, and the Nicaraguan poet, Rubén Darío, castigated the Monroe Doctrine. After the Nicaraguan intervention of 1927, which precipitated a vigorous debate on intervention at the sixth inter-American conference in Havana, the United States tried to mollify Latin America by reevaluating its interventionist policies and, under Franklin Roosevelt, by stressing hemispheric cooperation. But what sentimental or intellectual links existed between the Monroe Doctrine and Pan-Americanism were broken by two of the most effective (probably because both works appeared in English) Latin American criticisms of the Monroe Doctrine—Raúl Diez de Medina (Gaston Nerval, pseud.), *Autopsy of the Monroe Doctrine*, published in 1934, and Luís Quintanilla, *A Latin American Speaks*, which appeared during World War II when inter-American sentiment ran strong. Both required an abandonment of the more odious features of the Monroe Doctrine before a true Pan-Americanism could thrive.[23]

The Monroe Doctrine offers an illustration of that scholarly maxim that one's conclusions are often shaped by one's predilections or method of research. Considerable debate has been generated in determining the origins of principles expressed in Monroe's message. Thus, the biographers of John Quincy Adams, whose foreign-policy views presumably prevailed in the Monroe era, argue convincingly that the decision to reject Canning's overture for a joint declaration in favor of a unilateral announcement was owing to Adams's shrewdness and intellectual persuasiveness in the cabinet debate. The most forceful proponents of the Adams school are Worthington Ford and Samuel Flagg Bemis, both of whom had unrestricted access to the voluminous Adams papers. Ford edited probably the most widely used collection of Adams's works; and Bemis published in 1949 his magisterial biography, *John Quincy Adams and the Foundations of American Foreign Policy*. And, it should be recalled, the most vigorous defender of Adams's role in the making of the Monroe Doctrine was of course Adams himself, whose diary, which bristles with acidulous commentary on American politics and society, has reinforced in modern scholarship Adams's very high opinion of himself. Monroe's biographers, most recently Harry Ammon, identify the doctrine with the man whose name it bears. Jefferson's intellectual disciples trace its major ideas to the Sage of Monticello. And other scholars champion the cause of the Argentinian Carlos de Alvear, the publicist Abbé de Pradt, or even Canning, as the figure of the age whose ideas shaped the doctrine. There is credit given to Sir Thomas More, whose masterpiece, *Utopia*, with its lyrical praise of the New World advanced the doctrine of the "two spheres," an inherent theme of Monroe's famous statement.[24]

There is also a debate about how the Monroe Doctrine fits into the larger scheme of Pan-Americanism and the "Western Hemispheric Idea." Historians who matured in the years after World War I, such as Joseph B.

Lockey or Whitaker, were intrigued with the apparent contradictions in the thinking of a generation that extolled the isolationist sentiments of Washington's Farewell Address and rejected Latin America's plea for a defensive alliance but ultimately identified with the concept of inter-American cooperation. Revisionist diplomatic historians, such as Richard Van Alstyne or William Appleman Williams, by contrast, interpret the Monroe Doctrine as a statement of American empire, cleverly disguised in isolationist language, the origins of which lay in the imperial designs of Monroe's predecessors—James Madison and Benjamin Franklin, for example, who advanced expansionist concepts of American empire.[25]

Given the large number (more than three hundred fifty listings in the Library of Congress catalog) of books and pamphlets on the Monroe Doctrine, it would seem that the relevant issues have been thoroughly ventilated. One of the few nineteenth-century scholarly efforts to interpret Monroe's message was G. F. Tucker's *The Monroe Doctrine*, which appeared in 1885. In the two decades following the war with Spain, three histories, each bearing the title *Monroe Doctrine*, were published. Uniformly they expressed an American viewpont. Not until Perkins's 1927 volume did scholarship on the Monroe Doctrine reflect multiarchival—and to some degree, multinational—influence. Indeed, what explains the continued dominance of Perkins's study is the fact that the author thoroughly explored the European archives. Subsequent studies, such as the one by E. H. Tatum, which advanced the thesis that the doctrine was directed against Britain and not the continental allies, have been unable to challenge Perkins simply because of the thoroughness of his research. There are three hundred fifty works on the doctrine but that of one author overshadows the others.[26]

Perkins's dominance in Monroe Doctrine historiography has been challenged by historians employing new methodological techniques. A distinguished historian of twentieth-century American foreign policy, Ernest R. May, has used a combination of traditional and quantitative methods. Undertaking an assignment to write still another history of the doctrine, May was confronted with a conundrum: the decision to reject Canning's overture for a joint declaration on Latin America originated with Adams, yet there is no evidence that Adams convinced the other members of Monroe's cabinet, who appeared to be in favor of Canning's proposal, to come round to the secretary of state's views because of his intellectual persuasiveness. May has concluded that Monroe's associates, including Adams, were motivated less by their convictions than by a desire to identify with a stern statement that would enhance their presidential aspirations. The most hallowed document in American diplomacy, then, emanated from the maneuverings of self-serving politicians. This is not to denigrate the doctrine, May argues, for the famous message of Monroe represented the foreign policy of a democracy.[27]

The historiography of Jacksonian diplomacy has been characterized by a tendency to explain Jackson's foreign policies largely in terms of his personality. In John William Ward's brilliant assessment of Jackson and his impact upon the times, Old Hickory is called the "rationalization of American imperialism," but Ward makes little effort to pursue the point in an extended analysis. Jackson's biographers, notably Marquis James and John S. Bassett, have measured his foreign policy by his notorious outrage over the French spoliations treaty, his adjustments with Britain in the West Indies trade dispute, and his conduct toward Mexico and the Texas revolution.[28] In the diplomatic historiography of the 1830s the Texas question dominates, of course. During the centennial celebration of the revolution, the publishing industry of the state disgorged volumes to meet an almost insatiable demand for works on Sam Houston, the Alamo, or some other heroic topic in the history of the Lone Star State. At the same time an embittered young historian, Richard Stenberg, was grinding out scholarly articles condemning Jackson for his abusive policies toward Mexico and his conspiracy with Houston to incite the Texas revolution. The prominent Texas historian, E. C. Barker, tried valiantly to correct this distortion by showing that the revolution stemmed mostly from cultural differences between Mexicans and Anglos.[29]

The most noticeable flaw in the voluminous and often brilliant historiography of this era is the absence of an integrated synthesis spanning the entirety of American diplomacy from Ghent to the expansionist 1840s.[30] American leaders of this generation came to political maturity during the great debate over neutral rights and the second war for independence from Great Britain. The age that followed was, clearly, an age of nationalism, in which the nation's political aspirants articulated the country's fundamental policies toward the world. And it was an age of nationalists—Monroe, Adams, Calhoun, Clay, and Jackson. The biographer of each has credited his subject with the accolade of true nationalist. The best syntheses of the era, Dangerfield's *Era of Good Feelings* and his *Awakening of American Nationalism*, brilliantly capture this nationalistic spirit. But Dangerfield fails to carry his theme into the years of Jackson, whose diplomatic philosophy called for a dissemination of American diplomatic principles—free trade and nonentanglement—to a larger world. Indeed, Jackson may very well have been the supreme nationalist of his age, if not the most articulate.

Notes

1. Samuel Flagg Bemis, *John Quincy Adams and the Foundations of American Foreign Policy* (New York: Alfred A. Knopf, 1949), esp. pp. 566-72. The second

volume, *John Quincy Adams and the Union* (New York: Alfred A. Knopf, 1956), assesses Adams's "second career" as U.S. representative but touches occasionally on foreign policy.

2. Bemis, *Adams and Foreign Policy*, pp. 382-408; Worthington C. Ford, "John Quincy Adams and the Monroe Doctrine," *American Historical Review* 7 (July 1902): 676-96; Charles Francis Adams, ed., *Memoirs of John Quincy Adams*, 12 vols. (Philadelphia: J. B. Lippincott Co., 1874-1875), 6: 177-215.

3. Charles Webster, *The Foreign Policy of Castlereagh, 1815-1822: Britain and the European Alliance* (London: G. Bell & Sons, 1947); Harold Temperley, *The Foreign Policy of Canning, 1822-1827: England, the Neo-Holy Alliance, and the New World* (London: G. Bell & Sons, 1925); W. P. Cresson, *James Monroe* (Chapel Hill: University of North Carolina Press, 1946); Harry Ammon, *James Monroe: The Quest for National Identity* (New York: McGraw-Hill, 1971); Robert V. Remini, *Andrew Jackson and the Course of American Empire* (New York: Harper & Row, 1977); George Dangerfield, *The Era of Good Feelings* (New York: Harcourt, Brace & World, 1952).

4. Walter LaFeber, ed., *John Quincy Adams and American Continental Empire* (Chicago: Quadrangle Books, 1965).

5. Bradford Perkins, *Castlereagh and Adams: England and the United States, 1812-1823* (Berkeley: University of California Press, 1964).

6. Arthur P. Whitaker, *The United States and the Independence of Latin America, 1800-1830* (Baltimore: Johns Hopkins Press, 1941).

7. Arthur P. Whitaker, *The Spanish-American Frontier, 1783-1795* (Cambridge, Mass.: Harvard University Press, 1927) and *The Mississippi Question, 1795-1803* (New York: D. Appleton-Century, 1934).

8. Perkins, *Castlereagh and Adams*, chaps. 4-6. For wartime diplomacy *see* Charles Gates, "The West In American Diplomacy, 1812-1815," *Mississippi Valley Historical Review*, 24 (March 1940): 499-510; Fred Engleman, *The Peace of Christmas Eve* (London: Rupert Hart-Davis, 1960); Reginald Horsman, *The War of 1812* (New York: Alfred A. Knopf, 1969); F. A. Updyke, *The Diplomacy of the War of 1812* (Baltimore: Johns Hopkins Press, 1915); Henry Adams, *History of the United States during the Administrations of Thomas Jefferson and James Madison*, 9 vols. (New York: Charles Scribner's Sons, 1921), vols. 6-9; Raymond Walters, *Albert Gallatin: Jeffersonian Financier and Diplomat* (New York: Macmillan Co., 1957); Patrick C. T. White, *A Nation on Trial: America and the War of 1812* (New York: John Wiley & Sons, 1965).

9. Bradford Perkins, *The Great Rapprochement: England and the United States, 1895-1914* (New York: Atheneum, 1968).

10. This era witnessed no spirit of Franco-American compromise, though Americans remained fascinated with France and adulated Lafayette. *See* Anne Loveland, *Emblem of Liberty: The Image of Lafayette in the American Mind* (Baton Rouge: Louisiana State University Press, 1971) and Henry Blumenthal, *A Reappraisal of Franco-American Relations, 1830-1871* (Chapel Hill: University of North Carolina Press, 1959). On the American cultural impact in Britain, *see* David P. Crook, *American Democracy in British Politics, 1815-1850* (Oxford: Oxford University Press, Clarendon Press, 1965) and Frank Thistlethwaite, *The Anglo-American*

Connection in the Early Nineteenth Century (Philadelphia: University of Pennsylvania Press, 1959).

11. Walter Lippmann, *U.S. Foreign Policy: Shield of the Republic* (Boston: Little, Brown & Co., 1943); Samuel Flagg Bemis, "Walter Lippmann on United States Foreign Policy," *Hispanic American Historical Review* 23 (November 1943): 664-67. On this theme *see also* H. C. Allen, *Great Britain and the United States: A History of Anglo-American Relations* (New York: St. Martin's Press, 1955), esp. pp. 350-81.

12. Richard Rush, *Memoranda of a Residence at the Court of London . . . From 1819 to 1825* (Philadelphia: Lea & Blanchard, 1845).

13. *See* especially Webster, *Foreign Policy of Castlereagh*, pp. 437-53; Temperley, *Foreign Policy of Canning*, pp. 126-56.

14. *See*, for example, Clifford Egan, "The United States, France, and West Florida, 1803-1807," *Florida Historical Quarterly* 47 (January 1969): 227-52. Even more critical of Jefferson is Wanjohi Waciuma, *Intervention in Spanish Florida, 1801-1813: A Study in Jeffersonian Foreign Policy* (New York: Brandon, 1976). *See also*, Isaac J. Cox, *West Florida Controversy, 1798-1813: A Study in American Diplomacy* (Baltimore: Johns Hopkins Press, 1918). On East Florida *see* Rembert Patrick, *Florida Fiasco: Rampant Rebels on the Georgia-Florida Boundary, 1810-1815* (Athens: University of Georgia Press, 1954).

15. Bemis, *Adams and Foreign Policy*, pp. 300-340; Remini, *Andrew Jackson*, pp. 298-398; Marquis James, *Andrew Jackson: The Border Captain* (New York: Literary Guild, 1933), chaps. 18-19; Charles C. Griffin, *The United States and the Disruption of the Spanish Empire, 1810-1822: A Study of the Relations of the United States with Spain and the Rebel Spanish Colonies* (New York: Columbia University Press, 1937); Philip C. Brooks, *Diplomacy and the Borderlands: The Adams-Onís Treaty of 1819* (Berkeley: University of California Press, 1939). An older study, Herbert Fuller, *The Purchase of Florida: Its History and Diplomacy* (Cleveland: Burrows Co., 1906), uses only American sources.

16. Whitaker, *United States and . . . Latin America*; Harry Bernstein, *Origins of Inter-American Interest, 1700-1812* (Philadelphia: University of Pennsylvania Press, 1945) and *Making an Inter-American Mind* (Gainesville: University of Florida Press, 1961).

17. Two important works in Spanish are: Rafael Altamira y Crevea, *Resumen Histórico de la Independencia de América Española* (Buenos Aires: Menéndez y Galli, 1910), and Nicolás García Samudio, *La Independencia de Hispano América* (México: Fondo de Cultura Económica, 1945). On the military aspects of British and American involvement *see* G. S. Graham and R. A. Humphreys, *The Navy and South America: 1807-1823: Correspondence of the Commanders-in-Chief on the South American Station* (London: Naval Records Society, 1962) and Edward Billingsley, *In Defense of Neutral Rights: The United States Navy and the Wars of Independence in Chile and Peru* (Chapel Hill: University of North Carolina Press, 1967). For the Clay-Adams debate *see* Whitaker, *U.S. and . . . Latin America*, pp. 344-69 and H. L. Hoskins, "The Hispanic American Policy of Henry Clay, 1816-1828," *Hispanic American Historical Review* 7 (November 1927): 460-78.

18. William R. Manning, ed., *Diplomatic Correspondence of the United States Concerning the Independence of the Latin American Nations*, 3 vols. (New York:

Carnegie Endowment for International Peace, 1925). For the 1830-1861 era *see* William R. Manning, ed., *The Diplomatic Correspondence of the United States: Inter-American Affairs, 1831-1861*, 12 vols., (Washington, D.C.: Carnegie Endowment for International Peace, 1932-39); Charles K. Webster, *ed., Britain and the Independence of Latin America*, 2 vols. (London: Oxford University Press, 1938).

19. J. Fred Rippy, *Rivalry of the United States and Great Britain over Latin America, 1808-1830* (Baltimore: Johns Hopkins Press, 1929); John Lynch, *The Spanish American Revolutions, 1808-1826* (New York: W. W. Norton & Co., 1973). *See also* W. W. Kaufman, *British Policy and the Independence of Latin America, 1804-1828* (New Haven: Yale University Press, 1951).

20. Dexter Perkins, *The Monroe Doctrine, 1823-1826* (Cambridge, Mass.: Harvard University Press, 1927).

21. Dexter Perkins, *The Monroe Doctrine, 1826-1867* (Baltimore: Johns Hopkins Press, 1933); *The Monroe Doctrine, 1867-1907* (Baltimore: Johns Hopkins Press, 1937); and *Hands Off: A History of the Monroe Doctrine* (Boston: Little, Brown & Co., 1941); Hiram Bingham, *The Monroe Doctrine: An Obsolete Shibboleth* (New Haven: Yale University Press, 1913). John Logan traces the history of an important parallel principle in *No Transfer: An American Security Principle* (New Haven: Yale University Press, 1961). In 1811 the House of Representatives resolved not to permit the transfer of Spanish Florida to another nonhemispheric power. From the 1870s the "no transfer doctrine" was incorporated into the Monroe Doctrine and reasserted at the Havana conference of 1940. After World War II the Monroe Doctrine was used also as justification for America's global mission. The historian (and future U.S. Senator from Wyoming) Gale McGee argued, in "The Monroe Doctrine—A Stopgap Measure," *Mississippi Valley Historical Review* 38 (September 1951): 233-50, that the declaration was meant to be a prelude to an Anglo-American collaboration. And in the 1963 edition, Dexter Perkins, *A History of the Monroe Doctrine* (Boston: Little, Brown & Co., 1963) argued that the doctrine "never was intended to bar the way to the larger defense of American interests . . . in other parts of the globe."

22. Elihu Root, "The Real Monroe Doctrine," *American Journal of International Law* 8 (July 1914): 428-42; Charles Evans Hughes, *The Pathway of Peace* (New York: Harper & Brothers, 1928); J. R. Clark, *Memorandum on the Monroe Doctrine* (Washington, D.C.: Government Printing Office, 1930). Olney's letter was written to A. E. Keet, January 15, 1897, Letterbook Vol. 9, Richard Olney Papers, Library of Congress.

23. Donald W. Dozer, ed., *The Monroe Doctrine: Its Modern Significance* (New York: Alfred A. Knopf, 1965), features Latin American views. Raúl Diez de Medina [Gaston Nerval], *Autopsy of the Monroe Doctrine* (New York: Macmillan Co., 1934); Luís Quintanilla, *A Latin American Speaks* (New York: Macmillan Co., 1943). For a Soviet view *see* S. Gonionsky, "The Unburied Corpse of the Monroe Doctrine," *International Affairs* (October 1960): 60-66.

24. Allan Nevins, ed., *The Diary of John Quincy Adams* (New York: Longmans, Green & Co., 1929); Ammon, *James Monroe*, chap. 27; Laura Bornholdt, "The Abbé de Pradt and the Monroe Doctrine," *Hispanic American Historical Review* 24 (May 1944): 201-22; Thomas B. Davis, Jr., "Carlos de Alvear and James Monroe: New Light on the Origin of the Monroe Doctrine," *Hispanic American Historical*

Review 23 (November 1943): 632-49; Dangerfield, *Era of Good Feelings*, esp. pp. 293-308.

25. A handy collection illustrating this point is Armin Rappaport, ed., *The Monroe Doctrine* (New York: Holt, Rinehart, and Winston, 1964). Arthur P. Whitaker, *The Western Hemisphere Idea: Its Rise and Decline* (Ithaca: Cornell University Press, 1954) lists the major Latin American interpretations of the hemispheric idea, which are profoundly Bolivarian in spirit. Two revisionist interpretations of the doctrine are William A. Williams, "The Age of Mercantilism: An Interpretation of the American Political Economy, 1763-1828," *William and Mary Quarterly* 15 (October 1958): 419-37 and Richard Van Alstyne, *The Rising American Empire* (Chicago: Quadrangle Books, 1965).

26. Dexter Perkins, *Yield of the Years* (Boston: Little, Brown & Co., 1969); E. H. Tatum, *The United States and Europe, 1815-1823* (Berkeley: University of California Press, 1936); George F. Tucker, *The Monroe Doctrine: A Concise History of its Origins and Growth* (Boston: G. B. Reed, 1885); John Bassett Moore, *The Monroe Doctrine: Its Origin and Meaning* (New York: Evening Post Publishing Co., 1895); William F. Reddaway, *The Monroe Doctrine* (New York: G. E. Stechert, 1905).

27. Ernest R. May, *The Making of the Monroe Doctrine* (Cambridge, Mass.: Harvard University Press, 1975).

28. John S. Bassett, *The Life of Andrew Jackson*, 2 vols. (1911; reprint ed., New York: Archon Books, 1967); Marquis James, *Andrew Jackson: Portrait of a President* (Indianapolis: Bobbs-Merrill Co., 1937); George Dangerfield, *Awakening of American Nationalism, 1815-1828* (New York: Harper & Row, 1965); John William Ward, *Andrew Jackson: Symbol for an Age* (New York: Oxford University Press, 1955).

29. The literature on the Texas revolution is voluminous, but this controversy may be followed in Richard Stenberg, "Jackson, Anthony Butler, and Texas," *Southwestern Social Science Quarterly* 13 (December 1932): 264-86 and "The Texas Schemes of Jackson and Houston, 1829-1836," *Southwestern Social Science Quarterly* 15 (December 1934): 229-50; and Eugene C. Barker, *Mexico and Texas, 1821-1835* (Dallas: Southern Methodist University Press, 1928). David Pletcher devotes careful attention to this question in *The Diplomacy of Annexation: Texas, Oregon, the Mexican War* (Columbia: University of Missouri Press, 1973).

30. The most recent bibliography of the period is Robert Remini and Edwin Miles, eds., *The Era of Good Feelings and the Age of Jackson, 1816-1841* (Arlington Heights, Ill.: AHM Publishing Corp., 1979). *See also*, in the same series, Norman A. Graebner, ed., *American Diplomatic History before 1900* (Arlington Heights, Ill.: AHM Publishing Corp., 1978).

4 ______ Destiny and Diplomacy, 1840–1865

ANNA KASTEN NELSON

"We must ever maintain the principle that the people of this continent alone have the right to decide their own destiny . . ." wrote President Polk in his first message to Congress.[1] For the next twenty years, Americans wrestled with those decisions of "destiny." By 1865 they had determined to expand to the Pacific, but not beyond; to encompass those territories which were sparsely settled, while rejecting those with too many alien peoples; and to accept the Northern rather than the Southern blueprint for the nation's future. Thus, the final result was both more than could be imagined by Senator Dickerson of New Jersey who wrote in 1825, "Oregon can never be one of the United States. . . . The Union is already too extensive . . . ," and less than the desires of men such as James Buchanan who wrote in 1848, "We must have Cuba. We can't do without Cuba. . . . We shall acquire it by a coup d'etat at some propitious moment. . . ."[2]

Impressive figures of land acquisition—1,200,000 square miles between 1845 and 1848—and the colorful rhetoric of the supporters of unlimited expansion encourage students of history to neglect the equally important fact that between 1848 and 1860 the only territorial addition to the United States was the Gadsden Purchase, and that had more to do with building railroads than achieving manifest destiny. There were, in fact, important internal and external factors setting the peripheries of destiny. The history of American expansion in the decades preceding the Civil War is not only the history of destiny achieved; it is also the history of destiny contained.

As David M. Pletcher writes in a recent essay, although the term manifest destiny was first applied specifically to the proposed annexation of the Texas Republic and Oregon Territory, it came to mean "the whole range of American expansionist rationalizations." With the publication in 1935 of Albert K. Weinberg's *Manifest Destiny*, the broader definition was "firmly established."[3]

Certainly every examination of the ideological underpinnings of expansion must start with *Manifest Destiny*. Weinberg notes that the expansionists of the 1840s inherited certain justifications for expansion from earlier generations. To the doctrine of natural right, the theory of geographical predestination and the assumption that the white race had a superior right to the land because it used land "according to the intentions of the CREATOR," these expansionists added the "dogma of special mission." Through expansion, the United States would extend the area of freedom and regenerate backward peoples. Therefore, expansionism of the 1840s was distinguished by its purpose as well as its scope.

By the 1850s another ingredient had been added to this stew of ideas. The "spread-eagle" expansionists were no longer content with natural boundaries or the regeneration of peoples within those boundaries. Looking west to Hawaii and south to Cuba, they insisted that nations were like children and had to grow for good health. For a nation to progress, it must grow even beyond the restraints of natural boundaries.

The exhaustive manner in which Weinberg traces to its roots each of the ideas which influenced the course of expansionism makes *Manifest Destiny* a ponderous book. Weinberg writes that a sense of mission gives a nation a sense of moral purpose, and "in its moral purposiveness the idea of a national destiny is not unreasonable." One reason the book has been reprinted rather than replaced may be that its thoroughness provides a wealth of material for the critics of American expansion. The critical reader of today need only bring a different viewpoint to Weinberg's scholarship to find ample evidence of the racial arrogance and national greed behind this "moral purposiveness."[4]

In a book clearly labeled a reinterpretation Frederick Merk needs only one line to define the subject that occupies Weinberg's book. Manifest destiny "meant expansion, prearranged by heaven, over an area not clearly defined."[5] This terse sentence is indicative of Merk's nonideological approach which contrasts sharply with Weinberg's. In *Manifest Destiny and Mission in American History: A Reinterpretation*, Merk concludes that the concept of a manifest destiny did not reflect the national spirit and lacked both sectional and national support. Instead, it was largely propaganda to gain public support for the acquisition of a specific territory at a particular time. In Merk's view, manifest destiny was a movement limited in both time and place. "Manifest Destiny was continentalism. . . . It meant absorption of North America" and contained the principle that "a people not capable of rising to statehood should never be annexed."[6]

Manifest destiny, Merk contends, died in 1848 after the completion of the continental boundaries. It is the idea of mission, quite separate from that of manifest destiny, which, as the true expression of the national spirit, has permeated all of American history. A sense of mission preceded manifest destiny, and is still a part of the national spirit in the twentieth century. Keeping the idea of mission separate, Merk not only returns the phrase manifest destiny to a specific era, but provides it with specific limitations.

Norman Graebner also regards the expansionist drive of the 1840s as a limited one, a precise and calculated movement to preserve the national interests. He agrees with Merk that "manifest destiny was purely the creation of editors and politicians." Those who preached the crusade were "ideologues, not statesmen." While they preached, policymakers, including President Polk, proceeded with specific territorial objectives in order to accomplish the goal of maintaining the national interest.[7]

Richard W. Van Alstyne's *The Rising American Empire* attempts a complete refutation of this view, asserting that manifest destiny was never a limited movement. Covering two hundred years of history with a broad and colorful brush, he draws three conclusions. First, that the United States was an expansionist power—a rising empire—from its very inception. Second, that this expansion did not happen accidentally, but was so well planned that the outlines for American growth were virtually complete by 1800. Third, American expansion was never exclusively continental in nature, but was always global in its orientation.

Unconcerned with the ideological foundations, Van Alstyne concentrates on the political and economic manifestations of the American appetite for land and commerce. The organization of his book indicates that he does not even consider the era of manifest destiny a proper historical division: the annexation of Texas is discussed in one chapter while the Mexican War is discussed in another (devoted to the empire of commerce on the Pacific) and the expansive forays toward the south occupy a third ("The Thrust into the Caribbean, 1848-1917").[8]

Charles Vevier, in "American Continentalism: An Idea of Expansion, 1845-1910," adds a geopolitical factor to Van Alstyne's interpretation of expansionism by suggesting the existence of two related American worlds: "the nation-continent created through the interaction of foreign policy and territorial expansion that resulted in the acquisition of contiguous territory in North America," and "the continental domain that was fated to extend its influence over the entire world through the expansion of commerce and control of international communications." Aligning himself with those who see the era of manifest destiny as just a phase in the sweep of American expansion, Vevier writes that historians should therefore explore the "concept of American continentalism as an ideology of overseas expansion."[9]

Although Van Alstyne's most recent article on expansion was published in 1972, and Merk published five books after 1962, both historians began their original research on Oregon and annexation more than forty years ago—at approximately the time that Weinberg was publishing *Manifest Destiny*. The more recent research of Graebner and Vevier dates from the

1950s. It is striking that in spite of the revisionism which has affected so much of American diplomatic history, no new interpretations of manifest destiny have emerged from the 1960s.

Although the Tyler administration must be credited with the annexation of Texas, the halcyon days of territorial expansion came during the presidential term of James K. Polk. By settling the dispute over Oregon and going to war with Mexico, Polk virtually completed the territorial boundaries of the United States. He therefore is a pivotal figure in the historical controversies surrounding these events.[10]

For almost fifty years the history of the diplomacy of the Polk administration was dominated by a handful of books written between 1907 and 1920. Jesse S. Reeves's book on American diplomacy under Tyler and Polk and volumes on Texas, Mexico, and the United States by George L. Rives, Ephraim D. Adams, and Justin Smith became the standard works influencing the perceptions of historians and the textbooks of their students. Each of these volumes evidenced highly nationalistic views of American diplomacy. The most nationalistic, Smith's *War With Mexico*, was also perhaps the most influential.[11]

War With Mexico won the Pulitzer Prize in 1920 and appears to be a book of formidable scholarship. (It consists of two volumes with almost 350 pages of notes.) But the conclusions expressed in the text are not necessarily substantiated by the paragraphs of notes. Smith wrote a highly personal, extremely opinionated book, never hesitating to express his views about the individuals and events he describes.

Polk was "simply Polk the Mediocre," possessed of "seriousness, industry, and fidelity," but "incapable of seeing great things in a great way." He was not, in Smith's opinion, a person who would plot to take his country into war. Seeking peace, Polk was forced into war by the Mexicans, who could not be expected to handle properly a "complicated question requiring all possible sanity of judgment and perfect self-control." Even Polk's desire for the Mexican borderlands was justified by the fact that Mexico, rather than improving on its Spanish heritage, had simply degenerated. A patient president and public, Smith concludes, had no other recourse but war. "While ours could perhaps be called a war *of* conquest, it was not a war *for* conquest—the really vital point."[12]

Reeves's assessment of the war is slightly less nationalistic and much less opinionated. He is quite willing to conclude that Polk went to war for the conquest of California and indicates that his diplomatic dealings with Mexico suffered from his lack of knowledge of the "spanish character." But, as in other nationalistic histories of the early twentieth century, the criticism remains muted.

Several accounts of the war have been written using Smith as the essential source. Alfred Hoyt Bill clearly reflects the view that Mexico was the provocative belligerent, but thinks well enough of Polk to refer to him as the "hero of the piece." Even the most recent popularized version of the war by Seymour V. Connor and Odie B. Faulk returns to the view that while men and factions on both sides were responsible for war, Mexico was the more aggressive. Only Otis A. Singletary successfully uses the vast information collected by Smith without absorbing his opinions. Singletary's book remains the best brief, factual account of the events of the war.[13]

In a 1967 book, Glenn W. Price implicated Polk in an intrigue specifically designed to bring Mexico into a war to satisfy the president's insatiable expansionist desires. Expanding on the thesis of an article written in 1935 by Richard R. Stenberg, Price angrily concludes that for too long the nationalistic historians succeeded in covering up the aggressive manner in which Polk instigated war. Perhaps because of his tendency for overstatement, Price failed to convince historians of Polk's involvement in the intrigue. However, few historians now doubt that Polk's expansionist impulse led to a war for California, rather than a war over Texas.[14]

That war *was* fought for California is Graebner's central thesis in *Empire on the Pacific.* He develops the view that American expansion was inspired as much by commercial interests, eastern mercantilists, and the Whig desire for ports, as by the agrarian desire for land. Although Graebner supports the view that Polk would have preferred peace to war, he asserts that Polk willingly chose the latter in order to gain the ports of California. Polk's belligerent bargaining with Britain over Oregon was as much for the Juan de Fuca Strait as for the fertile soil of the Willamette valley. Although his tone and style are different, Van Alstyne basically agrees with this mercantile thesis. Frederick Merk, in *The Monroe Doctrine and American Expansionism, 1843-1849*, however, interprets Polk's concern over Texas, Oregon, and California as a concern for the security of the United States. Whether or not he was justified in his fears, Polk perceived Great Britain as a threat to American security. In Polk's mind, Merk concludes, the way to fend off dangerous potential aggressors was to "acquire the periphery."[15]

There is little question that David M. Pletcher's, *The Diplomacy of Annexation* is now the definitive account of the diplomacy of the Polk administration. His scholarly book on the events surrounding the annexation of Texas and Oregon and the Mexican War is the product of extensive multiarchival research in the United States, England, Spain, and France, as well as an exhaustive search through secondary sources.

Pletcher if not concerned with the ideology of manifest destiny or the domestic problems of the United States except in so far as they directly influenced the diplomatic events. This is a balanced, thorough, detailed account of the diplomats and their diplomacy, and therein lies both its strength and its weakness. Only after he has completed the narrative does Pletcher enliven his subject by assessing the participants and appraising their actions.

Pletcher concludes that the country paid too high a price for annexation in the 1840s because Polk neglected conventional diplomacy. Blunders delayed the treaty with Great Britain over Oregon Territory while the war with Mexico was the direct result of Polk's belief in aggressive negotiation. Comparing the achievements with the costs, he concludes that the gains in territory and the growth in European respect for the United States must be balanced against the rise of American chauvinism and the divisive forces of sectionalism. Although he does not accuse Polk of intrigue, he does place the responsibility for war firmly in his hands. Imagining nonexistent British threats, Polk went to war for territory which was ultimately destined for acquisition because of the inevitable migrations of Americans.[16]

The Diplomacy of Annexation renders the footnotes of Smith and Reeves obsolete, but students of the 1840s will still profit from the lively prose of Merk and the interpretations of Van Alstyne and Graebner. In addition, it would be remiss not to compare the conclusions of Pletcher with those of Polk's most recent biographer, Charles G. Sellers. Sellers has completed only two volumes of his projected three-volume biography, but the concluding chapters of the second, *James K. Polk, Continentalist, 1843-1846*, address the issues raised by Pletcher. Sellers, who does not always condone Polk's most recent biographer, Charles G. Sellers. Sellers has completed remarkable presidents. He disputes the charge that Polk bungled negotiations with Great Britain and Mexico. Instead, as 1846 came to a close, "by a remarkable combination of nerve, judgment, and disingenuous manipulation of men, Polk had completed the first two phases of his continental program, Texas and Oregon."[17]

Robert E. May writes in *The Southern Dream of a Caribbean Empire, 1854-1861*, that the year 1850 was a turning point in the expansionist movement. Before 1850, American expansionists looked south with a nationalist vision. After 1850, the movement was sectionalized and only the South, seeking to preserve a slave empire, was interested in expansion in the Caribbean. May discusses Mexico, Cuba, and Nicaragua from 1854-1861 and effectively places the adventures of the filibusters within the political framework of the decade. Romance meets reality. The failure of the expansionists and the containment of expansionism are firmly tied to the fear of potential political repercussions from the annexation of territories with slaves or with the potential for a slave economy. May exaggerates the sectional nature of expansionist support and his emphasis on Southern interests limits the book as a definitive treatment of the era. Although he clearly notes the expansionist views of two Northern presidents, Franklin Pierce and James Buchanan, he fails to account for the fact that many of the leading expansionist newspapers were in New York City or that New York entrepreneurs were the financial backers of the Southern dream. He discusses the attempts of many Southerners to reap financial benefits from the Caribbean movement, and notes that Pierre Soule acted as an attorney for New York supporters of the Tehuantepec canal across Mexico. However, because he limits the book to the Southern dream, the economic underpinnings of the movement, firmly planted in the North, are neglected.[18] But his analysis does point to the fact that expansion after 1850 became inexorably tied to the question of slavery and free soil.

Because of Whig opposition and Democratic timidity, the expansinists moved outside the constraining bonds of diplomacy. Hence filibusters and entrepreneurs became their agents abroad. Enamored with the adventures surrounding these individuals, some historians have romanticized their lives and exaggerated their achievements. One example is William H. Goetzmann's brief and extremely readable treatment of expansionism, *When the Eagle Screamed.* It is also an uncritical appreciation. From its first chapter on Jefferson and John Quincy Adams, "clear-eyed men of destiny," to the closing quotation from Rudyard Kipling, Goetzmann encourages the reader to join him in an unabashed appreciation of individual and national chauvinism. Oregon, Texas, California, Nicaragua, Cuba, Central America, Hawaii, China—all are depicted as proper goals in the growth of young America.[19]

For some of his dramatic details, Goetzmann, like several other historians, relies upon Edward S. Wallace's *Destiny and Glory. Destiny and Glory* is a book about people: well-known and obscure filibusters, a minister to Spain (Pierre Soule), and a person Wallace refers to as "the female of the species" (Jane Storms Cazneau.) Although Wallace lists some sources in a bibliography and assures us that his research was extensive, the absence of footnotes requires the reader to accept this assertion on faith. There is much in Wallace that does not bear scholarly scrutiny, for in order to engage his reader Wallace records and exploits every myth surrounding these adventurers. Thus the book, like the movement it describes, may be based upon fact, but is built upon conjecture.[20]

There is no single volume which satisfactorily treats the broad range of expansionist interests in the 1850s. Dexter Perkins's, *The Monroe Doctrine, 1826-1867,* discusses American interests in the Western Hemisphere, but interprets these interests solely within the limitations of his primary concern, the Monroe Doctrine. Oriented to American sources and American national interests, he is sympathetic to American attempts to repel European meddling. Although the book is largely a justification of American actions, it does contribute to the understanding of the extent of American involvement by noting that American presidents before 1867 rarely invoked the doctrine or exerted American pressure on events south of the Caribbean countries.[21]

Two quite different books provide useful interpretations of United States relations with Cuba. Basil Rauch, in a monograph specifically devoted to the period 1848-1854, provides the most detailed description of the diplomatic problems surrounding the filibustering expeditions of the period. Using Spanish language sources as well as English, Rauch discusses events in Cuba as well as those in the United States. Philip Foner uses many of the same sources as Rauch, but arrives at a quite different interpretation of the events. Foner stresses slavery as the key to annexationist interest in Cuba as well as the United States. That Southerners who supported the annexation of Cuba were eager to preserve slavery is well known, but Cuban annexationists also saw the incorporation of Cuba into the United States as a means of preserving slavery in Cuba. Lester D. Langley gives a short summary of the annexationist movement in *The Cuban Policy of the United States* and also emphasizes the importance of slavery by pointing to it as the major cause for the failure of annexation.[22]

No new studies of the United States and the Dominican Republic have replaced those of Charles Tansill and Sumner Welles. Tansill's *The United States and Santo Domingo* gives the more complete account of the attempts at annexation which were thwarted by French and British concerns over American expansionist fever. Welles covers much the same ground as Tansill, adding a few extra details but no different interpretations.[23]

William Walker, the adventurer who declared himself president of Nicaragua, has continued to interest historians and biographers. Walker was so flamboyant in his exploits that American interest in Nicaragua has been overemphasized. The American government, which sought Cuba and sent agents to Santo Domingo, found Walker an embarrassment. The definitive study of Walker and his associates is William O. Scroggs's *Filibusters and Financiers*, which states that the desire for the extension of slavery was not the "fundamental motive actuating all American filibusters." Walker, he points out, was joined by European soldiers of fortune, supporters of Cuban liberation, New Yorkers, and many New Englanders. Although in his attempt to prove this point he neglects the decisive influence of Southerners such as Pierre Soule and the importance of Walker's proslavery stand, his emphasis on the financiers as well as filibusters presents the kind of approach to expansion which is missing from other accounts. In Scroggs's account one finds ample evidence of the greedy desire for quick profits among the filibusters and their supporters and further evidence of the web of relationships formed by these entrepreneurs.[24]

It seems curious that revisionist historians who have emphasized the economic factors in diplomacy after 1877 should have neglected an era where the American entrepreneur was so central to expansion. Indeed one does not need to be an economic determinist to realize that the romantic aspect of the filibusters has obscured the reality of greedy Americans eager for the repetition of the successful Texas model: land concessions, settlement of immigrants, monopoly over resources, investment in bonds, and finally, the payoff in annexation to the United States. There were variations, such as in Cuba, but the motives of those agents of expansion in Texas, Santo Domingo, Tehuantepec, and Nicaragua were only superficially tied to the extension of slavery. Entrepreneurs wanted to become rich and powerful and were happy to join with Northern financiers, Southern slaveholders, or both.

The literature on the 1850s is therefore incomplete. Modern studies are needed to illuminate the web of relationship between adventurer, entrepreneur, and politician, as well as the economic ties of those individuals. These studies must go beyond conventional diplomatic sources.

Wherever Americans chose to move, north, south, or west, they found the British had preceded them. A knowledge of Anglo-American relations is crucial to an understanding of American expansion. Several books on the sweep of United States relations with Great Britain provide useful chapters on the expansionist years. Because H. C. Allen's *Great Britain and the United States, 1783-1950* provides only two chapters on these decades, studies by Kenneth Bourne and Charles S. Campbell give more useful coverage of events in the nineteenth century. Bourne, concerned with the various crises in Anglo-American diplomacy, concludes that by 1860 Britain had decided to acquiesce in American expansion, even though she refrained from action which would promote it. Reflecting the consensus among historians of Anglo-American diplomacy, he notes that the rapprochement between Great Britain and the United States which developed from 1898-1902 would have come forty years earlier if the Civil War had not interposed a new set of divisive issues. Campbell contributes the view that the impending rapprochement was as much a result of the United States decision to retreat from British North America as the British decision to acquiesce in American domination of Central America.[25]

Wilbur Devereux Jones, who has spent twenty-five years publishing articles and monographs on Anglo-American relations has emphasized the importance of the decades 1841-1861 in his thorough account of British encounters with American expansion. The view from the British side is a welcome change from the often myopic view which results from an overemphasis on American sources. Beginning with the Webster-Ashburton Treaty and ending with a brief mention of the Trent affair, Jones adds to his discussion of controversial events by offering the reader varying interpretations before stating his own opinions.[26]

The conflict between the Americans and the British in Hawaii in the 1850s is an often-neglected chapter in expansion. Although efforts at annexation were premature—by more than forty years—the internal and external conflicts over the attempt at annexation are an essential part of the decade. The encyclopedic two-volume *The Hawaiian Kingdom* by Ralph S. Kuykendall offers every known fact, but for interesting interpretations of those facts, the reader should turn to articles by Richard W. Van Alstyne and Merze Tate. Van Alstyne points out that Pierce and the expansionists wanted Hawaii very much. They were outclassed by the British, who encouraged Hawaiian independence, and by the demands of the Hawaiians who would settle for nothing less than statehood. Tate adds the conclusion that the demand for statehood reflected the fear of the Hawaiians that if they accepted a colonial status within the United States they would be enslaved because of their color. Thus another attempt at annexation was thwarted by the external pressure from Britain and the internal pressure from slavery.[27]

Dreams of expansion were brought to an untimely end by the outbreak of the Civil War. The literature on the diplomacy of the war indicates that the issues of 1861-1865 bore little relation to those of the previous decade even as they influenced the next. For the first time since 1815 American diplomacy, north and south, turned east toward Europe. Once again the pervasive problems of diplomacy were inextricably bound to Anglo-American relations. The neutrality of Europe and the questions of neutral and belligerent rights and obligations at sea were problems that revolved around Great Britain. For many years after its publication in 1925 the diplomatic history of the Civil War was dominated by E. D. Adams's *Great Britain and the American Civil War.*

Writing after World War I, a period of rapprochement between Britain and the United States, Adams sought "a fairly true estimate" of what the Civil War meant to Great Britain. In two lengthy volumes, he presents a narrative history of every major diplomatic event which affected the two countries between 1861 and 1865. The reader of this book, however, will gain a greater understanding of British policy than the policy of Lincoln and Seward.[28]

No one book has emerged in recent years to replace Adams, but understanding of the Anglo-American relationship has been greatly enhanced through the publication of a number of articles and monographs in the last twenty-five years. For example, several recently published books fully explore the maritime problems which resulted from the Union blockade and British recognition of Southern belligerency. Frank J. Merli considers the maritime problems of the South, while Stuart L. Bernath discusses the North. Bernath deliberately avoids discussion of the Trent affair, noting that historians had adequately covered that famous incident. However, this did not discourage Norman B. Ferris from writing a very detailed account in *The Trent Affair, A Diplomatic Crisis.*[29]

Bibliographies on Anglo-American relations indicate that historians have been far more interested in exploring the British reaction to the Civil War than American policy decisions. Thus, an understanding of the decisions of the Lincoln administration can best be obtained from biographies of the participants. One of the clearest short accounts of American diplomacy in England can be found in Martin Duberman's biography of Charles Francis Adams. Lincoln is Jay Monaghan's subject in *Diplomat in Carpet Slippers*, although this readable, if shallow, account greatly exaggerates the role of President Lincoln.[30]

The recent emergence of William Henry Seward from Lincoln's shadow has also served to enhance our knowledge of Civil War diplomacy. As D. P. Crook has noted, the picture of Seward as "a rash and expedient Secretary of State" has given way to that of a man who "during his nation's greatest trial . . . demonstrated a superb understanding of American nationalism."[31] Glyndon G. Van Deusen's *William Henry Seward* remains the only complete biography of Seward, but several monographs have appeared on specific aspects of his diplomacy. At least two of these were prompted by the recent interest in Seward as expansionist and visionary rather than as Lincoln's secretary of state. Ernest Paolino concentrates almost exclusively on Seward's postwar dreams, and Walter G. Sharrow stops short of the Civil War years. Norman B. Ferris, however, in a recent, favorable treatment of Seward covers the crucial first year of the war.[32]

In spite of its age, no student of the Confederacy can neglect Frank L. Owsley's, *King Cotton Diplomacy*. Emphasizing the Southern premise that neither England nor France could function without Southern cotton, Owsley provides a thorough account of Southern diplomacy and examines the causes behind European nonintervention. In this account of Confederate diplomacy, neither the English nor Union leaders fare very well. A more balanced interpretation of the failure of the diplomacy of the Confederacy can be found in an article by Henry Blumenthal.[33]

Fortunately, a rebirth of scholarly interest in the Civil War prompted by the commemoration of its centennial led to the publication of numerous books and articles on the international aspects of the war. A brief introduction to the issue of Northern diplomacy and European neutrality can be found in an essay by Norman Graebner. Two important works ôn Franco-American relations, one by Lynn M. Case and Warren F. Spencer and one by Henry Blumenthal, have helped correct the emphasis on Anglo-American relations. Case and Spencer give a more thorough account of the Civil War years, while the briefer book by Blumenthal places the war in a broader context. A book which is a direct result of the centennial, *Heard Round the World*, includes a series of essays which explore the effect of the war on Canada and Latin America as well as on Great Britain, France, Central Europe, and Russia.[34]

The difficulty of writing a one-volume synthesis of Civil War diplomacy no doubt accounts for the absence of such a book until 1974 when Crook's work appeared. Crook does a remarkable job of presenting both the events of the war and a synthesis of the most recent interpretations of those events. His conclusion reflects the current emphasis on European reaction, rather than American action: "The powers did not meddle because they were unable to subdue their rivalries or find a mutually acceptable basis for intervention." The key to nonintervention lay in Europe, not in America.[35]

The study of history is continually refreshed by the interpretations of each generation. Provoked to agree or disagree, historians return to original sources, examine forgotten contemporary material, and formulate interpretations to continue the dialogue.

Fascination with the Civil War will continue to promote interest in the diplomacy of the war and its international ramifications. In addition, the current interest in Seward promises to increase an appreciation of the political roots of American diplomacy during the Civil War. Meanwhile, Pletcher's account of the Mexican War provides a modern narrative which will remain the standard for some time to come.

Unfortunately, the rest of the period discussed in this chapter seems to be of little interest to historians—especially those who are the newest members of the profession. A glance at the subjects of recent dissertations or articles in major historical journals reveals the decline of interest in American expansion before the Civil War. This decline is due to a number of factors.

Diplomatic historians are more interested in the twentieth century. The generation of scholars from the 1960s finds itself drawn to the period when the United States was a world power rather than a struggling adolescent. In addition, the period after 1941 is of particular interest because of the accessibility of sources in presidential libraries and the excitement of using recently declassified documents.

The decline in the interest of historians in the political history of the United States is also a factor. The diplomacy of "young America" was generated by internal factors deeply tied to the domestic concerns of the United States rather than by external pressures from the great powers of Europe. The Jacksonians and Whigs who made foreign policy were political leaders first, and diplomats second. New insights into the diplomacy of the fifteen years which preceded the Civil War may have to wait for a renewed interest in the political history of that period.

It should also be noted that the "Wisconsin school," which has generated so much recent reinterpretation in diplomatic history, has largely ignored the period of manifest destiny. Content with Van Alstyne's interpretation of expansion, students of this school have concentrated almost entirely on post-Civil War America. As a result, those diplomatic historians who are most interested in the ties between economic institutions, political groups, and diplomacy have turned away from analyzing the effects of the entrepreneurs, filibusters, and speculators on the course of American history.

The era has suffered accordingly. There are no new insights into Merk's suggestion that racism was an element in determining the extent of expansion. There are no recent attempts to use newly arranged documents or newly filmed manuscript collections to examine the link between New York capitalists, leading politicians, and Southern men of empire. There are no new examinations of expansionist leaders, such as James Buchanan. A reconsideration of manifest destiny, the idea and the era, is clearly overdue.

Notes

1. James D. Richardson, ed., *A Compilation of the Messages and Papers of the Presidents, 1789-1897* (Washington, D.C.: Government Printing Office, 1897), 4: 398.

2. Ephraim D. Adams, "Manifest Destiny—An Emotion," in Armin Rappaport, ed., *Essays in American Diplomacy* (London: Collier-Macmillan, 1967), p. 78; John Bassett Moore, ed., *The Works of James Buchanan* (Philadelphia: J. B. Lippincott, 1909), 8: 361.

3. David M. Pletcher, "Manifest Destiny" in Alexander DeConde, ed., *Encyclopedia of American Foreign Policy* (New York: Charles Scribner's Sons, 1978), 2: 526; Albert K. Weinberg, *Manifest Destiny: A Study of Nationalist Expansionism in American History* (1935; reprint ed., Chicago: Quadrangle Books, 1963). For the origin of the phrase "manifest destiny" *see* Julius W. Pratt, "John L. O'Sullivan and Manifest Destiny," *Proceedings of the New York State Historical Association*, 14 (July 1933): 213-34.

4. Weinberg, *Manifest Destiny*. pp. 73, 128, 485.

5. Frederick Merk, *Manifest Destiny and Mission in American History: A Reinterpretation* (New York: Alfred A. Knopf, 1963).

6. Ibid., pp. 256-57. Merk writes that his book is a study in public opinion. His sources are newspapers, congressional speeches, and other manifestations of this opinion. It is a very unscientific, subjective study which obviously precedes the age of quantification in spirit as well as time. Nevertheless, Merk does not hestitate to make broad generalizations from the material which he presents. It would be exceedingly useful if the interdisciplinary techniques now available for studying public opinion were applied to the 1840-1860 period in order to test his conclusions.

For additional examples of Merk's interest in public opinion *see Fruits of Propaganda in the Tyler Administration* (Cambridge, Mass.: Harvard University Press, 1971) and *The Oregon Question: Essays in Anglo-American Diplomacy and Politics* (Cambridge, Mass.: Harvard University Press, 1967).

7. Norman A. Graebner, ed., *Manifest Destiny* (New York: Bobbs-Merrill Co., 1968), p. xviii and "Lessons of the Mexican War," *Pacific Historical Review* 47 (August 1978): 325-42.

8. Richard W. Van Alstyne, *The Rising American Empire* (New York: W. W. Norton & Co., 1960). *See also* his "Empire in Midpassage, 1845-1867," in William A. Williams, ed., *From Colony to Empire* (New York: John Wiley & Sons, 1972).

9. Charles Vevier, "American Continentalism: An Idea of Expansion, 1845-1910," *American Historical Review* 65 (January 1960): 329-30, 334.

10. James J. Horn, "Trends in Historical Interpretation: James K. Polk," *North Carolina Historical Review* 42 (October 1965): 454-64; Peter T. Harstad and Richard W. Resh, "The Causes of the Mexican War, A Note on Changing Interpretations," *Arizona and the West* 6 (Winter 1964): 289-302.

11. Jesse S. Reeves, *American Diplomacy Under Tyler and Polk* (Baltimore: Johns Hopkins Press, 1907); George L. Rives, *The United States and Mexico, 1821-1848* (New York: Charles Scribner's Sons, 1913); Ephraim D. Adams, *British Interests and Activities in Texas, 1838-1846* (Baltimore: Johns Hopkins Press, 1910); Justin H. Smith, *The Annexation of Texas* (New York: Baker and Taylor, 1911) and *The War With Mexico*, 2 vols. (New York: Macmillan Co., 1919).

12. Smith, *War With Mexico*, 1: 28, 57, 128-29; 2: 322.

13. Alfred Hoyt Bill, *Rehearsal For Conflict* (New York: Alfred A. Knopf, 1947), p. x; Seymour V. Connor and Odie B. Faulk, *North American Divided: The Mexican War, 1846-1848* (New York: Oxford University Press, 1971); Otis A. Singletary, *The Mexican War* (Chicago: University of Chicago Press, 1960).

14. Glenn W. Price, *Origins of the War with Mexico: The Polk-Stockton Intrigue* (Austin: University of Texas Press, 1967); Richard R. Stenberg, "The Failure of Polk's Mexican War Intrigue of 1845," *Pacific Historical Review* 4 (March 1935): 39-68.

15. Norman A. Graebner, *Empire on the Pacific* (New York: Ronald Press, 1955); Frederick Merk, *The Monroe Doctrine and American Expansionism 1843-1849* (New York: Alfred A. Knopf, 1966). For a critique of the Graebner thesis *see* Shomer S. Zwelling, *Expansion and Imperialism* (Chicago: Loyola University Press, 1970).

16. David M. Pletcher, *The Diplomacy of Annexation* (Columbia: University of Missouri Press, 1973).

17. Charles G. Sellers, *James K. Polk, Continentalist, 1843-1846* (Princeton: Princeton University Press, 1966).

18. Robert E. May, *The Southern Dream of a Caribbean Empire, 1854-1861* (Baton Rouge: Louisiana State University Press, 1973). Difficult to understand is the exclusion of a discussion of Santo Domingo. The agent William Marcy sent to the island in 1854, William Cazneau, was a Texan, a supporter of slavery, and later a supporter of the Confederacy.

19. William H. Goetzmann, *When The Eagle Screamed: The Romantic Horizon in American Diplomacy, 1800-1860* (New York: John Wiley & Sons, 1966).

20. Edward S. Wallace, *Destiny and Glory* (New York: Coward-McCann, 1957). An example of undocumented statements can be found on pp. 247-48. Wallace describes a meeting between Jane Storms and General Winfield Scott. According to Wallace, Mrs. Storms greatly influenced Scott although there is absolutely no evidence that she ever met him. Goetzmann and Wallace present dramatic accounts of Walker's exploits, but the most balanced summary can be found in May's *The Southern Dream of a Caribbean Empire.*

21. Dexter Perkins, *The Monroe Doctrine, 1826-1867* (Baltimore: Johns Hopkins Press, 1933). Two chapters devoted to the period 1821-1860 can be found in Lester D. Langley, *Struggle for the American Mediterranean* (Athens, Ga.: University of Georgia Press, 1976).

22. Basil Rauch, *American Interest in Cuba: 1848-1855* (1948; reprint ed., New York: Octagon Books, 1974); Philip S. Foner, *A History of Cuba and Its Relations*

with the United States (New York: International Publishers, 1963), 2; Lester D. Langley, *The Cuban Policy of the United States: A Brief History* (New York: John Wiley & Sons, 1968).

23. Charles C. Tansill, *The United States and Santo Domingo, 1798-1873* (Baltimore: Johns Hopkins Press, 1938); Sumner Welles, *Naboth's Vineyard: The Dominican Republic, 1844-1924* (1928; reprint ed., Mamaroneck, N.Y.: Paul P. Appel, 1966).

24. William O. Scroggs, *Filibusters and Financiers; The Story of William Walker and His Associates* (1916; reprint ed., New York: Russell and Russell, 1969).

25. H. C. Allen, *Great Britain and the United States, 1783-1952* (New York: St. Martin's Press, 1955); Kenneth Bourne, *Britain and the Balance of Power in North America, 1815-1908* (Berkeley: University of California Press, 1967); Charles S. Campbell, *From Revolution to Rapprochement: The United States and Great Britain, 1783-1900* (New York: John Wiley & Sons, 1974).

26. Wilbur Devereux Jones, *The American Problem in British Diplomacy, 1841-1861* (London: Macmillan & Co., 1974). Unfortunately, the reader who is seeking a current bibliography will find the 1974 publication date slightly misleading. The most recent secondary source in the bibliography is dated 1967, and most of the entries actually precede 1960. In addition, while Jones offers the most complete discussion of Anglo-American problems at the northern border, Mary Williams's study is still the most complete account of the problems encountered in Central America even though it dates from 1916. Mary W. Williams, *Anglo-American Isthmian Diplomacy, 1815-1915* (Washington: American Historical Association, 1916). For a view of United States relations with Europe in the 1850s see Alan Dowty, *The Limits of American Isolation: The United States and the Crimean War* (New York: New York University Press, 1971).

27. Ralph S. Kuykendall, *The Hawaiian Kingdom* (Honolulu: University of Hawaii Press, 1966); Richard W. Van Alstyne "Great Britain, the United States, and Hawaiian Independence, 1850-1855," *Pacific Historical Review* 4 (March 1935): 15-24; Merze Tate, "Slavery and Racism as Deterrents to the Annexation of Hawaii, 1854-1855," *Journal of Negro History* 47 (January 1962): 1-18. For a discussion of Mexican views of race during the Mexican war *see* Gene M. Brack, "Mexican Opinion, American Racism, and the War of 1846," *Western Historical Quarterly* (April 1970): 161-74. I am indebted to Howard M. Merriman, Professor Emeritus, George Washington University, for the references to Hawaii.

28. E. D. Adams, *Great Britain and the American Civil War*, 2 vols. (New York: Longmans, Green & Co., 1925).

29. Frank J. Merli, *Great Britain and the Confederate Navy, 1861-1865* (Bloomington: Indiana University Press, 1965); Stuart L. Bernath, *Squall Across the Atlantic: American Civil War Prize Cases and Diplomacy* (Berkeley: University of California Press, 1970); Norman B. Ferris, *The Trent Affair, A Diplomatic Crisis* (Knoxville, Tenn.: University of Tennessee Press, 1977).

30. Martin B. Duberman, *Charles Francis Adams* (Boston: Houghton Mifflin Co., 1961); Jay Monaghan, *Diplomat in Carpet Slippers: Abraham Lincoln Deals with Foreign Affairs* (Indianapolis: Bobbs-Merrill Co., 1945). *See also* the books by Bourne and Campbell, Note 25.

31. D. P. Crook, *The North, the South and the Powers, 1861-1865* (New York:

John Wiley & Sons, 1974). An abridged version was published under the title, *Diplomacy During the American Civil War* (New York: John Wiley & Sons, 1975).

32. Glynden G. Van Deusen, *William Henry Seward* (New York: Oxford University Press, 1967); Ernest N. Paolino, *The Foundations of the American Empire: William Henry Seward and United States Foreign Policy* (Ithaca: Cornell University Press, 1973); Walter G. Sharrow, "William Henry Seward and the Basis for American Empire, 1850-1860," *Pacific Historical Review* 36 (August 1967): 325-42; Norman B. Ferris, *Desperate Diplomacy: William H. Seward's Foreign Policy, 1861* (Knoxville: University of Tennessee Press, 1976).

For Seward's vision *see* William A. Williams, *The Contours of American History* (Cleveland: World Publishing Co., 1961), pp. 292-94 and Howard I. Kushner, "Visions of the Northwest Coast: Gwinn and Seward in the 1850s," *Western Historical Quarterly* 4 (July 1973): 295-306.

33. Frank L. Owsley, *King Cotton Diplomacy: Foreign Relations of the Confederate States of America* (Chicago: University of Chicago Press, 1931); Henry Blumenthal, "Confederate Diplomacy: Popular Notions and International Realities," *Journal of Southern History* 32 (May 1966): 151-71. Insight into Confederate diplomacy abroad can be found in Judith Fenner Gentry, "A Confederate Success in Europe: The Erlanger Loan," *Journal of Southern History* 36 (May 1970): 157-88.

34. Norman A. Graebner, "Northern Diplomacy and European Neutrality," in David Donald, ed., *Why the North Won the Civil War* (Baton Rouge: Louisiana State University Press, 1960); Lynn M. Case and Warren F. Spencer, *The United States and France: Civil War Diplomacy* (Philadelphia: University of Pennsylvania Press, 1970); Henry Blumenthal, *A Reappraisal of Franco-American Relations, 1830-1871* (Chapel Hill: University of North Carolina Press, 1959); Harold Hyman, ed., *Heard Round the World: The Impact Abroad of the Civil War* (New York: Alfred A. Knopf, 1969).

35. Crook, *The North, the South and the Powers*, p. 371.

5 ______ The Imperialist Impulse and American Innocence, 1865–1900

HUGH DE SANTIS

In a recent article in the *American Historical Review*, James A. Field, Jr., called the historiography of late nineteenth-century American foreign relations the worst chapter in almost any book.[1] While it may not be the worst, it might well be the most tedious. For nearly three-quarters of a century historians have trod the same ground, seeking to discover how and why America went wrong in 1898. Scholars of the traditionalist persuasion, who perceive the United States as the beacon of liberal-democratic progress in a benighted world, have attempted to isolate the nation's quest for empire as a momentary fall from grace. No less celebratory of the nation's Enlightenment mission, progressive historians and their new left descendants, who see history through the prism of the struggle between the "people" and the "interests," have treated the imperialist eruption as the culmination of a rational process in which the Manichean god of evil triumphed over the god of goodness. And the realists, given their amoral, power-political view of international behavior, have dismissed the imperialist impulse as a misguided and puerile outburst precisely because it sacrificed the national interest on the altar of America's civilizing mission. Their apparent differences notwithstanding, each of these interpretations shares the idea that the United States is unique, and hence so is American foreign policy: uniquely good in the case of the traditionalists, uniquely bad to the progressives, and uniquely naive according to the realists. A fourth school of thought has recently emerged, however, which views American foreign relations as a function of relatively unvarying cultural orientations and of changing social institutions. Moreover, by also placing the United States within the context of a dynamic system of international relations, these modernists have attached less significance to the concept of American uniqueness.

While the earliest historians of late nineteenth-century American foreign relations may have disapproved of the country's exuberant expansionism, they could not resist basking in the glory of national greatness. John H. Latané and Archibald Cary Coolidge acknowledged that war with Spain could have been avoided had the administration of President McKinley exhibited more patience and less submission to domestic pressure. But they did not consider its effects unpropitious, despite the unnecessary annexation of the Philippine Islands. For one thing, the war had awakened the European states and the American public to the country's status as a world power; for another, it had led to closer ties between the United States and Britain. At the same time, these traditionalist writers tried to vindicate the country's colonialist role, noting that officials in the Philippines, as in Cuba, had conducted themselves admirably in their sincere efforts to improve local political, social, and economic conditions.[2]

In contrast to their American counterparts, European historians reacted anxiously to the emergence of this bumptious upstart as a world power. Echoing the views of statesmen like the French diplomat Jules Cambon, they considered the American people and their leaders cultural barbarians ignorant of European history and politics who had embarked on an international democratic-egalitarian mission which threatened to undermine European colonialism. As Cambon, who was ambassador to the United States from 1897 to 1902, explained, "These people are ignorant and brutal and if they stick their hand in the complicated and patient game that the old world is playing it will little trouble them to set fire to the four corners of Europe." More disturbing still was America's economic might, which prompted statesmen like the Austrian foreign minister Count Agenor von Goluchowski and historians like Ugo Ojetti to call for a closing of ranks among the European powers—economically, politically, and psychologically—to guard against the American peril.[3]

In the aftermath of World War I, American scholars began to reassess the history of late nineteenth-century foreign relations. Writing at a time when Congress and the public had turned their backs on the League of Nations, Alfred L. P. Dennis pointed out in *Adventures in American Diplomacy* that the nation was historically ill-equipped to ply the course of world power on which it was set after the war against Spain. Still, Dennis's view was not fundamentally different from Latané's or Coolidge's. More typical of 1920s historiography was the revisionism of Harold Faulkner, Charles and Mary Beard, and others in the emerging school of progressive history. Disillusioned by the peace settlement that followed World War I, they argued that the United States went to war in 1898, just as she did in 1917, to satisfy the economic self-interest of a small but influential corporate class in American society.[4] In his provocative *The Idea of National Interest*, which appeared in 1934, Beard assailed the McKinley administration for its imperialist war, which had besmirched the nation's values and traditions. But the real culprits for Beard were the captains of commerce and their cosmopolite Hamiltonian forebears in the Republican party, who, unlike the "people" and their Jeffersonian-Democrat progenitors, had historically sought to expand territorially to gain control of new markets.[5]

Two years later Julius Pratt challenged Beard's view that the United States had waged war for commercial empire. Pratt persuasively demonstrated that businessmen opposed war with Spain lest it would disrupt the economic recovery of 1897. Caught up in the prevailing ideology of Social Darwinism, a frenzied American public and a handful of influential jingoes like Theodore Roosevelt and Henry Cabot Lodge drove the McKinley administration into a purposeless, unplanned war, Pratt asserted, though he never accounted for the fact that the survival-of-the-fittest ideology had been in vogue long before and that it retained its popularity in the aftermath of the imperialist outburst. However, once Commodore Dewey's victory in Manila Bay removed the prospect of a costly, protracted war, businessmen joined with the jingoes in support of Hawaiian and Philippine annexation, equal commercial rights in China, construction of an isthmian canal to expedite the shipment of goods from the east coast to the Pacific, and the development of a large navy to preserve American markets in East Asia. In their *apologiae pro vita Americana*, Samuel Flagg Bemis and Thomas Bailey similarly contended that a wave of expansionist hysteria had engulfed the American public and the McKinley administration and carried the country off on an "ill-fitting" imperialist course. More nationalistic than Pratt, Bemis especially so, they were not critical of America's "protective imperialism" in the Caribbean or, in Bemis's case, the acquisition of Hawaii, which strengthened the defense of the isthmian canal and safeguarded the security of the continental United States. As Dexter Perkins explained in a volume which mirrored Washington's concern with national security in the 1930s, American officials extended and distorted the Monroe Doctrine after 1867 in response to the perceived threat of European expansionism in the Western Hemisphere. To Bemis and Bailey the "great aberration" was the costly and militarily indefensible annexation of the Philippines, for which they held accountable a pusillanimous McKinley and the cabal of expansionists around him.[6]

Studies of public opinion, a field of inquiry which paralleled the emergence of opinion polls and sophisticated techniques of survey-analysis in the 1930s, further supported the traditionalist argument. In *The Martial*

Spirit, published in 1931, journalist Walter Millis contended that the yellow press, along with the exhortations of imperialists like Roosevelt and Lodge, produced a national hysteria that led to war and colonialism. A year later Marcus Wilkerson explained how the press in New York, Chicago, Boston, and San Francisco had exploited Spanish atrocities in Cuba to increase circulation. Joseph Wisan came to the same conclusion. In his interesting analysis of the New York press, he divided the dailies into those which supported McKinley for partisan political reasons but opposed war, those which were strongly anti-interventionist, and those, like Joseph Pulitzer's *World* and William Randolph Hearst's *New York Journal*, which favored the "large policy" of aggressive expansionism. These accounts also limned McKinley *à outrance* as a weak, indecisive leader held captive by party pressures and the vagaries of public opinion, an image that contrasted with Allan Nevins's hagiographic portrait of Grover Cleveland as a man of courage who defied the expansionists in his party following the Hawaiian coup of 1893.[7]

The idea that something had gone awry in 1898 was sustained in the decade-and-a-half following World War II from a different perspective. In contrast to the progressive historians, who attacked the "interests" for corrupting the fundamental verities of Jeffersonian America, and the traditionalists, who, in extremis, treated episodically the imperialist outburst in order to preserve the myth of American innocence, the realist school of historiography, influenced by the Axis grab for power during the 1930s and Soviet-American differences at the end of World War II, criticized the United States for its failure to understand the *realpolitik* nature of the international political system and its Panglossian approach to foreign affairs. Whereas the traditionalists and progressives focused their attention on the effect of domestic influences on foreign policy at the expense of exogenous factors, the realists have treated the United States as a dependent variable of the international system, ignoring in the process endogenous considerations including the role that ideology plays in the nation's foreign affairs.

University of Chicago political scientists Hans Morgenthau and Robert Osgood scornfully blamed the utopian crusade to liberate Cuba from Spain and the annexation of the Philippines on the tendency of American policymakers to drift in the current of mass emotionalism rather than pay heed to the national interest. In their view, only Theodore Roosevelt, whose own crusading spirit they minimized, appreciated the role of power in international politics. Outspokenly critical of the ideological thrust of post-World War II American foreign policy, diplomat-historian George Kennan similarly attacked the legalistic-moralistic basis of America's war with Spain. In a series of lectures given at Chicago, Kennan contended that further efforts to resolve diplomatically American differences with Spain were nullified by Washington's abdication of decision-making to an ignorant public and a handful of bellicose intriguers, including Roosevelt. Like Morgenthau and Osgood, he argued that McKinley and Secretary of State Hay simply did not understand that the old British policy of the Open Door no longer applied after March 1898, and that it was the European balance of power rather than the moralistic rhetoric of the Open Door notes which inhibited the partition of China. Norman Graebner, who did his graduate work at Chicago, continued the realist critique in the 1960s, noting that political pressure from Republicans and Democrats and public hysteria pushed McKinley into an annexationist war for Christian civilization. Yet, Graebner curiously slighted the importance of this ideological component in the decision to intervene; in his view, since Spain was moving as quickly as possible to satisfy American demands, there was no legitimate cause for war.[8]

The changing structure of the international political system after World War II, the proliferation of American overseas interests, and the growing coordination of military strategy and diplomacy also influenced the thinking of other scholars writing in the 1950s. In his ground-breaking *The United States Navy in the Pacific, 1897-1909*, William Braisted analyzed the impact of naval policy on American diplomatic relations. Minimizing the significance earlier historians had attached to then Assistant Secretary of the Navy Roosevelt's telegram authorizing Dewey to proceed to Manila Bay, Braisted showed that naval strategists had prepared for an assault in the Philippines against Spain as early as 1896. Inspirited by its successes in the war with Spain, the navy subsequently overrode the recommendation of American diplomatic officials to offer Germany territorial concessions in the Pacific and, though unsuccessfully, pressured the administration for a larger role in China. Howard K. Beale was less comfortable with America's postwar superpower status and with realist historiography. While praising Roosevelt as an energetic leader devoted to his country's interests, Beale, a pacifist during the 1930s, lamented the influence of a few expansionists on McKinley and Secretary of State Sherman and the public's imperialist hysteria of the 1890s, which, he believed, proved a portent of the global extension of American influence in the 1950s. Underscoring Beale's position, Paolo Coletta, who sought to remove the moral onus from the shoulders of William Jennings Bryan, accused McKinley of violating American traditions by annexing the Philippines. He argued that McKinley's biased composition of the Paris peace commission, his use of patronage, and his manipulation of public opinion made the acquisition a fait accompli, notwithstanding Bryan's endorsement of it as a temporary expedient to end the bloody Filipino insurrection.[9]

Despite the prevalence of realist or realist-influenced interpretations during the 1950s, the most provocative studies of American expansion emphasized the impact of domestic factors on foreign policy. Erecting a new social-psychological facade over Pratt's foundation, Richard Hofstadter argued that the country experienced a profound "psychic crisis" in the 1890s. The disastrous depression of 1893, the growth of the trusts, the disappearance of the frontier, the wave of violent labor stoppages, free-silver agitation, urban blight, and government corruption left Americans anxious that the hill on which this enlightened city rested was crumbling. Mounting national frustration was discharged partly in the movement for humanitarian reform, including support for the Cuban insurrection. It was also released in an aggressive revival of manifest destiny, as reflected in Blaine's caustic reply to Rome's protest over the lynching of eleven Italians in New Orleans in 1891, in President Harrison's belligerent posture toward Chile following the death of two American sailors involved in a drunken brawl in Valparaiso, in Secretary of State Olney's intemperate diplomacy during the Venezuelan crisis, and in the war against Spain, which allowed an outlet for both irrational aggressiveness and crusading humanitarianism. The themes of duty and destiny were subsequently merged to justify the annexation of Hawaii and the Philippines.[10]

While Hofstadter's theory was viewed with caution by historians, who relate to psychological formulations the way the tribal society of Manus studied by Margaret Mead reacted upon first catching sight of an airplane, the economic interpretation of William Appleman Williams became an immediate cause célèbre. In *The Tragedy of American Diplomacy*, Williams resurrected the Beardian view of American history as a conflict between the "people" and the "interests." Dismayed by Washington's unsympathetic response to the Cuban revolution of 1959, he contended that Americans had failed to comprehend their own revolutionary-democratic history, that the United States had strayed from her singularly humanitarian traditions of supporting other struggling peoples to achieve freedom. This, he argued, was because the government had increasingly fallen prey to the influence of corporations, which equated the nation's well-being with unremitting economic expansion. Williams traced the origins of America's informal economic empire, in its broad features, to the Cleveland presidency, citing as examples the president's acquiescence in the revolt of American sugar interests against the Hawaiian government in 1893, his militant defense of Yankee commerce in the Brazilian revolution of the same year, and the later Venezuelan crisis. In league with advocates of business expansionism like the National Association of Manufacturers, Brooks Adams, and Hay, McKinley knowingly precipitated the war with Spain ostensibly to end the Cuban insurrection, but really to divert the nation's energy to the commercial exploitation of China, whose markets seemed to offer a panacea for the protracted depression within the United States. Veiled in moralistic rhetoric, the Open Door policy was fundamentally a strategic maneuver designed to extend American economic and political control in China and, ultimately, throughout the world. In contrast to the conventional image of

McKinley as a weak leader unable to restrain a belligerent public and Congress, a view Margaret Leech reinforced in her biography, Williams portrayed the president as a confident, adept politician who guided the nation into an exploitative war to stabilize the parlous domestic situation.[11]

Coming at the end of a decade when Americanism had become a folk religion, and at a time when scholars like Daniel Bell were proclaiming the end of ideology, the revisionism of Williams, though woefully negligent in its consideration of noneconomic factors, was a useful corrective to the chest-thumping patriotism of the 1950s. In due course his book became a kind of vade mecum for historians such as Walter LaFeber, who elaborated on themes introduced by Williams. In *The New Empire* (a more sophisticated explication of the Williams thesis, aimed at refuting Pratt) LaFeber argued that the American quest for empire was neither sudden nor irrational, but the natural culmination of the transformation from an agrarian to an industrial society. Citing the 1854 reciprocity treaty with Canada, early interest in annexing Hawaii, and commercial expansion in China, he contended that the search for new markets started during the economic take-off of 1843-57 and intensified after 1873 as domestic consumption failed to keep pace with production. The blueprint for economic expansion drawn by Secretary of State Seward after the Civil War was followed under every successive administration, as attested by the 1875 reciprocity treaty with Hawaii and the growing interest in an isthmian canal. It was consummated in the imperial edifice purposefully wrought by McKinley, who shared the expansionist leanings of American businessmen, politicians like Lodge, and writers such as Josiah Strong, Brooks Adams, and Mahan. Thomas J. McCormick, a student of Williams, added another volume to the revisionist literature in 1967. In his view, annexation of Hawaii, the Philippines, and the other Pacific territories served as stepping-stones to establish economic hegemony in East Asia. The Open Door notes were intended to safeguard America's commercial exploitation of China, or what McCormick called the "imperialism of anti-imperialism." Both the Cleveland and McKinley administrations, he argued, consciously promoted the policy of "free-trade imperialism." Interestingly, however, both the Gorman and Dingley tariffs of 1894 and 1897—indeed, American tariff policy throughout the nineteenth century—were protectionist, a factor McCormick circumvented. Moreover, why, in spite of domestic concerns about surplus production, the absence of imperialism before or after the decade of the 1890s? To this question Williams replied in *The Roots of the Modern American Empire* that the importance of new markets to the metropolitan business elite was actually preceded in preindustrial America by a similar preoccupation with the export of surplus production on the part of the agricultural sector of the economy. In contrast to Beard's Jeffersonian-Hamiltonian dichotomy,

Williams now applied the taint of imperialism to the yeoman farmer. In short, he had, by 1969, grafted onto his populist proclivities, if he had not abandoned them altogether, the Hobson-Lenin model of capitalistic imperialism.[12]

But scholars who had imbibed the consensus history of the end-of-ideology-1950s were reluctant to accept undiluted the economic interpretation of the neo-Beardian new left. Thomas Bailey continued to decry America's "overseas aberration" as a misguided attempt "to keep up with the imperialistic Joneses." Indeed, traditionalists still clung to the idea that the American engine of enlightened progress temporarily went off the trolley in 1898. H. Wayne Morgan argued that the country went to war in a holiday mood which reflected its ignorance of world responsibilities, and that the road to empire was neither smooth nor decisive. Frederick Merk explained in a volume published in 1963 that there were two competing strains in American history. One was manifest destiny, that divinely inspired urge to expand aggressively, which seized the popular imagination in the 1840s and 1890s; the other was mission, that providentially endowed ideal to redeem the world by dint of America's enlightened example. The former justified bringing other peoples into the temple of freedom and democracy, kicking and screaming in some cases; the latter encouraged the rest of the world to construct its own temples in imitation of the American model. Never explaining how mission and manifest destiny became transmuted, Merk nonetheless concluded that mission was the true expression of the national spirit. In his study of American commercial, missionary, and naval activities in the eastern Mediterranean and the Near East, James Field similarly portrayed the United States, despite in fin de siècle militancy, as a child of the Enlightenment seeking mainly to inculcate in other peoples the values of political democracy, free trade, and scientific progress.[13]

Influenced by Pratt and Hofstadter, Ernest May concluded in *Imperial Democracy* that the United States, far from seeking great power status in the 1890s, had that role, to paraphrase Macauley, thrust upon her in a moralistic moment of national hysteria, while Spain, suffering the throes of imperial decay, proudly accepted the challenge of war to preserve her honor. However, May demonstrated that the European powers perceived America's assertion of might as evidence of her desire for a great power role. In a second volume May analyzed the process which transformed the United States from an isolationist to an imperialist nation, a phenomenon other writers had ignored. Drawing, like Hofstadter, from the social sciences, he speculated that the public-opinion elite transformed the views of American foreign policy in accordance with ideas which enjoyed currency among the European elite, particularly the British. By the 1890s the public-opinion elite divided into those who subscribed to liberal anticolonialism and those who advocated state-directed, colonialist-imperialist expansionism. As the foreign-policy elite fragmented, reason gave way to mass emotionalism, and an ill-informed public pressured an indecisive McKinley into war and annexationism. Like May, John A. S. Grenville and George Berkeley Young examined the effect of domestic pressures on foreign affairs. They pointed out that Congress became sensitized to the threat of European encroachment during the Harrison-Blaine years largely because of the admonitions of Commodore Stephen B. Luce, first head of the Naval War College, and Secretary of the Navy Benjamin Tracy, and only latterly by the writings of Mahan, whose purported early influence on foreign policy they found exaggerated. By the late 1890s a group of vocal expansionists in the Senate and House constrained Cleveland, who had no interest in statecraft, and the ill-tempered Olney to intervene in the Anglo-Venezuelan Guiana boundary dispute. Despite similar pressures to intercede in the Spanish-Cuban war, McKinley tried to avoid a conflict with Spain. Indeed, in line with H. Wayne Morgan's highly favorable view of McKinley, Grenville-Young depicted the president as a man of considerable courage and independence of judgment, hardly the indecisive leader portrayed by May. But with the onset of war and Dewey's sudden victory in Manila Bay, which transformed the expansionist mood of a few jingoes into a popular crusade, McKinley pursued an annexationist course which placed the United States in the power vacuum created by Spain's defeat.[14]

A number of writers, however, adopted a stance somewhere between the traditionalists and the so-called new left. David Pletcher explained developments during the Garfield-Arthur years—American interest in constructing a Nicaraguan canal, Caribbean reciprocity treaties, and the Berlin Congo Congress—in terms of prestige, security, and markets, and as links in the chain of American expansionism between 1865 and 1898. Milton Plesur focused on the overproduction thesis in tracing the origins of the "large policy" between 1865 and 1890, but examined as well, though too desultorily, social, cultural, and psychological factors. David Healy showed how concerns about American trade and investment affected the McKinley administration's involvement in Cuba and Congress's support for the Platt Amendment. At the same time, he also stressed the influence of political factors, pointing out that soldiers, politicians, and civil servants rather than businessmen made the important decisions in Cuba. Like LaFeber and McCormick, Marilyn Blatt Young argued in her interesting but ponderously written *The Rhetoric of Empire* that the timing of war with Spain was affected by the spoliation of China that began in 1897 with Germany's seizure of Kiaochow and by Washington's desire to be around when the commercial watermelon was cut, as Hay put it. But she contended that the social malaise within American society (Hofstadter) and the views of the public-opinion elite (May) who believed that the United States was a world power with a role to play in international politics also influenced the imperialist thrust. Similarly, in their volumes on Hawaii, Merze Tate and William Adam Russ demonstrated how powerful economic incentives combined with racism, the political domination American missionaries had established on the islands, and the corruption of the Kalakaua-Lilioukalani governments to pave the way for the coup of 1893.[15]

By the late 1960s, a new generation of scholars had less difficulty accepting the Williams-LaFeber-McCormick thesis. For one thing, the corporate structure Williams and LaFeber criticized was much more visible to them than it was to students in the 1950s. They were also outraged by America's war in Vietnam, by the government's neglect of social problems at home, and by Watergate. With dissent everywhere in the air, the progressive's dichotomy of the "establishment" versus the "people" had real meaning for younger historians, whose writings reflect an ideological hybrid of neo-Beardian populism and Marxism, as opposed to the monotonous Marxist-Leninist orthodoxy of, say, Philip Foner or economist Harry Magdoff.[16] Not surprisingly, Williams students abound. Edward Crapol, for one, asserted in *America for Americans* that nineteenth-century Americans both wished to remove the shackles of Britain's economic overlordship and to emulate her status as the preeminent international economic power. The love-hate relationship ended, in his view, not with the Venezuelan crisis or the Spanish-American War, but with the return of American prosperity in 1897 and the country's gradual supplantation of Britain as the reigning commercial force in the world. Tom Terrill, another Williams student, demonstrated how Republicans and Democrats, in a time of domestic upheaval, promised social harmony to the American electorate by respectively raising or lowering tariffs. Whether by means of free trade or protectionism, however, he suggested that the object for both parties was to rid the United States of its surplus production. A Williams student by way of Lloyd Gardner, Ernest Paolino presented a portrait of William Henry Seward in 1973 which endeavored to show that Seward's grand design for a greater America was predicated on the establishment of commercial hegemony throughout the world rather than territorial acquisition. However, as is the case with so many of these new left studies, he did not address the question of when commercial expansion became imperialistic.[17]

Americans were not alone in criticizing the nation's wayward departure from its liberal-democratic mission. No less distressed than their turn-of-the-century colleagues by the might of the American colossus, European writers like Georges Fournial and Roland LaBarre, in a Vietnam-influenced polemic, condemned the hypocrisy of American rhetoric in the face of the country's neocolonialism. More scholarly in presentation, Alberto Aquarone's volume stated that the American mission was simply a moralistic smokescreen to conceal the nation's insatiable desire for commercial empire, which the Venezuelan episode and the annexationism of

1898 revealed. Claude Julien's *L'Empire Américain* similarly maintained that Americans, like the Europeans before them, justified their imperialist behavior as "la mission civilisatrice." Nonetheless, he contended that American imperialism, unlike the European varieties, genuinely sought to uplift dependent peoples morally and politically. The tragedy for Julien, like Williams, was that the continued existence of an American empire and support for reactionary governments had subverted the nation's idealistic mission to bring law, democracy, and order to the world.[18]

The antiwar movement of the 1960s also altered traditional interpretations of late nineteenth-century anti-imperialism. In 1968 Robert Beisner published *Twelve Against Empire*, a balanced account of the anti-imperialist movement as refracted through the attitudes of a handful of Mugwumps and Old Guard Republicans who denounced the betrayal of American ideals. Challenging the Williams thesis, Beisner showed that the latter's opposition was more motivated by historical, constitutional, moral, and racial considerations than by the desire to establish an informal economic empire. Divided over such questions as the acquisition of Hawaii, bereft of an alternative vision for the nation's future, racially prejudiced, and in the waning years of their lives, the conservative elite was unable to compete with the more youthful and persuasive jingoist element led by Roosevelt, Lodge, and Senator Beveridge. But by the 1970s, Vietnam-influenced studies by E. Berkeley Tompkins and Daniel Schirmer presented idealized sketches of the anti-imperialists, whom they portrayed as radical humanists allied against the "interests," which Schirmer defined as essentially the military-industrial complex. Caught up in the popular protest against the Vietnam War, both authors have somehow overlooked the facts that the anti-imperialists were few in number, elitist in social predisposition (opposition to Bryan had at least as much to do with his rabble-rousing populism as it did with his wishy-washy stand on imperialism) and, in some cases, illiberal and even racist.[19]

Accounts of American atrocities in Vietnam have also stimulated interest in the Filipino insurrection of 1899-1902. Articles by James Zimmerman, William Gatewood, and Richard Welch demonstrated that the American public, torn by a sense of national duty and its traditional commitment to self-determination of all peoples, was ambivalent in its attitude toward the United States-Filipino conflict. The atrocities that did take place, according to Welch, were instigated by angry, bored, and racially prejudiced junior officers in the Philippines rather than by official policy in Washington or Manila. More recently John Gates argued that American atrocities were part of the negative incentives, which also included deportation and internment, used by the American army to quell the guerilla insurrection. However, the military, which was the first governing body, also employed positive incentives to weaken revolutionary resistance—the promise of true civil government, education, public health facilities—which antedated McKinley's policy of benevolent assimilation. Lured either by money, participation in the new Federal party, or hope of civil office, increasing numbers of Filipinos sided with the Americans after 1900. In retaliation the revolutionary leaders engaged in their own acts of terrorism including decapitation and live burials. Although Gates did not consider the effect of the Filipino insurrection on American society, Welch has made this topic the subject of his book, *Response to Imperialism*.[20]

By the mid-1970s Vietnam no longer provoked the same febrile emotions it had a few years earlier, and the socially disruptive mystery of Watergate had been revealed and resolved. Weary of the political divisions that had rent the country, Americans elected a president who promised to restore social cohesion. Analogously, the strident revisionism of the late 1960s and early 1970s gave way to a noncontroversial eclecticism exemplified at the beginning of the decade by David Healy's *US Expansionism*, a survey in search of a central argument. In a later study Charles Campbell reinvoked many of the themes in Healy's volume—messianic idealism, the born-again nationalism of Theodore Roosevelt, Social Darwinism, Anglo-Saxon racism, and market expansion. Although he had studied with Bemis, Campbell emphasized the growing preoccupation with national security among the post-Civil War administrations from Johnson to McKinley and the development of Anglo-American amity. More generous than his teacher in his assessment of McKinley, he likewise considered America's colonialist adventure in the Philippines an aberration of the national spirit. Lester Langley's survey of United States policy in the Caribbean, though mainly concerned with the increasing threat European encroachment in the Western Hemisphere posed for American security, falls into the same eclectic genre. While these authors have adequately summarized existing theories, Robert Beisner has provided a fresh look at late nineteenth-century diplomatic history by conceptualizing the period in terms of changing foreign-policy paradigms. Borrowing from the social science literature, Beisner set out to reconcile the conflict between the Beardians and Prattians, who respectively view the events of 1898-1900 either as part of a continuous historical process or as a break with the past. He sought to show that the combination of environmental changes in the United States and in the structure of international politics and the shifting perceptions of the material world by policymakers transformed the paradigm which had defined American foreign policy prior to the 1890s. Hitherto an isolationist or unilateralist United States had reacted to events rather than precipitate them, had engaged in an unsystematic diplomacy, and had marshalled military and naval forces woefully unprepared for warfare. The United States in the 1890s, however, as evidenced by Blaine's planned Pan-American conference of 1889, the lynching of Italians in New Orleans, the

Chilean imbroglio, and Harrison's vigorous support of Hawaiian annexation, had become a world power with geographically extended interests, had fashioned a centralized foreign policy that displayed a continuity of purpose, and had developed the military might and the will to act in defense of her interests.[21]

Fundamentally a study of the modernization of late-nineteenth century foreign relations, Beisner's book fits into an emerging historiographical pattern, which can be termed the modernist synthesis. The modernist view is characterized by its focus on the effect of pervasive social change on traditional cultural orientations (a theme social historians like Robert Wiebe and Ray Ginger have imaginatively explored), by the interrelation of domestic and geopolitical influences on the formulation of foreign policy, and by a comparative-historical approach to foreign relations which has de-emphasized the myth of American uniqueness. Methodologically, Beisner's study also reflects the trend toward a more systematic application of social science theory to historical analysis, which owes so much to the pioneering works by Hofstadter and May.[22]

An early critic of traditional approaches to diplomatic history, British historian A. E. Campbell, in a study published in 1960, focused on the sociocultural connections that gave rise to Anglo-American rapprochement. Campbell asserted that Britain's racial kinship with its progeny across the Atlantic, intensified by the rhetoric of Social Darwinism, perpetuated the myth that Britain would benefit from American expansionism. Though influenced by racial considerations, the United States, given its Enlightenment origins, viewed rapprochement essentially in ideological terms. Ideological identification with Britain's traditions of political freedom and social equality thus gave rise to support for London's struggle against the Boers in South Africa. In a volume based heavily on secondary works, Bradford Perkins pointed out that shared domestic tensions, mutual interest in social reform, and trans-Atlantic travel, among other considerations, brought the two states closer together in the 1890s. Basically, however, it was Anglo-Saxon racism that encouraged rapprochement on both sides of the Atlantic. The turning point came during the Spanish-American War, when Whitehall, influenced by an enthusiastic British public, cautiously supported the United States, and Washington, equally affected by the cult of Anglo-Saxonism, set out on an imperialist escapade in political and cultural imitation of Britain.[23]

Other writers have demonstrated how sociocultural differences among nations can produce conflict in international relations. John King Fairbank has noted in a critique of Washington's China policy in the nineteenth century that Americans in China self-righteously proclaimed a new vision for the world; but to the Chinese mind the United States, which in deed if not word accepted the Old World's unequal treaty system, was simply another

Western imperialist power. Of major importance are Akira Iriye's cross-cultural analyses of American-East Asian relations. In *Across the Pacific* Iriye explained in global terms that the process of technological and social change taking place at the end of the nineteenth century and the concomitant reassessment of national security this prompted affected Japan and China no less than the United States. Contact between the West and a similarly modernizing but culturally different Orient shattered American cultural monism and, as reflected in the widespread appeal of Social Darwinism, gave rise to the apprehension that Western civilization was declining. The result was the diplomacy of imperialism in East Asia in which the old system of informal political controls gave way to naval bases, colonies, and the militaristic accoutrements of formal empire. Whereas the United States government apologized for European imperialism as fundamentally civilizing, as Iriye demonstrated in another volume devoted to U.S.-Japanese relations, it was ill-prepared for Japanese expansionism, which provoked the anxiety that less-advanced peoples might overtake a lethargic Western civilization. In his judgment, apprehension about Japan's aims may well have proven the critical factor in America's decision to annex the Hawaiian Islands.[24]

Michael Hunt's study of United States-Chinese relations in Manchuria also focused on the impact of conflicting cultural images on international relations. Though clearly in their interests to do so, both the United States and China failed to keep Manchuria out of Russia's hands. This the Americans attributed to China's backwardness, passivity, and cultural unpreparedness for the modern world. For their part, the Chinese, who had once perceived the Americans as their protectors, now likened them to Russia and the other European imperialists, partly because of anti-Chinese sentiment within the United States and the latter's participation in suppressing the Boxer uprising. China's reaction, Hunt persuasively argued, was not surprising in light of the inconsistency of Washington's policies which, in the Hay notes, sustained Britain's traditional policy of the Open Door and yet, as evidenced by Hay's attempt to secure a naval station in Fukien province, flirted with staking out a sphere of American influence in China. The historical convergence in 1898 of Spain, the Philippines, and the United States provided the backdrop for Peter Stanley's volume on intercultural conflict and United States-Philippine relations. In *A Nation in the Making* he demonstrated that the movement toward revolutionary nationalism in the Philippine Islands (which owed its conception to difficulties experienced by the Spanish ruling class in accepting the decline of Spain's power on the islands and its gestation to Madrid's cultural tutelage) continued unabated among lower- and middle-class Filipinos after Dewey's victory. Though Washington was not responsive to Filipino nationalism and racial dignity, Stanley concluded, it did bring about a process of nation-building that gave

Filipinos, and particularly the elite who welcomed American sovereignty, confidence and pride in their accomplishment. Awkward in its imperialist role, the American government did not aim to subjugate the Filipinos, but to convert them to the American way. Carmelo Rosario Natal's study of United States-Puerto Rican relations employed a similar sociocultural approach. Natal examined the rise of Puerto Rican nationalism, the naive optimism with which rich and poor alike looked forward to their status as free citizens of the United States, and how Washington, swept away by the public's impulsive imperialism, annexed an island of neither strategic nor economic value and a people who were culturally unassimilable in American society.[25]

Gerald Linderman and David Patterson have also viewed late nineteenth-century American expansionism through the lens of a nation in social transformation. In *The Mirror of War* Linderman, a student of Wiebe's, explained that the industrial transformation of post-Civil War America upset traditional community life. Trusting in an elemental morality, Americans grew increasingly disturbed by the aggregation of capital and the consolidation of power in urban society. Seeking to exorcise the evils of modernization and to regain their freedom from the corporate interests, they identified psychologically with the Cuban struggle for independence against the centralized authority of Madrid, which they perceived, like their image of the business interests, as an immoral disrupter of social order. Patterson showed that the leaders of the anti-imperialist movement, despite their high ideals, were an elitist, conservative, and pessimistic lot who did not effectively mobilize public opinion. After 1900, however, an institutionalized peace movement emerged which reflected the growing centralization and bureaucratization of domestic society and which sought to internationalize American values and institutions. The group of moral men who formerly had taken the responsibility to preserve peace was replaced by "scientific" experts who tended to be more liberal, socially flexible, and optimistic, but who overestimated the applicability of American values to other societies.[26]

Sociocultural themes and the larger issue of modernity have also influenced historians writing on the relationship between military policy and diplomacy in late nineteenth-century America. Peter Karsten, for one, drew a correlation between the post-Civil War movement to modernize the navy and support for the large policy. Mahan's writings, in his judgment, were intended as much to sell the value of a professional naval institution to a niggardly Congress as they were to show the navy's strategic importance in enhancing American power and prestige. Karsten's examination of the social background and cultural values of navalists who attended Annapolis also added a new dimension to earlier studies of Anglo-American relations by explaining how social-class, ideological, and racial similarities produced a camaraderie between American and British naval officers. Richard Challener reinforced Karsten's view of the navy as a modernizing institution which sought to further its own aims. Challener contended that naval authorities (like the professionalizing diplomatic corps) mainly promoted American commercial expansion to demonstrate their national value and thereby to encourage congressional appropriations, a position Kenneth Hagan, following the Williams thesis, has challenged. At the level of policy, however, naval officials were still inhibited by the inheritance of traditions which denied military men political roles. Accordingly, he maintained that there was no significant civil-military relationship before World War I and no real reconciliation of force with diplomacy. Graham Cosmas has shown that there were also reformers who succeeded in modernizing the army. However, here too Cosmas noted that military-civil coordination was quite inadequate. This was largely because of the administrative inefficiency of the Department of War, which was not prepared for conflict with Spain, but also partly because of McKinley's sudden decision to give the military a more active role following Dewey's stunning victory, both of which mirrored the vacillation and experimentation of a country undergoing social change and emerging as a force in international politics. For a treatment that synthesizes diplomatic, military, political, and social developments between the Cuban insurrection and the Treaty of Paris, specialists must await David Trask's forthcoming study, tentatively titled *The War with Spain in 1898.*[27]

In his reply to James Field's essay in the *AHR*, Robert Beisner pointed out that the historiographical argument over American imperialism had not really changed much during the past four decades. Debate continued to revolve around the same dreary question of whether American imperialism was planned, was an accident, or, indeed, whether it ever existed. Beisner wondered if the hope for a new debate was a chimera.[28]

If the recent trend toward conceptualizing the history of late nineteenth-century American foreign relations in terms of social modernity and intercultural relations is any indication, the historiographical prospects for the future may not be as bleak as Beisner thinks. As early as 1952 Richard Hofstadter suggested that historians might usefully investigate whether the social-psychological pressures of a modernizing society which gave rise to the American strain of imperialism were also present in other countries. Bernard Semmel's work, like the study by Bradford Perkins, certainly indicates that the social upheaval of late nineteenth-century America had its analogue in Great Britain, which was also experiencing a crisis of modernity. Ernest May's *Imperial Democracy* drew interesting connections between social tensions within Spain and the United States and between their perceptions of national power and international relations. Urbanization, technological change, industrial expansion, labor unrest, and economic depression were problems that every European state had to contend with after 1876. Moreover, time-honored social institutions in Europe struggled to adjust to industrialization and, in contrast to the United States, democratic ideas as well. Indeed, the disruptive effects of modernity on traditional social patterns and values are revealed in the abstract expressionist and cubistic art which emerged at the turn of the twentieth century. Additional comparative studies such as May's will help to determine the similarities and dissimilarities between America's foreign relations and the policies of other countries (which were contending with similar unsettling effects of social change in different cultural milieux) without succumbing to the simplistic notion of American uniqueness. As Iriye has recently pointed out, international relations are, in the final analysis, intercultural relations. And the kinds of behavior nations exhibit in the international arena (extrasystemic behavior) are a function of their cultural values and traditions (intrasystemic orientation).[29]

Specialists in this period would also benefit from new analyses of American economic expansionism. By excessively focusing on United States commercial relations with the Third World countries of Latin America and Asia, and by oversimplifying their interpretation, the new left has ignored a number of important issues. One major area little examined is the effect of American economic expansion on Europe. Certainly this merits more attention than it has received, considering that the European states were the major trading partners of the United States at the end of the nineteenth century. To be sure, the entire world was becoming an outlet for American products at that time, but Europe remained the largest market, particularly in the distribution of finished manufactures. As Matthew Simon and David Novack have pointed out, the percentage increase in the finished manufactures to Europe during the decade 1896-1906 outstripped the entire production from 1820 to 1895. Between 1892 and 1912 American manufactured exports increased by 457.3 percent versus 126.5 percent for Britain, 108.5 percent for France, and 208.3 percent for Germany. One wonders, then, to what extent was the European partition of China influenced by the threat of American economic competition in new markets? Did the United States trigger the anxiety that manifested itself at Kiaochow (and Fashoda)? This would entail more empirical research reconciling the ideas and behavior of statesmen in both the United States and Europe. It would also be useful to examine United States-European economic relations to test the Hobson-Lenin thesis of capitalist rivalry in the colonial world on which new left historiography rests.[30]

As for the domestic part of the economic expansion equation, the production glut theory of Williams and LaFeber begs further investigation. As Paul Holbo and William Becker have noted, and as American balance-of-trade figures suggest, the production surplus may well have been a sign of strength and prosperity rather than weakness. While some businessmen vigorously supported the exploitation of new markets, most people in the 1870s and 1880s, including then Senator McKinley, appear to have been interested in protecting existing markets. Indeed, Congress did not lower tariff barriers until 1913, when it approved the Underwood bill (a point recognized by Tom Terrill, who defined America's economic imperialism in terms of nationalistic rather than free-trade expansionism). Nor for that matter did Congress appropriate funds to create an offensive navy of any size or to develop a trained consular service, both of which augmented commercial expansion, until after the turn of the twentieth century. Moreover, some Americans looked inward rather than outward for solutions to the problem of excess production. Bellamyites and single-taxers thought in terms of redistribution of the national product; some businessmen, antedating the New Deal's prescription, favored trusts, holding companies, and other varieties of cartelization to control production and prices. It would be helpful to analyze business motives for trade expansion, bearing in mind (if it turns out that businessmen were inclined to seek internal solutions to the nation's economic problems) Marilyn Young's question: why did the myth of the China market persist?[31]

More theoretical studies of the nature of power and imperialism, which have become virtually an inalienable part of the political scientist's demesne, might provide more direction to the present desultory debate over whether imperialism, expansionism, and annexationism are the same or different phenomena. Neo-Prattians like May, for example, still adhere to the position William Langer presented in *Foreign Affairs* in 1935 that territorial expansion is implicit in the definition of imperialism. But as Jeannette Nichols has pointed out, Langer paid short shrift to economic and other nonpolitical forms of imperialism. Neo-Beardians, of course, and Marxists like Foner, presenting their briefs from respective Hobsonian and Leninist benches, insist that imperialism is intrinsically economic. Yet, as economic historian David Landes has stated, one must be careful to distinguish between a monistic-economic interpretation of imperialism and economic imperialism, which is an aspect of a historical phenomenon. In his view, technology has created unequal economic relationships between states, and, in turn, has produced disparities of political power and an inevitable tendency toward dominance on the part of those states which possess material and psychological advantages. Josef Schumpeter, Bernard Semmel, and A. P. Thornton have respectively defined imperialism as an irrational atavism from the precapitalist age, a social phenomenon which served to strengthen national cohesion, and an intellectual construct which gave meaning to the constant struggle for survival. Economic historians Ronald Robinson and John Gallagher have treated imperialism as a historically continuous phenomenon, but one whose form changed in the late Victorian period from the informal mode of one state exercising preponderant control over another to the establishment of formal empire, including colonies and naval bases, owing to the appearance of adventitious and idiosyncratic situations which called for specific, individual, ad hoc responses. Iriye, to cite another position, has presented a case in his writings for the cultural and racial basis of imperialism. By combining Iriye's and Landes's theses, imperialism could also be conceptualized as a response to modernization. Whatever the explanation, each of these theoretical positions deserves empirical attention.[32]

In addition to these suggestions, political histories would help clarify the effects of Congress, party politics, and pressure groups on foreign policy. In *The Whirligig of Politics*, for example, J. Rogers Hollingsworth showed how divisions in the Democratic party reflected the conflict between agrarian-romantic America (Bryan) and urban-industrial America (Cleveland), and how a morally priggish, tactless Cleveland intensified party divisions which found an outlet in the war for humanity. As stimulated by May's speculative essay on imperialism, empirical inquiries into the role opinion leaders played in the evolution of American foreign relations (not an impossible task when the numbers of both the foreign-policy elite and the public were so small), would also prove illuminating. So would research on the relationship between technological change and alternative foreign-policy strategies. Finally, biographies such as Gerald Eggert's study of Olney, which breathe life into their subjects instead of treating them as mere symbols of their times (as Kenton Clymer and, to a lesser extent, Ronald Spector have done in their respective portraits of Hay and Dewey) would shed light on the motives of the prime actors in the drama of late nineteenth-century American diplomatic history.[33]

It might be well at this point to take a slice-of-life approach to this period rather than to design new architectonic monuments to the causes of American imperialism. In-depth analyses of specific episodes may yield fresh insights; they will at least produce less of the intellectual acrobatics that seem designed to avoid a confrontation between divergent schools of thought or that rehash the metaphysical struggle to reconcile America the Imperialist Power with America the Innocent Child of the Enlightenment.

Notes

1. I wish to thank David Trask for his helpful suggestions which I have incorporated in this essay. James A. Field, Jr., "American Imperialism: The Worst Chapter in Almost Any Book," *American Historical Review* 83 (June 1978): 644-68.

2. John H. Latané, *America as a World Power, 1897-1907* (New York: Harper & Brothers, 1907); Archibald Cary Coolidge, *The United States as a World Power* (New York: Macmillan Co., 1908).

3. J. Frederick MacDonald, "Jules Cambon et la Menace de l'Impérialisme Américain (1898-1899)," *Revue d'Histoire Diplomatique* (April-September 1972): 247-55. For a view critical of the United States, yet sympathetic to American colonial practices, *see* Henri Hauser, "L'Oeuvre Américaine aux Philippines," *Revue Politique et Parlementaire* 40 (April 1904): 126-39. Concerning the American economic threat, *see* Ugo Ojetti, *L'America Vittoriosa* (Milan: Fratelli Treves, 1899) and Ludwig Max Goldberger, *Das Land der unbegrunzten Möglichkeiten* (Berlin: F. Fontane, 1903). Some writers like E. Catellani considered the Monroe Doctrine a pretentious ruse which might be used to justify an American political, if not military, invasion of Europe. *See* "La Questione della Venezuela e la Dottrina Monroe," *Nuova Anthologia* 145 (1896): 445-66. Goluchowski's views, among others, can be found in many secondary works including Charles S. Campbell, *Special Business Interests and the Open Door Policy* (New Haven: Yale University Press, 1951).

4. Alfred L. P. Dennis, *Adventures in American Diplomacy, 1896-1906* (New York: E. P. Dutton, 1928); Harold Underwood Faulkner, *American Economic History* (New York: Harper & Brothers, 1924); Charles A. and Mary R. Beard, *The Rise of American Civilization*, 2 vols. (New York: Macmillan Co., 1927).

5. Charles A. Beard, *The Idea of National Interest: An Analytical Study in American Foreign Policy* (New York: Macmillan Co., 1934).

6. Julius W. Pratt, *Expansionists of 1898: The Acquisition of Hawaii and the Spanish Islands* (Baltimore: Johns Hopkins Press, 1936); Samuel Flagg Bemis, *A Diplomatic History of the United States* (New York: Henry Holt, 1936); Alexander DeConde and Armin Rappaport, eds., *Essays Diplomatic and Undiplomatic of Thomas A. Bailey* (New York: Appleton-Century-Crofts, 1969); Dexter Perkins, *The Monroe Doctrine, 1867-1907* (Baltimore: Johns Hopkins Press, 1937). Alfred Vagts has shown in his monumental *Deutschland und die Vereinigten Staaten in der Weltpolitik*, 2 vols. (New York: Macmillan Co., 1935) that Berlin, preoccupied with European affairs, was reluctant to contest United States dominance in the Caribbean.

7. Walter Millis, *The Martial Spirit: A Study of Our War with Spain* (Boston: Houghton Mifflin Co., 1931); Marcus M. Wilkerson, *Public Opinon and the Spanish-American War* (New York: Russell & Russell, 1932); Joseph E. Wisan, *The Cuban Crisis as Reflected in the New York Press, 1895-1898* (New York: Columbia University Press, 1934). A recent essay by Daniel Simundsen on the midwestern press reiterates the refrain that McKinley was goaded into war by "yellow journals." *See* "The Yellow Press on the Prairie: South Dakota Newspaper Editorials Prior to the Spanish-American War," *South Dakota History* 2 (Summer 1972): 211-29. *See also* Arnold M. Shankman, "Southern Methodist Newspapers and the Coming of the Spanish-American War: A Research Note," *Journal of Southern History* 39 (February 1973): 93-96. For a more favorable view of McKinley, *see* Tyler Dennett, *John Hay: From Poetry to Politics* (New York: Dodd, Mead & Co., 1933). *See also* Joseph A. Fry's historiographical essay, "William McKinley and the Coming of the Spanish-American War: A Study of the Besmirching and Redemption of an Historical Image," *Diplomatic History* 3 (Winter 1979): 77-97. Allan Nevins, *Grover Cleveland: A Study in Courage* (New York: Dodd, Mead & Co., 1932) shares the hagiographic style of other biographies written during this period such as Nevins's *Hamilton Fish: The Inner History of the Grant Administration* (New York: Dodd,

Mead & Co., 1936) and David S. Muzzey, *James G. Blaine: A Political Idol of Other Days* (New York: Dodd, Mead & Co., 1934).

8. Hans J. Morgenthau, *In Defense of the National Interest: A Critical Examination of American Foreign Policy* (New York: Alfred A. Knopf, 1951); Robert E. Osgood, *Ideas and Self-Interest in America's Foreign Relations: The Great Transformation of the Twentieth Century* (Chicago: University of Chicago Press, 1953). A decade-and-a-half earlier, A Whitney Griswold presented a similar case concerning the Hay notes in *The Far Eastern Policy of the United States* (New Haven: Yale University Press, 1938). George F. Kennan, *American Diplomacy* (Chicago: University of Chicago Press, 1951); Norman A. Graebner, "The Year of Transition," in Norman A. Graebner, ed., *An Uncertain Tradition: American Secretaries of State in the Twentieth Century* (New York: McGraw-Hill, 1961). Ernest R. May's essay, "Emergence to World Power," in John Higham, ed., *The Reconstruction of American History* (New York: Harper & Row, 1962) examined the changing interpretations of America as a world power. David F. Trask has presented a useful critique of the realists, among others, in his essay, "Writings of American Foreign Relations: 1957 to the Present," in John Braeman, Robert H. Bremner, and David Brody, eds., *Twentieth Century American Foreign Policy* (Columbus: Ohio State University Press, 1971). For other realist interpretations of developments during this period, *see* C. P. Stacey, "Britain's Withdrawal from North America, 1864-1871," *Canadian Historical Review* 36 (September 1955): 185-98 and Maureen M. Robson, "The Alabama Claims and the Anglo-American Reconciliation, 1865-71," *Canadian Historical Review* 42 (March 1961): 1-22. These writers attributed London's willingness to settle the Alabama claims in 1871 to its concern with changes in the European balance of power following the Franco-Prussian War and Russia's abrogation of the Black Sea clauses of 1856. Similarly, English historian R. G. Neale pointed out that Britain's acquiescence in 1895 to American demands concerning the Venezuelan border dispute and her support of the United States in the war against Spain were dictated by security needs rather than Anglo-American friendship. *See Britain and American Imperialism, 1898-1900* (Queensland, Australia: University of Queensland Press, 1965). These interpretations of Anglo-American rapprochement depart from the historical accounts of the post-Munich era which either scorned Britain's manipulation of a beneficent America in 1898 or romanticized Anglo-American unity. *See*, as an example of the former, R. H. Heindel, *The American Impact on Great Britain, 1898-1914* (Philadelphia: University of Pennsylvania Press, 1940, and as illustrations of the latter, Lionel M. Gelber, *The Rise of Anglo-American Friendship* (London: Oxford University Press, 1938) and John B. Brebner, *North Atlantic Triangle* (New York: Columbia University Press, 1945). In a like manner Russell Bastert contended that Secretary of State Blaine's Pan-American policy evolved from his growing concern over the outbreak of conflicts between the Latin American states in the early 1880s, such as the War of the Pacific, and the threat they posed for possible European intervention. *See* Russell H. Bastert, "A New Approach to the Origins of Blaine's Pan-American Policy," *Hispanic American Historical Review* 39 (April 1955): 375-412 and "Diplomatic Reversal: Frelinghuysen's Opposition to Blaine's Pan-American Policy in 1882," *Mississippi Valley Historical Review* 42 (March 1956): 653-71.

9. William R. Braisted, *The United States Navy in the Pacific, 1897-1909*

(Austin: University of Texas Press, 1958); Howard K. Beale, *Theodore Roosevelt and the Rise of America to World Power* (Baltimore: Johns Hopkins Press, 1956); Paolo E. Coletta, "Bryan, McKinley, and the Treaty of Paris," *Pacific Historical Review* 26 (May 1957): 131-46 and "McKinley, The Peace Negotiations, and the Acquisition of the Philippines," *Pacific Historical Review* 30 (November 1961): 341-50. Coletta elaborated on this theme in his *William Jennings Bryan, I: Political Evangelist, 1860-1908* (Lincoln: University of Nebraska Press, 1964), which sympathetically presented Bryan as a suffering Moses. *See also* Paul H. Glad, *The Trumpet Soundeth, William Jennings Bryan and His Democracy, 1896-1912* (Lincoln: University of Nebraska Press, 1960).

10. Richard Hofstadter, "Cuba, the Philippines, and Manifest Destiny," in Daniel Aaron, ed., *America in Crisis: Fourteen Crucial Episodes in American History*, 1st ed. (New York: Alfred A. Knopf, 1952). Gerald G. Eggert has revised the traditional view of Olney in *Richard Olney: Evolution of a Statesman* (University Park: Pennsylvania State University Press, 1974). Though Eggert succeeded in bringing the secretary of state to life, his portrayal of Olney—so irascible that he once shot a cow that trod upon his tennis lawn—as a shrewd, calm statesman in the Venezuelan crisis is not wholly convincing. *See also* J. A. S. Grenville, *Lord Salisbury and Foreign Policy* (London: Athlone Press, 1964).

11. William Appleman Williams, *The Tragedy of American Diplomacy*, rev. ed. (New York: World Publishing Co., 1962). *See also* Richard W. Van Alstyne, *The Rising American Empire* (New York: Oxford University Press, 1960) and, on McKinley, Margaret Leech's biography, *In the Days of McKinley* (New York: Harper & Row, 1959) which does present a refreshingly human portrait of the president.

12. *See* Daniel Bell, *The End of Ideology: On the Exhaustion of Political Ideas in the Fifties* (Glencoe: Free Press, 1965); Daniel J. Boorstin, *The Genius of American Politics* (Chicago: University of Chicago Press, 1953); Walter LaFeber, *The New Empire: An Interpretation of American Expansion, 1860-1898* (Ithaca: Cornell University Press, 1963). While LaFeber had branded Josiah Strong as a trade expansionist, others have portrayed him as an ecclesiastical politician trumpeting the dawn of a new international order based on the social gospel. *See* Dorothea Muller, "Josiah Strong and American Nationalism: A Reevaluation," *Journal of American History* 53 (December 1966): 487-503 and James E. Reed, "American Foreign Policy, The Politics of Missions and Josiah Strong, 1890-1900," *Church History* 41 (June 1972): 230-45. Thomas J. McCormick, *China Market: America's Quest for Informal Empire, 1893-1901* (Chicago: Quadrangle Books, 1967); William Appleman Williams, *The Roots of the Modern American Empire* (New York: Vintage, 1969).

13. Thomas A. Bailey, "America's Emergence as a World Power: The Myth and the Verity," *Pacific Historical Review* 30 (February 1961): 1-16; H. Wayne Morgan, *America's Road to Empire: The War with Spain and Overseas Expansion* (New York: John Wiley & Sons, 1965); Frederick Merk, *Manifest Destiny and Mission in American History* (New York: Random House, 1963); James A. Field, Jr., *America and the Mediterranean World, 1776-1882* (Princeton: Princeton University Press, 1969).

14. *See* Ernest R. May's *Imperial Democracy: The Emergence of America as a Great Power* (New York: Harper & Row, 1961) and his *American Imperialism: A Speculative Essay* (New York: Atheneum, 1968). For the impact of the diplomacy of

imperialism in Europe on American policymakers and on naval expansionists, *see also* Victor Morales Lezcano, "Ideologia y Estrategia Estadounidense: 1898," *Hispania* 29 (September-October 1969): 610-26. John A. S. Grenville and George Berkeley Young, *Politics, Strategy, and American Diplomacy* (New Haven: Yale University Press, 1966); H. Wayne Morgan, *William McKinley and His America* (Syracuse: Syracuse University Press, 1963).

15. David M. Pletcher, *The Awkward Years: American Foreign Relations under Garfield and Arthur* (Columbia: University of Missouri Press, 1962); Milton Plesur, *America's Outward Thrust: Approaches to Foreign Affairs 1865-1890* (DeKalb: Northern Illinois University Press, 1971); David F. Healy, *The United States in Cuba: 1898-1902* (Madison: University of Wisconsin Press, 1963); Marilyn Blatt Young, *The Rhetoric of Empire: American China Policy, 1895-1901* (Cambridge, Mass.: Harvard University Press, 1968). The best book on American missionaries and expansionism in China is Paul A. Varg, *The Making of a Myth: The United States and China, 1897-1912* (East Lansing: Michigan State University Press, 1968). *See also* William Adam Russ, Jr., *The Hawaiian Revolution* (*1893-94*) (Selinsgrove, Pa.: Susquehanna University Press, 1959) and Merze Tate's two volumes, *The United States and the Hawaiian Kingdom* (New Haven: Yale University Press, 1965) and *Hawaii: Reciprocity or Annexation* (East Lansing: Michigan State University Press, 1968). *See also* Sylvester Stevens, *American Expansion in Hawaii, 1842, 1898* (Harrisburg: Archives Publishing Co., 1945).

16. Philip S. Foner, *The Spanish-American-Cuban War and the Birth of American Imperialism, 1895-1902*, 2 vols. (New York: Monthly Review Press, 1972); Harry Magdoff, *The Age of Imperialism: The Economics of U.S. Foreign Policy* (New York: Monthly Review Press, 1969).

17. Edward P. Crapol, *America for Americans: Economic Nationalism and Anglophobia in the Late Nineteenth Century* (Westport, Conn.: Greenwood Press, 1973); Tom E. Terrill, *The Tariff, Politics and American Foreign Policy, 1874-1901* (Westport, Conn.: Greenwood Press, 1973); Ernest N. Paolino, *The Foundations of the American Empire; William Henry Seward and U.S. Foreign Policy* (Ithaca: Cornell University Press, 1973).

18. Georges Fournial and Roland La Barre, *De Monroe à Johnson: La Politique des Etats-Unis en Amérique Latine* (Paris: Éditions Sociales, 1966); Alberto Aquarone, *Le Origini dell'Imperialismo Americano: Da McKinley a Taft* (*1897-1913*) (Bologna: Società Editrice il Mulino, 1973); Claude Julien, *L'Empire Américain* (Paris: Éditions Bernard Grasset, 1968).

19. Robert L. Beisner, *Twelve Against Empire: The Anti-Imperialists, 1898-1900* (New York: McGraw-Hill, 1968); E. Berkeley Tompkins, *Anti-Imperialism in the United States: The Great Debate, 1890-1920* (Philadelphia: University of Pennsylvania Press, 1970); Daniel B. Schirmer, *Republic or Empire: American Resistance to the Philippine War* (Cambridge, Mass.: Schenkman Publishing Company, 1972). *See also* Thomas G. Paterson, ed., *American Imperialism and Anti-Imperialism* (New York: Thomas Y. Crowell Co., 1973). In opposition to the view that the imperialists and anti-imperialists made strange bedfellows, *see* William E. Leuchtenberg, "Progressivism and Imperialism: The Progressive Movement and American Foreign Policy, 1898-1916," *Mississippi Valley Historical Review* 39 (December 1952): 483-504. *See also* Joseph M. Siracusa, "Progressivism, Im-

perialism, and the Leuchtenberg Thesis: An Historiographical Appraisal," *Australian Journal of Politics and History* 20 (December 1974): 312-25. Lest one conclude that only the social elite were racially prejudiced, *see* Alice Wexler, "Pain and Prejudice in the Santiago Campaign of 1898," *Journal of InterAmerican Studies and World Affairs* 18 (February 1976): 59-73. Among the more interesting biographical treatments is John Braeman, *Albert J. Beveridge: American Nationalist* (Chicago: University of Chicago Press, 1971) which shows that the Indiana senator's imperialism stemmed from many motives including racial pride, Christian duty, Social Darwinism, and the desire for new markets.

20. On the U.S.-Filipino conflict, James Zimmerman examined public attitudes in Chicago in "The Chicago Liberty and Loyalty Meetings, 1899: Public Attitudes toward the Philippine-American War," *North Dakota Quarterly* 43 (Autumn 1975): 29-37. On the reaction of black-Americans, *see* William B. Gatewood, Jr., "Black Americans and the Quest for Empire, 1898-1903," *Journal of Southern History* 38 (November 1972): 545-66. *See also* Richard E. Welch, Jr., "The Philippine Insurrection and the American Press," *Historian* 36 (November 1973): 34-51; "American Atrocities in the Philippines: The Indictment and the Response," *Pacific Historical Review* 43 (May 1974): 233-53; and *Response to Imperialism: The United States and the Philippine-American War, 1899-1902* (Chapel Hill: University of North Carolina Press, 1979); Stuart C. Miller's antihistory, "Our Mylai of 1900: Americans in the Philippine Insurrection," in Marilyn Blatt Young, ed., *American Expansionism: The Critical Issues* (Boston: Little, Brown & Co., 1973); John M. Gates, *Schoolbooks and Krags: The United States Army in the Philippines, 1898-1902* (Westport, Conn.: Greenwood Press, 1973).

21. David F. Healy, US Expansionism: The Imperialist Urge in the 1890s (Madison: University of Wisconsin Press, 1963); Charles S. Campbell, *The Transformation of American Foreign Relations, 1865-1900* (New York: Harper & Row, 1976); Lester D. Langley, *Struggle for the American Mediterranean: United States-European Rivalry in the Gulf-Caribbean, 1776-1904* (Athens, Ga.: University of Georgia Press, 1976). Although in need of revision, the best synthesis of U.S. relations with Latin America remains Bemis's *The Latin American Policy of the United States: An Historical Interpretation* (New York: Harcourt, Brace & World, 1943). For more recent monographs *see* David Pletcher's historiographical essay, "United States Relations with Latin America: Neighborliness and Exploitation," *American Historical Review* 82 (February 1977): 39-59; Robert L. Beisner, *From the Old Diplomacy to the New, 1865-1900* (New York: Thomas Y. Crowell Co., 1975).

22. Robert H. Wiebe, *The Search for Order, 1877-1920* (New York: Hill & Wang, 1967); Ray Ginger, *Age of Excess: The United States from 1877 to 1914*, 2d ed. (New York: Macmillan Co., 1975).

23. A. E. Campbell, *Great Britain and the United States, 1895-1903* (London: Longmans, Green & Co., 1960); Bradford Perkins, *The Great Rapprochement: England and the United States, 1895-1914* (New York: Atheneum, 1968). In "Racial Anglo-Saxonism and the American Response to the Boer War," *Diplomatic History* 2 (Summer 1978): 219-36, Stuart Anderson also found Anglo-Saxonism to be a major, if not the main, explanation for America's support of Britain in the Boer War. Cushing Strout has examined the impact of European, and particularly British, culture on America's national identity in *The American Image of the Old World*

(New York: Harper & Row, 1963). On the same subject, the cultural implications of late nineteenth-century American travel have been explored in Hugh De Santis, "The Democratization of Travel: The Travel Agent in American History," *Journal of American Culture* 1 (Spring 1978): 1-18.

24. John King Fairbank, "America's China Policy to 1898: A Misconception," *Pacific Historical Review* 39 (November 1970): 409-20; Akira Iriye, *Across the Pacific: An Inner History of American-East Asian Relations* (New York: Harcourt, Brace & World, 1967) and *Pacific Estrangement: Japanese and American Expansionism, 1897-1911* (Cambridge, Mass.: Harvard University Press, 1972).

25. Michael H. Hunt, *Frontier Defense and the Open Door: Manchuria in Chinese-American Relations, 1895-1911* (New Haven: Yale University Press, 1973). Hunt's view of Hay as an ambivalent statesman who mirrored the uncertainty of his time contrasts with the realist portrayal of the secretary as a cipher caught in the vortex of power politics, or a crass trade expansionist, as Kenton Clymer has described him in *John Hay: The Gentleman as Diplomat* (Ann Arbor: University of Michigan Press, 1975), or a canny statesman who succeeded in keeping American naval expansionists at bay, as Tyler Dennett, Marilyn Young, and Akira Iriye have portrayed him. *See* Tyler Dennett, *Americans in Eastern Asia* (New York: Barnes & Noble, 1941); Young, *Rhetoric of Empire*, and Iriye, *Across the Pacific*. Peter W. Stanley, *A Nation in the Making: The Philippines and the United States, 1899-1921* (Cambridge, Mass.: Harvard University Press, 1974) replaces the standard diplomatic history by Garel E. Grunder and William E. Livezey, *The Philippines and the United States* (Norman: University of Oklahoma Press, 1951) and easily improves on Teodoro A. Agoncillo, *Malolos: The Crisis of the Republic* (Quezon City: University of Philippines Press, 1960). Carmelo Rosario Natal, *Puerto Rico y la Crisis de la Guerra Hispanoamericana (1895-1898)* (Hato Rey, P.R.: Ramallo Bros., 1975).

26. Gerald F. Linderman, *The Mirror of War: American Society and the Spanish-American War* (Ann Arbor: University of Michigan Press, 1974); David S. Patterson, *Toward a Warless World: The Travail of the American Peace Movement, 1887-1914* (Bloomington: Indiana University Press, 1976). *See also* Warren F. Kuehl, *Seeking World Order: The United States and International Organization to 1920* (Nashville: Vanderbilt University Press, 1969).

27. Peter Karsten, *The Naval Aristocracy: The Golden Age of Annapolis and the Emergence of Modern American Navalism* (New York: Free Press, 1972); Richard D. Challener, *Admirals, Generals, and American Foreign Policy, 1898-1914* (Princeton: Princeton University Press, 1973); Kenneth J. Hagan, *American Gunboat Diplomacy and the Old Navy, 1877-1889* (Westport, Conn.: Greenwood Press, 1973); Graham A. Cosmas, *An Army for Empire: The United States Army in the Spanish-American War* (Columbia, Mo.: University of Missouri Press, 1971). Secretary of War Alger's quarrelsome apologia for the Department of War's mismanagement of the Spanish-American conflict can be found in *The Spanish-American War* (New York: Harper & Brothers, 1901).

28. Robert Beisner, Reply to Field, "The Worst Chapter," pp. 672-78.

29. Bernard Semmel, *Imperialism and Social Reform: English Social-Imperial Thought, 1895-1914* (Cambridge, Mass.: Harvard University Press, 1960); Akira Iriye, "Culture and Power: International Relations as Intercultural Relations," *Diplomatic History* 3 (Spring 1979): 115-28. The lack of "historical placeness" limits

the value of the sketches of Seward, Fish, Blaine, and Mahan in Frank J. Merli and Theodore A. Wilson, eds., *Makers of American Diplomacy: From Benjamin Franklin to Henry Kissinger* (New York: Charles Scribner's Sons, 1974).

30. Matthew Simon and David E. Novack, "Some Dimensions of the American Commercial Invasion of Europe, 1871-1914: An Introductory Essay," *Journal of Economic History* 24 (December 1961): 591-608. William L. Langer's *The Diplomacy of Imperialism*, 2 vols. (New York: Alfred A. Knopf, 1935) is indispensable.

31. Paul S. Holbo, "Economics, Emotion, and Expansion: An Emerging Foreign Policy," in H. Wayne Morgan, ed., *The Gilded Age* (Syracuse: Syracuse University Press, 1970); William H. Becker, "American Manufactures and Foreign Markets, 1870-1900: Business Historians and the 'New Economic Determinists,'" *Business History Review* 47 (Winter 1973): 466-81. The views of middle-class businessmen in Chicago suggest less concern for existing markets after the panic of 1893 and increased support for market expansion. *See* Hugh De Santis, "George Bowen and the American Dream," *Chicago History* 6 (Fall 1977): 143-54. *See also* Marilyn Blatt Young, "The Quest for Empire," in Ernest R. May and James C. Thompson, ed., *American-East Asian Relations: A Survey* (Cambridge, Mass.: Harvard University Press, 1972).

32. William L. Langer, "A Critique of Imperialism," in Theodore P. Greene, ed., *American Imperialism in 1898* (Boston: D. C. Heath, 1955); Jeannette P. Nichols, "The United States Congress and Imperialism, 1861-1897," *Journal of Economic History* 21 (December 1961): 526-38; David S. Landes, "Some Thoughts on the Nature of Economic Imperialism," *Journal of Economic History* 21 (December 1961): 496-512; Josef Schumpeter, *Zur Sociologie der Imperialism* (Tubingen: Mohr, 1919); Semmel, *Imperialism and Social Reform*; A. P. Thornton, *Doctrines of Imperialism* (New York: John Wiley & Sons, 1965); Ronald Robinson and John Gallagher with Alice Denny, *Africa and the Victorians: The Climax of Imperialism* (New York: Anchor Books, 1961).

33. J. Rogers Hollingsworth, *The Whirligig of Politics: The Democracy of Cleveland and Bryan* (Chicago: University of Chicago Press, 1963); Ronald Spector, *Admiral of the New Empire: The Life and Career of George Dewey* (Baton Rouge: Louisiana State University Press, 1974).

6 ______ The Diplomacy of Theodore Roosevelt and William Howard Taft

PAOLO E. COLETTA

Debate continues over the foreign policy of Theodore Roosevelt. Members of the consensus school of historians stress the homogeneity and continuity of the national past and conclude that United States foreign policies were realistic, well-intentioned, and successful. They see Roosevelt as understanding the realities of international relations better than his fellow Americans and, by making the United States a responsible weight in the international arena, strengthening the forces of law and order therein.[1]

On the other hand, realist historians credit the United States with good intentions but hold that it used excessive zeal and, by failing to recognize the realities of power and of national interests in world affairs, rarely formulated a foreign policy in which commitments and power were brought into balance. Walter Lippman, George F. Kennan, Hans J. Morgenthau, and Robert E. Osgood, particularly, disapprove of the legalistic-moralistic approach to international problems and foreign policy and also disapprove of policy based upon public opinion or party bias. They regret the making of policy decisions upon faulty information, the enormous confusion inherent in the decision-making process, the difficulty of controlling bureaucratic structures serving statesmen, and the naiveté, idealism, and utopianism of twentieth-century American foreign policy. Moreover, they see as foolish and tragic the piecemeal and eccentric character of America's foreign policies, swinging, for example, between isolationism and a self-righteous crusade, an intervention directed by "theologians of diplomacy."

In sum, they conclude that the United States has not had a generally accepted foreign policy since 1898.[2] They nonetheless agree that Roosevelt, as Raymond A. Esthus, Charles E. Neu, Robert A. Hart, Frederick W. Marks III, and Osgood see him and as Howard K. Beale put it, was "an international strategist with a peculiar *long-range* conception of the United States as a world power. That conception centers about the balance of power."[3]

A group of mostly young and professedly radical writers which appeared in the 1960s, largely followers of William Appleman Williams, have been labeled revisionists, new left, neo-Progressives, and neo-Marxists. Emphasizing ideological cleavages of the past, they decry Roosevelt's attempt (with his Big Stick) and Taft's effort (with his dollar diplomacy) to obtain and defend a world marketplace. To influence other nations to make themselves over politically or economically in the American image is evil because the attempt violates the principle of self-determination. By violating this principle, revisionists hold, both Roosevelt and Taft served the interests of big business; Taft's State Department, especially, was a trading post for Wall Street interests. Instead of providing domestic stability and tranquillity, the Roosevelt-Taft policies led to penetration, domination, interventions, and wars.[4]

Greatly influenced in foreign policy matters by Alfred Thayer Mahan and Brooks Adams, and having already contributed to expansion as an architect of the "large policy," Roosevelt pursued an imperialist foreign policy. He thus pleased most progressives, who supported expansion, and distressed those who, like modern revisionists, discounted his talk about duty, national obligation, and the need to protect the helpless against the imperialism of others. This latter group was appalled by what they considered his chauvinism, racism, and aggressive power diplomacy.[5] Still, these progressives continued to support Roosevelt because of his image of a warrior brandishing a big stick at American corporations on the one hand and foreign potentates on the other. They therefore saw no dichotomy in his domestic and foreign policies. Additional adhesives came in the form of their deification of Roosevelt, their demand for compulsory military training, their insistence that the Republican party remain lily-white (Negroes and Filipinos were considered wards to be educated toward freedom and independence, respectively), their hostility to oriental labor, their penchant for evaluating actions not by the means employed but by the results obtained, and their unshakable belief in the democratic mission of America.[6]

In his biography of Roosevelt, Henry F. Pringle caricatures him as a perpetual adolescent. With gentle irony he portrays him as entering the international arena in defense of American interests like a little boy who, his will crossed and pride aroused, reacts by resorting to fisticuffs.[7] Also critical is William A. Williams, who condemns Roosevelt as a racist nationalist, while a revisionist follower, Walter LaFeber, approves Arthur F. Beringause's characterization of Brooks Adams, Henry Cabot Lodge, and Roosevelt as the "three musketeers in a world of perpetual war."[8] However, such consensus historians as William H. Harbaugh, George E. Mowry, John M. Blum, and Julius W. Pratt—and such assimilators of the old progressive and consensus diplomatic history as Robert H. Ferrell, Richard W. Leopold, Alexander DeConde, Wayne S. Cole, and Thomas G. Paterson, J. Garry Clifford, and Kenneth J. Hagan—underscore his passion for law and order and his belief in individual self-responsibility. They view him, in the absence of accepted international law, as an aggressive nationalist seeking to balance America's strategic needs against its responsibilities, desiring to mediate between nations and so avoid war, and also as willing to eschew isolationism and enter into international conferences in order to prevent a war that might involve the United States. G. Wallace Chessman agrees with David H. Burton that Roosevelt was "a policeman in Central America and a peacemaker among the great nations." The first president to see that the future of the United States lay in the whole world, not in merely a part of it, he sought to equip it as "a strong man armed" for international maturity. Especially to Blum, who concentrates on the use and motivations of power, he was a conservative.[9]

Based on the tests of scholarship, objectivity, and literary excellence, the best study of the Roosevelt era is that by Mowry; the best on his foreign policies, that by Beale; the best single-volume biography, that by Harbaugh; the best study of his imperialist thought, that by Burton. Beale shows him as a nationalist who placed the honor and interests of the United States above those of any other nation and was convinced that his country was incapable of acting unjustly or wrongly. Since whatever position America took was right, opponents of its policies were morally derelict. On this point Beale believes Roosevelt to be in error. Beale sees Roosevelt's expansionist tendencies as based upon three needs: to control those strategic locations from which an isthmian canal could be attacked, to drive every European power "off this continent," and to insure that weaker nations did not thwart the designs of a great power with a mission of its superior peoples. Both Beale and Harbaugh agree, however, that, given the absence of serious challenge by other powers and the lack of need to defend the Panama Canal and American economic interests, Roosevelt occasionally overreacted.

Both Beale and Harbaugh assert that Roosevelt had a firm grasp of the relationship between national policy and power and that he knew that the loftiest ideals in international relations were worthless unless backed by force.[10] Quite close in agreement is the realist Dana G. Munro, a former foreign service officer in the Caribbean area. Rather than economic considerations, Munro stresses Roosevelt's strategic, humanitarian, and moralistic objectives for intervention.[11] Revisionists such as Lloyd C. Gardner, however, hold that Roosevelt, knowing that the United States could not dominate world trade without getting into a fight with other world powers, therefore built up his army and navy. John W. Robbins sees anti-imperialists as actually being imperialists because they favored overseas commercial expansion, and Christopher Lasch calls them racists, thereby overlooking their more generous impulses.[12] Be that as it may, Roosevelt was the first president to have an army efficiently organized along a general staff system and sufficient naval power to be able to stop thinking about the navy only in terms of defense.

As many writers on American naval history have shown, Roosevelt feared not the British but the growing German navy.[13] He increased the United States Navy until it grew from seventh to second in the world. Moreover, acting as his own secretary of the navy, he used the navy not only to protect American persons and interests abroad, but as a deterrent to war, the latter well illustrated by his concentrating the fleet in the Caribbean during the Venezuela crisis of the winter of 1902 and by his sending the Great White Fleet around the world in 1907-1909.[14]

Because Congress was, in Roosevelt's opinion, "not well-fitted for the shaping of foreign policy," he conceived and conducted a personal foreign policy. As particularly Beale, Paolo E. Coletta, Harbaugh, Mowry, and Peter A. Poole point out, where not constrained by Congress or the Constitution, Roosevelt used his executive powers to their limits—if not beyond—as illustrated by his threat to use troops during his controversy with Great Britain over the Alaska boundary and his admitted "taking" of Panama.[15] His advisers and executors in foreign policy matters—either those in formal posts or in his famous Tennis Cabinet—cannot be totally overlooked.[16] However, it is widely held that he assumed personal responsibility for the conduct of diplomacy and the derivation of foreign policy.[17]

At various times, the United States had used military power (as it was allowed to do by a treaty with Colombia of 1846) to keep the Isthmus of Panama open for transit of American citizens and property, but it had done nothing about building an isthmian canal when Roosevelt took office. With Roosevelt, thought meant action. He faced two major problems—to get Britain to modify the Clayton-Bulwer Treaty of 1850 in America's favor, and to obtain control over a route. Britain made the required concessions in the second Hay-Pauncefote Treaty of November 1901 in order to gain American friendship and the military and commercial advantages in any but an Anglo-American war.[18] Roosevelt then condoned a revolution in Panama and, as he confessed in 1911, "took the Canal Zone." The cost was the ill will of much of Latin America, the severing of friendship with Colombia, and his pillorying by liberals and partisan Democrats, albeit he was praised by those regardless of party who were happy with his getting results.[19] Robert A. Friedlander echoes Joseph B. Bishop and Willis Fletcher Johnson in concluding that Roosevelt's actions "were morally straightforward and legally justified."[20] Doris A. Graber, however, holds that an alternative route through Nicaragua was available to him and that "with the use of ordinary patience and diplomatic skill"—and a considerably larger payment, it should be added—he could have reached a satisfactory agreement with Colombia.[21] Harbaugh and Frederick W. Marks III agree that the opportunity for Panamanians to fill their aspirations for independence and the activities of American and French conspirators permitted Roosevelt "to acquiesce silently, yet in reasonably good conscience, to what he could not advocate publicly." Harbaugh therefore concludes that he obtained a "noble end by less noble means."[22] To Samuel Flagg Bemis "this intervention of 1903 is the only really black mark in the Latin American policy of the United States, and a great big black mark, too."[23] To Wilfrid H. Callcott, Roosevelt's "disclaimers of responsibility . . . sound extremely thin even though his skirts may have been technically clean."[24] To Sheldon Liss, Roosevelt has "never been completely absolved from complicity."[25] In his foreword to a work by Paul B. Ryan that stresses the maritime and strategic importance of the canal, Thomas A. Bailey notes the increasing stridency over seven decades of the Panamanian grievance that the United States inflicted a grave wrong on them at birth and then kept them perpetually humiliated. He agrees with Ryan that Panamanians had forgotten what Burton believes Roosevelt had in mind, "the benevolent role of Uncle Sam in bringing sovereignty, status, stability, sanitation, protection, and prosperity to the Panamanians."[26] In contrast, David McCullough finds that Roosevelt's haste "to make the dirt fly" was "tragically mistaken and inexcusable." Because many others conspired with him, however, he was not solely responsible for the "taking" of Panama.[27] LaFeber agrees with Friedlander, Bailey, Ryan, and McCullough only in part. After admitting that the drive for Panamanian independence grew partly out of chauvinistic nationalism, he concludes that while Panamanians have not been anti-North American by nature, they have increasingly opposed United States control of the Canal Zone and the blatant anti-Panamanian discrimination carried on there. Finally, "Panama needs the Zone for financial reasons." LaFeber's objectivity and readability make his work a standard reference.[28]

Despite Roosevelt's contention with Great Britain over various issues, he shared a sense of pride in the superiority he believed Anglo-Saxons had over other peoples. As Beale, particularly, points out, rather than being a racist, one who believed that people were "backward" because of their color, he criticized both those whites and nonwhites who were unable to rule themselves effectively.[29] These ideas, his belief that the expansion of English-speaking people meant attainment of world peace and the spread of civilization, and perhaps the threat of Germany's growing industrial and military power, led to a decided turn for the better in his relations with Great Britain.[30]

A number of older consensus historians who wrote about Roosevelt's Far Eastern policies agree with Tyler Dennett's original conclusion that the Open Door policy was "as old as our relations with China." Controversy about it concerned means, not ends. Roosevelt's alternatives were to fight with other nations or to cooperate with them, and Roosevelt helped preserve the balance of power in Asia as well as in Europe.[31] These conclusions are upheld by Beale, Louis J. Halle, Harbaugh, Mowry, and Neu.[32] Others disagree with these writers. A. Whitney Griswold asserts that Britain wanted a "deposit of American political support in Eastern Asia on which [it] could draw, whenever necessary, to protect her interests there," and that with the Open Door, Hay "kept pace with the expansionist forces . . . that had propelled the United States into the conquest and annexation of the Philippines."[33] Dennett, who changed his mind, in 1933 said that Hay adopted the Open Door policy at the urging of others and that "it represented part of the price paid by the United States to secure the practical withdrawal of England from the Caribbean."[34] Such revisionists as Williams, LaFeber, Thomas J. McCormick, and Edward F. Friedman and Mark Selden, however, hold that the Open Door policy is the key to a general United States foreign policy in the twentieth century. After saying that "the Roosevelt group defended their economic interest in terms of preventing the stagnation of the American economic system, and their program to accomplish that objective was vigorous overseas economic expansion," and that with the decline of public interest in traditional colonies the attractiveness of the Open Door policy increased, Williams reaches the dubious conclusion that the policy "ended the debate between imperialists and anti-imperialists" and "industrialized the Monroe Doctrine." More realistically, he adds that when the Open Door got nowhere, "Roosevelt was forced to maneuver in Asia according to the more traditional techniques of balance-of-power politics."[35]

As the economic historian Benjamin H. Williams evaluates it, the Open Door policy sought to save the weak Chinese nation from the onslaughts of European powers, and hence appeared to be an act of intervention arising from generosity. Yet behind it were exporters and manufacturers avid for trade with four hundred million Chinese.[36] According to Paul Varg, Hay thought of it as a main point for negotiating a temporary modus vivendi with China, an interpretation also favored by Bemis, Akira Iriye, and Charles S. Campbell.[37] Although calling it a policy born of ignorance and impractical idealism, Kennan agrees with revisionists on its attractiveness to economic interests. By emphasizing economic factors, however, revisionists overlook such other motivating forces behind the Open Door as missionary zeal, the mission to spread civilization to "backward peoples," nationalistic pride, domestic politics, and how developments in the Far East would affect the security of the Philippines. Marilyn Blatt Young in particular disagrees with revisionists by showing the need to distinguish between rhetoric that spoke of the "illimitable" markets of China and of America's need for them at a time when less than three percent of American overseas trade was with China. Moreover, too close involvement with Great Britain and Japan in opposing Russia's drive into Manchuria posed a danger of involvement in a possible war.[38]

Divergent views are found on Roosevelt's attitude toward the Chinese boycott of American goods of 1905-1906. Unsympathetic to Roosevelt's policy, Beale says that Roosevelt could not deal with the Chinese nationalist movement because he failed to recognize it as such and was contemptuous of China's weakness.[39] In any event, by admitting that the Open Door policy could not be upheld militarily, on sound geopolitical considerations Roosevelt conceded Japan's economic supremacy in Korea and in Manchuria.

Roosevelt originally backed Japan in its war with Russia, which had designs on Korea and Manchuria. Japan seemed to be maintaining the Open Door, and hence was playing our game in the Far East. Japan won many battles, but the war proved so costly that it hinted that Roosevelt offer to mediate. Roosevelt did so with the objective of keeping a balance of power in the Far East, and to this end he pledged the United States to a silent partnership in the Anglo-Japanese Alliance—a pledge Dennett revealed in 1925.[40] When Japan obtained less in the Treaty of Portsmouth than it demanded and Russia had to give up more than it wished, Roosevelt earned criticism from both sides, especially from Japan, where violent riots protested the terms. Ironically, the former Rough Rider was awarded the Nobel Peace Prize shortly before Russia and Japan agreed to divide Manchuria and Japan assumed control of Korea and Russia of Inner Mongolia. Eugene P. Trani cites Russian and Japanese as well as American sources in describing how Roosevelt balanced Japanese and Russian peace terms in probably the most complex twentieth-century diplomatic negotiations conducted prior to those at Panmunjon.[41] Also solidly based on multiarchival sources, but covering much more than the Portsmouth conference, are studies by Raymond Esthus and by Neu. Esthus, who analyzes Japanese policy, concludes that "Japan and the United States came through this agonizing period without serious mishap" largely because of "the friendliness and frankness which characterized the relations between the two governments." Rather than showing his customary impulsiveness and bumptious approach to foreign relations, in the case of Japan Roosevelt displayed caution and finesse, and the Japanese, despite their being hurt by the stigma of racial inferiority, continued to look upon the United States as their historic friend.[42] Neu, who concentrates on the attitudes of the British and Canadians as well as of the Japanese, and Griswold and William L. Neumann as well, see Roosevelt's diplomacy during his last three years as president as shrewd and responsible.[43] In contrast, Williams holds that Roosevelt took sides with Japan against Russia in 1904 "in an attempt to exhaust both nations and thereby open the way for American supremacy." Fumbling in an effort to correct his error by controlling the peace settlement, he "gave the Japanese the initiative and on top of that antagonized them."[44]

With the federal government hesitant to stem the flow of Japanese immigration, in October 1906 the San Francisco Board of Education segregated oriental school children. Here was an excellent example of the twilight zone in which federal power could not be used against a local jurisdiction. All writers on the subject applaud not only Roosevelt's method but his equanimity during the crisis. He not only desired the continued friendship of Japan; he carefully balanced conflicting foreign and domestic forces to achieve this goal. In conference with the members of the board in Washington, he promised to end the inflow of Japanese workers, but not of students and upper-class Japanese, if the board would desegregate. The series of notes he exchanged with Japan, the Gentlemen's Agreement of 1907-1909, provided that Japan would not issue passports to unskilled laborers seeking to reach the United States and that the segregation order would be dropped. Thus tension was eased—temporarily.[45]

Roosevelt sent the Great White Fleet around the world in part to insure that the Japanese did not evaluate his friendliness toward them as fear of them and to give notice that neither Japan nor any other rivals could challenge America's role in the political and economic affairs of the Far East. Outten J. Clinard overstresses Japan's influence on the size, power, and deployment of Roosevelt's navy, while Robert A. Hart oversimplifies by concluding that Roosevelt took a dangerous gamble in ordering the voyage, even if he meant it to be merely a public-relations gimmick.[46] Much more thoroughly researched and better balanced are studies by William R. Braisted and by Samuel Carter.[47] Nevertheless, with the navy opting for Subic Bay and the army for Manila Bay, nothing was done from Roosevelt's day to World War II to strengthen the defenses of the Philippines, and congressional parsimony left Guam undefended. This left only Pearl Harbor as the Gibraltar of the Pacific. The impossibility of defending American interests in two oceans with a one-ocean navy is discussed by Braisted, Seward Livermore, and W. E. Snowbarger.[48]

When Roosevelt assumed office, Germany was growing rapidly as an industrial and naval power and seeking an overseas empire. It was therefore perceived as a menace to American security if not to world peace by Roosevelt and by most American military and naval officers. The one major exception was Rear Admiral French Ensor Chadwick, who thought the Entente Powers were encircling it and denying it the living room it needed for its growing population and industry.[49]

Roosevelt's part in the first Moroccan crisis is still subject to dispute. In 1904 when a presumably American citizen named Ion Perdicaris was seized by a native chief, Raisuli, Roosevelt decided to put "a little ginger" into the proceedings of the Republican national convention by ordering American naval vessels to Tangier and telegraphing that he must have "Perdicaris alive or Raisuli dead." The unpublished part of the telegram, however, directed the American consul at Tangier not to use force unless authorized to do so.[50] More important, when denied the Open Door in Morocco by Britain, France, and Spain, Emperor William II visited Tangier, in 1905, and made a saber-rattling speech that produced the most serious diplomatic crisis in Europe since the late 1870s. Fearing war, he asked Roosevelt to call an international conference. Although American economic interests in Morocco were small, Roosevelt wished to keep the Open Door open and particularly to avoid a war. He therefore agreed and the conference took place, at Algeciras, Spain, early in 1906. There Henry White led the European delegates into agreement, and Germany, not yet ready to fight, backed down. Thus the Open Door remained open and the danger of a war that might have involved the United States evaporated.

The literature on the Moroccan problem overwhelmingly upholds Roosevelt, Britain, and France rather than Germany. In addition to the works by Kenneth Bourne, Ebert Malcolm Carroll, Oron Hale, W. O. Henderson, George Monger, and Bernadotte Schmitt, support for Roosevelt is found in Eugene N. Anderson, Ima C. Barlow, Ross N. Dunn, Griswold, Harbaugh, Holger H. Herwig, A. J. P. Taylor, and Samuel R. Williamson. The only work that upholds Germany is, paradoxically, by a Frenchman, Edmund D. Morell.[51]

In great contrast to his mediation at Portsmouth and Algeciras, Roosevelt had no more use than Mahan did for arbitration as a method of settling international disputes. He held that national interests must never be compromised or arbitrated. But he was aware that there was a respectable, even fashionable and popular, peace movement in the United States and respected men such as Elihu Root who were engaged in it. Only because public opinion favored them, however, did he support various arbitration treaties negotiated by Hay in 1905; he paid little attention to the Second Hague Peace Conference, which he was instrumental in calling; and he agreed to Root's arbitration treaties of 1911 only because the Senate must approve an agreement before an issue could be referred to arbitration. For his stand he was applauded by nationalists and criticized by pacifists and internationalists.

In 1911 after his relations with Roosevelt soured, Taft wrote that "he believes in war and wishes to be a Napoleon and die on the battlefield." History proved Taft wrong. Roosevelt easily could have had a war with Germany or Japan. Although he put righteousness before peace, Beale, Harbaugh, Mowry, Neu, and Nevins, among others, point out that he did more to prevent than to make war.

A much simpler man than the polydimensional Roosevelt, and much more pacifically inclined, William Howard Taft preferred to use arbitration and economic power rather than sword rattling to insure peace.[52]

One old biography contains nothing on Taft's foreign policies.[53] Another devotes but eight pages to them.[54] In his first volume on Taft, Henry F. Pringle reveals the training in diplomacy McKinley and then Roosevelt gave Taft; in the second, he devotes one chapter to "Dollar Diplomacy" and one to "Mexico and Japan." In his study of Taft's presidency, Coletta devotes two out of thirteen chapters to foreign affairs, whereas Horace Samuel and Marion Galbraith Merrill deal wholly with domestic issues. Although incomplete because it deals only with Latin America and the Far East, Walter and Marie Scholes provide the fullest published study of Taft's foreign policies to date.[55]

Differences between the dynamic and personal statesmanship of Roosevelt and Taft's impersonal and inept procedures and lack of subtlety in exercising that intangible known as "power" are noted in studies dealing with the administrations of the two men. Wilfred H. Callcott, Coletta, Harbaugh, and Mowry agree with the Scholeses on Taft's pacifism, materialism, laziness, and political bungling. They also support Pringle's and Pratt's negative assessment of his foreign policies.

Taft relied largely upon a lesser image of himself, his legalistic secretary of state, Philander C. Knox, to direct Caribbean policy, and upon William Phillips and then Willard Straight to handle Far Eastern policy. A lawyer who was happy to follow the demands of big business, Knox, like Taft, suffered bad relations with the press, Congress, and especially with Latin American representatives, the last of whom saw him lacking in fellowship by substituting litigation for diplomacy and considering them as adversaries.[56]

Rather than *realpolitik*, the "blundering Taft and Knox"—the adjective is Bemis's—emphasized commercial connections, legal techniques, and arbitration to solve international controversies.[57] All writers on Taft's foreign policies note his supreme objective of supplanting territorial imperialism with "nonimperialistic imperialism," that is, gold would replace guns as a way of obtaining needed outlets for surplus capital and goods, thus avoiding formal colonialism and political control. Moreover, funds would be lent to existing governments with which to crush rebellions, thus providing both profits and peace. In this matter he had the support of Republican progressives, or insurgents, throughout his administration. Iriye adds the interesting point that Roosevelt's foreign policy was based on a balance of power through spheres of interest, and Taft's on universalistic and economic tenets. As the Scholeses and Jerry Israel point out, Roosevelt thought of foreign policy largely in the context of Europe; Taft thought of it in the context of undeveloped countries and their need of trade. Although Griswold says that "only in emphasis is [dollar diplomacy] distinguishable from the foreign policy of every other nation on earth and every other American administration," Callcott calls dollar diplomacy "merely an irritating barnacle that attached itself to the Monroe Doctrine." Robert Hart holds that Taft presented "historians of economic determinism with their most authentic specimen."[58]

The major personalities involved in Taft's diplomatic ventures are described by the Scholeses, Katherine Crane, Gilbert Stuart, Archibald Willingham Butt, Oscar S. Straus, and Herbert Croly.[59] A popularly written book by William Manners focuses on personal and political differences between Roosevelt and Taft.[60] Unfortunately, biographies are lacking for Knox and such other important Taft men as his other cabinet members, second-level leaders in the Department of State, Straight excepted, and foreign service and consular corps.

Taft did not interfere with the execution of foreign policy unless a crisis demanded his intervention. On the other hand, he did provide subsidies for a merchant marine, obtain freer access for United States firms to engage in overseas banking, and so improved federal management procedures as to increase American investments abroad. The last resulted in the establishment of politico-geographic State Department "desks" designed to make every diplomat a salesman and to make the United States a major commercial and financial power.[61]

Tyler Dennett was among the first to sense Taft's shift from Roosevelt's balance-of-power strategy in the Far East to a "naive and simple" unilateral course. Pringle calls the new policy "a forced and unhappy marriage between commercialism and idealism," whereas Dulles, Griswold, and Charles Vevier stress the economic motive. The few revisionists who deal with Taft evaluate dollar diplomacy as an insidious device to obtain imperialistic objectives. The latest interpretation, that by Iriye, is that it was "the beginning of a moralistic diplomacy in East Asia."[62]

Unlike Roosevelt, Taft believed in obtaining world peace through treaties providing for the unlimited adjudication of any question, not excepting "vital interests" and "national honor," that could be settled by negotiation. If the Anglo-Saxon countries took the lead in making peace possible, he thought, other nations would follow and wars could be avoided. He did not reckon with his former friend nor with a Senate determined to put its prerogatives above peaceful arbitration.[63]

How Taft settled various disputes with Great Britain—over pelagic sealing, the Newfoundland fisheries, and the United States-Canadian boundary—by arbitration is described in several works.[64] If he then proved inconsistent in rejecting Britain's suggestion of arbitrating the Panama tolls question, he nevertheless remained neutral in the Mexican civil war that began in 1910 and passed that problem on to Wilson.[65]

Had Taft merely protected the lives and property of Americans and relied upon American investments abroad (while earning profits) to promote economic and political stability, he might have achieved his primary objective—world peace. He eschewed Roosevelt's balance-of-power technique, however, in favor of acquiring political power through financial control. Deeming Roosevelt's handling of Japan "appeasement" and his disinterest in China "moral cowardliness," for example, he opposed Japan's expansion in China with dollar diplomacy. Although he then reorganized his fleets so as to make the United States a Pacific power, in the end what Vevier calls his "shopkeeper diplomacy" looked somewhat like Roosevelt's Big Stick and drove those nations with greater vested interests in China into a close defensive alliance. His following of Roosevelt's policies with respect to oriental immigration to the United States showed that the exclusion policy would be retained.

Controversy continues over Roosevelt's diplomatic policies, which receive support from consensus and realist historians, but criticism from revisionists. There is a remarkable agreement in opposition, however, among historians who deal with Taft's foreign policies. That Taft obtained greater efficiency in the State Department by reforming its structure, that his seeking peace through the arbitration of national disputes was praiseworthy, that American overseas trade expanded greatly during his tenure, and that American dollars displaced European investments particularly in the republics of Central American cannot be gainsaid. But by trying to pump dollars into areas in which other nations already had vested interests he exacerbated his relations with the latter and, in the Far East, drove formerly antagonistic Russia and Japan to a new cooperation in despoiling China. Paradoxically, if Roosevelt was respected for the power politics he played to augment American power in international relations and to keep peace in the world, Taft was disliked because he tried to substitute dollar diplomacy and legalistic means to achieve the same ends.

Notes

1. In his extremely popular text, *A Diplomatic History of the American People*, 8th ed. (New York: Appleton-Century-Crofts, 1969), Thomas A. Bailey presents a consensus viewpoint and domestic perspective, the latter including the influence of public opinion and domestic politics on the formulation of foreign policy. Arthur A. Ekirch, who specializes in intellectual history, agrees more with consensus than with revisionist historians, for he says that "the roots of American expansion abroad were . . . economic and ideological rather than territorial" and "originally implied

acceptance of the white man's burden and supporting the concept of the imperial mission or destiny for the United States." (*Ideas, Ideals, and American Diplomacy: A History of Their Growth and Interaction* [New York: Appleton-Century-Crofts, 1966], pp. 82-84). *See also* J. Rogers Hollingsworth, "Censensus and Continuity in Recent American Historical Writing," *South Atlantic Quarterly* 61 (January 1962): 40-49.

2. Walter Lippman, *U.S. Foreign Policy* (Boston: Little, Brown & Co., 1943); George F. Kennan, *American Diplomacy, 1900-1950* (Chicago: University of Chicago Press, 1951) and *Realities of American Foreign Policy* (Princeton: Princeton University Press, 1954); Hans Morgenthau, *In Defense of the National Interest: A Critical Examination of American Foreign Policy* (New York: Alfred A. Knopf, 1951) and "The Mainsprings of American Foreign Policy: The National Interest vs. Moral Abstractions," *American Political Science Review* 44 (December 1950): 833-54; Robert E. Osgood, *Ideals and Self-Interest in America's Foreign Relations* (Chicago: University of Chicago Press, 1953). Louis J. Halle, *Dream and Reality: Aspects of American Foreign Policy* (New York: Harper & Bros., 1959) holds that our attitude toward the Latin American nations "has been quixotic and unstable, varying back and forth between an eager fraternalism . . . and an impatient or outraged paternalism." *See also* Robert Wiebe, *The Search for Order, 1877-1920* (New York: Hill & Wang, 1967).

3. Raymond A. Esthus, *Theodore Roosevelt and the International Rivalries* (Waltham: Ginn-Blaisdell, 1970); Charles E. Neu, *The Troubled Encounter: The United States and Japan* (New York: John Wiley & Sons, 1975); Howard K. Beale, *Theodore Roosevelt and the Rise of America to World Power* (Baltimore: Johns Hopkins Press, 1956); Robert A. Hart, *The Eccentric Tradition: American Diplomacy in the Far East* (New York: Charles Scribner's Sons, 1976); Robert E. Osgood, *Ideals and Self-Interest in America's Foreign Relations*; Frederick W. Marks III, *Velvet on Iron: The Diplomacy of Theodore Roosevelt* (Lincoln: University of Nebraska Press, 1979).

4. Various schools of historians are discussed by Francis L. Loewenheim, "A Legacy of Hope and a Legacy of Doubt: Reflections on the Role of History and Historians in American Foreign Policy Since the Eighteenth Century," in Loewenheim, ed., *The Historian and the Diplomat: The Role of History and Historians in American Foreign Policy* (New York: Harper & Row, 1971).

Characterizations of the consensus, realist, and revisionist schools of historians are found in Charles E. Neu, "The Changing Interpretive Structure of American Foreign Policy," in John Braeman, Robert H. Bremner, and David Brody, eds., *Twentieth Century American Foreign Policy* (Columbus: Ohio State University Press, 1971); Jerald A. Combs, *Nationalist, Realist, and Radical: Three Views of American Diplomacy* (New York: Harper & Row, 1972); Edward N. Saveth, "A Decade of American Historiography," and Daniel M. Smith, "Rise to World Power, 1865-1918," in William H. Cartright and Richard L. Watson, eds., *The Reinterpretation of American History and Culture* (Washington, D.C.: National Council for the Social Studies, 1973), pp. 17-36 and 443-64. Bernard Sternsher, *Consensus, Conflict, and American Historians* (Bloomington: Indiana University Press, 1975) follows Gene Wise, *American Historical Explanations: A Strategy for Grounded Inquiry* (Homewood, Ill.: Dorsey Press, 1973) who labels the schools progressive, counter-progressive, and new left (neo-progressive). Revisionists admit their obligation to old left progressives including Frederick Jackson Turner, Arthur Schlesinger, Sr., Vernon L. Parrington, and Charles A. Beard. They should add Marx, Lenin, and J. A. Hobson. Exponents of economic determinism, old left progressives also sought out domestic political and intellectual forces that helped shape a foreign policy and stressed that the corporate structure called for continuous expansion abroad. To them, American foreign policy was self-interested to the point of rapaciousness and in addition was antirevolutionary and antiprogressive. Like the old left progressives, modern revisionists demand that history be made relevant to present needs, as in promoting liberal democratic reforms and, by seeking policies of accommodation with potential enemies, avoid war. William Appleman Williams, *The Roots of the Modern American Empire* (New York: Random House, 1969) and *The Tragedy of American Diplomacy* (Cleveland: World Publishing Co., 1959), and Richard Hofstadter, *The Progressive Historians: Turner, Beard, Parrington* (New York: Alfred A. Knopf, 1968) discuss what they perceive to be the shortcomings of consensus historians, while Robert W. Tucker, *The Radical Left and American Foreign Policy* (Baltimore: Johns Hopkins Press, 1971), is critical of the new left.

While revisionists serve a purpose in showing the past as being more pluralistic and fragmented than do consensus historians, they have been inconsistent in applying their conclusions to the entire range of American diplomatic history. As historians with a cause, they often mar their work by neglecting the role of diplomacy, offering monolithic economic interpretations and sweeping moral judgments, and erecting logically coherent arguments upon questionable premises.

5. Roosevelt used the word "racist" in many ways, sometimes synonymously with "nationality," sometimes to denote peoples whose civilizations and cultures he considered less fully developed than those of Anglo-Saxons. *See* John Higham, *Strangers in the Land; Patterns of American Nativism, 1860-1925* (New Brunswick, N.J.: Rutgers University Press, 1955), and Oscar Handlin, *Race and Nationality in American Life* (Boston: Little, Brown & Co., 1950).

6. William E. Leuchtenberg, "Progressivism and Imperialism: The Progressive Movement and American Foreign Policy, 1898-1916," *Mississippi Valley Historical Review* 39 (December 1952): 483-504; David H. Burton, *Theodore Roosevelt* (New York: Twayne Publishers, 1972). That many progressives in the Middle West and South opposed imperialism is made clear in Arthur S. Link, *Woodrow Wilson and the Progressive Era, 1910-1917* (New York: Harper & Bros., 1954); Russel B. Nye, *Midwestern Progressive Politics* (East Lansing: Michigan State University Press, 1951); Barton J. Bernstein and Frank A. Lieb, "Progressive Republican Senators and American Imperialism, 1898-1916," *Mid-America* 50 (July 1968): 163-205; Fred H. Harrington, "The Imperialistic Movement in the United States," *Mississippi Valley Historical Review* 22 (September 1935): 211-20; Richard T. Welch, Jr., "Motives and Policy Objectives of Anti-Imperialists, 1898," *Mid-America* 51 (April 1969): 119-29 and *Response to Imperialism: The United States and the Philippine-American War, 1899-1902* (Chapel Hill: University of North Carolina Press, 1979); Paolo E. Coletta, "Bryan, McKinley, and the Treaty of Paris," *Pacific Historical Review* 26 (1957): 131-46 and "Bryan, Anti-Imperialism, and Missionary Diplomacy," *Nebraska History* 44 (September 1963): 167-87; Robert Seager II, "The Progressives and American Foreign Policy, 1898-1917: An Analysis of the At-

titudes of the Leaders of the Progressive Movement toward External Affairs" (Ph.D. diss., Ohio State University, 1956). I. E. Cadenhead, Jr., *Theodore Roosevelt: The Paradox of Progressivism* (Woodbury, N.J.: Barron's Educational Series, 1974), p. 91, says that rather than seeking additional territory, Roosevelt wanted only to insure that the new American empire could be defended. Roosevelt's treating of Filipinos as wards is the theme of Oscar M. Alfonso, *Theodore Roosevelt and the Philippines, 1897-1909* (Quezon City: University of the Philippines, 1970); the burden of David Southern is clear from his title, *The Malignant Heritage; Yankee Progressives and the Negro, 1901-1914* (Chicago: Loyola University Press, 1968).

7. Henry Pringle, *Theodore Roosevelt: A Biography* (New York: Harcourt, Brace & Co., 1931).

8. Walter LaFeber, *The New Empire: An Interpretation of American Expansion, 1860-1898* (Ithaca: Cornell University Press, 1963); Arthur F. Beringause, *Brooks Adams: A Biography* (New York: Alfred A. Knopf, 1955).

9. William Harbaugh, *Power and Responsibility: The Life and Times of Theodore Roosevelt* (New York: Farrar, Straus and Cudahy, 1961); George E. Mowry, *The Era of Theodore Roosevelt, 1900-1912* (New York: Harper & Row, 1958); John M. Blum, *The Republican Roosevelt* (Cambridge, Mass.: Harvard University Press, 1954); Robert Ferrell, *American Diplomacy: A History* (New York: W. W. Norton & Co., 1975); Alexander DeConde, *A History of American Foreign Policy* (New York: Charles Scribner's Sons, 1971); Richard W. Leopold, *The Growth of American Foreign Policy: A History* (New York: Alfred A. Knopf, 1962); Wayne S. Cole, *An Interpretive History of American Foreign Relations* (Homewood, Ill.: Dorsey Press, 1968); Thomas G. Paterson, J. Garry Clifford, and Kenneth J. Hagan, *American Foreign Policy: A History* (Lexington, Mass.: D. C. Heath & Co., 1977); Julius W. Pratt, *A History of United States Foreign Policy* (Englewood Cliffs, N.J.: Prentice-Hall, 1965); David H. Burton, *Theodore Roosevelt: Confident Imperialist* (Philadelphia: University of Pennsylvania Press, 1968); G. Wallace Chessman, *Theodore Roosevelt and the Politics of Power* (Boston: Little, Brown & Co., 1969). The quotation is from Burton, *Theodore Roosevelt*, p. 106.

10. Beale, *Roosevelt and the Rise of America to World Power*; Harbaugh, *Roosevelt*, p. 270. Ample support for the moral stance assumed by Roosevelt is found in Elting E. Morison et al., eds., *The Letters of Theodore Roosevelt*, 8 vols. (Cambridge, Mass.: Harvard University Press, 1951-1954); in Henry Cabot Lodge, ed., *Selections from the Correspondence of Theodore Roosevelt and Henry Cabot Lodge, 1884-1918*, 2 vols. (New York: Charles Scribner's Sons, 1925); and in Dewey Grantham, Jr., "Theodore Roosevelt in American Historical Writing, 1945-1960," *Mid-America* 43 (January 1961): 3-35. A contrary view is expressed by Frederick W. Marks III, "Morality in the Diplomacy of Theodore Roosevelt," *Diplomatic History* 2 (Winter 1978): 44n3, who asserts that Blum and Harbaugh wrote about Roosevelt as though he was "operating in a moral vacuum" and that the only recent account that "is sensitive to the prominence of a moral strain in Roosevelt's approach to foreign policy" is Burton's *Roosevelt*.

11. Dana G. Munro, *Intervention and Dollar Diplomacy in the Caribbean, 1900-1921* (Princeton: Princeton University Press, 1965).

12. Lloyd C. Gardner, "American Foreign Policy, 1900-1921," in Barton J. Bernstein, ed., *Towards a New Past* (New York: Pantheon, 1968); John W. Robbins, "The Anti-Imperialists and Twentieth Century American Foreign Policy," *Studies on the Left* 3 (Fall 1962): 9-24; Christopher Lasch, "The Anti-Imperialists, the Philippines, and the Inequality of Man," *Journal of Southern History* 24 (August 1958): 319-31. More judicious accounts of imperialists and anti-imperialists are found in David Healy, *U.S. Expansionism: The Imperialist Urge in the 1890s* (Madison: University of Wisconsin Press, 1970); Ernest R. May, *Imperial Democracy, The Emergence of America as a Great Power* (New York: Harper & Row, 1973); Robert Beisner, *Twelve Against Empire: The Anti-Imperialists 1898-1900* (New York: McGraw-Hill, 1968) and *From the Old Diplomacy to the New, 1865-1900* (New York: Thomas Y. Crowell Co., 1975); Paolo E. Coletta, *William Jennings Bryan: Political Evangelist, 1860-1908* (Lincoln, Neb.: University of Nebraska Press, 1964); Samuel Morison, Frederick Merk, and Frank Freidel, *Dissent in Three Wars* (Cambridge, Mass.: Harvard University Press, 1970); and E. Berkeley Tompkins, *Anti-Imperialism in the United States: The Great Debate, 1890-1920* (Philadelphia: University of Pennsylvania Press, 1970). Healy, particularly, challenges the rhetoric used by devotees of the market-expansion historians, while Paul S. Holbo, "Economics, Emotion, and Expansion: An Emerging Foreign Policy," in H. Wayne Morgan, ed., *The Gilded Age*, rev. ed. (Syracuse: Syracuse University Press, 1970), counters the conclusions of such revisionists as LaFeber and Williams.

13. A greater understanding of how Roosevelt used his navy to support his foreign policies and dedicated its use to assuring world peace can be obtained from Richard D. Challener, *Admirals, Generals, and American Foreign Policy* (Princeton: Princeton University Press, 1973); Paolo E. Coletta, *The American Naval Heritage in Brief* (Washington: University Press of America, 1978); Gordon C. O'Gara, *Theodore Roosevelt and the Rise of the Modern Navy* (Princeton: Princeton University Press, 1943); Robert Seager II, *Alfred Thayer Mahan: The Man and His Letters* (Annapolis, Md.: Naval Institute Press, 1977); and Harold and Margaret Sprout, *The Rise of American Naval Power, 1776-1918* (Princeton: Princeton University Press, 1939). *See also* the historiographical article on American naval history by James E. Merrill, "Successors of Mahan: A Survey of Writings on American Naval History, 1914-1940," *Mississippi Valley Historical Review* 50 (June 1963): 79-99.

14. For Roosevelt's secretaries of the navy *see* Paolo E. Coletta, "John D. Long," and Paul T. Heffron, "William H. Moody," "Paul Morton," "Charles J. Bonaparte," "Victor R. Metcalf," and "Truman H. Newberry" in Coletta, Robert G. Albion, and K. Jack Bauer, eds., *The American Secretaries of the Navy*, 2 vols. (Annapolis, Md.: Naval Institute Press, 1980).

15. Paolo E. Coletta, *The Presidency of William Howard Taft* (Lawrence: University Press of Kansas, 1973), pp. 11-13; Harbaugh, *Roosevelt*, pp. 182-83; Mowry, *Era of Theodore Roosevelt*, pp. 230, 232-36; Peter A. Poole, *America in World Politics: Foreign Policy and Policy-Makers Since 1898* (New York: Frederick A. Praeger, 1975), p. 22.

16. *See* Nelson M. Blake, "Ambassadors at the Court of Theodore Roosevelt," *Mississippi Valley Historical Review* 42 (September 1955): 179-206.

17. In addition to the works by Pringle and Harbaugh *see*, particularly, Tyler

Dennett, *John Hay: From Poetry to Politics* (New York: Dodd, Mead & Co., 1933); John A. Garraty, *Henry Cabot Lodge: A Biography* (New York: Alfred A. Knopf, 1953); Philip Jessup, *Elihu Root*, 2 vols. (New York: Dodd, Mead & Co., 1938); Paul A. Varg, *Open Door Diplomat: The Life of W. W. Rockhill* (Urbana: University of Illinois Press, 1951); Allan Nevins, *Henry White: Thirty Years of American Diplomacy* (New York: Harper & Bros., 1930); Stephen Lucius Gwynn, ed., *The Letters and Friendships of Sir Cecil Spring Rice: A Record*, 2 vols. (Boston: Houghton Mifflin Co., 1929); and Wayne August Wiegand, "Patrician in the Progressive Era: A Biography of George von Lengerke Meyer" (Ph.D. diss., Southern Illinois University, 1974).

18. This conclusion follows Alexander E. Campbell, *Great Britain and the United States, 1895-1903* (London: Longmans, Green & Co., 1960) and *America Comes of Age: The Era of Theodore Roosevelt* (New York: American Heritage Press, 1971); Charles S. Campbell, *Anglo-American Understanding, 1898-1903* (Baltimore: Johns Hopkins Press, 1957) and "Anglo-American Relations, 1897-1901," in Paolo E. Coletta, ed., *Threshold to American Internationalism: Essays on the Foreign Policies of William McKinley* (New York: Exposition University Press, 1970); Bradford Perkins, *The Great Rapprochement: England and the United States, 1895-1914* (New York: Atheneum, 1968); J. A. S. Grenville, "Great Britain and the Isthmian Canal, 1898-1901," *American Historical Review* 61 (October 1955): 48-69. The theme that Hay was a "mindless Anglophile" is repeated in a psychohistorical manner in Howard I. Kushner and Anne Hummel Sherill, *John Milton Hay: The Union of Poetry and Politics* (New York: Twayne Publishers, 1977). *See also* Foster Rhea Dulles, "John Hay (1898-1905)," in Norman A. Graebner, ed., *An Uncertain Tradition: American Secretaries of State in the Twentieth Century* (New York: McGraw-Hill, 1961).

19. Mostly critical are Paolo E. Coletta, *William Jennings Bryan: Progressive Politician and Moral Statesman, 1909-1915* (Lincoln, Neb.: University of Nebraska Press, 1969); Miles P. DuVal, *And the Mountains Will Move* (Stanford: Stanford University Press, 1947); Lawrence O. Ealy, *Yanqui Politics and the Isthmian Canal* (University Park: Pennsylvania State University Press, 1971); John P. Lambert, *Arthur Pue Gorman* (Baton Rouge: Louisiana State University Press, 1953); Lester D. Langley, *Struggle for the American Mediterranean: The United States-European Rivalry in the Gulf-Caribbean, 1776-1904* (Athens, Ga.: University of Georgia Press, 1976); Gerstle Mack, *The Land Divided* (New York: Alfred A. Knopf, 1940); and Dwight C. Miner, *The Fight for the Panama Canal Route: The Story of the Spooner Act and the Hay-Herran Treaty* (New York: Columbia University Press, 1940). The last includes a clear analysis of the background of the episode in Colombian politics.

20. Robert A. Freidlander, "A Reassessment of Roosevelt's Role in the Panamanian Revolution of 1903," *Western Political Quarterly* 14 (June 1961): 535-43; Joseph B. Bishop, *Theodore Roosevelt and His Time Shown in His Own Letters*, 2 vols. (New York: Charles Scribner's Sons, 1920); William Fletcher Johnson, *Four Centuries of the Panama Canal* (New York: Henry Holt and Co., 1906).

21. Doris A. Graber, *Crisis Diplomacy: A History of U.S. Intervention Policies and Practices* (Washington: Public Affairs Press, 1959).

22. Harbaugh, *Roosevelt*, p. 207; Marks, "Morality as a Drive Wheel in the Diplomacy of Theodore Roosevelt."

23. Samuel Flagg Bemis, *The Latin American Policy of the United States: An Historical Interpretation* (New York: Harcourt, Brace & Co., 1943), p. 151.

24. Wilfrid H. Callcott, *The Caribbean Policy of the United States, 1890-1920* (Baltimore: Johns Hopkins Press, 1942), p. 157.

25. Sheldon Liss, *The United States and the Panama Canal* (Notre Dame, Ind.: University of Notre Dame Press, 1967), p. 18. For the conspirators *see* Philippe Bunau-Varilla, *Panama: The Creation, Destruction, and Resurrection* (New York: McBride, Nast, 1914); C. D. Ameringer, "The Panama Canal Lobby of Philippe Bunau-Varilla and William Nelson Cromwell," *American Historical Review* 68 (January 1963): 346-63; and Ernesto J. Castillero Reyes, *Historia de Panama* (Panama, 1955).

26. Paul B. Ryan, *The Panama Canal Controversy: U.S. Diplomacy and Defense Interests* (Stanford: Hoover Institution Press,1977); Burton, *Theodore Roosevelt*, p. 128. On the touchy question of Panamanian sovereignty *see* Ralph Minger, "Panama, the Canal Zone, and Titular Sovereignty," *Western Political Quarterly* 14 (June 1961): 144-54.

27. David McCullough, *The Path Between the Seas: The Creation of the Panama Canal, 1870-1914* (New York: Simon and Schuster, 1977). Henry F. Pringle, *Roosevelt*, p. 224, concluded that "Roosevelt did nothing to incite the revolution, perhaps, but he was extremely well informed regarding the plans."

28. Walter LaFeber, *The Panama Canal: The Crisis in Historical Perspective* (New York: Oxford University Press, 1978), which has an excellent bibliography. For the diplomacy that finally assuaged Colombia, *see* German Arciniegas, *Caribbean: Sea of the New World*, trans. Harriet de Onis (New York: Alfred A. Knopf, 1954); J. Fred Rippy, *The Capitalists and Colombia* (New York: Vanguard Press, 1931); Paolo E. Coletta, "William Jennings Bryan and the United States-Colombia Impasse, 1903-1921," *Hispanic American Historical Review* 57 (November 1967): 486-501. An excellent study of the diplomatic relations of the United States and Colombia is found in U.S. Congress, Senate, *Diplomatic History of the Panama Canal*, Senate Document 474, 63d Cong., 2d sess., 1914.

29. Beale, *Roosevelt and the Rise of America to World Power*, pp. 81-171. *See also* Burton, *Theodore Roosevelt*, pp. 106-08 and Thomas George Dyer, "Theodore Roosevelt and the Idea of Race" (Ph.D. diss., University of Georgia, 1975).

30. In addition to Howard K. Beale, Alexander Campbell, Charles S. Campbell, and Bradford Perkins, already mentioned, this rapprochement is traced in Kenneth Bourne, *Britain and the Balance of Power in North America, 1815-1908* (London: Longmans, Green & Co., 1967); Merle Curti, *Peace or War: The American Struggle, 1636-1936* (Boston: J. S. Canner & Co., 1959), especially chaps. 6-7; Lionel M. Gelber, *The Rise of Anglo-American Friendship: A Study in World Politics, 1898-1906* (New York: Oxford University Press, 1938); Richard H. Heindel, *The American Impact on Great Britain, 1898-1914* (Philadelphia: University of Pennsylvania Press, 1940); Warren F. Kuehl, *Seeking World Order: The United States and International Organization to 1920* (Nashville: Vanderbilt University Press, 1969), especially chaps. 5-7; R. G. Neale, *Great Britain and United States Expansion* (East Lansing: Michigan State University Press, 1966); and David S. Patterson, *Toward a Warless World: The Travail of the American Peace Movement 1887-1914* (Bloomington: Indiana University Press, 1976), especially chap. 2. *See also* Manfred

Jonas, "The Major Powers and the United States, 1898-1910," in Jules Davids, ed., *Perspectives in American Diplomacy: Essays on Europe, America, China, and the Cold War* (New York: Arno Press, 1976), pp. 30-77. Stressing Anglo-American conflict rather than rapprochement, in contrast, is Edward P. Crapol, *America for Americans: Economic Nationalism and Anglophobia in the Late Nineteenth Century* (Westport, Conn.: Greenwood Press, 1973).

31. Tyler Dennett, *Americans in East Asia* (New York: Macmillan Co., 1922), pp. v, viii, 4, and *Roosevelt and the Russo-Japanese War* (Garden City, N.Y.: Doubleday, Page, 1925); Thomas A. Bailey, *Theodore Roosevelt and the Japanese-American Crises* (Stanford: Stanford University Press, 1934).

32. Charles E. Neu, "Theodore Roosevelt and Involvement in the Far East, 1901-1909," *Pacific Historical Review* 35 (November 1966): 433-69.

33. A. Whitney Griswold, *Far Eastern Policy of the United States* (New York: Harcourt, Brace & Co., 1938), pp. 50, 86.

34. Dennett, *John Hay: From Poetry to Politics*, p. 296 and "The Open Door as Intervention," *Annals of the American Academy of Political and Social Science* 168 (July 1933): 78-83. John K. Fairbank, *Chinese-American Interactions: A Historical Summary* (New Brunswick, N. J.: Rutgers University Press, 1975), pp. 62-63, says that the Open Door was "a British idea from the beginning, a free trade idea," and that following the Boxer rebellion it was expanded into a "two-headed idea. First, that we would seek me-too trade opportunities according to the treaty system that we had lived under so long in China. Second, that we were against the breakup of China. We wanted it to remain a unified nation."

35. Williams, *The Tragedy of American Diplomacy*, pp. 37, 38 and *The Shaping of American Diplomacy*, p. 387. *See also* LaFeber, *The New Empire*; Thomas J. McCormick, *The China Market: America's Quest for Informal Empire, 1893-1901* (Chicago: Quadrangle Books, 1967); Edward F. Friedman and Mark Selden, eds., *America's Asia: Dissenting Essays in Asian-American Relations* (New York: Random House, 1969).

36. Benjamin H. Williams, *Economic Foreign Policy of the United States* (New York: Howard Fertig, 1929), p. 3.

37. Paul A. Varg, *Open Door Diplomat: Life of W. W. Rockhill*, p. 36 and "The United States as World Power, 1900-1917: Myth or Reality?" in Braeman, Bremner, and Brody, eds., *Twentieth-Century American Foreign Policy*, p. 215; Akira Iriye, *Across the Pacific: The Inner History of American-East Asian Relations* (New York: Harcourt, Brace & World, 1967); Campbell, *Anglo-American Understanding*; Bemis, *Diplomatic History of the United States*.

38. Marilyn Blatt Young, *The Rhetoric of Empire: American China Policy, 1895-1901* (Cambridge, Mass.: Harvard University Press, 1968). John A. Garraty, "American Historians and the Open Door," Dorothy Borg, comp., *Historians and American Far Eastern Foreign Policy* (New York: Columbia University Press, 1966), pp. 1-13, traces how various historians treated the Open Door notes from 1899 to 1966.

39. George F. Kennan, *American Diplomacy, 1900-1950* (Chicago: University of Chicago Press, 1951); Beale, *Roosevelt and the Rise of America to World Power*; Young, *The Rhetoric of Empire*; Paul A. Varg, *Missionaries, Chinese, and Diplomats: The American Missionary Movement in China, 1890-1952* (Princeton:

Princeton University Press, 1958). *See also* William R. Braisted, "China, the United States Navy, and the Bethlehem Steel Company, 1909-1929," *Business History Review* 42 (Spring 1968): 50-66 and "The United States and the American China Development Company," *Far Eastern Quarterly* 11 (February 1952): 147-65.

40. Dennett, *Roosevelt and the Russo-Japanese War*, p. 332. *See also* Griswold, *Far Eastern Policy of the United States*, pp. 105-19 and Harbaugh, *Roosevelt* pp. 273-75, 277.

41. Eugene P. Trani, *The Treaty of Portsmouth: An Adventure in American Diplomacy* (Lexington: University of Kentucky Press, 1969). *See also* the well-balanced text of Paul Hibbert Clyde, *International Rivalries in Manchuria, 1689-1922*, 2d ed. rev. (New York: Octagon Books, 1928) and Thomas A. Bailey, *America Faces Russia: Russian-American Relations from Early Times to Our Day* [1950] (Gloucester, Mass.: P. Smith, 1964); William Appleman Williams, *American-Russian Relations 1781-1947* (New York: Rinehart, 1952); and John A. White, *The Diplomacy of the Russo-Japanese War* (Princeton: Princeton University Press, 1964) the last as scholarly a work as that of Edward Zabriskie, *American-Russian Power Rivalry in the Far East: A Study in Diplomacy and Power Politics, 1895-1914* (Philadelphia: University of Pennsylvania Press, 1946). Zabriskie holds that for lack of competent aides Roosevelt assumed personal direction of his diplomacy. For Russia's position on the war with Japan and the Treaty of Portsmouth *see* Robert K. Godwin, "Russia and the Portsmouth Peace Conference," *American Slavic and East European Review* 9 (1950): 279-91; Ernest R. May, "The Far Eastern Policy of the United States in the Period of the Russo-Japanese War: A Russian View," *American Historical Review* 62 (January 1957): 345-51; and Raymond A. Esthus, "Roosevelt, Russia, and Peacemaking, 1905," in Davids, ed., *Perspectives in American Diplomacy*, pp. 2-29.

42. Raymond A. Esthus, *Theodore Roosevelt and Japan* (Seattle: University of Washington Press, 1966).

43. Charles E. Neu, *An Uncertain Friendship: Theodore Roosevelt and Japan, 1906-1909* (Cambridge, Mass.: Harvard University Press, 1967); Griswold, *Far Eastern Policy of the United States*; William L. Neumann, *America Encounters Japan: From Perry to MacArthur* (Baltimore: Johns Hopkins Press, 1963).

44. Williams, *The Tragedy of American Diplomacy*, p. 44. The idea is "recycled" by Williams in *The Contours of American History* (Cleveland: World Publishing Co., 1961), p. 417.

45. Thomas A. Bailey, *Theodore Roosevelt and the Japanese-American Crises*; Roger Daniels, *The Politics of Prejudice: The Anti-Japanese Movement in California and the Struggle for Japanese Exclusion* (Berkeley: University of California Press, 1962); Akira Iriye, *Pacific Estrangement: Japanese and American Expansion, 1897-1911* (Cambridge, Mass.: Harvard University Press, 1972).

46. Outten J. Clinard, *Japan's Influence on American Naval Power, 1897-1907* (Berkeley: University of California Press, 1947); Robert A. Hart, *The Great White Fleet: Its Voyage Around the World, 1907-1909* (Boston: Little, Brown & Co., 1965).

47. William R. Braisted, *The United States Navy in the Pacific, 1897-1909* (Austin: University of Texas Press, 1958) and *The United States Navy in the Pacific,*

1909-1922 (Austin: University of Texas Press, 1971); Samuel Carter III, *The Incredible Great White Fleet* (New York: Crowell-Collier Press, 1971).

48. William R. Braisted, "The United States Navy's Dilemma in the Pacific, 1906-1909," *Pacific Historical Review* 26 (August 1957): 235-44 and "The Philippine Naval Base Problem, 1898-1909," *Mississippi Valley Historical Review* 41 (June 1954): 21-40; Seward L. Livermore, "American Naval Base Policy in the Far East, 1850-1941," *Pacific Historical Review* 13 (June 1944): 113-35; W. E. Snowbarger, "Pearl Harbor in Pacific Strategy, 1898-1908," *Historian* 19 (May 1957): 361-84.

49. Kenneth Bourne, *Britain and the Balance of Power in North America*; Ebert Malcolm Carroll, *Germany and the Great Powers, 1866-1914* (New York: Prentice-Hall, 1938); Oron J. Hale, *Germany and the Diplomatic Revolution: A Study in Diplomacy and the Press, 1904-1906* (New York: Octagon Books, 1931); W. O. Henderson, *The Rise of American Industrial Power, 1834-1914* (Berkeley: University of California Press, 1975); George Monger, *The End of Isolation: British Foreign Policy, 1900-1907* (London: T. Nelson, 1963); Bernadotte Everly Schmitt, *England and Germany, 1740-1914 [1916]* (New York: Howard Fertig, 1967); Paolo E. Coletta *Admiral Bradley A. Fiske and the American Navy* (Lawrence: Regents Press of Kansas, 1979), and *French Ensor Chadwick: Scholarly Warrior* (Washington, D.C.: University Press of America, 1980).

50. *See* Barbara Tuchman, "Perdicaris Alive or Raisuli Dead," *American Heritage* 10 (August 1959): 18-21, 98-101; William J. Hourihan, "Marlinspike Diplomacy: The Navy in the Mediterranean, 1904," U.S. Naval Institute *Proceedings* 105 (January 1979): 42-51.

51. Eugene N. Anderson, *The First Moroccan Crisis, 1904-1906* (Chicago: University of Chicago Press, 1930); Ima C. Barlow, *The Agadir Crisis* (Chapel Hill: University of North Carolina Press, 1940); Beale, *Roosevelt and the Rise of America to World Power*, pp. 356-89; Ross N. Dunn, *Resistance in the Desert: Moroccan Responses to French Imperialism, 1881-1912* (Madison: University of Wisconsin Press, 1977); Griswold, *Far Eastern Policy of the United States*, pp. 108-12; Harbaugh, *Roosevelt*, pp. 192-94; Holger H. Herwig, *Politics of Frustration: The United States in German Naval Planning, 1889-1941* (Boston: Little, Brown & Co., 1976); A. J. P. Taylor, *The Struggle for Mastery in Europe, 1848-1918* (Oxford: Oxford University Press, Clarendon Press, 1954); Samuel R. Williamson, *The Politics of Grand Strategy: Britain and France Prepare for War, 1904-1914* (Cambridge, Mass.: Harvard University Press, 1969); Edmund D. Morell, *Morocco in Diplomacy* [1911] (London: Smith, Elder, 1976).

52. Beale, *Roosevelt and the Rise of America to World Power*; Harbaugh, *Roosevelt*. Close attention to the arbitration procedures is given by Perkins, *The Great Rapprochement*; Patterson, *Toward a Warless World*; Osgood, *Ideals and Self-Interest in America's Foreign Relations*; W. Stull Holt, *Treaties Defeated by the Senate* (Baltimore: Johns Hopkins Press, 1933); and Robert Seager, *Mahan*. Among many contemporary accounts *see* William Howard Taft, *The United States and Peace* (New York: Charles Scribner's Sons, 1914) and William J. Bryan, "The Arbitration Treaties," *Outlook* 98 (12 August 1911): 801-02.

53. Herbert S. Duffy, *William Howard Taft* (New York: Minton Balch & Co., 1930).

54. Francis McHale, *President and Chief Justice: The Life and Public Services of William Howard Taft* (Philadelphia: Dorrance and Co., 1931).

55. Henry F. Pringle, *The Life and Times of William Howard Taft: A Biography*, 2 vols. (New York: Farrar & Rinehart, 1939); Coletta, *The Presidency of William Howard Taft*, chaps. 9, 10; Horace Samuel and Marion Galbraith Merrill, *The Republican Command 1897-1913* (Lexington, Ky.: University of Kentucky Press, 1971); Walter V. and Marie V. Scholes, *The Foreign Policies of the Taft Administration* (Columbia, Mo.: University of Missouri Press, 1970).

56. *See* the following in the section on Roosevelt: Pringle, *Roosevelt*; Harbaugh, *Roosevelt*; Mowry, *Era of Theodore Roosevelt*; Challener, *Admirals, Generals, and American Foreign Policy*; Nevins, *Henry White*; Callcott, *Caribbean Policy of the United States*, esp. pp. 258, 306-07; Munro, *Intervention and Dollar Diplomacy in the Caribbean*; Cline, *The United States and Mexico*; Cox, *Nicaragua and the United States*; and Griswold, *Far Eastern Policy of the United States*. Taft's conception of the presidential office is available in his work, *The Presidency: Its Duties, Its Powers, and Its Opportunities and Limitations* (New York: Charles Scribner's Sons, 1916) and in Donald F. Anderson, *William Howard Taft: A Conservative's Conception of the Presidency* (Ithaca: Cornell University Press, 1973). An evaluation of his diplomatic troubleshooting while serving under McKinley and Roosevelt is found in Ralph Minger, *William Howard Taft and United States Foreign Policy: The Apprenticeship* (Urbana: University of Illinois Press, 1975). *See also* Scholes and Scholes, *Foreign Policies of the Taft Administration*, chap. 1; William Phillips, *Ventures in Diplomacy* (Boston: Beacon Press, 1952); and Paul S. Reinsch, *An American Diplomat in China* (Garden City, N.Y.: Doubleday, Page, 1922). Julius W. Pratt, *Challenge and Rejection: The United States and World Leadership, 1900-1921* (New York: Macmillan Co., 1967) entitled his chapter on the Taft administration "The Epigoni" (i.e., second-rate imitators).

57. Bemis, *Latin American Policy of the United States*, p. 166.

58. Griswold, *Far Eastern Policy of the United States*, p. 134; Callcott, *Caribbean Policy of the United States*, p. 210; Hart, *The Eccentric Tradition*, p. 77; Akira Iriye, *From Nationalism to Internationalism: U.S. Foreign Policy to 1914* (Boston: Routledge & Kegan Paul, 1977); Scholes and Scholes, *Foreign Policies of the Taft Administration*, pp. 21, 27. *See also* Jerry Israel, *Progressivism and the Open Door: America and China, 1905-1921* (Pittsburgh: University of Pittsburgh Press, 1971), and Gordon Connell-Smith, *The United States and Latin America: An Historical Analysis of Inter-American Relations* (London: Heinemann Educational Books, 1974), esp. p. 122.

59. Scholes and Scholes, *Foreign Policies of the Taft Administration*, chap. 1; Katherine Crane, *Mr. Carr of State: Forty-Seven Years in the Department of State* (New York: St. Martin's Press, 1960); Gilbert Stuart, *The Department of State: A History of Its Organization, Procedure, and Personnel* (New York: Macmillan Co., 1949); Archibald W. Butt, *Taft and Roosevelt: The Intimate Letters of Archie Butt, Military Aide*, 2 vols. (Garden City, N.Y.: Doubleday, Doran, 1930); Oscar Straus, *Under Four Administrations* (Boston: Houghton Mifflin Co., 1922); and Herbert Croly, *Willard Straight* (New York: Macmillan Co., 1924).

60. William Manners, *TR and Will: The Friendship That Split the Republican Party* (New York: Harcourt, Brace & World, 1969).

61. U.S., Department of State, *The Foreign Service of the United States: Origins, Development, and Functions,* prepared for the Bureau of Public Affairs, Historical Office by William and Morgan Barnes and John Heath (Washington, D.C.: Government Printing Office, 1961); John Mabry Matthews, *The Conduct of Foreign Relations* (New York: Century Co., 1922) and *American Foreign Relations: Conduct and Policies* (New York: Century Co., 1928); Gaillard Hunt, *The Department of State of the United States: Its History and Functions* (New Haven: Yale University Press, 1914), esp. pp. 244-47; Gilbert Stuart, *Department of State.*

62. Taft's ventures in China including the Hukuang Loan, railroad neutralization scheme, Chinchow-Aigun railroad, currency loan, and governmental reorganization loan are dealt with, in addition to the works mentioned in the note above, by Coletta, *Taft;* Croly, *Straight*; Griswold, *Far Eastern Policy of the United States*, pp. 138-75; and Foster Rhea Dulles, *America's Rise to World Power, 1898-1954* (New York: Harper & Row, 1954). The quotations are from Henry F. Pringle, *Taft*, 1: 686, and Akira Iriye, *Across the Pacific: An Inner History of American-East Asian Relations* (New York: Harcourt, Brace & World, 1967), p. 122. *See also* the excellent historiographical article by Charles E. Neu, "From the Open Door to the Washington Treaties, 1906-1913," in Ernest R. May and James C. Thompson, eds., *American-East Asia Relations: A Survey* (Cambridge, Mass.: Harvard University Press, 1972). The author indicates that the best work on the period lies in various unpublished doctoral dissertations.

63. In addition to the works by W. Stull Holt and Thomas G. Paterson, already mentioned, *see* Scholes and Scholes, *Foreign Policies of the Taft Administration*, and "The General Arbitration Treaties," *Outlook* 98 (26 August 1911): 914 and "The Senators and the Arbitration Treaties," ibid., 100 (16 March 1912): 561-62. John P. Campbell, "Taft, Roosevelt, and the Arbitration Treaties of 1911," *Journal of American History* 53 (September 1966): 279-98, concludes that popular support for these treaties determined Roosevelt to challenge Taft's nomination in 1912.

64. James M. Callahan, *American Foreign Policy in Canadian Relations* (New York: Macmillan Co., 1937); Charles C. Tansill, *Canadian-American Relations, 1875-1911* (New Haven: Yale University Press, 1943); Thomas A. Bailey, "The North Pacific Sealing Convention of 1911," *Pacific Historical Review* 4 (1935): 1-14.

65. Coletta, *Taft*, pp. 168-69; Scholes and Scholes, *Foreign Policies of the Taft Administration*, pp. 81-104; P. Edward Haley, *Revolution and Intervention: The Diplomacy of Taft and Wilson with Mexico, 1910-1917* (Cambridge: M.I.T. Press, 1970); Edward J. Berbusse, "Neutrality Diplomacy of the United States and Mexico, 1910-1911," *The Americas* 12 (January 1956): 265-83.

7 Wilsonian Wartime Diplomacy: The Sense of the Seventies

EDITH JAMES

Intervention, self-determination, economic expansion, economic regulation, government candor, international cooperation—so many of the forces which shape current affairs flow directly from World War I. The search for origins of contemporary international crises has led several generations of historians to investigate the Great War.[1]

For the past fifty years, historians have developed a variety of explanations to account for American involvement in the war. Some emphasized the German threat and national security needs, while others cited economic pressures, American commitment to international law, or the desire for an enduring and equitable postwar system of international relations. For half a century, too, historians have analyzed the diplomacy of the peace negotiations and disputed the efficacy of the final settlement and the wisdom of the treaty's provisions. Because the role of Woodrow Wilson was central to the war and peace, historians closely scrutinized the president and debated his character, vision, policies, and performance.

Scholars began to group the varying views concerning American involvement according to interpretive schools, which they often entitled traditionalist, revisionist, multicausal, and new left.[2] Some historians were categorized as critics, others defenders of the Versailles settlement.[3] The failure of the United States to adopt the treaty was laid to the fault of personalities, and, contrarily, to impersonal forces.[4] Some Wilson biographies were labeled eulogies; others were condemnations.[5] Other biographers differed over the extent to which Wilson was a realist or an idealist.[6]

Personal predilections accounted for some of the varied interpretations. Different readings of the same evidence produced others. Availability of evidence determined, in part, other emphases. Each time vital new personal papers or governmental archives became open, historians reevaluated the earlier literature.

Some of the historical interpretations, however, reflected the tone and concerns of the times in which the histories were written. For example, in the immediate postwar period, the most popular explanation of American involvement was the traditionalist view, which approximated that provided the American people by Wilson, and emphasized the threat posed by Germany's unrestricted submarine warfare. By the mid-1930s, the country was enveloped in the economic depression and engulfed by isolationism. The contemporary crisis had its impact on World War I historiography. The revisionists questioned the sincerity of Wilson's neutrality, noting that America's economic ties with the Allies made impartiality impossible. Post-World War II literature, conditioned in some respect by American involvement in a second conflagration, lessened the criticism of the previous decade. Entry into the war was multicausal, more complex than defined by the submarine-thesis advocates or by the revisionist interpretations. America intervened in accordance with a realistic assessment of American vital interests and national security. Following the cold war disillusionment, realists of the 1950s tended to regard Wilson's diplomacy as a prime example of the legalistic-moralistic approach in American thinking about foreign affairs. Shades of revisionism remained, to be revivified by new left historians of the 1960s. The themes of that decade were change and social justice. New left historians held Wilsonian diplomacy responsible for the suppression of revolutionary social change and for the construction of an American economic empire.

From the historiographical debates, several accounts emerged as authoritative. The fullest biography of Wilson is Arthur S. Link's multivolume work, five volumes of which have been completed. The last three volumes contain a fine account of the neutrality period. Two books by Arno J. Mayer, *Political Origins of the New Diplomacy* and *Politics and Diplomacy of Peacemaking*, set the problems of Wilsonian peacemaking in their world context. Paul Birdsall's *Versailles* is an excellent brief account of the Paris peace conference. Robert E. Osgood's *Ideals and Self-Interest in America's Foreign Relations* gives a good discussion of the impact of the war on American thinking about foreign policy. For a brief one-volume survey of the period see Daniel M. Smith's *The Great Departure.*[7]

The interpretive tendencies were explained in numerous historiographical reviews written during the 1950s, 1960s, and 1970s. The most useful is Smith's "National Interest and American Intervention, 1917."[8] In addition to essays specifically devoted to World War I, several essays placed World War I scholarship within the larger context of the historiography of diplomatic relations in general.[9] Because historiographical reviews of World

War I diplomacy are abundant and adequate, and since the essays analyze the histories produced during the period 1920 to 1970, this essay will survey the literature published since 1970.

Thomas McCormick, assessing the state of American diplomatic history in 1970 issued an ecumenical call for less conventional studies. He asked that historians who study foreign affairs explore new and unfamiliar materials and methodologies, that they offer comparative, cosmopolitan, and culturally relative analyses, and, finally, that they make diplomatic history the study of the total impact of societies upon other societies.[10]

McCormick held up as exemplary N. Gordon Levin's *Woodrow Wilson and World Politics*.[11] Levin concentrated on the response of the United States during 1917-1919 to the challenges of war and German imperialism on the right and Bolshevik social revolution on the left. In this context, Wilson sought to spread the values and institutions of American liberal capitalism in order to create a new world order, characterized by open world trade and great power cooperation within a framework of world law and international-capitalist commercial relationships. In Wilsonian thought, the needs of America's expanding capitalism were joined ideologically with a more universal vision of American service to suffering humanity and to world stability. Most of the volume was devoted to the attempt to apply the program to Russia and Germany. Levin's work, which received the Bancroft Prize in 1968, was, as McCormick proposed, an integrated, refined, and provocative historical analysis of Wilson's plan for reshaping international relations.

Students of Wilson and World War I have recently moved in the directions McCormick suggested. Colleagues associated with the documentary series, *The Papers of Woodrow Wilson*, have used some rich but less traditionally consulted resources and have applied special techniques to their study of Wilson.[12] Non-American historians, such as Patrick Devlin, Inga Floto, and George Egerton wrote from different cultural frameworks. David Trask, Burton Kaufman, and Joseph Tulchin extended a vision of diplomatic history which encompassed more than a narrative of high-level political negotiation.

Historians of twentieth-century diplomacy are chronically awaiting the opening of additional public or private records which will provide answers to their questions. Until recently, explanations of World War I diplomacy suffered from limitations on access to certain records. One important aspect of current World War I scholarship is the availability of hithertofore closed materials. A fifty-year prohibition on access to the British archives, for instance, left unanswered many questions concerning Anglo-American relations. An example of the benefits of using fresh records is John Cooper's "The British Response to the House-Grey Memorandum."[13] Sir Edward Grey and David Lloyd George had written conflicting recollections of the

British government's rejection of the March 1916 American offer of mediation. Historians, too, wrote differing interpretations of the event. Cooper found three documents showing that Grey sympathized with the offer, and that contrary to Lloyd George's account, Grey alone did not scotch the plan. The war committee turned down the American proposal because their squabbling and ineptitude ruled out the kind of bold choice required to accept the offer.

The records that Cooper used are traditional sources for diplomatic history. Other historians have been studying more unconventional resources. By using public addresses, essays, course examinations, love letters, and medical records for documentary publication, intellectual biography, diplomatic history, and psycho-medical biography, Arthur Link, John Mulder, Eugene Trani, and Edwin Weinstein provided insights into the wellsprings of Wilsonian diplomacy.

An appreciation of Wilson's character and motives is vital to any thorough understanding of his diplomacy. Editor Link and the staff of the *Papers* have contributed to that understanding. The series, projected at fifty-two volumes, will be completed in the late 1980s. The most recently published volume, number twenty-eight, carries through to 6 December 1913.[14] Earlier volumes deal with the prepresidential years. Strikingly apparent in those years, and fully presented in the *Papers,* are many of the concepts and concerns which would come to dominate Wilson's presidential career. For example, a deeply held Presbyterian faith pervades Wilson's private correspondence, his student essays, scholarly lectures, and public addresses.

The fundamental religious values upon which the president acted are explained by Mulder in a supplementary volume of the *Papers.*[15] Prior to his entry into politics, Wilson was profoundly influenced by the Presbyterian covenant tradition. Wilson used a secularized concept of the religious covenant in his personal relationships, his professional ambitions, and his understanding of American society. This analysis of Wilson's sense of American exclusivism, mission, and vocation, and his tendency to defend the exercise of power in moral terms, provides diplomatic historians with a clearer basis for assessing Wilson's principled rhetoric and seemingly less-principled action.

One specialized study, Trani's "Woodrow Wilson, China, and the Missionaries," considers the effect of evangelical Protestantism on Wilsonian diplomacy.[16] Wilson gained his knowledge of China from missionaries at Princeton. He viewed Christianity as a unifying force and the Chinese revolution of 1911 as the first step toward the spread of Christianity, and, concomitantly, democracy for China. During World War I, missionaries successfully urged Wilson to oppose Japanese demands.

Throughout his correspondence, Wilson comments on the state of his emotional and physical health and its effect on his work. Wilson suffered from nervous stomach, tension headaches, and, prior to the presidential years, had a history of cerebral-vascular disease. Wilson's health interested historians of diplomacy, since his incapacity following a massive stroke in 1919 affected the outcome of the treaty fight. Until recently no sophisticated medical explanation of his physical condition was available.

Much of the earlier literature centered on Wilson's mental health. In the portrait of Wilson drawn by Sigmund Freud and William C. Bullitt, psychobiography reached its nadir. When the book appeared in 1967 it was discredited by most authorities, psychologists and historians alike. The authors framed a savage assault that depicted Wilson as a messianic, effeminate zealot hovering on the brink of insanity. The central neurosis, which unconsciously gripped the whole course of Wilson's life, was his fixation upon his father.[17]

The remarkable relationship between Wilson and his minister-father already had interested Alexander and Juliette George. The Georges' work, *Woodrow Wilson and Colonel House*, adopted a compensation hypothesis as the basis of their psychological interpretation of Wilson.[18] Power for Wilson, they said, was a means of restoring self-esteem damaged in childhood. His behavior is explained as an effort to gain freedom from domination by figures whom he may have seen as reincarnations of his domineering father. Having attained power, he was unable to suppress inner impulses toward aggressive leadership and indulged his wish to force others into complete compliance. His provocative behavior encouraged opposition and ultimately led to self-defeat. Much of his break with his advisor, Colonel House, his battle with Senator Lodge, and his uncompromising stand on the treaty, are seen as manifestations of this personality trait.

The Georges' *Wilson* is often cited as a pioneering effort in the now voguish area of psychobiography. But was that effort successful? Two articles, "The Georges' Wilson Reexamined" by Robert Tucker and "Woodrow Wilson's Political Personality" by Edwin Weinstein, James Anderson, and Arthur Link, propose answers. Tucker posited an alternative psychological model based on the hypothesis that Wilson, responding to adverse childhood experiences, formed an idealized image of himself. It was his *high* self-esteem that led to active involvement in the political arena where he could demonstrate that he was in fact the idealized self. When in the role of leader, his tendency was to provoke opposition, not to self-defeating ends but rather to reenact the experience of winning. Weinstein, Anderson, and Link asserted that the Georges' book presented an inaccurate portrait of Wilson's personality because the monograph rested on inadequate research, because the Georges failed to recognize the limitations of their psychological model, and because they ignored Wilson's physical disorders as conditions affecting his behavior.[19]

Weinstein has focused on physical health factors. In a broad-gauged medical history he discussed Wilson's general health in terms of his family and gender roles, his religious convictions, his social-class orientation, and style of language and communication. He then specifically analyzed the neurological disturbances that occurred in 1896 and 1906 and during the presidential period.[20] Weinstein concluded that, given Wilson's cultural preconditioning, the neurological impairment sustained after his strokes accounts for many of Wilson's behavioral patterns: intensity, aggressiveness, intolerance of criticism. Recent investigations and the use of hitherto unavailable material such as the diary of Admiral Cary T. Grayson, Wilson's White House physician, have led Weinstein to modify some of his previous diagnoses. For example, at Paris in April 1919 Wilson apparently had influenza and encephalitis, not a stroke. Some of the concessions he made during the week following his recovery may have been caused by his state of post-recovery euphoria.

The assumption that international relations could be viewed as aspects of one nation's history underlay much of the early writing about American foreign policy. That assumption has been challenged by a multinational approach. Victor S. Mamatey's monograph, for example, relying on little-known Eastern European sources, sought to reconstruct the story of the United States attitude toward the breakup of the Hapsburg empire.[21] For Mamatey, Wilson's foreign policy was a reaction to events at home and abroad. Wilson neither balkanized east central Europe, nor represented bourgeois-nationalist opposition to social revolution. The new nations of central Europe were not created by the Paris peace conference, but created themselves by their own efforts. The Allies made their independence possible by crushing the main obstacle, the Central Powers. Today it is agreed that the actions of the United States in World War I must be viewed in the perspective of the actions of other nations.

That perspective has led to an increased interest in the writings of foreign scholars and to an international scholarly exchange. Foreign literature on Wilsonian diplomacy is burgeoning. French, West German, and British authors have focused upon those aspects of Wilsonian diplomacy most relevant to the writer's nation. One important French work now receiving American attention is Pierre Renouvin's *Le Armistice de Rethondes, 11 Novembre 1918.*[22] Renouvin constructed a framework for the study of international affairs based upon the statesman's struggle with "forces profondes," and applied this approach to the peacemaking which ended World War I. The military situation itself, melded with public opinion, shaped the armistice. The armistice, in turn, channeled the future peace. Wilson was locked into the dilemma.

Like Renouvin's work, lack of translation made Fritz Fischer's work, primarily *Griff nach der Weltmacht*, relatively inaccessible for several years.[23] Fischer theorized that the genesis of the war was primarily Germany's drive toward territorial and commercial expansion. He argued that Germany's expansionist war goals grew directly out of imperialist aspirations, especially the desire to create a massive, German-dominated central Europe. His position clashed with the traditional German claim that Germany, surrounded by the hostile powers of Russia, France, and Great Britain, was on the defensive in war. Fischer stated that expansionist schemes were promoted not only by pan-German extremists, but also by civilian and military leaders. The leaders desired the destruction of France as a great power, and at least equal footing for Germany. Fischer's work challenged American revisionists, like Harry Elmer Barnes, who defended Germany's actions and whose works were popular in Germany between the two world wars.[24] Americans have begun to incorporate Fischer's findings into their own work, as, for example, Lancelot Farrar's *The Short War Illusion*.[25]

While Fischer contributed new understanding of German leadership and foreign policy, other Germans began to look more closely at American leaders. One prominent German historian, Klaus Schwabe, has done meticulous research on both sides of the Atlantic. He is currently translating his *Deutsche Revolution und Wilson-Frieden*, which will become part of the supplementary series to *The Wilson Papers*.[26] He wrote as a German attempting to straighten out the confused German understanding of Woodrow Wilson as a participant at Versailles. In so doing, he helped to clarify for Americans the intricacies which characterized German-American relations during the final year of the war. Wilson, he concluded, adhered to the unshakable opinion that Germany should and would be admitted to the League of Nations. But because Wilson viewed Germany as the guilty party, he agreed that Germany would have to bear the burden of that guilt.

A one-volume work which brings together the perspectives of scholars from France and Germany is *Wilson's Diplomacy: An International Symposium*.[27] Two of the essays explore Wilson's fluctuating image in France and West Germany. According to Jean-Baptiste Duroselle, Wilson's "peace without victory" message aroused irritation and the outcome of the treaty created hostility in France. Frenchmen felt that Wilson, like the typical Anglo-Saxon, posed as a humanitarian while promoting the interests of his own country. Ernst Fraenkel explained that in Germany there was some pro-Wilson euphoria among socialists and radical-leftist liberals, but this turned to hatred. To them, and to the German nation as a whole, the treaty was the opposite of all Wilson's avowed ideals. Wilson had either presented his views deceptively or betrayed his principles, and he became a scapegoat for German troubles. How the world and its leaders perceived the character and purposes of Wilson was crucial in determining the conduct of war and the outcome of peace negotiations.

Because of the primacy of Britain in the war, American historiography is greatly enriched by British explanations of the struggle. The distinguished jurist, Patrick Devlin, in *Too Proud to Fight*, provides a sensitive study of the character of Wilson and his neutrality policy.[28] Lord Devlin's professional background helped him explain international laws governing war at sea. His skillful analysis of the tangle reveals that there was considerable ambiguity in the Allied claims against the German submarine policy. The bulk of the book is devoted to an account of the diplomatic exchanges between the government of the United States and those of Germany and Great Britain. He explains the international usages applying to neutral shipping in time of war, the liberties taken by the British authorities in order to enforce a blockade that they thought essential to their nation's survival, and the efforts of the belligerents to find legal justification for what they felt they must do. According to Devlin, for Wilson the war was not primarily a legal problem. Rather, the struggle for neutrality was primarily a moral problem, a "battle for Wilson's mind." Wilson saw neutrality as a positive stance which would protect America and enable it to exercise leverage against both warring parties, and he saw the war as a profound human tragedy in which victory was not worth the cost. Devlin attributes Wilson's failure to maintain neutrality to his inability to incorporate compromise and expediency into his statecraft, and to "flaws" in Wilson's Christianity, particularly the tone of moral condescension that characterized Wilson's speeches and diplomatic notes and his offers of service. Wilson was moved toward war in order to preserve a moral principle—democracy. Wilson shared the unparalleled optimism prevalent in late nineteenth-century America, and believed that America should spread "the ideal democracy [she had] in her own opinion already attained." By March 1917 Wilson was firmly convinced that Germany and its submarines had begun to threaten that civilization, and that by avoiding war he would lose his power to make the peace. He was then compelled to fight, to overcome "the military masters of Germany," because only by fighting could "the good be reached."

The contributions of French, German, and British scholars to the literature of Wilsonian diplomacy seem greatest in those areas where their own country's history intersected that of the United States. Here they have widened the discussion for American historians. Scholars from other countries provide an important objectivity. For example, Canadian George Egerton's *Great Britain and the Creation of the League of Nations* has definitively explained the British contribution to the birth of the league, and *Colonel House in Paris*, the monograph of a Danish scholar, Inga Floto, now supplements Birdsall's analysis of the peace conference.[29]

Until recently, those interested in portraying the British side have had to do so from incomplete evidence, but Egerton, using recently opened government and private sources, began to fill in the picture which previously was but a sketch of speculation. He concludes that Lloyd George was not allied with the old order against Wilson and the new diplomacy as claimed by historians like Ray Stannard Baker.[30] Although Lloyd George and the British government were firmly committed to the principle of establishing a league, the specific function, powers, and structure of the organization which emerged from the peace conference presented major problems for the British Empire. Lloyd George, the war cabinet, and the British inner circle wanted a league to promote peace and to further international cooperation, but one that did not attempt to institute the obligations and commitments of a system of collective security. Despite his government's reservations, Robert Cecil negotiated an Anglo-American draft of the league which incorporated the thinking of Wilson, Jan Smuts, and himself, and which went beyond the desires of the British government. The triumph of the Wilson-Cecil collective-security approach alienated the British policymaking elite from the league who then shunted the league to the periphery of British diplomacy. The collective-security approach also insured a ferocious treaty battle in the United States.

While Egerton clarified some of the uncertainties and differences of interpretation concerning the British role in the peacemaking, Inga Floto unveiled some of the mysteries surrounding the American side. Charles Seymour and the Georges had relied heavily on Colonel House's own interpretation of history (his massive diary) and had presented House in a favorable light.[31] Floto used most of the pertinent sources and drew other conclusions. House was a compromiser, incapable of working through complex problems, a clever man but a poor diplomat and vulnerable to flattery. Moreover, he failed to fully inform Wilson about his negotiations, and finally, while Wilson was away from the conference in February and March 1919, he disloyally moved toward shelving the league and joining with Clemenceau.

An American historian who draws on the most recent international scholarship is Arthur Walworth. In his latest work, *America's Moment: 1918*, Walworth uses some of the findings of Renouvin, Duroselle, Schwabe, Devlin, and Floto, but he interprets the evidence differently.[32] For Walworth, the critical moment for American diplomacy was October 1918 to January 1919, the period between the time when the Central Powers sued for armistice agreements and the official beginning of the Paris peace conference. This theme was well-chosen. At that moment the United States had a victorious and unparalleled army, fleet, and economic structure, and its president had immense popular support. In the style of more traditional diplomatic studies, Walworth chronicles the intricate negotiations which led up to the peace conference. He does not, however, attempt to formulate systematic conclusions about the end of the war and its immediate aftermath.

Although Walworth is concerned with essentially the same questions and hypotheses of his predecessors, many historians have recently gone on to new concerns. Some are looking behind high-level diplomatic negotiations in hopes of explaining America's foreign policy. Others are looking beyond the diplomatic maneuvering altogether, and are focusing their attention on transformations wrought by the war and by peacemaking diplomacy.

David Trask, for example, has been concerned with the effect on diplomacy of Wilson's style as commander-in-chief. In his article, "Woodrow Wilson and the Reconciliation of Force and Diplomacy," Trask refined and elaborated some of the ideas he had presented earlier.[33] Trask suggests that historians have attached too much significance to Wilson's lack of interest in the day-to-day conduct of military operations and have overlooked the fact that Wilson was an excellent grand-strategist. Many studies have portrayed Wilson as a near-pacifist; a reluctant commander who insisted on a rigid, unrealistic distinction between military and civilian affairs, and who failed to coordinate diplomatic aims with military force. Ernest May, in *The Ultimate Decision*, argued that Wilson evaded his duty as commander and was hesitant to provide strategic direction for the military since he felt that involvement in Allied strategy would compromise his conditions for peace.[34] That view of Wilson prevails in such recent works as Samuel and Dorothy Rosenman's *Presidential Style* and R. Gordon Hoxie's *Command Decision and the Presidency*.[35] Trask, however, has argued effectively that Wilson developed a cogent political program of war aims and conditions for peace, accurately calculated the disposition of American naval and military power to achieve his diplomatic objectives, avoided any serious civilian-military rift within the government, and possessed the iron will essential to execute the grand design. This enabled Wilson to become, by November 1918, *arbiter mundi.*

While Wilson's accomplishments as commander-in-chief affected diplomacy, so too did his relationship with his secretaries of state. In *Aftermath of War*, Daniel Smith attempted to fill in gaps in our understanding of the period's diplomacy with the first comprehensive study of Bainbridge Colby, Wilson's third and last secretary of state.[36] Smith stated that Colby was, for Wilson, the most satisfactory of his appointments to that post. The two men established a far more workable relationship than had William Jennings Bryan or Robert Lansing and Wilson. Moreover, although Colby's tenure was brief, he made a significant impression upon Latin America, in strengthening the Open Door policy in East Asia, and in persuading Japan to adopt a more cooperative course. The Wilson-Colby approach was prologue to that of the Republican administration's middle-of-the-road, limited internationalism. Smith saw their "neoisolationism" as a reflection of Wilson's personal bitterness over the treaty defeat and his growing suspicion of the motives of the major powers.

While Smith looked at the office of the secretary of state, Rachel West has delved into the bureaucratic hierarchy for insights into diplomacy. In her monograph, *The Department of State on the Eve of the First World War*, West argues that Department of State officials were largely ignorant of European events because of the serious understaffing of those bureaus responsible for communications with European capitals, and because of the practice of appointing amateurs to diplomatic posts as political favors.[37] The outbreak of the war proved the necessity for reforms in the diplomatic service and for increases in departmental and embassy staffs.

Trask, Smith, and West looked at the political structure for explanations, while other historians looked to the economy. A great deal of literature in the 1960s centered on the issue of whether Wilson was an economic expansionist. Levin's work and Carl Parrini's *Heir to Empire* culminated that debate at the end of the decade.[38] Parrini's volume investigated how American business leaders cooperated with the government to take advantage of the shift of financial power from London to New York, creating a new economic community dominated by the United States. Today many historians accept the fact that Wilson did enthusiastically seek open door expansion.

Historians of the 1970s continued to explore the economic theme. For example, Sidney Bell, in *Righteous Conquest*, primarily addressing an earlier period than Parrini's, suggested that American involvement in World War I could be laid to Wilson's desire for righteous conquest of the markets of the world in order to prevent domestic conflict that would result from a surplus of American population, capital, and goods.[39] When war broke out in 1914 Wilson hoped to expand the nation's economic empire at the expense of its great power rivals. Great Britain's tactics, however, soon convinced Wilson that economic expansion required Anglo-American cooperation and a system of collective security. Wilson was forced to weigh neutrality against the broader benefits of Anglo-American cooperation and the dangers of postwar German rivalry. Bell seems to bring World War I historiography back, full circle, to the earliest revisionist interpretations.

Adding significantly to the growing body of literature on the political economy of World War I, but taking a quite different tack, is Robert Cuff's *The War Industries Board*.[40] He takes exception with those who try to conceptualize the political economy of the war years as a fully integrated institutional order and then make it a paradigm for future historical development. He insists on the historical uniqueness of business-government relations in the Great War and questions the notion that the War Industries Board represented an early experiment in state economic planning as well as the suggestion that the board was simply the tool of dominant economic interests. Wilson wanted to do as little violence to traditional peacetime institutions as possible. Cuff argues that Wilson envisioned the board as a device to bring order to the mobilization effort, as an attempt to protect his business advisors from public censure, and as a means to undermine the potential radical reordering of America's institutional system implicit in the idea of a munitions industry.

Burton Kaufman's *Efficiency and Expansion* builds on the work of both Parrini and Cuff.[41] Before the war German trade, aided by cooperation between the German government and German merchants, grew dramatically. Before, during, and after the war, the United States and Great Britain became intense rivals for trade supremacy, especially in Latin America. Faced on all fronts by rival European trade interests, the United States found itself at a disadvantage because it was comparatively new on the commercial and diplomatic scene. Economic competition and an awareness of Europe's superior structure for promoting foreign trade stimulated the federal government to forsake its traditionally passive role in this area. Wilson championed the gospel of efficiency, and actively advanced the federal government as a coordinating and integrating force. Wilson's foreign policy served as an extension of the domestic reform movement, in its search for efficiency, centralization, and order, translated into international terms.[42]

Jeffrey Safford's *Wilsonian Maritime Diplomacy* extends Kaufman's thesis.[43] According to Safford, in order to remove the impediments to greater American success Wilson undertook to lower tariffs and democratize domestic economic credit. He also sought to improve the maritime services, "the arms of commerce," that would transport the goods released through tariff and financial reforms. Safford maintains that because of Wilson's merchant marine policies, the wartime Shipping Board was able to lever into service, to equip, and to man over one thousand oceangoing vessels for the European front, and to carry on vital worldwide trade for materials required to prosecute the war. Shipping was an important American contribution to Allied victory and strengthened America's position, but it also occasioned a "commercial war after the war" between the Allies.

The Allied commercial war produced repercussions in Latin America as Joseph Tulchin explains in *The Aftermath of War: World War I and U.S. Policy Toward Latin America*.[44] He demonstrates how wartime deficiencies in petroleum, investment capital, and cable communications led to the determination of the United States to gain independence from European ownership of Latin America's resources. The United States absorbed most of the European investment and trade and consolidated its own economic predominance in a quest for economic security. The effect was to ensure American hegemony in the hemisphere for the next half-century.

While some historians have examined the political and economic forces behind foreign-policy decision-making, others have abandoned diplomatic negotiations as a major area of concern and are studying the effects of the war at home and abroad. Throughout history, war has been the catalyst for the transformation of states and societies. The new frontier of historical research may be the impact of World War I, rather than issues relating to neutrality, war, and peacemaking diplomacy.[45]

What sense, then, emerges from the World War I scholarship of the 1970s? First is a consensus regarding the methods of historical inquiry. This consensus calls for multiarchival research, multinational perspectives, multicausal analysis, and multidimensional explanations. These methods of inquiry have proved their value. From today's perspective, American involvement in World War I can no longer be seen as stemming strictly from political interests or from purely economic motives, but rather from a complex combination of factors involving national security, moral and legal issues, and diplomatic and economic influences. Single-cause explanations of American intervention no longer appear valid. Nor do simplistic explanations of Wilson's character and purposes suffice. The past half-century of research into Wilsonian wartime diplomacy settles the debate over whether Wilson was an idealist or a realist; he demonstrated both characteristics as a diplomatist. Historians, too, have demonstrated that from World War I the structure of the power and methods used by a dominant America and its leadership emerged. From World War I the shape of the modern international world order also emerged.

Notes

1. For a good bibliography of the period, *see*, Wilton B. Fowler, comp., *American Diplomatic History Since 1890* (Northbrook, Ill.: AHM Publishing Corp., 1975), pp. 48-71 and Arthur S. Link and William M. Leary, Jr., comps., *The Progressive Era and the Great War, 1896-1920* (New York: Appleton-Century-Crofts, 1969).

2. Examples are, respectively: traditionalist, Charles Seymour, *American Diplomacy during the World War* (Baltimore: Johns Hopkins Press, 1934) and *American Neutrality, 1914-1917* (New Haven: Yale University Press, 1935), who concluded that from political and legal standpoints, Wilson had little choice but to oppose unrestricted submarine warfare; revisionist, Charles C. Tansill, *America Goes to War* (Boston: Little, Brown & Co., 1938), who argued that intervention was due to sinister machinations by Allied propagandists, and arms makers and bankers with a financial stake in Allied victory; multicausal analyst, Ernest R. May, *The World War and American Isolation, 1914-1917* (Cambridge, Mass.: Harvard University Press, 1959), who demonstrated that entry into war could not have been avoided without sacrificing American honor, vital interests, and security; and new left, William Appleman Williams, *The Tragedy of American Diplomacy*, 1st rev. ed.

(New York: Dell Publishing Co., 1962), who viewed American involvement as an episode in the larger American quest for world economic predominance.

3. Early critical accounts by John Maynard Keynes, *The Economic Consequences of the Peace* (New York: Harcourt, Brace & Co., 1920) and by Harold Nicolson, *Peacemaking: 1919* (New York: Harcourt, Brace & Co., 1930) held that the peace was impractical and unjust. Thomas A. Bailey, *Woodrow Wilson and the Lost Peace* (New York: Macmillan Co., 1944) separated the avoidable from the unavoidable, but viewed the treaty as neither a thoroughgoing victor's peace nor a peace of accommodation. Their influential interpretations should be compared with Paul Birdsall, *Versailles Twenty Years After* (New York: Reynal & Hitchcock, 1941) which saw the settlement as a difficult compromise in the struggle between Wilsonian principles of a new world order and the principles of reactionary nationalism, or with Seth P. Tillman, *Anglo-American Relations at the Paris Peace Conference of 1919* (Princeton: Princeton University Press, 1961), which saw that whatever its specific defects, the treaty as a whole was a reasonable embodiment of the Fourteen Points and of the democratic principles of Anglo-American society.

4. D. F. Fleming, *The United States and the League of Nations, 1918-1920* (New York: G. P. Putnam's Sons, 1932) was especially critical of the role of Henry Cabot Lodge, Wilson's chief adversary in the Senate, while Thomas A. Bailey, *Woodrow Wilson and the Great Betrayal* (New York: Macmillan Co., 1945) argued that Wilson killed the treaty by refusing to cooperate with Lodge or to accept mild reservations to Article X of the League Covenant. On the other hand, Selig Adler, *The Isolationist Impulse: Its Twentieth Century Reaction* (New York: Abelard-Schuman, 1957) concluded that the rejection was best explained by a resurgence of an isolationist coalition of immigrants, liberals, and nationalists.

5. Arthur Walworth's Pulitzer prize-winning biography, *Woodrow Wilson*, 2 vols. (New York: Longmans, Green & Co., 1958) was rather adulatory, while the work of Sigmund Freud and William C. Bullitt, *Thomas Woodrow Wilson, Twenty-eighth President of the United States: A Psychological Study by Sigmund Freud and William C. Bullitt* (Boston: Houghton Mifflin Co., 1967) was a vindictive vilification.

6. John Morton Blum stressed the force of moral principles and Wilson's obedience to "a rigid conscience" in *Woodrow Wilson and the Politics of Morality* (Boston: Little, Brown & Co., 1956). Foreign policy analysts frequently focused on what they saw as the hopelessly moralistic tone of Wilson's policy. *See*, for example, George F. Kennan, *American Diplomacy, 1900-1950* (Chicago: University of Chicago Press, 1951). On the other hand, Wilson's primary biographer, Arthur S. Link, did not underestimate idealism as a mainspring of Wilson's foreign policy, but emphasized the extent to which Wilson came to grips with the realities of world and domestic politics. *See* Arthur S. Link, *Wilson the Diplomatist: A Look at His Major Foreign Policies* (Baltimore: Johns Hopkins Press, 1957) and "'Wilson the Diplomatist' in Retrospect," in Arthur S. Link, *The Higher Realism of Woodrow Wilson and Other Essays* (Nashville: Vanderbilt University Press, 1971).

7. *See* Arthur S. Link, *Wilson*, 5 vols.: *The Road to the White House, The New Freedom, The Struggle for Neutrality, 1914-1915, Confusions and Crises, 1915-1916, Campaigns for Progressivism and Peace, 1916-1917* (Princeton: Princeton University Press, 1947, 1956, 1960, 1964, 1965); Arno J. Mayer, *Political*

Origins of the New Diplomacy, 1917-1918 (New Haven: Yale University Press, 1959) and *The Politics and Diplomacy of Peacemaking: Containment and Counterrevolution at Versailles, 1918-1919* (New York: Alfred A. Knopf, 1967); Birdsall, *Versailles*; Robert E. Osgood, *Ideals and Self-Interest in America's Foreign Relations* (Chicago: University of Chicago Press, 1953); Daniel M. Smith, *The Great Departure: The United States and World War I, 1914-20* (New York: John Wiley & Sons, Inc., 1965).

8. Daniel M. Smith, "National Interest and American Intervention, 1917: An Historiographical Appraisal," *Journal of American History* 52 (June 1965): 5-24. *See also*, Richard W. Leopold, "The Problem of American Intervention, 1917: An Historical Retrospect," *World Politics* 2 (April 1950): 405-425; Richard L. Watson, Jr., "Woodrow Wilson and His Interpreters, 1947-1957," *Mississippi Valley Historical Review* 44 (September 1957): 207-236; Warren I. Cohen, *The American Revisionists: The Lessons of Intervention in World War I* (Chicago: University of Chicago Press, 1967); Victor John Porto, "Woodrow Wilson, the War, and the Interpretations; 1917-1970," *Social Studies* 63 (January 1972): 22-31; Thomas M. Hill and Wiliam H. Barclay, "Interests, Ideals and American Intervention in World War I: An Historiographical Appraisal," *International Review of History and Political Science* 14 (February 1977): 1-24.

9. *See*, for example, Ernest R. May, "Emergence to World Power" in John Higham, ed., *The Reconstruction of American History* (New York: Harper & Row, 1962); and David F. Trask, "Writings on American Foreign Relations: 1957 to the Present," in John Braeman, Robert H. Bremner, and David Brody, eds., *Twentieth-Century American Foreign Policy* (Columbus, Ohio: Ohio State University Press, 1971).

10. Thomas J. McCormick, "The State of American Diplomatic History" in Herbert J. Bass, ed., *The State of American History* (Chicago: Quadrangle Books, 1970).

11. N. Gordon Levin, Jr., *Woodrow Wilson and World Politics: America's Response to War and Revolution* (New York: Oxford University Press, 1968).

12. Arthur S. Link, ed., *The Papers of Woodrow Wilson* (Princeton: Princeton University Press, 1966-).

13. John Milton Cooper, Jr., "The British Response to the House-Grey Memorandum: New Evidence and New Questions," *Journal of American History* 59 (March 1973): 958-71. *See also* Cooper's *Walter Hines Page: The Southerner as American, 1855-1918* (Chapel Hill: University of North Carolina Press, 1977).

14. Volume 26, an index, will postdate volumes 27 and 28.

15. John M. Mulder, *Woodrow Wilson, The Years of Preparation* (Princeton: Princeton University Press, 1978).

16. Eugene P. Trani, "Woodrow Wilson, China, and the Missionaries, 1913-21," *Journal of Presbyterian History* 49 (Winter 1971): 328-51.

17. Sigmund Freud and William C. Bullitt, *Thomas Woodrow Wilson*.

18. Alexander L. George and Juliette L. George, *Woodrow Wilson and Colonel House: A Personality Study* (New York: John Day, 1956).

19. Robert C. Tucker, "The Georges' Wilson Reexamined: An Essay on Psychobiography," *American Political Science Review* 71 (June 1977): 606-618; Edwin A. Weinstein, James William Anderson, and Arthur S. Link, "Woodrow

Wilson's Personality: A Reappraisal," *Political Science Quarterly* 93 (Winter 1978-79): 585-598.

20. Edwin A. Weinstein, "Woodrow Wilson's Neurological Illness," *Journal of American History* 57 (September 1970): 324-351.

21. Victor S. Mamatey, *The United States and East Central Europe, 1914-1918: A Study in Wilsonian Diplomacy and Propaganda* (Princeton: Princeton University Press, 1957).

22. Pierre Renouvin, *Le Armistice de Rethondes, 11 Novembre 1918* (Paris: Editions Gallimard, 1968).

23. Fritz Fischer, *Griff nach der Weltmacht: die Kriegsziel-politik des Kaiserlichen Deutschland, 1914-1918* (Dusseldorf: Droste Verlag, 1961), available in English as *Germany's Aims in the First World War* (New York: W. W. Norton & Co., 1967); *Weltmacht oder Niedergang: Deutschland im ersten Weltkrieg* (Frankfurt: Europaische Verlagsanstalt, 1965), or *World Power or Decline: The Controversy Over Germany's Aims in the First World War*, trans. Lancelot L. Farrar, and Robert and Rita Kimber (New York: W. W. Norton & Co., 1974); *Krieg der illusionen: die deutsche Politik von 1911 bis 1914* (Dusseldorf: Droste Verlag, 1969), or *War of Illusions: German Policies from 1911 to 1914*, trans. Marian Jackson (New York: W. W. Norton & Co., 1975).

24. Harry Elmer Barnes, *Genesis of the World War: An Introduction to the Problem of War Guilt* (New York: Alfred A. Knopf, 1926).

25. Lancelot L. Farrar, *The Short War Illusion* (Santa Barbara, Calif.: ABC-Clio, 1973).

26. Klaus Schwabe, *Deutsche Revolution und Wilson-Frieden: Die Amerikanische und Deutsche Friedensstrategie Zwischen Ideologie und Machtpolitik 1918/19* (Dusseldorf: Droste Verlag, 1971). A Schwabe title now available in English is "Woodrow Wilson and Germany's Membership in the League of Nations, 1918-19," *Central European History* 8 (March 1975): 3-22.

27. J. Joseph Huthmacher and Warren I. Susman, eds., *Wilson's Diplomacy: An International Symposium* (Cambridge, Mass.: Schenkman Publishing Co., 1973).

28. Patrick Devlin, *Too Proud to Fight: Woodrow Wilson's Neutrality* (New York: Oxford University Press, 1974).

29. George W. Egerton, *Great Britain and the Creation of the League of Nations: Strategy, Politics, and International Organization, 1914-1919* (Chapel Hill: University of North Carolina Press, 1978); George W. Egerton, "The Lloyd George Government and the Creation of the League of Nations," *American Historical Review* 79 (April 1974): 419-44; Inga Floto, *Colonel House in Paris, A Study of American Foreign Policy at the Paris Peace Conference 1919* (Ärhus: Universitetsforlaget i Ärhus, 1973); Birdsall, *Versailles*.

30. Ray Stannard Baker, *Woodrow Wilson and World Settlement*, 3 vols. (Garden City, N.Y.: Doubleday & Co., 1923-27).

31. Charles Seymour, *The Intimate Papers of Colonel House*, 4 vols. (Boston: Houghton Mifflin Co., 1926-1928), and Alexander and Juliette George, *Wilson and House*.

32. Arthur Walworth, *America's Moment: 1918, American Diplomacy at the End of World War I* (New York: W. W. Norton & Co., 1977).

33. David F. Trask, "Woodrow Wilson and the Reconciliation of Force and

Diplomacy: 1917-1918," *Naval War College Review* 27 (January-February 1975): 23-31; and *The United States in the Supreme War Council* (Middletown, Conn.: Wesleyan University Press, 1961).

34. Ernest R. May, *The Ultimate Decision* (New York: George Braziller, 1960).

35. Samuel and Dorothy Rosenman, *Presidential Style* (New York: Harper & Row, 1976); R. Gordon Hoxie, *Command Decision and the Presidency: A Study in National Security Policy and Organization* (New York: Reader's Digest Press, 1977).

36. Daniel M. Smith, *Aftermath of War: Bainbridge Colby and Wilsonian Diplomacy, 1920-1921* (Philadelphia: American Philosophical Society, 1970).

37. Rachel West, *The Department of State on the Eve of the First World War* (Athens, Ga.: University of Georgia Press, 1978).

38. Levin, *Wilson and World Order*; Carl P. Parrini, *Heir to Empire: United States Economic Diplomacy, 1916-1923* (Pittsburgh: University of Pittsburgh Press, 1969).

39. Sidney Bell, *Righteous Conquest: Woodrow Wilson and the Evolution of the New Diplomacy* (Port Washington, N.Y.: Kennikat Press, 1972).

40. Robert D. Cuff, *The War Industries Board: Business-Government Relations during World War I* (Baltimore: Johns Hopkins Press, 1973).

41. Burton I. Kaufman, *Efficiency and Expansion: Foreign Trade Organization in the Wilson Administration, 1913-1921* (Westport, Conn.: Greenwood Press, 1974).

42. For a summary of works covering the relationship between domestic reform and foreign policy during the era, *see* Jerry Israel, *Progressivism and the Open Door: America and China, 1905-1921* (Pittsburgh: University of Pittsburgh Press, 1971).

43. Jeffrey J. Safford, *Wilsonian Maritime Diplomacy, 1913-21* (New Brunswick, N.J.: Rutgers University Press, 1978).

44. Joseph S. Tulchin, *The Aftermath of War: World War I and U.S. Policy Toward Latin America* (New York: New York University Press, 1971).

45. Burl Noggle, *Into the Twenties, The United States from Armistice to Normalcy* (Urbana: University of Illinois Press, 1974) and "The Twenties: Historiographical Frontier," *Journal of American History* 53 (September 1966): 299-314.

8 ______ Isolation, Expansion, and Peace: American Foreign Policy Between the Wars

ERNEST C. BOLT, JR.

In a 1957 survey of writing in American diplomatic history, Alexander DeConde mentioned fewer than fifteen books dealing with the 1920s and 1930s. In the same year, Robert H. Ferrell pointed to wide gaps in the study of interwar American diplomacy and expressed the hope that source materials for 1919-1939 would be "more fully exploited in the future."[1] By 1961 Wayne S. Cole continued to point out that the 1929-1938 period, in comparison with the 1939-1941 period, was being neglected by historians. He found a "striking dearth of specialized studies of the history of American foreign affairs in the New Deal era." In the same volume Richard Lowitt made similar comments concerning research on foreign affairs during the 1920s.[2] The comments of DeConde, Ferrell, Cole, and Lowitt, although now dated, provide a basis from which to judge recent progress in research on the interwar period. Diplomatic historians and others have produced a vast new literature, much of it revising previous scholarship, and have filled gaps in knowledge as new sources have become available. Comparing DeConde's 1957 pamphlet with his *American Diplomatic History in Transformation*, published in 1976, shows that after almost two decades research on American interwar diplomatic history has grown to include the publication of sixty-seven titles.[3]

Arnold A. Offner and Selig Adler have written the most useful broad surveys of the interwar period. Offner's *Origins of the Second World War*, written from a multinational approach, reviews American interwar diplomacy, especially in the context of "the almost shockingly bad" relations with Great Britain as well as relations with Germany and Japan. Avoiding any single school of thought, and without imposing a conspiracy thesis, Offner is no less critical of American interwar leadership than the older, Pearl Harbor revisionists, led by Charles Beard. His analysis is unlike that of the more recent neorevisionists or new left, who see twentieth-century American diplomacy as dominated by Open Door expansion and globalism. Offner acknowledges a "more skeptical or fatalistic, if not tragic, view of human and national behavior" on the part of himself and others writing from the multinational perspective in the 1970s. Adler's earlier survey, *Uncertain Giant*, less analytical than Offner's, is a synthesis based on the more optimistic scholarship produced before the mid-1960s. Adler's synthesis thus better depicts both the isolationist mood of America and interwar America's "uncertainty," marked by "constant gyrations of public opinion around foreign affairs."[4] Predating Adler, Allan Nevins had presented a chronicle of international affairs from 1933 to 1945. Nevins wrote from an internationalist-liberal viewpoint popular during and immediately after World War II, a viewpoint generally favorable to interwar presidents and critical of the more isolationist Congress and the American people.[5]

American historians in recent years have remained fascinated by the roots, ideology, and significance of isolationism during the interwar years. This continued interest stems from the complex and sometimes contradictory nature of the isolationist position, the increasing availability of source materials, and changing American attitudes toward internationalism. The earlier judgments of William Appleman Williams, Selig Adler, and Wayne S. Cole also encouraged further study. Adler's *The Isolationist Impulse* was broad in scope, a successful blend of diplomatic and intellectual history, and a harsh criticism of the isolationists. Williams challenged prevailing assumptions by questioning the existence of isolationism in the 1920s. Cole's *America First* was more sympathetic to the isolationists, and also encouraged further study.[6]

Historians have offered many explanations for the strength and varieties of isolationism, and are currently being encouraged by Justus Doenecke to investigate further the ethnic, agrarian, and geographic dimensions of isolationist groups and individuals.[7] Most scholars now believe that Samuel Lubell overemphasized ethnic roots of isolationism. Cole has emphasized agrarian roots in his biography of Senator Gerald P. Nye, and others have examined geographic roots of isolationism. Manfred Jonas more recently summarized and evaluated the various explanations of ethnic and regional aspects of isolationism, concluding that neither ethnic nor geographic factors were major roots of isolationism. Jonas avoids an explanation of isolationism based on socioeconomic or political factors and emphasizes instead the isolationists' common "faith in unilateralism and fear of war." Only. this, he argues, comes close to explaining the varieties of isolationism.[8]

A biographical approach, used by several historians, has provided significant contributions to the understanding of isolationism during the interwar period. Yet we shall not know more about the roots of isolationism until gaps are filled in our knowledge of House and Senate isolationists. There is a need, also, for broader studies of House isolationism similar to Thomas Nathan Guinsburg's unpublished study of the Senate isolationist bloc, which the author argues was neither large nor cohesive.[9] Furthermore, President Roosevelt's relationship to isolationism, frequently debated by historians in the past, remains of interest. Robert Divine set forth the belief, accepted increasingly in the 1960s, that Roosevelt was, at least for a time, an isolationist. The more conventional judgment by scholars, summarized by DeConde, was that Roosevelt—always the internationalist—"could not lead the country into commitments of collective security any faster than an isolationist people would permit." Writing in the 1970s, Robert Dallek viewed Roosevelt not as an occasional isolationist but rather as a cautious internationalist, thus suggesting a new challenge to Divine's view of a wavering Roosevelt.[10]

Two accounts of isolationists illustrate the currently more favorable "press" given them by historians. James T. Patterson's biography of Robert A. Taft presents him as a pragmatic, wise, political figure. Attempting to revise our understanding of five conservative critics of American "globalism," Ronald Radosh examines Taft, Charles A. Beard, Oswald Garrison Villard, John T. Flynn, and Lawrence Dennis. He argues that these courageous critics "lost the battles they waged" but deserve appreciation for their warnings against executive erosion of congressional powers and their opposition to military intervention abroad.[11] If, as Doenecke believes, there has been a more objective trend in the historiography of isolationism, continuing studies are desirable to examine the alternatives it offered.[12]

Historians are also studying other personalities, and their work illustrates some of the recently renewed debates among interwar specialists. Controversy no longer focuses so much on isolationism versus internationalism as on the complex social and ideological contexts in which diplomats work. These studies are characterized by increased professional maturity and tolerance and by intensive multiarchival research. To Doenecke, the resulting less-polemical historiography is in large part due to both the decline of violent partisanship over Pearl Harbor common in the 1940s and 1950s and the more recent new left revisionism. It took "military defeat in Vietnam and the possibility of a 'new isolationism'" to force most historians toward the renewed debates of the past two decades.[13] Much of this scholarship is critical of American policy and policymakers and yet less conspiratorial and polemical than the older Beardian revisionism.

Many standard biographies are thin on foreign affairs. The biography-and-foreign affairs approach in recent years has accordingly enlarged our knowledge of key diplomatists, both official and unofficial. Robert Maddox, for example, has filled the foreign-policy gap in earlier studies of Senator William E. Borah of Idaho. Examples of the biographical approach for the study of foreign affairs are E. David Cronon's *Josephus Daniels in Mexico*, Robert Dallek's definitive biography of William E. Dodd, and Waldo Heinrichs's outstanding book on Joseph C. Grew. Heinrichs evaluates Grew as diplomat, especially in Japan, examines American diplomacy from 1904 to 1945, and traces the development of the United States Foreign Service. Grew is seen as a cautious diplomat in searching for alternatives to war, and American relations with Japan are seen in less moralistic terms. Two other books which illustrate the diplomatic-biographic approach are Thomas C. Kennedy's study of Charles A. Beard and James K. Libbey's *Alexander Gumberg and Soviet-American Relations, 1917-1933*. Libbey concludes that diplomatic recognition of the Soviet Union in 1933 was anticlimactic because of the efforts of Gumberg, an unofficial American agent who worked with businessmen and others to normalize relations in the 1920s.[14]

Julius Pratt's two-volume biography of Secretary of State Cordell Hull and the course of American diplomacy from 1933 to 1945, the most significant work on an interwar diplomatist, is generally favorable to Hull. Written from the traditionalist-internationalist viewpoint, it is a model study and an outstanding contribution to the *American Secretaries of State and Their Diplomacy* series. Pratt was the first scholar to use the Hull papers, for the most part copies from Department of State records, and his study should still be used to correct and clarify Hull's own memoirs. Howard Jablon, writing a brief essay on Hull ten years later, is more critical of Hull and his advisors because of their excessive moralism in dealing with Japan. L. Ethan Ellis's narrative biography of Frank B. Kellogg remains the standard source. Ellis argues that Kellogg served effectively despite personal limitations. He is seen as less able and vigorous than Secretary Charles Evans Hughes, as overly dependent upon Hughes, Elihu Root, and others for advice and policymaking, and as handicapped by age and temperament. Robert Ferrell has written sympathetic studies of Kellogg and Henry L. Stimson, pointing out, in the case of Stimson, the declining world influence of American policy by 1933. Betty Glad's 1966 biography of Charles Evans Hughes remains the only recent book-length study that stresses diplomacy. Glad relies chiefly on the Hughes papers and uses psychological as well as more traditional analysis. Because of the author's failure to use key manuscript and State Department files, the book is not a definitive study of Hughes's diplomatic career.[15]

Richard Dean Burns and Edward M. Bennett effectively employ a biographical approach by presenting thirteen sketches of Chinese, Japanese, and American diplomats. Their edited volume, *Diplomats in Crisis*, demonstrates the effectiveness of a cooperative study of American diplomacy with Pacific nations since Asian languages frequently are barriers for diplomatic historians. American diplomatic historians remain interested in biographical subjects. There are seventy-one entries in the research list of the Society for Historians of American Foreign Relations. Ten of these concern interwar diplomatists. Listed studies, which are much needed and eagerly awaited, include those of ambassadors Clarence E. Gauss, Hugh Gibson, Stanley K. Hornbeck, Alanson B. Houghton, and George Messersmith as well as political isolationists Louis Ludlow and Hiram Johnson.[16]

Robert Dallek's 1979 *Franklin D. Roosevelt and American Foreign Policy* is a welcome addition to the unfinished biographies by Frank Freidel and Arthur M. Schlesinger, Jr. Dallek's portrait is both sympathetic and critical and is based on multiarchival research. Roosevelt's policies, according to Dallek, encouraged the very aggression in Spain which the president sought to prevent, but Dallek sympathetically explains his use of "small gestures" in 1937-1938 (such as in the Quarantine speech) as due to domestic and international constraints. In fact, one is repeatedly struck by Dallek's emphasis upon the ever-present limitations upon Roosevelt's freedom to achieve what he calls the president's "diplomacy of hope." Depicting Roosevelt in the context of his internationalism and his hopes to make the United States "a major force for world prosperity and peace," Dallek also presents countering influences—nationalism, intense isolationism, general public indifference to outside events, the depression, and external events. The internationalist Roosevelt appears only briefly, 1935-1938, as an isolationist, able only to muddle through and unable to serve the cause of peace.[17]

In a 1971 essay, Dallek had begun his praise of Roosevelt's prewar leadership, maintaining that his frequent caution and restraint were both necessary and politically correct. This view is in marked contrast to that of earlier writers, such as Robert A. Divine and James MacGregor Burns, who were critical of Roosevelt's vacillations on neutrality and statesmanship. Dallek especially challenges much of the earlier harshly critical scholarship which emphasized Roosevelt's shortcomings, errors of judgment, excessive timidity, and guarded dealings. This is done chiefly by emphasizing the constraints under which Roosevelt worked. Dallek praises Roosevelt most, however, in his coverage of the World War II period, presenting "the idealist as realist," and arguing that Roosevelt's wartime foreign-policy leadership was significant in both the survival of international democracy and the American acceptance of a major role in foreign affairs. Dallek's reappraisal seems not to have been influenced by the criticism of globalism so current in the 1970s. Instead, by reconstructing more fully than others the context in which Roosevelt worked, his book offers the most understanding and balanced assessment yet available. Arguing that the Roosevelt presidency was a mixture of realism and idealism, the Dallek study is part of the trend in Roosevelt scholarship, recently noted by Doenecke, which emphasizes "a mixture of presidential initiative and caution."[18]

Greater revision of previous scholarship has characterized recent studies of Republican presidents Warren G. Harding and Herbert Hoover. Part of the Harding revision begun a decade ago by Robert K. Murray, *The Presidency of Warren G. Harding* by Eugene P. Trani and David L. Wilson is a balanced treatment of foreign and domestic history. The authors present Harding as knowledgeable, although they see Secretary of State Hughes dominating formulation of foreign policy. They also emphasize Secretary of Commerce Hoover's influence over Harding. Revision of the assessment of Hoover as diplomatist began with Richard Hofstadter and Richard N. Current, and what Adler calls Hoover's "outright rehabilitation" was carried out by William Appleman Williams and others after 1954. Whether following Williams's new left disciples or simply because they matured in the cold war world of nuclear tensions or the nightmare of Vietnam, many scholars have joined in the Hoover reassessment.[19] Joan Hoff Wilson, for example, presents the best synthesis of Hoover in a brief biography, *Herbert Hoover: Forgotten Progressive*. In this and an earlier essay, Wilson expands on insights from Williams and Ellis Hawley to present Hoover as a pragmatic progressive and independent internationalist. Wilson maintains that Hoover's independent internationalism was progressive by contemporary standards, that it required greater use of experts and professionals in diplomacy, that it emphasized economic solutions, and that it utilized noncoercive methods in diplomacy. Hoover, according to Wilson, advocated limited rather than righteous internationalism, offering a middle course between isolationism and world domination under Wilsonian internationalism. In an important insight, Wilson further argues that historians have not really discovered a "new" Hoover but rather have come recently to better understand him. This is a result, she believes, of a "value change in domestic and foreign policies along the cooperative, decentralized, anti-interventionist lines Hoover suggested in the 1920's."[20]

Another recent contribution to Hoover scholarship relies too much on Hoover's memoirs and reflects too little the recent revisionist scholarship. After more than two decades of research in many manuscript collections and use of the Hoover presidential papers, Edgar Eugene Robinson and

Vaughn Davis Bornet produced a pro-Hoover biography which gives insufficient attention to foreign policy. Emphasizing Hoover's 1931 world leadership, Robinson and Bornet argue that nonrecognition left no doubt about United States repudiation of aggression or its rewards, and they defend Hoover against the implied link between nonrecognition and Pearl Harbor. More reliable in its use of Hoover papers and the published Hoover literature is the biography by David Burner, *Herbert Hoover: A Public Life*. Like Wilson, Burner sees Hoover's Quaker religion and values as significant. Although he does not accept Secretary Stimson's characterization of Hoover as a pacifist (since he did not exhibit the witness that Quakers make against all war), Burner does acknowledge that Hoover "was certainly the President closest to being a pacifist."[21] With only one major chapter on diplomacy in Burner's biography, Wilson remains the most perceptive, original, and thorough among Hoover's recent biographers who examine his foreign policy.

As with recent investigations of isolationism and certain foreign-policy biographies, studies of the peace movement, pacifism, and individual peace workers and their organizations have enlarged our knowledge of the interwar period. Students and scholars should turn to several pioneering brief studies before examining recent monographs. As early as 1952, Robert H. Ferrell ably related the peace advocates to the origins of the Kellogg-Briand Pact, and in doing so encouraged much of the subsequent study of the peace movement. He noted that there had been little effort by historians to study the peace movement. An essay five years later expressed his continuing interest in the subject and stimulated more studies that tested his conclusion that "the peace movement proved intellectually incapable of fitting its ideas to the facts of international life after 1918." Such an assessment of the peace movement, generally popular in the 1950s, maintained that the peace movement "went wrong in its ideas."[22] Although taken seriously by some historians, the peace movement seemed inept and ineffectual.

In more recent years, however, studies of the peace movement by Charles Chatfield, Ernest Bolt, and Charles De Benedetti have placed the disparate peace advocates and their efforts in a broader intellectual and political context. They have provided valuable correctives to the earlier interpretations of peace workers as naive, intellectually inept, irresponsible, and lacking in influence. Chatfield provides the definitive study of the role of pacifism in the peace movement, placing the interwar pacifists, their programs, and their organizations in an intellectual, social, and political setting. His book is both critical and sympathetic. For example, he points to both ill-conceived and well-thought-out peace activities. He establishes high scholarly standards for other historians interested in the peace movement, and his discussion of the Emergency Peace Campaign's lobbying for neutrality legislation especially expands our knowledge of the neutrality debates. Skillfully,

Chatfield examines individual pacifism, antiwar coalitions, and social justice efforts of the peace movement. Bolt ties the popular war-referendum peace measure to interwar diplomacy, politics, and peace activism, expanding on earlier secondary literature. He discusses interwar efforts to obtain the war-referendum measure, dealing in part with what Chatfield has called "peace movement lobbying" as well as placing the public interest in this peace plan in the context of modern American liberalism. Bolt especially examines this peace plan in relation to Secretary of State Hughes's European security-pact efforts of the early 1920s, antiwar profits legislation, neutrality legislation, and the Ludlow amendment. More recently DeBenedetti has traced the origins and early history of the larger peace movement, 1915-1929, examining the peaceseekers' coalition attempts, their interest in American membership in the International Court of Justice, their concern over American multinational business activities, and their interest in arbitration. De Benedetti argues that the Kellogg-Briand Pact was the "endpoint of the first phase of the modern peace movement," closing a period when peace activism helped keep the reform spirit alive. Yet, in the 1920s the peace activists discovered limits to their reform cause except when able to blend peace with interests of business and government.[23] In short, Chatfield, Bolt, and DeBenedetti have argued that although the ideas and actions of peace advocates in the interwar period often provided America with alternatives to war, American liberalism after World War I was too powerful an obstacle and too resistant to those ideas and alternatives.

It is true, as DeConde maintained, that "study of peace groups and dissenters marks one of the distinctive changes in diplomatic history."[24] An enlarged and more sympathetic knowledge of the peace movement has taught historians more about techniques of dissent and domestic sources of foreign policy. Nevertheless, as Chatfield has pointed out in his fine analytical study, final evaluation of the influence of the peace movement in the interwar period must await more study. He has called for a "comprehensive history of traditional internationalism with its varying points of view and organizations, and with its points of informal contact in government." Doenecke has pointed to other gaps in our knowledge of the peace movement and pacifism.[25]

Another interest of interwar diplomatic historians is their continued examination of other domestic sources of foreign policy, such as the role of public opinion in interwar diplomacy. Thomas A. Bailey's research during the two interwar decades pointed scholars toward such a study and the appearance of the Gallup polls after 1935 furnished useful data.[26] Bernard C. Cohen has argued that academic interest in the impact of public opinion on policymakers stems from "both a civic concern and a professional curiosity over the apparent intractability of foreign policy."[27] Interwar specialists among diplomatic historians today, like many of the interwar Americans they study, are especially drawn to opinion-policy studies because questions of war and peace, which affect us all but elude our grasp as citizens, dominated both the interwar period and recent decades. As Ernest R. May has suggested, interest in public opinion has also indicated a concern that official documents might reveal less than the full story of our diplomacy.[28] Finally, the attraction flows from disagreement among scholars over what Lawrence E. Gelfand calls fundamentals: the nature of mass opinion, the identity of opinion leaders and elites, and the variety of constituent sources when foreign-policy issues involving presidents and congressmen are being considered. Many would accept Gelfand's conclusion that "chaos" prevails among monographs discussing the relationship between public opinion and foreign policy.[29]

Nevertheless, several older studies remain models of precision and insights,[30] and new scholars, with greater detachment, wider scope, and—for some—the use of quantitative-analysis techniques, continue to make important contributions.[31] Among recent studies are three which deal with the Roosevelt years. David H. Culbert examines six radio commentators, their coverage of foreign news, and their interaction with officials in the government. Though Culbert is less than convincing in his conclusion that commentators played a primary role in combating isolationism, he makes clear that they helped create and articulate interventionist opinion. Culbert admits that these radio commentators—Boake Carter, H. V. Kaltenborn, Raymond Gram Swing, Elmer Davis, Fulton Lewis, Jr., and Edward R. Murrow—did not directly influence foreign policy. But he maintains they greatly aided Roosevelt, after May 1940, in creating "a popular majority favorable to full-scale intervention in Europe." Using recorded broadcasts as well as manuscript and printed sources, Culbert's book augurs well for greater examination of the impact of radio in understanding public opinion and foreign policy in the 1930s.[32] George Q. Flynn's study of Roman Catholic opinion in the Roosevelt years surveys views on neutrality legislation, the peace movement, the Spanish civil war, and the Myron Taylor mission. Flynn's work is a significant attempt to recount the impact of religion on policy, and is part of another little-worked area of public opinion studies.[33] In examining three case studies involving public opinion and policy decisions, 1937-1947, Michael Leigh looks at Roosevelt's Quarantine speech of 1937. He adds little, however, to the corrective provided earlier by Dorothy Borg who argued that the view of the speech as a trial balloon, deflated immediately as a result of adverse public opinion, was "historical legend." Borg emphasized the intent of Roosevelt and analyzed the drafting of the speech, concluding that he was groping for some means to maintain peace rather than challenging isolationist opinion directly. Leigh attempts to expand on Borg's analysis by examining the earliest opinion polls as well as surveys of press opinion and White House mail. He finds evidence of ambivalent public attitudes and mixed public reaction to the 1937 speech, concluding that "being divided, public opinion was more permissive and hence more susceptible than Roosevelt believed to a strong presidential lead between 1937 and 1939." But, according to Leigh, Roosevelt projected his own caution and hesitancy on the public, "magnifying congressional opposition" and deferring action "even when popular isolationism was crumbling." He argues that repeal of the arms embargo in 1939 gave the president his first experience as opinion maker in foreign affairs.[34] Overall, Leigh's book is important for emphasizing the ambiguous nature of opinion polls, 1939-1941, and for describing Roosevelt as an activist not restrained by a hostile public opinion (as often argued by the State Department and historians) but limited by the administration's own lack of alternatives and by its caution.[35]

In 1969 Wayne Cole challenged foreign affairs specialists to study further the influence of domestic interests, attitudes, and motivations on foreign policy.[36] Historians have responded with a minimum of social science and behavioral science jargon. Several studies reveal a marked interest in the impact of popular controls on foreign affairs, an interest no doubt increased for some writers by the Vietnam War. Alan Raucher examines the research departments of the Foreign Policy Association and the Institute of Pacific Relations, two interwar internationalist groups seeking to inform and educate Americans in foreign affairs. He maintains that these were the first foreign-affairs think tanks. These two groups, serving as "nonpartisan opinion forums for cosmopolitan elites," saw their roles as analytical and intellectual rather than merely fact-finding. Remaining impartial became more difficult after 1939, and Raucher concludes that the groups were never as influential as their critics charged or as their staffs hoped. Bolt's history of the war referendum movement, 1914-1941, traces the appeal of the ballot as a form of democratic control over foreign-policy decisions. Barry B. Hughes emphasizes the period since 1945, concluding that several models of opinion-policy relationships are relevant. Ralph B. Levering considers public participation in foreign-policy making since World War I. Emphasizing contemporary foreign-policy debates and decisions, he discusses the "attentive public" (the fifteen percent or less who maintain an interest in foreign affairs), the importance of college education within this elite, and the increased public interest and involvement in times of stress or change in foreign policy.[37]

In addition to isolationism, the peace movement, and public opinion, other themes important to interwar scholars in recent years include arms limitations, security, and economic foreign policy. Almost fifty years after the Washington Conference, Thomas H. Buckley examines British, Japanese, and American diplomatic negotiations. Buckley's neglect of domestic American politics is understandable in light of the earlier opinion-policy study by J. Chal Vinson. Roger Dingman builds on the Vinson approach and gives an excellent examination of British, Japanese, and American naval bureaucracies and the impact of domestic politics, 1914-1922, upon the Washington Conference.[38] In separate but related studies, Raymond G. O'Connor and Stephen E. Pelz have examined the 1930 London Naval Conference and the breakdown of naval disarmament negotiations which followed. Pelz emphasizes the Japanese in his treatment of the resulting naval race involving the United States, Great Britain, and Japan, but his placing of responsibility on the Japanese military questions James B. Crowley's earlier assignment of responsibility to the civilian Japanese cabinet.[39]

Two other books examine the United States Navy during part of the interwar period. Gerald E. Wheeler has solidly researched civil-military relations. He emphasizes public and congressional apathy as well as a need for stronger executive leadership in 1921-1931. James R. Leutze considers Anglo-American naval collaboration and traces the pre-1941 naval talks which led to exchanges of technical information but failed to produce the political commitments London wanted. Leutze attributes this largely to official uncertainties brought about by American public opinion and Roosevelt's caution.[40] Because of Wheeler's concentration on the 1920s and Leutze's emphasis on 1940 and 1941, neither book adequately examines naval security policy or Anglo-American relations for the 1930s. However there is an excellent and exhaustive bibliography for the interwar navy by Myron J. Smith, Jr., and Armin Rappaport's study of the Navy League provides useful information on the interwar period.[41]

Two standard topics dealing with international security have attracted little recent interest. Robert Ferrell's *Peace in Their Time* remains after twenty-five years the definitive study of the negotiations of the Kellogg-Briand Pact. Scholars will also profit from two thoughtful and cogent essays on the subject, one by Richard N. Current and one by David C. DeBoe. These essays have less to do with the origins than the consequences of the Kellogg-Briand Pact. Current has traced the subsequent invocation of the treaty as well as later efforts to provide machinery to strengthen the pact—consultation, nonrecognition, and discriminatory arms embargoes. Current, who had earlier studied Secretary Stimson's role in making American policy, concluded that Stimson's view of the pact's significance prevailed by the end of World War II. The pact reflected and reinforced the legalistic-moralistic diplomacy which George F. Kennan has deplored and helped prepare the American people for the idea of collective security. DeBoe has examined Stimson's efforts, using the Kellogg-Briand Pact in 1929-1936, to alter directions of American foreign policy, a fight which he describes as "a fascinating study in frustration." He briefly traces Stimson's efforts to use the pact "to bring the United States into collective action for the preservation of peace," efforts which failed because of opposition from Hoover, Congress, the State Department, and public opinion.[42].

Denna F. Fleming's treatment of American World Court policy remains the only published monograph on that topic. In the Senate's handling of the World Court issue, Fleming sees a continuity with the Senate's "catastrophic obstruction" of the League covenant in 1919 and 1920. His history of United States interactions with the League of Nations is also still useful; it makes a strong argument for American membership in the League. Although broader and more recent, Richard Van Alstyne's survey of America's search for collective security covers the interwar years too briefly. A comprehensive analysis of interwar collective security efforts is needed.[43] Essays in *Isolation and Security* by Vinson and Current consider the interwar search for peace. Vinson has examined American efforts "to maintain in the interwar years a foreign policy divorced from military force." Current has traced the history of the idea of collective security, pointing out that it was an uncommon phrase until about 1934. Fred Greene has briefly examined American policy from a military perspective. The only existing broader study is Roland N. Stromberg's *Collective Security and American Foreign Policy*, a survey of international politics from World War I to 1949 written from the realist viewpoint. Despite Stromberg's reasoned and critical approach this is not the comprehensive analysis needed for the interwar period. Collective security is described as an illusory concept and inadequate to prevent change by violent means, balance of power politics, or alliance systems.[44] Raymond G. O'Connor has provided insight into American interwar use (and nonuse) of force and diplomacy, though without furnishing a comprehensive study of interwar collective security efforts.[45]

In contrast to the lack of interest in topics related to interwar security, historians have been extremely interested in economic foreign policy. Following the lead of Williams, a number of American diplomatic historians have examined government-business relationships for the interwar period. Though his *Tragedy of American Diplomacy* is an overstatement and excessive in its economic determinism, Williams's denial of the existence of isolationism during the 1920s, first made in 1954, has challenged the most apologetic American historians to rethink their assumptions and reassess earlier conclusions.[46] Attempting to refute the view that the 1920s were isolationist, Williams depicts Republican leadership as aggressive and realistic, pursuing every opportunity to expand American economic power in the world.[47] The debate has continued. Robert Freeman Smith has expanded the Williams interpretation, while Robert J. Maddox offers the best critique of the "myth of isolationism." Charging that Williams misread those whom he revised and shaped the legend for demolition by creating a caricature definition of isolationism (seclusion), Maddox concluded the "legend" was "an exercise in semantic ingenuity."[48]

Among writers influenced by Williams, several are known for their analyses of interwar economic foreign policies. In *Economic Aspects of New Deal Diplomacy*, Lloyd C. Gardner corrected earlier studies which minimized economic objectives and motives in the Roosevelt years. Although dedicated to Williams, this book is, in Williams's opinion, "more interest-group-oriented" and therefore a "variation on a theme." Closer to Williams's own emphasis upon the Open Door *Weltanschauung* is Carl P. Parrini's *Heir to Empire*. Relying chiefly on Department of Commerce records, this student of Williams sees a continuity with Woodrow Wilson's position in the early Republican economic foreign policies. Parrini asserts American foreign economic policy was a continuum to 1929. Wilson and the Republicans who succeeded him created an economic community of interest managed by the United States. It was not a community in which the United States acted as world policeman; rather it sought to make Western Europe and Japan "associates with full rights."[49]

Joan Hoff Wilson offers the best analysis of early interwar economic diplomacy. With insight and balance, and leading a group of historians that she has called middle-of-the-road, Wilson's *American Business and Foreign Policy, 1920-1933* stresses ideological and economic considerations, diversity of business opinion, and a pragmatic independent internationalism as the American diplomatic method and policy of the 1920s. Hers is a broad account designed to stimulate further study as well as to reappraise (and praise) aspects of Hoover's foreign policies. It is a valuable supplement to the orthodox works on Republican foreign policy by Ferrell and Ellis but does not follow Williams exactly.[50]

Wilson has credited Williams with maintaining almost single-handedly in the 1950s "a critical approach to the impact of corporate liberalism on U.S. diplomacy." She has argued that the anticapitalist revisionists influenced directly by Williams are, like the probusiness entrepreneurial historians, "searching for an explanation of continuity, rather than change" in America's past. Wilson has also pointed out that "critics of the impact of corporate liberalism on the formulation of foreign policy are not found exclusively among advocates of left-of-center politics." She faulted the Williams-led radical revisionists as well as their opposites, the realists led by George Kennan and Hans J. Morgenthau, for not overcoming the "tempting, yet highly questionable assumption that foreign-policy formulation is a completely rational, calculated process." Wilson has challenged diplomatic historians to a judicious employment of "ideological value judgments and economic statistics" in studying diplomatic history but has warned against economic determinism. Her work on the 1920s is an examination of "the complex impact of ideological and economic motivation as it is affected by structural relationships and role playing within Government agencies and business organizations." Expanding on this historiographical background in her essay on "Economic Foreign Policy" in the *Encyclopedia of American Foreign Policy*, Wilson has, no doubt, correctly predicted that interpretations concerning economic foreign policy will remain tendentious.[51] Her eclectic approach offers scholars a reasonable alternative between the realists and the new left. DeBenedetti also maintains that the historiography of American foreign relations of the 1920s is well on the way toward "a new, more eclectic synthesis."[52]

Most recent studies of interwar economic diplomacy have been narrower than those by Gardner, Parrini, and Wilson, and with the exception of Wilson's examination of 1918-1933 Soviet-American relations they are less original in methodology.[53] Frederick C. Adams, following earlier revisionists, concludes that the Export-Import Bank was merely a new tool used by the New Deal in its pursuit of expanded markets, a goal common to the 1920s. Richard Kottman studies British-American-Canadian trade in the 1930s, finding the State Department most interested in the reciprocal trade agreements program. In a moderately revisionist study of the reciprocal trade agreements in Latin America, 1933-1945, Dick Steward found the reciprocity agreements failing to promote recovery, retarding industrialization, and causing Latin American resentment. Further evidence of the increased scholarly attention being given to American economic expansion into developing nations is Stanley E. Hilton's monograph on the 1930s trade rivalries of the United States and Europe in Brazil. Irvine Anderson has studied American-East Asian oil policy from the perspective of the Standard-Vacuum Oil Company, the largest American investment in eastern Asia before 1941.[54]

Several studies of the interwar economic dynamics in the 1920s are narrower and less analytical than those of Parrini or Wilson, but have made important contributions to our knowledge of economic diplomacy. Robert Freeman Smith's study of United States reactions to Mexican nationalism, 1916-1932, is part of the literature on causal analysis which emphasizes economic factors and closely reflects Williams's revisionism. Michael J. Hogan contributes to the revisionist emphasis on the expansionist nature of American diplomacy in his book on British-American economic cooperation, 1918-1928. Hogan investigates a decade of postwar loans, and developing cable, radio, and oil policies, emphasizing cooperation between Great Britain and the United States as a major foreign policy goal. In treating rubber policies, Hogan discovers more conflict in goals and a retreat from cooperation.[55] A study by Benjamin M. Weissman of Secretary of Commerce Hoover's American Relief Administration concludes that the ARA made a significant contribution to the stability of the Bolshevik regime in Soviet Russia. Wesley Phillips Newton examines American aviation diplomacy: efforts to dominate, at the expense of European rivals, the Latin American interwar market for aviation equipment. Other students of United States economic relations with Latin America include Robert Freeman Smith (Cuba), Lorenzo Meyer (Mexico), and Stephen J. Randall (Colombia). In a balanced book which typifies the emerging eclectic synthesis, Melvyn P. Leffler examines post-World War I economic issues with Europe—war debts, reparations, currencies and markets—carefully analyzing American government-business relationships and influences with relation to French security and German economic demands. Narrower in scope is Stephen Schuker's history of the London Economic Conference of 1924 and the subsequent adoption of the Dawes Plan.[56]

In many of these monographs attention has been focused as never before on American economic diplomacy. The result has been, in contrast to cold war revisionism, a more balanced, less polemical revisionism in the historiography of interwar American diplomacy. The new revisionists are also more diverse and restrained than the older ones in discussing World War II. Furthermore, their critique stresses diversity rather than monolithic economic influences, and they see bureaucratic differences more clearly than did earlier scholars.[57] The work being done on interwar economic foreign policy is among the most original and exciting in the field. Begun and first dominated by the new left, this work, as DeBenedetti notes, has recently moved toward an eclectic economic synthesis.[58] Historians await a larger synthesis of traditional, economic, and multinational approaches.

Robert Ferrell's hope for fuller use of source materials on American diplomacy, 1919-1939, has been realized in the past twenty-three years. There is no longer a dearth of 1920s and New Deal era studies. Instead, one is struck by the bulk of monographic literature available, in comparison to 1957. Much of it has revised our understanding of the interwar years. Scholars have continued to be fascinated by isolationism and have provided a more favorable assessment of isolationists and their alternatives to war. Study of diplomatists by a biography-and-foreign affairs approach has increased, and there has been continued interest in the nature of American colonialism, the Good Neighbor theme, and opinion-policy questions. We have seen an increased use of a multinational approach, with multiarchival research and the bicultural approach pioneered by Akira Iriye on American-East Asian relations setting new standards for diplomatic historians. Others, with this model, have combined biographical and cross-cultural approaches and collaborative methods. Another important trend is the increased interest in peace. Stimulated by Ferrell's realist assessment popular in the 1950s, scholars have examined interwar peace leaders, their causes, and their influence. Now peace advocates and their work are studied in broader intellectual, social, and political settings. A healthy debate has continued on these and other topics. Analysis has been characterized by greater balance and fewer polemics. In the area of economic foreign policies historians have stimulated the most productive debates. No longer dominated by the Williams-led "Wisconsin School," and no longer characterized by economic determinism or a conspiracy theory, a more moderate and diverse revisionism has resulted.

Still, there is much to be done. Needed are studies of House isolationism and foreign policy biographies of a number of interwar House and Senate isolationists. A definitive study of Charles Evans Hughes, stressing diplomacy, is essential. Anglo-American relations for the 1930s have been neglected as have naval security policies. There is a need for greater use of quantitative-analysis techniques to study opinion-policy questions. Except for a study of Roman Catholics, the impact of religious opinion upon foreign policies of the interwar era has been neglected. Finally, the bulk of monographic studies, and the related literature reflected therein, points to the need for a synthesis of interwar diplomacy based on traditional, economic, and multinational approaches. Today's research opportunities have resulted from a greater appreciation of the cultural, social, political, economic, and ideological context in which interwar diplomatists have worked.

Notes

1. Alexander DeConde, *New Interpretations in American Foreign Policy* (Washington: American Historical Association, 1957); Robert H. Ferrell, *American Diplomacy in the Great Depression: Hoover-Stimson Foreign Policy, 1929-1933* (New Haven: Yale University Press, 1957), p. 283.

2. Wayne S. Cole, "The United States in World Affairs, 1929-1941," and Richard Lowitt, "Prosperity Decade, 1917-1928," in William H. Cartwright and Richard L. Watson, Jr., eds., *Interpreting and Teaching American History* (Washington: National Council for the Social Studies, 1961). *See also* essays by Burle Noggle, "Configurations of the Twenties," who comments only briefly on foreign policy, and Robert Ferrell, "Foreign Policy, 1929-1941," in Cartwright and Watson, *The Reinterpretation of American History and Culture* (Washington: National Council for the Social Studies, 1973).

3. Alexander DeConde, *American Diplomatic History in Transformation* (Washington: American Historical Association, 1976). *See also* Robert Freeman Smith, "American Foreign Relations, 1920-1942," in Barton J. Bernstein, ed., *Towards a New Past: Dissenting Essays in American History* (New York: Random House, 1968); Selig Adler, *The Uncertain Giant, 1921-1941: American Foreign Policy Between the Wars* (New York: Macmillan Co., 1965); Wilton B. Fowler, ed., *American Diplomatic History Since 1890* (Northbrook, Ill.: AHM Publishing Corp., 1975); and Alexander DeConde, ed., *Encyclopedia of American Foreign Policy: Studies of the Principal Movements and Ideas*, 3 vols. (New York: Charles

Scribner's Sons, 1978). *See also* William Langer and Hamilton Fish Armstrong, eds., *Foreign Affairs Bibliography: A Selected and Annotated List of Books on International Relations, 1919-1932* (New York: Harper & Brothers, 1933) and a similar volume for 1932-1942, edited by Robert Gale Woolbert (New York: Harper & Brothers, 1945); Byron Dexter, ed., *The Foreign Affairs 50-Year Bibliography: New Evaluations of Significant Books on International Relations 1920-1970* (New York: R. W. Bowker Co., 1972).

Among the monographs on interwar diplomacy, the following contain the most useful historiographical or bibliographical essays: John E. Wiltz, *From Isolation to War, 1931-1941* (New York: Thomas Y. Crowell Co., 1968); L. Ethan Ellis, *Republican Foreign Policy, 1921-1933* (New Brunswick, N.J.: Rutgers University Press, 1968); Selig Adler, *The Isolationist Impulse: Its Twentieth Century Reaction* (New York: Abelard-Schuman, 1957); Robert H. Ferrell, *Frank B. Kellogg-Henry L. Stimson* (*The American Secretaries of State and Their Diplomacy*, 18 vols.) (New York: Cooper Square, 1963), vol. 11; Charles Chatfield, *For Peace and Justice: Pacifism in America, 1914-1941* (Knoxville: University of Tennessee Press, 1971); and Charles DeBenedetti, *Origins of the Modern American Peace Movement, 1915-1929* (Millwood, N.Y.: KTO Press, 1978).

The interwar scholar is deeply indebted to Justus D. Doenecke for several outstanding bibliographical guides: *The Literature of Isolationism: A Guide to Non-Interventionist Scholarship, 1930-1972* (Colorado Springs, Colo.: Ralph Myles, 1972); "Isolationists of the 1930's and 1940's: An Historiographical Essay," in R. W. Sellen and T. W. Bryson, eds., *American Diplomatic History: Issues and Methods* (Carrollton, Ga.: West Georgia College Studies in the Social Sciences, 1974); and "Beyond Polemics: An Historiographical Re-Appraisal of American Entry into World War II," *History Teacher* 12 (February 1979): 217-51.

Also useful are Blanche Wiesen Cook, *Bibliography on Peace Research in History* (Santa Barbara, Calif.: American Bibliographical Center, 1969), regrettably out of print, and William J. Stewart, ed., "The Era of Franklin D. Roosevelt: A Selected Bibliography of Periodical and Dissertation Literature, 1945-1966" (Hyde Park, N.Y.: Franklin D. Roosevelt Library, 1967). Less valuable for bibliography although suggestive of research opportunities is Milton O. Gustafson, ed., *The National Archives and Foreign Relations Research* (Athens, Ohio: Ohio University Press, 1974).

4. Offner, *The Origins of the Second World War: American Foreign Policy and World Politics, 1917-1941* (New York: Praeger, 1975), pp. ix-xiv and Adler, *Uncertain Giant*, p. vii.

5. Allan Nevins, *The United States in a Chaotic World: A Chronicle of International Affairs, 1918-1933* (New Haven: Yale University Press, 1950) and *The New Deal and World Affairs: A Chronicle of International Affairs, 1933-1945* (New Haven: Yale University Press, 1950). John E. Wiltz's *From Isolation to War,* W. Berger in William A. Williams, ed., *From Colony to Empire: Essays in the History of American Foreign Relations* (New York: John Wiley & Sons, 1972).

Other surveys of this period, still useful today, include Foster Rhea Dulles, *America's Rise to World Power, 1898-1954* (New York: Harper & Row, 1955); the best European survey, Jean-Baptiste Duroselle, *From Wilson to Roosevelt: Foreign Policy of the United States, 1913-1945* (Cambridge, Mass.: Harvard University

Press, 1963); and David A. Shannon, *Between the Wars: America, 1919-1941*, 2d ed. (Boston: Houghton Mifflin Co., 1979).

6. Adler, *The Isolationist Impulse*; William Appleman Williams, "The Legend of Isolationism in the 1920's," *Science and Society* 18 (Winter 1954): 1-20; Wayne S. Cole, *America First: The Battle Against Intervention, 1940-1941* (Madison: University of Wisconsin Press, 1953). *See also* D. C. Watt, "American 'Isolationism' in the 1920's: Is It a Useful Concept?" *Bulletin of the British Association for American Studies* 6 (1963): 3-19. Wayne Cole's forthcoming book on Franklin D. Roosevelt and the isolationists will be the result of thirty years' study and will, no doubt, reflect more than what he has already said in *America First*.

7. Justus Doenecke is currently providing scholars with the most thorough research on isolationism as well as a deeper assessment of isolationists. His bibliographic essays and research manual, all previously cited, and many of his articles have filled gaps in our knowledge. *See also* Wayne S. Cole, *Senator Gerald P. Nye and American Foreign Relations* (Minneapolis: University of Minnesota Press, 1962) and *Charles A. Lindbergh and the Battle Against American Intervention in World War II* (New York: Harcourt Brace Jovanovich, 1974); Manfred Jonas, *Isolationism in America, 1935-1941* (Ithaca: Cornell University Press, 1966); Robert J. Maddox, *William E. Borah and American Foreign Policy* (Baton Rouge: Louisiana State University Press, 1969); Walter Johnson, *The Battle Against Isolation* (Chicago: University of Chicago Press, 1944); William L. Langer and S. Everett Gleason, *The Challenge to Isolation: The World Crisis of 1937-1940 and American Foreign Policy* (New York: Harper & Brothers, 1952); Donald F. Drummond, *The Passing of American Neutrality, 1937-1941* (Ann Arbor: University of Michigan Press, 1955). Also helpful are the essays by Alexander DeConde, Robert Ferrell, Richard Current, and J. Chal Vinson in *Isolation and Security: Ideas and Interests in Twentieth-Century American Foreign Policy* (Durham: Duke University Press, 1957).

8. Samuel Lubell, *The Future of American Politics* (New York: Harper & Brothers, 1952); Doenecke, "Isolationists," pp. 13-14, 16-17; Cole, *Nye*, pp. 6-13, 227-235; Jonas, *Isolationism in America*, pp. 17-31.

9. Biographical studies include Cole's *Nye* and Maddox's study of Senator Borah. Doenecke lists others and names nine congressional isolationists still needing study (Doenecke, "Isolationists," pp. 15-16). *See also* Guinsburg, "Senatorial Isolationism in America, 1919-1941" (Ph.D. diss., Columbia University, 1969). Leroy N. Rieselbach, *The Roots of Isolationism: Congressional Voting and Presidential Leadership in Foreign Policy* (Indianapolis: Bobbs-Merrill Co., 1966) covers the 1939-1958 period.

10. Robert A. Divine, "Franklin D. Roosevelt and Collective Security, 1933," *Mississippi Valley Historical Review* 48 (June 1961): 42-59; Divine, *The Illusion of Neutrality* (Chicago: University of Chicago Press, 1962); Divine, *Roosevelt and World War II* (Baltimore: Johns Hopkins Press, 1969), esp. chap. 1; DeConde, *American Diplomatic History in Transformation*, p. 34; Robert Dallek, "Franklin D. Roosevelt as World Leader," *American Historical Review* 76 (December 1971): 1503-13; and Dallek, *Franklin D. Roosevelt and American Foreign Policy, 1932-1945* (New York: Oxford University Press, 1979).

11. James T. Patterson, *Mr. Republican: A Biography of Robert A. Taft* (Boston: Houghton Mifflin Co., 1972); Ronald Radosh, *Prophets on the Right: Profiles of Conservative Critics of American Globalism* (New York: Simon and Schuster, 1975).

12. Justus D. Doenecke, "Review Essay: The Isolationists and a Useable Past," *Peace and Change* 5 (Spring 1978): 67-73. *See also* his comments on isolationism in "Beyond Polemics," pp. 232-37.

13. Doenecke, "Beyond Polemics," pp. 220, 226. *See also* Divine, *Roosevelt and World War II*, for another summary of literature on FDR's foreign policy leadership.

14. Cole, *Nye*; Cole, *Lindbergh*; Maddox, *Borah*; E. David Cronon, *Josephus Daniels in Mexico* (Madison: University of Wisconsin Press, 1960); Robert Dallek, *Democrat and Diplomat: The Life of William E. Dodd* (New York: Oxford University Press, 1968); Waldo Heinrichs, Jr., *American Ambassador: Joseph C. Grew and the Development of the United States Diplomatic Tradition* (Boston: Little, Brown & Co., 1967); Thomas C. Kennedy, *Charles A. Beard and American Foreign Policy* (Gainesville: University Presses of Florida, 1975); James K. Libbey, *Alexander Gumberg and Soviet-American Relations, 1917-1933* (Lexington, Ky.: University of Kentucky Press, 1977). *See also* Russell D. Buhite, *Nelson T. Johnson and American Policy Toward China, 1925-1941* (East Lansing, Mich.: Michigan State University Press, 1968) and Beatrice Farnsworth, *William C. Bullitt and the Soviet Union* (Bloomington: Indiana University Press, 1967).

15. Julius W. Pratt, *Cordell Hull 1933-44*, 2 vols. (New York: Cooper Square, 1964); Howard Jablon, "Cordell Hull, His 'Associates,' and Relations with Japan, 1933-1936," *Mid-America* 56 (July 1974): 160-74; L. Ethan Ellis, *Frank B. Kellogg and American Foreign Relations, 1925-1929* (New Brunswick, N.J.: Rutgers University Press, 1961); Robert H. Ferrell, *Frank B. Kellogg-Henry L. Stimson*; Charles Cheney Hyde, *Charles Evans Hughes* (New York: Alfred A. Knopf, 1929); Betty Glad, *Charles Evans Hughes and the Illusions of Innocence: A Study in American Diplomacy* (Urbana: University of Illinois Press, 1966).

16. Richard Dean Burns and Edward M. Bennett, eds., *Diplomats in Crisis: United States-Chinese-Japanese Relations, 1919-1941* (Santa Barbara, Calif.: American Bibliographical Center-Clio Press, 1974); Warren F. Kimball, ed., "1976 Membership Roster and List of Current Research Projects," Published (n.d.) by the Society for Historians of American Foreign Relations (Newark, N.J.: Rutgers University 1976).

17. Dallek, *Roosevelt and American Foreign Policy*, pp. 58, 143, 168. *See also* Frank Freidel, *Franklin D. Roosevelt*, 4 vols. (Boston: Little, Brown & Co., 1952-1973); Arthur M. Schlesinger, Jr., *The Age of Roosevelt*, 3 vols. (Boston: Houghton Mifflin Co., 1957-1960).

18. Dallek, "Franklin Roosevelt as World Leader," pp. 1503-13; Dallek, *Roosevelt and American Foreign Policy*, pp. 529-38; Robert A. Divine, *The Illusion of Neutrality*; James MacGregor Burns, *Roosevelt: The Lion and the Fox* (New York: Harcourt, Brace & Co., 1956); Doenecke, "Beyond Polemics," pp. 230-32.

19. Eugene P. Trani and David L. Wilson, *The Presidency of Warren G. Harding* (Lawrence: Regents Press of Kansas, 1977); Selig Adler, "Hoover's Foreign Policy and the New Left," in Martin L. Fausold and George T. Mazuzan, eds., *The Hoover*

Presidency: A Reappraisal (Albany: State University of New York Press, 1974).

20. Joan Hoff Wilson, *Herbert Hoover: Forgotten Progressive* (Boston: Little, Brown & Co., 1975), pp. 168, 174, 189, 208, 269, whose bibliography is especially useful for recently published articles; Wilson, "A Reevaluation of Herbert Hoover's Foreign Policy," in Fausold and Mazuzan, eds., *The Hoover Presidency*, pp. 164-86.

21. Edgar Eugene Robinson and Vaughn Davis Bornet, *Herbert Hoover: President of the United States* (Stanford, Calif.: Hoover Institution Press, 1975); David Burner, *Herbert Hoover: A Public Life* (New York: Alfred A. Knopf, 1978). Other examples of interwar diplomatic biography are the brief biographical sketches of James T. Shotwell, Henry L. Stimson, Stanley K. Hornbeck, and Franklin D. Roosevelt in Frank Merli and Theodore A. Wilson, eds., *Makers of American Diplomacy: From Benjamin Franklin to Henry Kissinger* (New York: Charles Scribner's Sons, 1974).

22. Robert H. Ferrell, *Peace in Their Time: The Origins of the Kellogg-Briand Pact* (New Haven: Yale University Press, 1952); Ferrell, "The Peace Movement," in Alexander DeConde, ed., *Isolation and Security: Ideas and Interests in Twentieth-Century American Foreign Policy* (Durham: Duke University Press, 1957), p. 106. Among the outstanding early books on the American peace movement are the excellent survey by Merle Curti, *Peace or War: The American Struggle, 1636-1936* (New York: W. W. Norton & Co., 1936) and Denna F. Fleming's *The United States and World Organization, 1920-1933* (New York: Columbia University Press, 1938).

23. Charles Chatfield, *Peace and Justice*, and *Peace Movements in America* (New York: Schocken Books, 1973); Ernest C. Bolt, Jr., *Ballots before Bullets: The War Referendum Approach to Peace in America, 1914-1941* (Charlottesville: University Press of Virginia, 1977); Charles DeBenedetti, *Origins of the Modern American Peace Movement, 1915-1929* (Millwood, N.Y.: KTO Press, 1978). Among other recent peace studies, the following are useful for the interwar period: John K. Nelson, *The Peace Prophets: American Pacifist Thought, 1919-1941* (Chapel Hill: University of North Carolina Press, 1967), a brief narrative based largely on the religious-periodical press; Harold Josephson, *James T. Shotwell and the Rise of Internationalism in America* (Rutherford, N.J.: Fairleigh Dickinson University Press, 1975); and Michele Flynn Stenehjem, *An American First: John T. Flynn and the America First Committee* (New York: Arlington House, 1976) each dealing with efforts of the past to make foreign policy accountable to public opinion; Lawrence S. Wittner, *Rebels Against War: The American Peace Movement, 1941-1960* (New York: Columbia University Press, 1969) which contains a background chapter on the 1930s.

24. DeConde, *American Diplomatic History in Transformation*, p. 30.

25. Chatfield, *Peace and Justice*, p. 369; Doenecke, "Isolationists," p. 18; Doenecke, "Beyond Polemics," p. 233.

26. In addition to his popular textbook, Bailey's interest in studying the role of public opinion in American foreign policy is best shown in his *The Man in the Street: The Impact of American Public Opinion on Foreign Policy* (New York: Macmillan Co., 1948). *See also* Hadley Cantril, ed., *Public Opinion, 1935-1946* (Princeton: Princeton University Press, 1951).

27. Bernard C. Cohen, "The Relationship Between Public Opinion and Foreign Policy Maker," in Melvin Small, ed., *Public Opinion and Historians: Interdisciplinary Perspectives* (Detroit: Wayne State University Press, 1970), p. 65. In this and more recent books, Cohen is critical of the accuracy, validity, and relevance of certain assertions by Dexter Perkins, Denna F. Fleming, and Thomas A. Bailey, and attributes to them responsibility for a "folklore of our time" concerning public opinion and foreign policy of the interwar period. His skepticism is countered by Alfred H. Kelly, ibid., pp. 81-88. *See also* Cohen, *The Press and Foreign Policy* (Princeton: Princeton University Press, 1963).

28. Ernest R. May, "The Decline of Diplomatic History," in George Athan Billias and Gerald N. Grob, eds., *American History: Retrospect and Prospect* (New York: Free Press, 1971), p. 410.

29. Lawrence E. Gelfand, "American Foreign Policy and Public Opinion: Some Concerns for Scholars," *Reviews in American History* 5 (September 1977): 420-21.

30. Still useful are the path-breaking study of the Senate and the Washington Conference treaties by John Chalmers Vinson, *The Parchment Peace: The United States Senate and the Washington Conference, 1921-1922* (Athens: University of Georgia Press, 1955) and the penetrating essay on the State Department and public opinion by Dexter Perkins, "The Department of State and American Public Opinion," in Gordon A. Craig and Felix Gilbert, eds., *The Diplomats, 1919-1939* (Princeton: Princeton University Press, 1953). *See also* Ferrell, *Peace in Their Time*; Cole, *America First*; Adler, *Isolationist Impulse*.

31. Thomas Schoonover's brief report, "How Have State Department Officials (or Diplomatic Historians) Behaved? A View from the Computer," SHAFR *Newsletter* 7 (September 1976): 12-17, is an example of computer use to examine treaties before the Senate, 1776-1929. He concludes that in the 1920s, the busiest treaty-making decade before the Great Depression, the volume of Senate activity supports William Appleman Williams's "myth of isolation" thesis. Interwar specialists have yet to utilize effectively quantitative tools which could aid in examinations of the role and influence of public opinion.

32. David H. Culbert, *News for Everyman: Radio and Foreign Affairs in Thirties America* (Westport, Conn.: Greenwood Press, 1976).

33. George Q. Flynn, *Roosevelt and Romanism: Catholics and American Diplomacy, 1937-1945* (Westport, Conn.: Greenwood Press, 1976). Alfred O. Hero, Jr., concludes in his examination of trends in rank-and-file opinion of religious groups, 1937-1969, that ministers were more "internationalist" than their parishioners: Alfred O. Hero, Jr., *American Religious Groups View Foreign Policy: Trends in Rank-and-File Opinion, 1937-1969* (Durham: Duke University Press, 1973).

34. Michael Leigh, *Mobilizing Consent: Public Opinion and American Foreign Policy, 1937-1947* (Westport, Conn.: Greenwood Press, 1976). On the Quarantine speech, *see* Dorothy Borg, "Notes on Roosevelt's 'Quarantine' Speech," *Political Science Quarterly* 72 (September 1957): 405-33 and the dissenting view of John McVickar Haight, Jr., "Franklin Delano Roosevelt and a Naval Quarantine of Japan," *Pacific Historical Review* 40 (May 1971): 203-26.

35. Gelfand, "American Foreign Policy and Public Opinion," p. 422.

36. Wayne S. Cole, "Domestic Influences on United States Foreign Relations in the Twentieth Century," in Gustafson, ed., *National Archives and Foreign Relations Research*, pp. 111-20.

37. Alan Raucher, "The First Foreign Affairs Think Tanks," *American Quarterly* 30 (Fall 1978): 493-513; Bolt, *Ballots before Bullets*; Barry B. Hughes, *The Domestic Context of American Foreign Policy* (San Francisco: W. H. Freeman & Co., 1978); Ralph B. Levering, *The Public and American Foreign Policy, 1918-1978* (New York: William Morrow & Co., 1978).

38. Thomas H. Buckley, *The United States and the Washington Conference, 1921-1922* (Knoxville: University of Tennessee Press, 1970); Vinson, *Parchment Peace*; Roger Dingman, *Power in the Pacific: The Origins of Naval Arms Limitation, 1914-1922* (Chicago: University of Chicago Press, 1976). *See also* Wunsz King, *China at the Washington Conference: 1921-1922* (New York: St. John's University Press, 1963).

39. Raymond G. O'Connor, *Perilous Equilibrium: The United States and the London Naval Conference of 1930* (Lawrence: University Press of Kansas, 1962); Stephen Ernest Pelz, *Race to Pearl Harbor: The Failure of the Second London Naval Conference and the Onset of World War II* (Cambridge, Mass.: Harvard University Press, 1974); James B. Crowley, *Japan's Quest for Autonomy: National Security and Foreign Policy, 1930-1938* (Princeton: Princeton University Press, 1966). Three studies of the Geneva World Disarmament Conference, 1932-1933, are useful. *See* John Wheeler-Bennett, *Disarmament and Security Since Locarno, 1925-1931*, reprint ed. (New York: Howard Fertig, 1973) and *The Pipe Dream of Peace: The Story of the Collapse of Disarmament*, reprint ed. (New York: Howard Fertig, 1971); Hugh R. Wilson Jr., *Disarmament and the Cold War in the Thirties* (New York: Vantage Press, 1963).

40. Gerald E. Wheeler, *Prelude to Pearl Harbor: The United States Navy and the Far East, 1921-1931* (Columbia: University of Missouri Press, 1963); James R. Leutze, *Bargaining for Supremacy: Anglo-American Naval Collaboration, 1937-1941* (Chapel Hill: University of North Carolina Press, 1977).

41. Myron J. Smith, Jr., *The American Navy, 1918-1941: A Bibliography* (Metuchen, N.J.: Scarecrow Press, 1974); Armin Rappaport, *The Navy League of the United States* (Detroit: Wayne State University Press, 1962).

42. Richard N. Current, "Consequences of the Kellogg Pact," in George L. Anderson, ed., *Issues and Conflicts: Studies in Twentieth Century American Diplomacy* (Lawrence: University Press of Kansas, 1959); David C. DeBoe, "Secretary Stimson and the Kellogg-Briand Pact," in Margaret F. Morris and Sandra L. Myres, eds., *Essays on American Foreign Policy* (Austin: University of Texas Press, 1974). *See also* Current, *Secretary Stimson: A Study in Statecraft* (New Brunswick, N.J.: Rutgers University Press, 1954).

43. Denna F. Fleming, *The United States and the World Court* (Garden City, N.Y.: Doubleday, Doran & Co., 1945); Fleming, *The United States and World Organization, 1920-1933* (New York: Columbia University Press, 1938); Richard W. Van Alstyne, *American Crisis Diplomacy: The Quest for Collective Security, 1918-1952* (Stanford: Stanford University Press, 1952). Warren F. Kuehl's work on the United States and world organizations will undoubtedly update these older studies.

44. John Chalmers Vinson, "Military Force and American Policy, 1919-1939," and Richard N. Current, "The United States and 'Collective Security,'" in DeConde, ed., *Isolation and Security*, pp. 33-55 and 56-81. *See also* Fred Greene, "The Military View of American National Policy, 1904-1940," *American Historical Review* 66 (January 1961): 354-77 and Roland N. Stromberg, *Collective Security and American Foreign Policy: From the League of Nations to NATO* (New York: Frederick A. Praeger, 1963).

45. Raymond G. O'Connor, *Force and Diplomacy: Essays Military and Diplomatic* (Coral Gables, Fla.: University of Miami Press, 1972). *See also* his *Perilous Equilibrium*.

46. William Appleman Williams, *The Tragedy of American Diplomacy* (New York: Dell Publishing Co., 1972), esp. chap. 4. *See also* p. 15 and note 6 herein. Williams is the father of what Athan G. Theoharis has labelled "left revisionism," distinguished from World War I revisionism and the right revisionists who focus on World War II. Although Williams's chief influence has been upon the study and understanding of the cold war, his own broad scope and syntheses have also produced a general revisionism during the past two decades by a number of young scholars. This interpretation of American diplomacy emphasizes American omnipotence and omniscience, overseas expansionism, elite manipulation and determination of policy, and domestic economic influences on policy. *See* Theoharis, "Revisionism," in DeConde, ed., *Encyclopedia of American Foreign Policy* 3: 900-13. For Williams's own disclaimer concerning the profession's personalization of the "Open Door interpretation," *see* his essay, ibid., 2: 703-10.

47. See Adler, *Isolationist Impulse* and John D. Hicks, *Republican Ascendancy, 1921-1933* (New York: Harper & Brothers, 1960) for examples of the traditional view.

48. Smith, "American Foreign Relations, 1920-1942," pp. 232-62; Robert J. Maddox, "Another Look at the Legend of Isolationism in the 1920's," *Mid-America* 53 (January 1971): 35-43.

49. Lloyd C. Gardner, *Economic Aspects of New Deal Diplomacy* (Madison: University of Wisconsin Press, 1964); Carl P. Parrini, *Heir to Empire: United States Economic Diplomacy, 1916-1923* (Pittsburgh: University of Pittsburgh Press, 1969); Williams, "Open Door Interpretation," p. 710.

50. Joan Hoff Wilson, *American Business and Foreign Policy, 1920-1933* (Lexington: University of Kentucky Press, 1971). *See also* Joseph Brandes, *Herbert Hoover and Economic Diplomacy: Department of Commerce Policy: 1921-1928* (Pittsburgh: University of Pittsburgh Press, 1962) and the essays of Adler and Wilson in Fausold and Mazuzan, eds., *The Hoover Presidency: A Reappraisal.* For excellent handling of isolationism and independent internationalism, *see* Thomas G. Paterson's chapters on the interwar years in the textbook by Paterson, J. Garry Clifford and Kenneth J. Hagan, *American Foreign Policy: A History* (Lexington, Mass.: D. C. Heath & Co., 1977). Two essays by Robert F. Smith and Henry W. Berger in Williams, ed., *From Colony to Empire*, pp. 254-336, especially reflect the influence of Williams.

51. Wilson, *Ideology and Economics: U.S. Relations with the Soviet Union, 1918-1933* (Columbia, Mo.: University of Missouri Press, 1974), pp. 133-54. This concluding chapter describes the historiographical background for Wilson's effort,

in this book, to construct a "structural-functional synthesis" of opposing diplomatic schools, using as an example the "institutional and economic aspects of ideological opposition to recognition of the Soviet Union." *See* esp. pp. 136-41 and "Economic Foreign Policy," in DeConde, ed., *Encyclopedia of American Foreign Policy*, 1: 281-90.

52. De Benedetti, *Modern American Peace Movement*, p. 256.

53. *See* comment on *Ideology and Economics* in note 51.

54. Frederick C. Adams, *Economic Diplomacy: The Export-Import Bank and American Foreign Policy* (Columbia: University of Missouri Press, 1976); Richard N. Kottman, *Reciprocity and the North Atlantic Triangle, 1932-1938* (Ithaca: Cornell University Press, 1968); Dick Steward, *Trade and Hemisphere: The Good Neighbor Policy and Reciprocal Trade* (Columbia: University of Missouri Press, 1975); Stanley E. Hilton, *Brazil and the Great Powers, 1930-1939: The Politics of Trade Rivalry* (Austin: University of Texas Press, 1975); Irvine H. Anderson, Jr., *The Standard-Vacuum Oil Company and United States East Asian Policy, 1933-1941* (Princeton: Princeton University Press, 1975). *See also* the excellent review article by David M. Pletcher, "United States Relations with Latin America: Neighborliness and Exploitation," *American Historical Review* 82 (February 1977): 39-59, esp. p. 49.

55. Joseph Brandes, *Herbert Hoover and Economic Diplomacy: Department of Commerce Policy, 1921-1928* (Pittsburgh: University of Pittsburgh Press, 1962); Robert Freeman Smith, *The United States and Revolutionary Nationalism in Mexico, 1916-1932* (Chicago: University of Chicago Press, 1972); Michael J. Hogan, *Informal Entente: The Private Structure of Cooperation in Anglo-American Economic Diplomacy, 1918-1928* (Columbia, Mo.: University of Missouri Press, 1977). For a perceptive and critical review of Hogan, *see* Carl Parrini, "Anglo-American Corporatism and the Economic Diplomacy of Stabilization in the 1920's," *Reviews in American History* 6 (September 1978): 379-87.

56. Benjamin M. Weissman, *Herbert Hoover and Famine Relief to Soviet Russia, 1921-1923* (Stanford, Calif.: Hoover Institution Press, 1974); Wesley Phillips Newton, *The Perilous Sky: U.S. Aviation Diplomacy and Latin America, 1919-1931* (Coral Gables, Fla.: University of Miami Press, 1978); Robert Freeman Smith, *The United States and Cuba: Business and Diplomacy, 1917-1960* (New Haven: College and University Press, 1960); Lorenzo Meyer, *Mexico and the United States in the Oil Controversy, 1917-1942* (Austin: University of Texas Press, 1977); Stephen J. Randall, *The Diplomacy of Modernization: Colombian-American Relations, 1920-1940* (Toronto: University of Toronto Press, 1977); Melvyn P. Leffler, *The Elusive Quest: America's Pursuit of European Stability and French Security, 1919-1933* (Chapel Hill: University of North Carolina Press, 1978); Stephen A. Schuker, *The End of French Predominance in Europe: The Financial Crisis of 1924 and the Adoption of the Dawes Plan* (Chapel Hill: University of North Carolina Press, 1976). *See also* Melvyn P. Leffler, "Political Isolationism: Economic Expansionism or Diplomatic Realism? American Policy Toward Western Europe, 1921-1933," *Perspectives in American History* 8 (1974): 413-61.

57. Comments on the new revisionism are in Robert Freeman Smith, "American Foreign Relations, 1920-1942," pp. 232-62; and Richard E. Welch, Jr., "New Deal

Diplomacy and Its Revisionists,'' a review-essay of Leonard Liggio and James J. Martin, eds., *Watershed of Empire: Essays on New Deal Foreign Policy* (Colorado Springs, Colo.: Ralph Myles, 1976), in *Reviews in American History* 5 (September 1977): 410-17. Essays in *Watershed of Empire* which are especially significant and pertinent to this chapter are those of Lloyd Gardner (''New Deal Diplomacy: A View from the Seventies'') and Robert Freeman Smith (on the Good Neighbor Policy). *See also* Joan Hoff Wilson, ''Economic Foreign Policy,'' pp. 281-90.

58. DeBenedetti, *Modern American Peace Movement*, p. 256.

9 ______ Roads to War: United States Foreign Policy, 1931–1941

GERALD K. HAINES

American belligerency in World War II was the turning point which ended, for the duration of the war, the great debates over America's international political and economic role. As with United States entry into World War I, the second war generated a large amount of literature on the causes of America's participation and the motives of the statesmen who led the nation into war. Historians debated sharply not only the question of responsibility for Pearl Harbor but also the foreign policy of the Roosevelt administration in general.

That the interpretation of such an important historical event would change over time is an obvious truism. The introduction of new materials forces a reexamination of the past. New events alter our understanding of the past and the meaning of historical events changes as their long-range implications are discovered. Although historians are trained to avoid present-mindedness, they seldom escape completely from contemporary influences.

This examination of the historical interpretations and literature relating to United States entry into World War II focuses on these changes. Despite the enormous amount of available material, attempts to treat the period historically continue to be perplexing and difficult. What emerges from this study is confirmation of the adage that historical truth is, at best, never more than relative. In seeking to identify trends and interpretations in historical writing and to examine theories concerning United States involvement in the war, the pertinent historical literature has been organized according to four schools of analysis: traditionalist, revisionist, realist, and new left.[1] It also includes works of scholars that do not fit any particular school but that add to our understanding of the causes of United States involvement. This is especially true for the more recent literature, which tends to be eclectic in nature.

The traditionalist interpretation of United States involvement in World War II has long dominated the literature.[2] In this conventional view, World War II originated in the aggression of totalitarian have-not powers against the democratic, status quo powers and the Soviet Union. It is a straightforward cause-effect explanation. Writers of this school attribute the fundamental causes of American belligerency to developments in parts of the world beyond the control of American power. They do not find the explanation within the United States—except in so far as noninterventionist opposition inhibited administration actions that might have prevented the war from beginning or from reaching a critical stage. According to this view the United States had little choice but to enter the war. Japan, Germany, and Italy threatened not only American security but the American Way of Life. War with the Axis powers therefore, was inevitable, realistic, and right.[3]

In general, the traditionalist accounts were written in the early postwar period by a generation of scholars and journalists who had lived through the war. They assumed that United States participation in the war was just and necessary, and that Roosevelt was a far-sighted leader. Despite various attacks, this position still predominates in most college and high school textbooks.[4]

Charles A. Beard, Charles C. Tansill, and Harry Elmer Barnes led the revisionist attack on the diplomacy of the New Deal. In striking contrast to the traditionalist interpretation, these revisionists argued that American participation in the war had been avoidable and that war was brought about either through blundering or sinister intention by policies that deceived the American public and provoked Japan. They rejected the idea that the Axis powers constituted a serious threat to American security. The revisionists maintained that the Roosevelt administration had the power to choose for itself whether it would or would not enter the war. They found the explanation for American entry into the war primarily within the United States rather than in the action of other nations.[5] Unlike the revisionists after World War I, however, the revisionists of World War II were unable to convince the majority of the historical profession or the general public that United States participation in World War II was a mistake.

Inevitably, the cold war cast its shadow over the historiography of World War II. Writing in the 1950s, scholars such as Hans J. Morgenthau, George F. Kennan, Robert E. Osgood, Walter Lippmann, and Reinhold Niebuhr, generally known as realists, stressed that the United States needed a greater awareness of the use of power in foreign affairs in order to survive.[6] Believing that American foreign policy had been naive, overly idealistic, and moralistic, these realists bore down heavily on traditionalists and revisionists alike. They argued that from the Spanish American War to World War II, the United States largely failed to make a mature adjustment to its international environment because it failed, as a whole, to understand or act upon a realistic view of international relations. The year 1941, according to this theory, marked America's passing from the age of innocence. The transformation in the American outlook during the crisis years preceding Pearl Harbor consisted chiefly in the fact that the great majority of the American people came to understand that their everyday lives were seriously affected by what happened overseas. Agreeing with the traditionalists on one point, these scholars emphasized the primacy of external factors in United States foreign policy and argued that the domination of Europe or Asia by a hostile and aggressive power would be disastrous for America's security. Balance-of-power considerations and self-interest necessitated United States involvement in World War II. Seeking to explain the lessons of history for both the past and the present, these writers often drew analogies between the Roosevelt administration's efforts to stem the tide of aggression in the late 1930s and the necessity for the United States to do so in the postwar period. They believed, in short, that the failure to contain Nazi Germany and imperial Japan before Pearl Harbor demonstrated the need to be resolute with and contain the Soviet Union. The United States had to resist power with power in order that the national interests of American society might be preserved.[7]

The new left interpretation, which gained popularity in the late 1960s and early 1970s, challenged the realists' position by arguing that United States foreign policy had always been realistic and self-interested, not naive or moralistic. According to William Appleman Williams, United States entry into World War II was neither desirable nor avoidable, but rather inevitable. American foreign policy had as its central theme a belief that the security and well-being of the United States required a world order hospitable to the expansion of the American system of liberal capitalism. Given the assumption that American welfare depended upon a world marketplace system open to American economic power—the Open Door—the rise of German and Japanese militant alternatives led naturally to military action to preserve the American system.[8] Following Williams's lead other new left historians maintained that New Deal diplomacy found its primary explanation not in the threats and actions of other nations but in the internal needs of the American economy. Thus, when the New Deal failed to pull the nation out of the depression, American policymakers pursued the expansion of an informal Open-Door empire. In brief, the Roosevelt administration defined the security of the country in terms of overseas markets deemed necessary for domestic prosperity.[9]

It is clear from the existence of these four basic theories that historians often imposed their value systems upon an age that viewed events from quite different perspectives. In order to appreciate more fully the changing nature of interpretations relating to United States involvement in World War II, this essay will examine the historical debates over the isolationists and interventionists, the influence of business interests, the role of public opinion, and the portrayal of Franklin D. Roosevelt.

In general, both the traditionalists and the realists supported the internationalist position which stressed the interdependence of modern nations and the need for the United States to assume a full share of the responsibility for an international organization, collective security, and world peace. They were convinced that America could not escape the effects of foreign quarrels. They vilified the isolationists who opposed American "entanglement" in the political affairs of other nations. They pictured the isolationists as naive and backward-looking. To these writers, the United States was shaken out of its "isolationism" just in time to save the world for democracy. Robert Sherwood, for example, blamed the isolationists for preventing Roosevelt from taking stronger actions sooner against the Axis powers.[10] Selig Adler went so far as to declare that had the isolationists been successful they "might have destroyed the fighting will of those nations still resisting the Axis."[11]

The revisionists, many of whom were isolationists prior to Pearl Harbor, continued to adhere to a noninterventionist approach to American foreign policy. Led by Charles Beard and Harry Elmer Barnes they had advocated a policy of "continentalism" during the 1930s.[12] As William Borah put it, they continued to believe that "America existed in a world of rapacious nation-states whose behavior warranted the affection one might hold for a swarm of barracuda."[13] The revisionists thought the major European powers treacherous and found the idea of aligning the United States with those attempting to hold back the tides of world revolution repellent. For the revisionists, the isolationists were the true heirs of the American foreign-policy tradition of "peace, commerce, and honest friendship with all nations; entangling alliances with none."[14] The bitterness of the debate between the traditionalists and the revisionists in the late 1940s and 1950s obscured the positions of both the internationalists and the isolationists of the 1930s.[15]

Only gradually with the passage of time did a new image emerge of the two groups. Wayne S. Cole's detailed study of the isolationist America First Committee pioneered the new scholarship. Cole carefully examined the makeup and position of the America First Committee and concluded it was not simply fascist or ostrichlike in its behavior, as its critics had charged.[16] Building on Cole's work, Manfred Jonas found the isolationists had a positive view of the world and the role the United States should play in it. According to Jonas, the isolationists based their arguments on a thorough analysis of the nature of the crisis confronting Europe and Asia and they carefully considered America's internal problems. Although he disagreed with its premises, Jonas contended that "to regard isolationism as pure obstructionism was grossly misleading."[17]

With the Vietnam era and the emergence of the neo-Beardian new left, the reputation of the isolationists continued to undergo rehabilitation. Isolationist views commanded a new respect in an age which demanded a usable past. William A. Williams, for example, endorsed much of Beard's criticism of American foreign policy and his noninterventionism. Praising Beard's "cooperative commonwealth" approach, Williams saw a system of domestic regionalism as the only hope for American society.[18] Christopher Lasch, however, criticized Williams for putting too much emphasis on the ways in which foreign policy has been shaped by domestic requirements and above all by the ideology of the Open Door. For Lasch, Beard's continentalism or Williams's regionalism would in all likelihood have led to economic nationalism with fascist overtones. Lasch commented: "A Fortress America would have made imperial America look genial by comparison." Although an internationalist foreign policy proved hardly better in its long-range political effects, he argued, it constituted not an indictment of American policymakers for turning their backs on domestic problems but an indictment of capitalism itself.[19] Lasch's Marxist views notwithstanding, the Vietnam and Watergate era has provided a much more sympathetic treatment of isolationists like Herbert Hoover, Robert Taft, Charles Lindbergh, John T. Flynn, Charles Beard, and Oswald Garrison Villard.[20] As viewed from the 1970s these men's opinions appeared "sober, wise, and realistic." In a period of "wanton interventionism" Robert Taft's complaint that "no one has ever suggested before that a single nation should range over the world like a knight errant, protecting democracy" seemed most relevant.[21]

The interventionists have also come under renewed examination but with little change in the basic traditionalist interpretation that most interventionists were farsighted men who perceived the dangers to American society and attempted to awaken the country to the dangers from abroad. For example, Mark Chadwin presented a detailed study of the stoutly interventionist Century Group and the Fight for Freedom Committee. Although Chadwin felt the interventionists had, in fact, little direct influence on the decisions which led the United States into war, he argued they had a clearer vision of America's interests and future place in the world than most of their fellow countrymen. By counterbalancing the influence of the isolationists they helped free the Roosevelt administration to decide foreign-policy issues on their merits rather than because of internal pressure.[22]

Stephen I. Sniegoski delved beyond the rhetoric used by the interventionists for American involvement in the war and explored the deeper ideological commitments most of them held. He contended that the interventionists linked the war with the extension of democracy and that the "social purpose generated by the war would lead to a more cohesive society which would preserve and spread the democratic ideal."[23] Such recent studies suggest that the interventionists and the isolationists were not so different in their analysis of the world situation; they differed primarily in the programs they recommended.[24] The internationalists believed that war against the Axis powers was the only way to preserve and extend democracy, while the isolationists portrayed the United States as the world's last outpost against feudal and revolutionary ideologies. Only by a policy of noninvolvement, according to the isolationists, could this last bastion of republicanism be preserved. The older views that the isolationist consensus position was xenophobic and the interventionist consensus was militaristic now seem vastly oversimplified.[25]

American business, its foreign-policy attitudes and its relationship to government has also undergone reexamination, especially in the light of new left emphasis on economic policies and the interconnection of business and government. In a study of business attitudes and the approach of World War II, Roland N. Stromberg concluded in 1953: "In the drift toward unneutrality and then war, business played no independent role. . . . It was dragged along in the wake of circumstances, like everyone else." Basing his study almost exclusively on the business press and business publications, Stromberg asserted that the business position on foreign affairs was not significantly distinguishable from that of a majority of the general public and that "certainly the business community had not formulated a very clear notion of its foreign policy before 1939."[26]

John Masland in an even earlier article published in 1942 found that American policy toward Japan prior to war was not greatly influenced by economic considerations. Motivated by requirements of its own enterprises, American business was preoccupied with the desire to preserve the normal processes of business and to avoid considerations of what might be called moral issues in its conduct of trade with Japan.[27]

Gabriel Kolko, however, writing from a new left point of view, found business's role far more complex than Stromberg pictured it. For Kolko, there was a vast distinction between the business press and business behavior. Despite their public pronouncements, Kolko asserted, large American corporations pursued a course whose dominant objective was to satisfy their private interests. For example, Kolko depicted General Motors's explain how or why American business developed that antagonism to be made, irrespective of political circumstances.[28] In his brief study of American business participation in German industry, in which he depicted large American corporations as inextricably bound to German industry despite their public antagonism toward Germany, Kolko, however, failed to explain how or why American business developed that antagonistism to Germany in the late 1930s.

Mira Wilkins's and Peter Hoffer's more recent studies added support to the earlier works of Masland and Stromberg. Examining the role of American business in East Asia, Wilkins concluded that no single business policy or attitude toward the area dominated but rather a spectrum of views prevailed. Diversity was the key. Wilkins found that American businessmen shared only two sentiments. They desired to survive and make profits in an increasingly hostile environment; they did not want war and did not urge measures that might result in war. For Wilkins, businessmen's thoughts and actions were more influenced by than influential upon the course of events. Hoffer's study, "American Businessmen and the Japan Trade," further buttressed these claims. Hoffer, in addition, offered a clue to understanding the shift in American business attitudes in the late 1930s when he wrote that only when business profits and self-respect came to be increasingly dependent on the United States defense effort did businessmen's perceptions of Japan change.[29]

In a similar vein the entire concept of public opinion has also been reexamined. The early historical arguments between the traditionalists and revisionists centered around Franklin Roosevelt and his relationship and response to public opinion. Traditionalists long claimed that isolationist sentiments inhibited the president from taking stronger actions earlier against the aggressor nations and the revisionists protested that Roosevelt manipulated the public in order to get the United States involved in the conflict.[30]

Moving away from the often virulent arguments concerning Roosevelt and public opinion and putting public opinion in a more abstract setting, the realists argued that the idealistic concepts held by the American public and with which American policymakers had to deal contributed to an irrational American foreign policy. As they saw it, the basic problem was a public uneducated in international politics. In *American Diplomacy, 1900-1950* George Kennan argued, for example, that undue public influence over decisions had led to an irresponsible foreign policy. To avoid that problem Kennan advocated in the 1950s the establishment of an elite core of professionals to conduct foreign policy matters.[31]

While few would argue that public opinion in the United States affected the policymaking process of the Roosevelt administration, studies by Gabriel Almond, Melvin Small, and Bernard Cohen have forced a review of the elusive concept of public opinion. On the whole, until the appearance of these studies, a rather powerful impact on foreign affairs had been attributed to public opinion, to the press, and to political interest groups.[32] Contemporary scholarship, however, suggests that public opinion may be overrated. During most of the 1930s, with the possible exception of the Manchurian crisis, the influence of American foreign-policy public opinion was of limited consequence. Domestic crisis dominated the popular consciousness.

Looking at the decade of the 1930s as a whole, Waldo Heindrichs suggested that the salient fact of much of the period was that national energies and concerns were directed inward toward resolution of domestic problems. Generally, external affairs lacked the immediate urgency of internal ones and most governments lacked the necessary margin of political power to undertake initiatives abroad. For example, the battle over the neutrality act of 1937 was virtually ignored in the general excitement over the Supreme Court battle. Even as late as 1937, domestic issues clearly rated far more importance than foreign ones.[33]

According to Almond, policymakers also have an enormous capacity to shape the public opinion they are supposedly responsive to and to interpret the opinions they hear in ways that support their own views. Cohen suggested that Roosevelt and other policy leaders may not have realized how free they were to pursue the policies they wanted. Dismissing the argument that public opinion "sets the boundaries within which foreign policy operates" as unproven, Cohen stated that post-hoc criticisms and reactions may be far more important in influencing policymakers since these actions tend to shape the next decisions.[34]

Robert Dallek in his recent study, *Franklin D. Roosevelt and American Foreign Policy, 1932-1945*, took up this argument. He claimed that contrary to contemporary and subsequent complaints that Roosevelt's inaction and reluctance left him behind public opinion, a close assessment of national sentiment at the time suggested that he was abreast and possibly even a little ahead of public feeling. Wayne Cole found the same to be true with regard to the president's policies toward Asia. Roosevelt, according to Cole, had much more leeway in shaping policies toward that area than generally assumed.[35]

Public opinion research and analysis has, in part, led historians back to focusing on Franklin D. Roosevelt and his influence on American foreign policy. Traditionalists portrayed Roosevelt as demonstrating realistic and skillful democratic leadership in recognizing the menace of the Fascist states. His decisions prior to Pearl Harbor were wise and sound. Most traditionalists believed that Roosevelt took exactly the proper course during these years of crisis. He was a farseeing president who slowly educated a reluctant nation.[36]

The revisionists challenged this view. They pictured Roosevelt as deceitful, naive, and inept. Beard claimed that Roosevelt deceived the American people by professing a policy of isolation and neutrality while actually conspiring with Winston Churchill to lead the nation into war. Moreover, Roosevelt threatened the American constitutional system with his usurpation of congressional power "to conduct foreign affairs and initiate war at will." To Beard, Roosevelt was disingenuous if not actually dishonest.[37]

While admitting that Roosevelt may have engaged in a degree of duplicity, some pro-Roosevelt scholars have argued that it was necessary for Roosevelt to be deceitful "because the masses are notoriously shortsighted." Roosevelt's behavior was the result of the fear that his critics could have blocked his maneuvers if the issue had been clarified and discussed in an open forum.[38]

The realists have treated Roosevelt in an ambiguous fashion. While Osgood contended that Roosevelt had a grasp of world politics and a respect for the imperatives of power which Wilson never sought or attained, Kennan and most of the realists found Roosevelt's diplomacy insufficiently oriented to the realities of strategic power. Kennan chided Roosevelt for misjudging the ambitions of Stalinist Russia. To Kennan, Roosevelt clouded the national interests of the United States in a policy of ill-defined universalism.[39]

In the wake of Watergate and Vietnam, new left historians turned back to the Roosevelt era for the origins of the abuse of presidential powers and the heavy concentration of power in the executive branch. They pointed to Roosevelt's use of executive agreements to bypass Congress and his sanctioning of FBI violations of civil and political rights as setting precedents for the arbitrary use of executive power by later presidents. Returning to the issue of Roosevelt's deceitfulness, Williams asked the basic question: is the highest leader in a system of representative government justified in using devious means to impose his own best estimate of the situation on the country?[40]

Dallek took up this point in his classic eclectic work. While agreeing with the traditionalists that the isolationists failed to appreciate the threat posed by the Axis and that Roosevelt was perhaps justified in misleading the country in its own interest, Dallek accepted much of the revisionist and new left criticism of Roosevelt. The "Greer" incident, Dallek wrote, created a precedent for manipulating public opinion and made it easier for Lyndon Baines Johnson to practice the same kind of deviousness in a bad cause. According to Dallek, it is an irony of history that in his determination to save democracy from nazism Roosevelt contributed to the rise of some undemocratic practices in the United States.[41]

Although, in general, Roosevelt still enjoys a favorable reputation,[42] the historical debate has moved away from whether Roosevelt was an evil conspirator or a farsighted statesman to an examination of his ideological makeup and his long-range views on what role the United States should play in the world.

Robert Divine claimed that the president shared in the isolationist temper of his times. Divine contended that Roosevelt acted out of a deep and sincere belief when he declared that he hated war, and it was precisely this intense conviction that prevented him from embracing an interventionist foreign policy in the late 1930s. Roosevelt, according to Divine, never fully committed himself to American involvement prior to Pearl Harbor. His hesitancy was not just a catering to isolationist strength but a reflection of his own inner uncertainty.[43]

While generally favorable to Roosevelt, James MacGregor Burns also found him drifting from crisis to crisis. He saw Roosevelt as "a deeply divided man" reluctant to challenge the isolationists and inclined to sidestep great issues.[44] This reluctance diminished his stature as president. Stephen Pelz also saw Roosevelt making a series of haphazard decisions which increased the probability of an unwanted war. What intrigued Pelz was the question of how rational United States leaders were in making decisions. He denied that they carefully assessed their goals and resources or reviewed their options before making critical decisions.[45]

Dallek believes that too much has been made of Roosevelt's shortcomings and too little of the constraints under which he had to work in foreign affairs. For Dallek, a shifting array of pressures moved Roosevelt from one position to another; his own ideas, domestic considerations, and foreign events, either individually or in various combinations, determined Roosevelt's behavior in foreign affairs. What seemed most striking to Dallek in this period was not Roosevelt's arbitrariness in pushing the country toward war but rather his caution and restraint.[46]

Historians have not only reexamined Roosevelt and the American domestic scene in their quest to understand the origins and paths leading to American involvement in World War II, but have also taken a new look at United States relations with Germany and Japan. The traditional account and still the popular view regarding the origins of the war places the responsibility for the conflict squarely on Germany and Adolf Hitler.[47] Until the publication of A. J. P. Taylor's *The Origins of the Second World War* in 1961 there was a consensus among historians that Hitler outlined a blueprint for aggression which he carefully pursued. The image projected of Hitler was one of an irrational, evil madman who would, if he could, destroy the world. Germany, under Hitler and the Nazis, sought to rule not only Europe but the entire world, including the United States. This view, primarily based on the Nuremberg records, the court findings, and Hitler's own words as recorded in *Mein Kampf*, portrayed the Nazi system as the most aggressively wicked political order on human record.[48]

American historians, in general, accepted this traditional view. Only revisionists like Beard and Barnes challenged the consensus. Beard claimed that Germany represented no serious threat to the United States and Barnes argued that Russia and Germany would have fought to a stalemate if left alone. Barnes added that American entry into the European war led directly to "the rise and influence of Communism, military state capitalism, the police state, and the impending doom of civilization."[49] Beard's and Barnes's theses concerning Germany, however, were virtually ignored or dismissed as having no merit during the 1950s.[50]

Taylor vigorously challenged the traditional view. Taylor asserted that far from being a madman, Hitler was merely a traditional German statesman seeking to restore Germany to its "natural" position in Europe. The German leader had no systematic plan for aggression and world conquest, no blueprint for a German empire, and no American policy. Hitler intended to leave the United States alone. Taylor claimed the Germans were no more wicked in aspiring to dominate Europe than others were in resolving to stop them, and concluded: "Hitler simply leaned on the door hoping to gain entrance and the whole house fell in."[51] Taylor saw the accepted view of Hitler and Germany as a myth and the Nuremberg records as nothing more than a lawyer's brief. It was, to Taylor, accident and misconception on both sides that led to the war.

Taylor's interpretation sparked a renewed interest among historians over the origins of the war and Hitler's intentions toward America. Discarding the Nuremberg devil thesis or "guilty men" theory as inadequate, historians such as Christopher Thorne, Keith Eubank, and Laurence Lafore reconsidered German policies and assigned the western powers a share of the responsibility for the outbreak of the war. While Thorne admitted that Taylor helped correct the oversimplified traditionalist views regarding Hitler and Germany, he felt Taylor "came close to throwing out the baby with the bath water." According to Thorne, Hitler never abandoned his expansionist aims, and was, therefore, primarily responsible for the war.[52]

Essentially agreeing with Thorne on Germany's guilt, and writing from a realist perspective, scholars such as Arnold Offner, Donald Watt, and John McVickar Haight argued that the United States could have and should have taken a stiffer and more resolute attitude toward Hitler's earlier encroachments and provocations. Both Offner and Watt pictured United States policy toward Nazi Germany as appeasement oriented, and Haight indicted the Roosevelt administration for supporting Munich.[53]

German policy toward the United States was also probed more deeply for a better understanding of American involvement. Saul Friedlander and James V. Compton both confirmed Hans L. Trefousse's conclusion that Nazi Germany made a determined effort to avoid provoking the United States as imperial Germany had in World War I. Hitler kept a firm hand on his admirals by insisting that German U-boats refrain from attacks on American ships right up to his declaration of war.[54]

Neither Friedlander nor Compton, however, supported Beard's and Barnes's contention that Germany did not constitute a threat to the United States. While finding no direct evidence of Hitler's intentions regarding the Western Hemisphere, both suggested that Hitler expected an eventual contest with the United States. While Compton portrayed Hitler's vision as landbound and continental in outlook, he still claimed that Hitler imagined himself as eventual master of the world.[55] Friedlander suggested that Hitler began by late 1940 to see American intervention in the war as inevitable and that this conviction influenced his decision to turn against the Soviet Union. He planned to deal with the United States later.[56]

While Gerhard Weinberg agreed with Compton and Friedlander, he attempted to broaden the understanding of German-United States relations by examining Hitler's perceptions of America. Weinberg asserted that Hitler saw the United States with a mixture of ignorance, prejudice, and incomprehension. Hitler underestimated America's power potential despite reports from his professional diplomats to the contrary, and by the mid-1930s concluded that the United States was simply a "mongrel society" made up of inferior exiles from every country.[57]

New left historians have not as yet produced any major work on United States-European relations. Paul Varg, while not a new left historian, suggested in 1976 that while the policies adopted by the Roosevelt administration are perhaps best explained in terms of multiple causation, the conflict between the foreign economic policies pursued by Germany and the United States had received minimal attention. Varg implied that it was Hitler's foreign economic policy combined with German determination to achieve dominance in Europe for the purpose of subordinating the continental economy to German economic interests that set the stage for war. Varg suggested American security was at stake, primarily in the form of American economic interests overseas.[58]

Only recently has the new left begun to explore this topic in any detail. Writing in *Watershed of Empire*, Murray Rothbard, Robert Freeman Smith, and Lloyd Gardner all speculated that American policymakers' anger at successful German competition through bilateral agreements and the Roosevelt administration's desire to liquidate such competition were important factors in the drive toward war against Germany. To yield on the question of multilateralism, Gardner asserted, would give a worldwide impetus to trade patterns such as economic nationalism and bilateralism, which were antagonistic to the American Way of Life.[59]

Recent studies have attempted to put the German-American conflict in a broader context. Laurence Lafore, for example, offered an appraisal of the war as a product of the changed position of European nations in the world, of the importance of the chasm between their unchanged responsibilities and their diminished capacities, and, most importantly, of the absence of the nascent superpowers, Russia and the United States, from the decision-making process. The years 1930 to 1940 were clearly a period of transition from a European-centered structure to an American-Soviet bipolar structure.[60] For Geoffrey Barraclough the current obsession with Hitler has closed our minds to the broader dynamic of the historical process and made it impossible to "view the international crisis of the 1930s internationally." It was not simply a European crisis. The emphasis is now on the interconnection of events in Asia and in Europe.[61]

In many respects historical interpretations of United States-Japanese relations prior to Pearl Harbor have followed a similar pattern to those offered for German-American relations. However, there appears to be a greater willingness on the part of scholars to reassess and reassign the responsibilities for war in the Far East than in Europe. The Nazis and Hitler still appear too distasteful to deal with dispassionately. A greater tolerance toward Japanese actions, coupled with United States involvement in Vietnam, has led scholars to reexamine United States policies toward Asia.

The traditionalist view reflected the judgment of the International Military Tribunal of the Far East and wartime images in the United States. Applying the conspiracy thesis, the tribunal concluded that from 1928 to 1945 Japan, led by a military clique, had been engaged in a conspiracy designed to secure Japanese domination of all Asia and that part of the conspiracy had been to wage aggressive war against the allied powers.[62]

The tribunal's verdict that Japanese actions in the 1930s were part of a single long-planned conspiracy was echoed by American policymakers and traditional historians alike. All hostilities after Manchuria were treated as related actions. According to this view, the road from Manchuria led directly through Ethiopia to Spain to Munich to Warsaw and back across the Pacific to Pearl Harbor.[63]

The traditionalists saw Japanese aggression as threatening world order, the territorial integrity of China, and American interests in the Far East. As the situation in Europe worsened, the scale of Japanese aggression mounted. The United States was finally forced to aid China and institute sanctions against Japan in the hope that firmness would halt Japanese ambitions. In their negotiations with Tokyo, the Department of State and the president acted in good faith and made every effort to preserve the peace. These efforts failed because of Japanese obduracy and insistence on continuing the war in China and expanding into Southeast Asia. The sudden and unexpected attack on Pearl Harbor was, in the traditional interpretation, an unprovoked act of treachery by Japan.[64]

Following the majority findings of the joint congressional committee that investigated the attack, the traditionalists exonerated the president and his advisers and placed the blame for inadequate preparation and faulty intelligence on the Hawaiian commanders, Admiral Husband Kimmel and General Walter Short. Although the leaders knew that Japanese armed forces were underway and that war was imminent, the Japanese attack on Pearl Harbor was a genuine surprise to members of the Roosevelt administration who believed the attack would fall on the southwest Pacific, not Pearl Harbor.[65]

As could be expected, the revisionists took quite a different view of the Roosevelt administration's policies with regard to Japan. Concentrating on United States policies in the Far East, the revisionists portrayed the

Japanese attack on Pearl Harbor as being brought on by American restrictions that threatened Japanese security interests. According to this line of reasoning, Roosevelt invited the attack by a series of moves that left Japan little choice but war. To Charles Tansill, Roosevelt deliberately provoked the Japanese in order to enter the European conflict via the back door.

One of the most emotional debates between the traditionalists and revisionists was over the question of responsibility for the Pearl Harbor disaster. In its most extreme form, the revisionist position held that Roosevelt deliberately placed the fleet at Pearl Harbor as bait for the Japanese attack which he knew about through the decoded Japanese messages. A conspiracy of Roosevelt, Henry Stimson, Frank Knox, George Marshall, and Harold Stark withheld the vital information from the Hawaiian commanders.[66]

Roberta Wohlstetter's careful analysis of operation "Magic" and the activities of the American intelligence community in the final months before Pearl Harbor appears to have settled the controversy. Wohlstetter's study concluded that while "signals" of the Japanese intention could be read into these messages from hindsight, the signals were distorted by contradictory "background noises." The many clues to the attack were simply missed or overlooked, due to technical and human problems. It was not a dark conspiracy.[67]

As more and more of the records become available for investigation, historians continue to review and revise their assessment of American policy in the Far East. Reacting against idealistic interpretations and panacea solutions for international politics, the realists have criticized United States Far East policies and especially Herbert Hoover's secretary of state, Henry L. Stimson, for not recognizing the power realities in the Orient. Stimson's exaggerated concern for moral principle only gained the enmity of the Japanese. According to this view, his efforts were based on premises, many of which were unfounded in fact or history, and his policy outran the resources at his disposal. For the realists, it was foolish to risk war in the Pacific over principles when the United States' primary interests were in Europe.[68]

Paul Schroeder, writing from a *realpolitik* perspective, further argued that until July 1941 the United States consistently sought to attain two limited objectives in the Far East: splitting the Axis and stopping Japan's advance southward. The United States then abandoned these goals and concentrated on a third, the liberation of China. According to Schroeder, this last aim was not in line with American strategic interests and, most importantly, was completely incapable of being achieved by peaceful means and doubtful of attainment even by war. The unrelenting application of extreme economic pressure on Japan, instead of forcing the evacuation of China, rendered war inevitable.[69]

Schroeder did not use Japanese sources in his study, however. Two of the first American scholars to use the records of the Japanese were David Lu and Robert Butow. Lu, like Schroeder, focused on China, but asserted that the Japanese army, which pressed for an expansionist policy, totalitarian control, and a planned economy, was to blame for the conflict. Butow also put the blame squarely on the Japanese military for the war. Both Lu's and Butow's analyses were not far from the traditional interpretation in placing the responsibility for the war on the Japanese.[70]

The role of the Japanese military has long been the subject of extensive research. Utilizing sources in Great Britain, Japan, and the United States, Stephen E. Pelz lends support to those who maintained that the Japanese military establishment was primarily responsible for the Pacific war. Pelz argued that Japan's admirals wanted to build a great fleet and to expand into China and Southeast Asia, even at the risk of war with the United States. Consequently, they attacked the Washington and London naval treaties, initiated a huge naval race, and aided greatly in bringing about the war. According to Pelz, Japan's military leaders thought expansion was both necessary and possible.[71] Fujiwara Akira concurred with Pelz. He asserted that the key decisions leading to war in 1941 were made by middle-echelon officers in the Operations Section of the General Staff and the Military Affairs Bureau of the Army Ministry.[72]

Ohata Tokushiro and Hosoya Chihira, while tending to support the contention that middle-level officers in both the army and navy were influential in these plans, showed clearly that the Japanese government in 1940 was no simple dictatorship of the middle-level officers or even of the military as a whole. In tracing the development of the Anti-Comintern Pact, Ohata illustrated the incredible infighting, faulty communications, deliberate deception, and boundless ambiguity in the relationships between the Japanese foreign ministry, the navy, and the army over policy. Hosoya demonstrated that the navy was sincere in not wanting war with the United States and was at first opposed to the Tripartite Pact. The picture that emerges is that of a group of decision makers who were far from certain of their own convictions. In short, institutional and factional rivalries made the Japanese government far less centralized than believed.[73]

In contrast to those who blamed Japan solely for the war, Akira Iriye, James B. Crowley, and Waldo Heinrichs assigned a larger share of responsibility for war to the United States. Iriye maintained that when the United States closed the door to peaceful Japanese economic expansion it aided in the triumph of Japanese militarism. The militarists in Japan sought the same ends as diplomats had throughout the 1920s and early 1930s, albeit with aggressive military force. Crowley went even further in his analysis. He depicted the leaders of Japan as rational, honorable men who sought to achieve traditional limited goals of national security and economic prosperity in Asia. America's failure to recognize legitimate Japanese national aims hardened positions on both sides. While critical of Japan's actions in China, Crowley asserted that the United States oil embargo of July 1941 drove Japan into a war of desperation in which it had "almost no hope of victory." Waldo Heinrichs added that there was a good possibility for compromise with the Japanese if the Americans had accepted a limited amount of Japanese expansion in China.[74]

Writing from a somewhat different perspective, Dorothy Borg emphasized the aims of American Far East policy and the methods by which the United States government attempted to achieve these aims. Examining the period 1933-1938, Borg found the primary goal of the United States was not the championing of China but rather was reducing the threat of war between the United States and Japan. Borg's major thesis was that the Roosevelt administration refrained from any action which might have aroused Japan and followed a strategy of moral suasion. The administration did not depart from this basic pattern until the late 1930s when administration officials perceived Japan as being intimately connected with the Axis. Borg emphasized the degree of passivity which the United States maintained toward Japan during the mid-1930s.[75]

The new left presented yet another interpretation. Stressing Open Door imperialism and the entanglement of security and prosperity, Williams, Smith, and Gardner found United States actions were based on the effort to maintain the Open Door in the Far East. American policymakers, according to this view, insisted on an international framework in Asia which would allow the preservation of American free-market capitalistic principles.[76] Noam Chomsky, in a new left work, argued that Japan was merely following the traditional policies of Western powers. This policy challenged the position of the United States in Asia and the Roosevelt administration began to take stringent measures to protect American economic interests in China. Opposed at every turn by the Americans, Japan either had to abandon its claims and interests in Asia and become a part of the emerging American world system or strike out on its own.[77]

Current works present a much more complex picture of United States policies in the Far East than the new left's basic thesis. In his generally new left but balanced study of the Export-Import Bank, Frederick Adams saw no clear-cut set of attitudes and beliefs in the American approach to the Far East, but rather a blend of evangelicalism, political calculation, benevolent paternalism, and crude self-interest. All of these came to surround the American use of the term Open Door.[78] And while Irvine Anderson showed that the Standard-Vacuum Oil Company as well as other oil firms did, in fact, cooperate closely with the American government, they were often also at odds with administration policy.[79] Clearly, the economic connection projected by the new left is not as clear-cut as originally portrayed.

In *Pearl Harbor as History*, scholars from Japan and the United States set forth an eclectic approach to the understanding of the Pacific war. Using in-depth studies of governmental institutions as well as a comparative analysis, these scholars attempted to examine political, economic, and cultural factors in Japanese and American society that in the end made the war inescapable.

While they offered no consensus theory on the origins of the war, they were in general agreement that the causes of the conflict were far more numerous and difficult to discern than many of the earlier historians had recognized and that the blame for the war could not be attributed primarily to either the United States or Japan. They also agreed that the Japanese-American confrontation could not be understood except in a triangular relationship with Britain and that the Far Eastern configuration of power was part of a larger global problem.[80]

Pearl Harbor as History and the recent works of Christopher Thorne and Akira Iriye have set the tone for the study of United States-Japanese relations during the 1930s and 1940s. Thorne's thorough analysis in *The Limits of Foreign Policy* and *Allies of a Kind* went beyond traditional writings in diplomatic history for this area. Using multinational sources and focusing on the interplay of the major powers in the Far East with their attendant images of and approaches to that part of the world as well as internal domestic factors, Thorne set a high standard. He put the 1931-1933 crisis within the whole relationship between Washington, Paris, London, and Tokyo. He related it to the changing domestic political situation in each country, the focus and degree of intensity of public opinion, the efforts of pressure groups, and the domestic consequences of current international financial and economic crises. According to Thorne, the crisis of the 1930s occurred at a time when the power and influence of the West in the Far East were in decline. In both tangible and intangible ways, this decline had already set some of the major limits to what various Western states could achieve in the area. Both Britain and the United States wrongly perceived the situation by projecting on to others in Asia a self-flattering image based on themselves. The tendency was to assume that the Japanese would ultimately make their decisions on the basis of an idealized process of Western rationality. They perceived policy on an entirely occidental basis. Inherent in this philosophy was a pervasive racial arrogance—explicit or implicit—which relegated not only Japan but all Asia to second-class status. Thorne also clearly showed United States-British cooperation was never as close as depicted in the hands across-the-sea version projected during the war. There was a widespread and often patronizing British weariness with American idealism and moralizing over international relations which was matched in the opposite direction by a belief in the ineradicably corrupt and war-engendering nature of European politics.[81]

Applying a cultural systems approach and examining images and cross-cultural influences, Akira Iriye also found that crude and condescending images were not the exclusive property of the West. There were stereotyped images on both sides. From 1933 to 1939, Iriye wrote, Japan maintained a predominantly intransigent and sometimes menacing attitude toward the West. Iriye believed the Pacific war, in its larger setting, was a cultural-racial war. Japan at Pearl Harbor was only one aspect of a widespread Asian revolt, both spiritually and materially, racial in outline, and directed against an occidental world order—political, economic, and cultural. Japan's assault on the West, according to Iriye, needs to be seen in the context of her rapid development as a modern power—absorbing western technology and techniques in part to resist the West. Though defeated, Japan won important gains for the people of Asia.[82]

Both Thorne and Iriye stressed that the Far East crisis preceded, had links with, but did not cause the events which followed in Europe. Relations between the powers in the Far East, however, were not conducted in a vacuum. Their policies were affected by other considerations and by their policies toward other regions. Both also saw the fatalistic belief in the inevitability of war on each side as having a self-fulfilling prophesy. Both sides, said Iriye, had a tendency to oversimplify the other's motivation, overrationalize its decisions, and neglect its completely different frame of reference.[83] Despite themselves, it is clear that even Thorne and Iriye were influenced by post-1945 developments, notably the decline of western power in Asia, the successes of anticolonialism, and the modern concern and emphasis on racism.

Present-day scholarship regarding United States policies in the Far East is in basic agreement that the Roosevelt administration was cautious, passive, and appeasement-oriented. The ambiguities and ambivalences in the American approaches to Asia derived from the lack of clearly established policy priorities.[84] While some scholars have argued that the United States had absolutely no vital interests in the Far East, Chrisopher Thorne put it more aptly. The problem which has dogged the United States, he wrote, is that "America's interest in the Far East was based on the undeniable fact that it had become a Great Power, and thus it had to be interested in the region."[85]

The course pursued by Japan and the United States was not a simple one leading directly to Pearl Harbor. War was never inevitable; it did not come like two trains rocketing toward each other on a single track. Choices always existed and decisions were complex.

The preoccupation of many American historians with the question of American uniqueness has given way to a hypothesis suggested by Dorothy Borg that "the motives underlying our policy in Eastern Asia may more often than not have been the same as those which formed the basis of our policies toward the rest of the world." This policy, Borg suggests, derives from certain traditional concepts, stylistic peculiarities of decision-making bodies, and the country's position in the world. In short, historians are attempting to treat American policy in this period in a global, comparative context.[86]

In summary, on the American side, few periods have been as closely studied or as fully documented as the years immediately preceding World War II. Despite the vast amount of literature, new studies continue to add to our perceptions of the events prior to Pearl Harbor. Present studies illustrate the immense complexity of motives and events leading to that fateful day. Statesmen and nations were never as clear in their actions and policies as public proclamations would indicate and events were never fully explainable in terms of abstract forces alone. Often, as has been seen, the historian sees logic and clarity where there was none and offers explanations in terms of rationality when chance, muddle, and irrationality may have been dominant. For example, Nazi Germany and militarist Japan appeared at the time as both monolithic and revolutionary, yet their policies are seen now to have been makeshift, divided, and hesitant. The same holds true for the Roosevelt administration and its policies. The narrowness of approach with regard to time has also given way to a broader, long-range perception which enables scholars to examine larger themes emerging from the period. There is certainly something artificial about limiting the period under discussion to the decade of the 1930s. Events of the decade become more intelligible by pushing the historical investigation back before 1931 and moving beyond 1941. New studies stretch the time period back to World War I in order to more fully understand the developments of the 1930s while other works push the time sequence forward into the 1940s and stress not only the causes but also the consequences of the conflict.[87] Perhaps, as Geoffrey Barraclough has suggested, future historians will regard World War II as a negative phenomenon which provided the peoples of Africa and Asia with an opportunity to asert their own cultural and national identity. Perhaps, as Wayne Cole has indicated, future studies will focus on such problems as industrialization, the rise of the common man, and the development of secular ideologies.[88] Robert Divine's speculative essay on "Democratic Wars," Stephen Pelz's forthcoming examination of war and American decision makers, and Akira Iriye's stimulating essay on nations' extrasystemic behavior as a function of their intrasystemic behavior promise new avenues of research.[89] In the last analysis, however, the study of the period will, as it has been in the past, be shaped by time, circumstance, and the changing position of the United States in a turbulent world.

Notes

1. See Justus D. Doenecke's extensive historiographical review of the period, "Beyond Polemics: A Historiographical Re-Appraisal of American Entry into

World War II," *History Teacher* 12 (February 1979): 217-51. I use the term traditionalist to mean those scholars who have put forth the long-prevailing explanation for American entry into the war. Wayne Cole describes them as "internationalists," Robert Divine uses the term "orthodox historians," and Jerald Combs calls them "nationalists." *See* Wayne S. Cole's excellent, although somewhat dated, article, "American Entry into World War II: A Historiographical Appraisal," *Mississippi Valley Historical Review* 43 (March 1957): 595-619; Robert A. Divine, *Causes and Consequences of World War II* (Chicago: Quadrangle Books, 1969); Jerald A. Combs, *Nationalist, Realist, and Radical: Three Views of American Diplomacy* (New York: Harper & Row, 1972). I have also confined the study to English language sources which are, in general, readily available.

2. John E. Wiltz, *From Isolation to War, 1931-1941* (New York: Thomas Y. Crowell Co., 1968).

3. Forrest Davis and Ernest K. Lindley, *How War Came* (New York: Simon and Schuster, 1942); William L. Langer and S. Everett Gleason, *The Challenge to Isolation, 1937-1940* (New York: Harper & Row, 1952); Basil Rauch, *Roosevelt from Munich to Pearl Harbor: A Study in the Creation of a Foreign Policy* (New York: Creative Age, 1950); Robert E. Sherwood, *Roosevelt and Hopkins: An Intimate History* (New York: Harper & Brothers, 1948); Herbert Feis, *Road to Pearl Harbor* (Princeton: Princeton University Press, 1950); Donald F. Drummond, *American Neutrality, 1937-1941* (Ann Arbor: University of Michigan Press, 1955).

4. *See*, for example, Robert H. Ferrell, *American Diplomacy: A History*, 3d ed. (New York: W. W. Norton & Co., 1975); Thomas A. Bailey, *A Diplomatic History of the American People*, 9th ed. (New York: Prentice-Hall, 1974); Alexander DeConde, *A History of American Foreign Policy*, 2d ed. (New York: Charles Scribner's Sons, 1971). This is not to deny that some recent textbooks have incorporated much of the changing historiography. *See*, for example, Thomas G. Paterson, J. Garry Clifford, and Kenneth J. Hagan, *American Foreign Policy: A History* (Lexington, Mass.: D. C. Heath & Co., 1977) and William Appleman Williams, *Americans in a Changing World: A History of the United States in the Twentieth Century* (New York: Harper & Row, 1978). For a sampling of high school texts, *see* James Shenton, Judith Benson, and Robert Jakoubek, *These United States* (Boston: Houghton Mifflin Co., 1978); Lewis P. Todd and Merle Curti, *Rise of the American Nation*, 2d ed. (New York: Harcourt, Brace, & World, 1966); Leonard C. Wood, Ralph H. Gabriel, and Edward L. Biller, *America: Its Peoples and Values* (New York: Harcourt Brace Jovanovich, 1975); L. JoAnne Buggey et al., *America! America!* (Glenview, Ill.: Scott, Foresman, & Co., 1977).

5. Charles A. Beard, *American Foreign Policy in the Making, 1932-1940* (New Haven: Yale University Press, 1946) and *President Roosevelt and the Coming of War, 1941* (New Haven: Yale University Press, 1948); Charles C. Tansill, *Back Door to War: The Roosevelt Foreign Policy, 1933-1945* (Chicago: Regnery, 1952); Harry Elmer Barnes, ed., *Perpetual War for Perpetual Peace: A Critical Examination of the Foreign Policy of Franklin Delano Roosevelt and Its Aftermath* (Caldwell, Idaho: Caxton, 1953). Writing at approximately the same time as the traditionalists, the revisionists serve as a good example for Ernest May's essay on historians. Just because writers live through the same period doesn't necessarily mean they will see events in a similar fashion. Two men writing on the same topic in the same year can

state diametrically opposite views. *See* Ernest R. May, "Factors Influencing Historians' Attitudes: Tyler Dennett," in Dorothy Borg, ed., *Historians and American Far Eastern Policy* (New York: Columbia University Press, 1966), pp. 32-37.

6. Hans J. Morgenthau, *In Defense of the National Interest* (New York: Alfred A. Knopf, 1951); Robert E. Osgood, *Ideals and Self-Interest in America's Foreign Relations* (Chicago: University of Chicago Press, 1953); George F. Kennan, *American Diplomacy 1900-1950* (Chicago: University of Chicago Press, 1951); Reinhold Niebuhr, *Christian Realism and the Political Problem* (New York: Charles Scribner's Sons, 1955); Walter Lippmann, *America in the World Today* (Minneapolis: University of Minnesota Press, 1957).

7. Arthur Schlesinger carried this idea into the 1960s when he argued in *Crisis of Confidence* (New York: Houghton Mifflin Co., 1969) that "the United States has an active and vital interest in the destiny of every nation on the planet."

8. William Appleman Williams, *The Tragedy of American Diplomacy*, rev. ed. (New York: Dell Publishing Co., 1962).

9. Robert Freeman Smith, "American Foreign Relations, 1920-1942," in Barton J. Bernstein, ed., *Towards a New Past: Dissenting Essays in American History* (New York: Pantheon, 1968), pp. 232-62; Lloyd C. Gardner, *Economic Aspects of New Deal Diplomacy* (Madison: University of Wisconsin Press, 1964).

10. Sherwood, *Roosevelt and Hopkins*, pp. 124-39.

11. Selig Adler, *The Isolationist Impulse: Its Twentieth Century Reaction* (New York: Abelard-Schuman, 1957). *See also* Samuel Eliot Morison, *The Rising Sun in the Pacific: History of the United States Naval Operations in World War II* (Boston: Little, Brown & Co., 1948), vol. 3; Walter Millis, *This Is Pearl, The United States and Japan 1941* (New York: William Morrow and Co., 1947); Robert Ferrell, "The Peace Movement 1918-1941," in Alexander DeConde, ed., *Isolation and Security* (Durham: Duke University Press, 1957).

12. Beard, *The Open Door at Home: A Trial Philosophy of National Interest* (New York: Macmillan Co., 1934) and *A Foreign Policy for America* (New York: Alfred A. Knopf, 1940). *See also* Barnes, *Perpetual War for Perpetual Peace.*

13. Borah's statement is printed in Robert Maddox, *William E. Borah and American Foreign Policy* (Baton Rouge: Louisiana State University Press, 1969).

14. Barnes, *Perpetual War for Perpetual Peace.*

15. Cole, "American Entry into World War II," pp. 595-617; Doenecke, "Beyond Polemics," pp. 217-51.

16. Wayne S. Cole, *America First: The Battle Against Intervention, 1940-1941* (Madison: University of Wisconsin Press, 1953) and Justus D. Doenecke, "Isolationists of the 1930's and 1940's: An Historiographical Essay," in R. W. Sellen and T. W. Bryson, eds., *American Diplomatic History: Issues and Methods* (Carrolton, Ga.: West Georgia College Studies in the Social Sciences, 1974), pp. 5-39.

17. Manfred Jonas, *Isolationism in America, 1935-1941* (Ithaca: Cornell University Press, 1966).

18. Williams, *Tragedy of American Diplomacy.*

19. Christopher Lasch, "William Appleman Williams on American History," *Marxist Perspectives* (Fall 1978): 118-26. *See also* Eugene Genovese's penetrating article, "Charles A. Beard and the Economic Interpretation of History," in Marvin C.

Swanson, ed., *Charles A. Beard: An Observance of the Centennial of His Birth* (Greencastle, Ind.: DePauw University Press, 1976).

20. James T. Patterson, *Mr. Republican: A Biography of Robert A. Taft* (Boston: Houghton Mifflin Co., 1972); Wayne S. Cole, *Charles A. Lindbergh and the Battle Against American Intervention in World War II* (New York: Harcourt Brace Jovanovich, 1974); Michele Flynn Stenehjem, *An American First: John T. Flynn and the America First Committee* (New Rochelle, N.Y.: Arlington House, 1976); and Ronald Radosh, *Prophets on the Right: Profiles of Conservative Critics of American Globalism* (New York: Simon and Schuster, 1975).

21. Patterson, *Mr. Republican*. As a comparison, James MacGregor Burns in *Roosevelt: The Soldier of Freedom* (New York: Harcourt Brace Jovanovich, 1970) dismissed Taft as a "rising young fogy." Arthur Schlesinger pictured Taft as an isolationist who failed to understand the role of power in the modern world. *See* Schlesinger, "The New Isolationism," *Atlantic* 189 (May 1952): 34-38.

22. Mark L. Chadwin, *The Hawks of World War II* (Chapel Hill: University of North Carolina Press, 1968). *See also* Donald J. Friedman, *The Road from Isolation: The Campaign of the American Committee for Non-Participation in Japanese Aggression, 1938-1941* (Cambridge, Mass.: East Asian Research Center, 1968) and William M. Tuttle, Jr., "Aid to the Allies Short of War versus American Intervention: A Re-Appraisal of William Allen White's Leadership," *Journal of American History* 56 (March 1970): 841-58.

23. Stephen I. Sniegoski, "Unified Democracy: An Aspect of American World War II Interventionist Thought, 1939-1941," *Maryland Historian* 9 (Spring 1978): 33-48.

24. Sniegoski, "Unified Democracy"; and Justus D. Doenecke, "Power, Markets, and Ideology: the Isolationists Response to Roosevelt Policy, 1940-1941," in Leonard Liggio and James J. Martin, eds., *Watershed of Empire: Essays on New Deal Foreign Policy* (Colorado Springs: Ralph Myles, 1976).

25. Robert Freeman Smith, "The Good Neighbor Policy: The Liberal Paradox in U.S. Relations with Latin America," in Liggio and Martin, eds., *Watershed of Empire*, pp. 65-94. Pacifists and pacifist organizations have undergone a similar reexamination to that of the isolationists. Charles Chatfield's *For Peace and Justice: Pacificism in America, 1914-1941* (Knoxville, Tenn.: University of Tennessee Press, 1971) and Lawrence S. Wittner's *Rebels Against War: The American Peace Movement, 1941-1960* (New York: Columbia University Press, 1967) portray the movement as being far more realistic in its views than critics gave it credit. *See also* Doenecke, "Isolationists of the 1930's and 1940's," pp. 5-39 and Ernest C. Bolt, Jr., *Ballots before Bullets: The War Referendum Approach to Peace in America 1914-1941* (Charlottesville, Va.: University Press of Virginia, 1977).

26. Roland Stromberg, "American Business and the Approach to War, 1935-1941," *Journal of Economic History* 13 (1953): 58-78.

27. John Masland, "Commercial Influences upon American Far Eastern Policy 1937-1941," *Pacific Historical Review* 11 (September 1942): 281-300.

28. Gabriel Kolko, "American Business and Germany, 1930-1941," *Western Political Quarterly* 15 (December 1962): 713-28. One has only to view the ads of the major oil companies today to understand Kolko's argument.

29. Mira Wilkins, "The Role of U.S. Business," in Dorothy Borg and Shumpei

Okamoto, eds., *Pearl Harbor as History, Japanese American Relations 1931-1941* (New York: Columbia University Press, 1973); Peter Hoffer, "American Businessmen and the Japan Trade, 1931-1941: A Case Study of Attitude Formation." *Pacific* don G. Van Duesen and Richard Wade, eds., *Foreign Policy and the American Spirit* *America Fought Germany in World War II* (St. Louis: Forum Press, 1973).

30. Langer and Gleason, *Challenge to Isolation*, and Beard, *Roosevelt and the Coming of War*.

31. Kennan, *American Diplomacy*, and Stephen E. Pelz, *Race to Pearl Harbor, The Failure of the Second London Naval Conference and the Onset of World War II* (Cambridge, Mass.: Harvard University Press, 1974).

32. Sherwood, *Roosevelt and Hopkins*; Langer and Gleason, *Challenge to Isolation*; Julius Pratt, *Cordell Hull, 1933-1944* (New York: Cooper Square, 1964); Glyndon G. Van Duesin and Richard Wade, eds., *Foreign Policy and the American Spirit* (Ithaca: Cornell University Press, 1957).

33. Waldo Heinrichs, "1931-1937," in Ernest R. May and James C. Thomson, Jr., eds., *American East Asian Relations: A Survey* (Cambridge, Mass.: Harvard University Press, 1972).

34. Gabriel Almond, *The American People and Foreign Policy* (New York: Frederick A. Praeger, 1960); Melvin Small, ed., *Public Opinion and Historians: Interdisciplinary Perspectives* (Detroit: Wayne State University Press, 1970); Bernard Cohen, *The Public Impact on Foreign Policy* (Boston: Little, Brown & Co., 1973); Michael Leigh, *Mobilizing Consent: Public Opinion and American Foreign Policy, 1937-1947* (Westport, Conn.: Greenwood Press, 1976).

35. Robert Dallek, *Franklin D. Roosevelt and American Foreign Policy, 1932-1945* (New York: Oxford University Press, 1979) and Cole, "The Role of the U.S. Congress and Political Parties," in Borg and Okamoto, *Pearl Harbor as History*. Cole argued that Roosevelt had far more room to maneuver because public opinion approved a hard line approach toward Japan.

36. Davis and Lindley, *How War Came*, and Langer and Gleason, *Challenge to Isolation*. While generally favorable to Roosevelt, Langer and Gleason believed he was unduly sensitive to isolationist criticism.

37. Beard, *Roosevelt and the Coming of War*.

38. Thomas A. Bailey, *The Man on the Street: The Impact of American Public Opinion on Foreign Policy* (New York: Macmillan Co., 1948); Selig Adler, *The Uncertain Giant: 1921-1941: American Foreign Policy Between the Wars* (New York: Macmillan Co., 1965); Samuel Eliot Morison, "Did Roosevelt Start the War? History Through a Beard," *Atlantic* 182 (August 1948): 91-97.

39. Kennan, *American Diplomacy*, and Osgood, *Ideals and Self-Interest*.

40. Williams, *Americans in a Changing World* and *From Colony to Empire* (New York: John Wiley & Sons, 1972).

41. Dallek, *Franklin D. Roosevelt*.

42. Gloria J. Barron, *Leadership in Crisis: FDR and the Path to Intervention* (Port Washington, N.Y.: Kennikat Press, 1973). *See also* Joseph Lash's uncritical account which eulogizes Roosevelt, *Roosevelt and Churchill, 1939-1941: The Partnership That Saved the West* (New York: W. W. Norton & Co., 1976).

43. Divine, *Roosevelt and World War II* (Baltimore: Johns Hopkins Press, 1969). Divine plays down Roosevelt's alignment with those who advocated the use of force

(especially during his formative years), his admiration for Theodore Roosevelt, his correspondence with Alfred Mahan, his pressure for naval expansion while assistant secretary of the navy, and his chafing at Wilson's policies of neutrality.

44. Burns, *Roosevelt: The Soldier of Freedom.*

45. Stephen E. Pelz, *America Goes to War: The Politics and Process of Decision, 1914-1941*, forthcoming.

46. Dallek, *Franklin D. Roosevelt. See also* Christopher Thorne, *Allies of a Kind: The United States, Britain, and the War Against Japan, 1941-1945* (New York: Oxford University Press, 1978). Thorne, whose disapproval of FDR is unremitting, also sees Roosevelt as evasive, slippery, and irresponsible. In addition, *see* Francis L. Loewenheim, Harold Langley, and Manfred Jonas, eds., *Roosevelt and Churchill: Their Secret Wartime Correspondence* (New York: E. P. Dutton, 1975). They picture the two leaders as conducting diplomacy on an ad hoc basis.

47. *See*, for example, Winston Churchill, *The Second World War*, 6 vols. (Boston: Houghton Mifflin Co., 1948-50) and Alan Bullock, *Hitler: A Study in Tyranny* (London: Odhams Press, 1952). For the popular view, *see* William Shirer's *The Rise and Fall of the Third Reich* (New York: Simon and Schuster, 1959).

48. A. J. P. Taylor, *The Origins of the Second World War* (New York: Atheneum, 1962); Hans Trefousse, *Germany and American Neutrality 1939-1941* (New York: Bookman Associates, 1951); Michael J. Cunningham, "Revisionism and the Origins of World War II: A Study of A. J. P. Taylor and His Critics," *Midwest Quarterly* 17 (January 1975): 8-23; the series of essays on Taylor in *Journal of Modern History* 49 (Spring 1977): 1-72; Elizabeth Wiskemann, *The Rome-Berlin Axis* (New York: Oxford University Press, 1949). *See also* Ernest R. May, *American Intervention, 1917 and 1941*, 2d ed. (Baltimore: Waverly Press, 1969) and Louis Morton, *Writings on World War II* (Baltimore: Waverly Press, 1967).

49. Langer and Gleason, *Challenge to Isolation*; Beard, *Giddy Minds and Foreign Quarrels* (New York: Macmillan Co., 1939); Barnes, *Perpetual War for Perpetual Peace.* Bruce Russett takes up this argument in his *No Clear and Present Danger, The United States Entry into World War II* (New York: Harper & Row, 1973). By the end of 1941, Russett claimed, Britain's survival was assured and Germany was hopelessly bogged down in Russia. There was, therefore, no longer any danger that Germany would dominate the European continent. A negotiated settlement would then have been in the best interest of the United States.

50. Morison, "History Through a Beard."

51. Taylor, *Origins*, and "Far Away Countries," *New York Review of Books* 10 (6 June 1968): 12. Taylor drew heavily on Burton Klein's study *Germany's Economic Preparedness for War* (Cambridge, Mass.: Harvard University Press, 1959) which attempted to show there was no massive German rearmament effort nor a planned mobilization of German resources for war. For an opposing view, *see* Bernice Carroll, *Design for Total War* (Paris: Mouton, 1968). *See also* D. C. Watt, "Appeasement: The Rise of a Revisionist School?" *Political Quarterly* 36 (April-June 1965): 191-213.

52. Thorne, *The Approach of War 1938-1939* (London: Macmillan & Co., 1967); Esmonde M. Robertson, *Hitler's Pre-War Policy and Military Plans* (London: Macmillan & Co., 1963) and *Origins of the Second World War: Historical Interpretations* (London: Macmillan & Co., 1971); Pierre Renouvin, *World War II and Its Origins: International Relations, 1929-1945*, trans. Remy Inglis Hall (New York:

Harper & Row, 1969); Keith Eubank, *The Origins of World War II* (New York: Thomas Y. Crowell Co., 1969); Laurence Lafore, *The End of Glory: An Interpretation of the Origins of World War II* (Philadelphia: J. B. Lippincott Co., 1972). Alan Bullock also revised his opinion. Hitler and Germany still bore, while not the sole, the primary responsibility for the war. *See* Bullock, "Hitler and the Origins of the Second World War," *Proceedings of the British Academy* 53 (Spring 1967): 258-88.

53. Arnold Offner, *American Appeasement: United States Foreign Policy and Germany 1933-1938* (Cambridge, Mass.: Harvard University Press, 1969). *See also* D. C. Watt, "Appeasement," pp. 198-200; John McVickar Haight, "France and the Aftermath of Roosevelt's Quarantine Speech," *World Politics* 11 (April 1959): 245-50 and *American Aid to France 1938-1940* (New York: Atheneum, 1970). This legacy of appeasement has had a strong influence on United States foreign policy. For example, policymakers such as Dean Rusk compared any move toward peace in Vietnam with Munich. *See* Stephen E. Ambrose, *Rise to Globalism: American Foreign Policy* (London: Penguin Press, 1971).

54. Trefousse, *Germany and American Neutrality*; Saul Friedlander, *Prelude to Downfall: Hitler and the United States, 1939-1941* (New York: Alfred A. Knopf, 1967); James V. Compton, *The Swastika and the Eagle: The United States and the Origins of World War II* (Boston: Houghton Mifflin Co., 1967). *See also* Alton Frye's *Nazi Germany and the Western Hemisphere, 1933-1941* (New Haven: Yale University Press, 1967). This point still remains controversial.

55. Compton, *The Swastika and the Eagle.*

56. Friedlander, *Prelude to Downfall.*

57. Gerhard L. Weinberg, "Hitler's Image of the United States," *American Historical Review* 69 (July 1964): 1006-21; Ernest R. May, "Nazi Germany and the United States: A Review Essay," *Journal of Modern History* 41 (June 1969): 207-14.

58. Paul Varg, "The Coming of the War with Germany," *Centennial Review* 20 (Fall 1976): 219-27.

59. Murray N. Rothbard, "The New Deal and the International Monetary System," Robert Freeman Smith, "The Good Neighbor Policy: The Liberal Paradox in U.S. Relations with Latin America," and Lloyd C. Gardner, "New Deal Diplomacy: A View from the Seventies," in Liggio and Martin, eds., *Watershed of Empire. See also* Gardner, *Economic Aspects of New Deal Diplomacy.*

60. Lafore, *End of Glory* and Offner, *The Origins of the Second World War, American Foreign Policy and World Politics, 1917-1941* (New York: Frederick A. Praeger, 1975).

61. Geoffrey Barraclough, "Hitler and Hirohito," *New York Review of Books* 20 (31 May 1973): 9-14.

62. International Military Tribunal for the Far East, *Record of Proceedings, Exhibits, Judgement, Dissenting Judgements, Preliminary Interrogations, Miscellaneous Documents* (Tokyo, 1946-48). *See also* David Bergamini, *Japan's Imperial Conspiracy* (New York: William Morrow, 1971) for a current work with this thesis.

63. Henry L. Stimson and McGeorge Bundy, *On Active Service in Peace and War* (New York: Harper & Brothers, 1948); Sumner Welles, *The Time for Decision* (New York: Harper & Brothers, 1944); Robert H. Ferrell, *American Diplomacy in the Great Depression: Hoover-Stimson Foreign Policy, 1929-1933* (New Haven: Yale University Press, 1957); Sara Rector Smith, *The Manchurian Crisis 1931-1933*

(Westport, Conn.: Greenwood Press, 1970). For a similar view from a present-day writer, *see* Saburo Ienaga, *The Pacific War, World War II, and the Japanese, 1931-1945* (New York: Random House, 1978).

64. Louis Morton, "1937-1941," in May and Thomson, eds., *American-East Asian Relations. See also* Langer and Gleason, *Challenge to Isolation*, and Feis, *Road to Pearl Harbor*.

65. U.S. Congress, *Hearings Before the Joint Committee on the Pearl Harbor Attack*, 79th Cong., 2d sess., 1946. *See also* Feis, *Road to Pearl Harbor*.

66. Tansill, *Back Door to War*; William Neumann, *America Encounters Japan: From Perry to MacArthur* (Baltimore: Johns Hopkins Press, 1963); Cole, "United States Entry into World War II," pp. 600-603.

67. Roberta Wohlstetter, *Pearl Harbor: Warning and Decision* (Stanford: Stanford University Press, 1968). *See also* Ladislas Farago, *The Broken Seal: The Story of "Operation Magic" and the Pearl Harbor Disaster* (New York: Random House, 1967).

68. Kennan, *American Diplomacy*. Kennan drew much of his criticism of Roosevelt's Asian policy from Whitney Griswold, a traditionalist who, nevertheless, argued that the American commitment to the Open Door and the territorial integrity of China could not be justified if it jeopardized more vital American interests, as in Europe. *See* Waldo Heinrichs, "The Griswold Theory of Our Far Eastern Policy: A Commentary," in Borg, ed., *Historians and American Far Eastern Policy*, pp. 38-41. *See also* Armin Rappaport, *Henry Stimson and Japan, 1931-1933* (Chicago: University of Chicago Press, 1963) and Richard N. Current, *Secretary Stimson: A Study in Statecraft* (New Brunswick, N.J.: Rutgers University Press, 1954).

69. Paul W. Schroeder, *The Axis Alliance and Japanese-American Relations* (Ithaca: Cornell University Press, 1958). Schroeder also argued that the tripartite pact, while initially a major issue in the U.S.-Japanese dispute, soon declined in importance and was used only for propaganda purposes at the end. Hosoya Chihiro and Johanna Margarete Menzel Meskill disagreed. They both argued that while elements within the Japanese government were never really convinced that a close relationship with Germany was a good idea and that pledges made in the public text were effectively revoked in the secret protocol, the Tripartite Pact did indeed mark another important step on the road to war. The pact strengthened the expansionists in Japan and at the same time presented the image to the United States of the sealing of an aggressive, unholy alliance between Japan and Nazi Germany. *See* Hosoya Chihiro, "The Tripartite Pact, 1939-1940," in James W. Morley, ed., *Deterrent Diplomacy: Japan, Germany, and the USSR, 1935-1940* (New York: Columbia University Press, 1977), pp. 191-257 and Johanna Margarete Menzel Meskill, *Hitler and Japan: The Hollow Alliance* (New York: Atherton Press, 1966).

70. David J. Lu, *From the Marco Polo Bridge to Pearl Harbor: Japan's Entry into World War II* (New York: Public Affairs Press, 1961) and Robert Butow, *Tojo and the Coming of the War* (Princeton: Princeton University Press, 1961).

71. Pelz, *Race to Pearl Harbor*.

72. Fujiwara Akira, "The Role of the Japanese Army," in Borg and Okamoto, *Pearl Harbor as History*, pp. 189-96.

73. Ohata Tokushiro, "The Anti-Comintern Pact, 1935-1939," and Hosoya Chihiro, "The Tripartite Pact, 1939-1940," in Morley, ed., *Deterrent Diplomacy*.

74. Akira Iriye, *After Imperialism: The Search for a New Order in the Far East, 1921-1931* (Cambridge, Mass.: Harvard University Press, 1965); James B. Crowley, *Japan's Quest for Autonomy: National Security and Foreign Policy, 1930-1938* (Princeton: Princeton University Press, 1966); Waldo Heinrichs, *American Ambassador: Joseph C. Grew and the Development of the United States Diplomatic Tradition* (Boston: Little, Brown & Co., 1966).

75. Dorothy Borg, *The United States and the Far Eastern Crisis of 1933-1938: From the Manchurian Incident Through the Initial Stage of the Undeclared Sino-Japanese War* (Cambridge, Mass.: Harvard University Press, 1964).

76. Williams, *The Tragedy of American Diplomacy. See also* Robert Freeman Smith, "American Foreign Relations, 1920-1942," pp. 232-62.

77. Noam Chomsky, *American Power and the New Mandarins* (New York: Pantheon, 1969).

78. Frederick Adams, *The Export-Import Bank and American Foreign Policy, 1934-1939* (Columbia, Mo.: University of Missouri Press, 1976).

79. Irvine H. Anderson, Jr., *The Standard-Vacuum Company and United States East Asian Policy, 1933-1941* (Princeton: Princeton University Press, 1975).

80. Borg and Okamoto, *Pearl Harbor as History.*

81. Thorne, *Allies of a Kind* and *The Limits of Foreign Policy: The West, The League and the Far Eastern Crisis, 1931-1933* (London: Hamish Hamilton, 1972).

82. Iriye, *Across the Pacific: An Inner History of American-East Asian Relations* (New York: Harcourt, Brace & Co., 1967); *Pacific Estrangement: Japanese and American Expansionism 1897-1911* (Cambridge, Mass.: Harvard University Press, 1972); "Culture and Power: International Relations as Intercultural Relations," *Diplomatic History* 3 (Spring 1979): 115-28.

83. Iriye, *Across the Pacific.*

84. Borg, *Far Eastern Crisis*; Thorne, *Limits of Power*; Iriye, "The Failure of Military Expansionism," in James W. Morley, ed., *Dilemmas of Growth in Prewar Japan* (Princeton: Princeton University Press, 1971) and Neumann, *America Encounters Japan.* This is also a predominant characteristic of United States policy in the 1930s with regard to Europe. *See* Offner, *American Appeasement.*

85. Thorne, *Allies of a Kind. See also* Jamie W. Moore, *The New Deal and East Asia: The Basis of American Policy* (Charleston: Citadel Press, 1973).

86. Borg, *Historians and American Far Eastern Policy. See also* Pierre Renouvin's *World War II and Its Origins.* Renouvin discussed eastern Asia as a relatively insignificant aspect of American foreign affairs.

87. *See*, for example, Offner, *Origins of World War II* and Divine, *Causes and Consequences of World War II.*

88. Barraclough's remarks can be found in Robertson, *The Origins of the Second World War.* For Wayne Cole's assessment, *see* his essay "American Entry into World War II," p. 612. Justus Doenecke disagrees here. He calls for the study of narrower topics. For Doenecke, wholesale assaults upon major interpretations usually lead to serious distortion. *See* Doenecke, "Beyond Polemics," pp. 243-45.

89. Stephen Pelz, *America Goes to War: The Politics and Process of Decision, 1914-1941*, forthcoming, and Robert Divine, "War, Peace and Political Parties in 20th Century America," *Society for Historians of American Foreign Relations Newsletter* 8 (March 1977): 1-6; Iriye, "Culture and Power."

10 ______ World War II Diplomacy in Historical Writing: Prelude to Cold War

MARK A. STOLER

For over thirty years United States diplomacy during World War II has been one of the major battlegrounds of American historiography. Like other areas of intense dispute, the history of this period has inspired a large volume of literature, has been assessed in the light of present-day issues, and has been affected by the emergence of distinct schools of interpretation.[1] In at least two areas, however, the historiography of World War II diplomacy is unique. Owing to an apparently insatiable public interest in the war and the availability of massive documentation, the number of historical works is not simply large; it is enormous, and continues to grow rapidly. And while these works can be divided into schools of thought which parallel those for other major historiographical issues, interpretations of United States World War II diplomacy often have a distinctive quality because of the influence of the cold war on its interpreters. Throughout the postwar era, in fact, World War II diplomacy has been treated not as an event unto itself, but as an explanation of the events that followed.

During the first two decades of the cold war, United States World War II diplomacy came under sharp attack. While starting from diverse assumptions, all of the critics reached the same basic conclusion—that American diplomatic blunders during the war had resulted in a massive and unnecessary extension of Soviet power. Once again, it appeared, the United States had managed to lose a peace in the process of winning a war.

The earliest of these criticisms came from historians who had been influenced at least as much by events which preceded American entry into World War II as they were by events of the cold war which followed. As early as 1945, conservatives who in the 1930s had opposed the New Deal resumed their efforts to discredit President Roosevelt and his programs by accusing him of having appeased Soviet dictator Joseph Stalin throughout the war, and especially at the Yalta Conference. Simultaneously, anti-interventionists of the pre-Pearl Harbor years reinforced their earlier criticisms of Roosevelt's foreign policy by emphasizing the new Russian menace which had been created in the process of defeating the Axis. Conquering one despotism only to pave the way for the triumph of "another totalitarian regime no less despotic and ruthless," Charles Beard noted in 1948, highlighted the folly of the president's policies.[2]

Post-Pearl Harbor diplomacy was admittedly not the major issue for Beard or most of his fellow critics of American entry into World War II. In 1950, however, journalist William Henry Chamberlin made it a central focus of his anti-interventionist critique of Roosevelt's World War II diplomacy. Seeking to explain "why the peace was lost while the war was being won," Chamberlin concluded that the president had never understood that communism was at least as dangerous as fascism, and that American policy should have pitted the Soviet Union against Nazi Germany. Instead, Roosevelt had manipulated the American people into a needless war with nations which did not constitute military threats to the United States, and had then compounded his error by fighting the war as an unlimited crusade instead of as a limited conflict to restore the balance of power. The result had been the creation of a massive power vacuum which Stalin had been able to fill. Roosevelt had further blundered by refusing to follow a military strategy which would have placed Anglo-American instead of Russian forces in key areas. Equally damaging, he had naively and immorally attempted to appease Stalin's territorial appetite in the vain hope of insuring a postwar world of international harmony, and had thereby violated the very ideals which had formed the basis of the "crusade." As a result of these follies, Stalin had been able to gain control of most of eastern and central Europe as well as China.[3]

While Chamberlin's interpretation of United States World War II diplomacy was closely linked to the anti-interventionist position of the 1930s, its appeal was by no means limited to prewar isolationists. To the contrary, numerous wartime advisers and associates of Roosevelt, as well as many internationalist-minded journalists, voiced similar objections.

One of the earliest and most influential of these critiques was former ambassador William C. Bullitt's 1948 article, "How We Won the War and Lost the Peace." According to Bullitt, Roosevelt's appeasement of Stalin in giving unlimited wartime aid and postwar territorial concessions had been a conscious if extraordinarily naive act of noblesse oblige to convince a "Caucasian bandit" to trust the United States and cooperate in building a peaceful postwar world. Equally damaging, Roosevelt had ignored the dictum that war is an instrument of policy and the warnings of the politically astute British prime minister, Winston Churchill, and had made total military victory a substitute for any carefully designed international political objectives.[4] According to *New York Times* military analyst Hanson Baldwin, this "political bankruptcy," as epitomized in the unconditional surrender formula, lay behind the American failure to win the peace.[5]

In 1952, Australian journalist and military historian Chester Wilmot, in what was at that time the most detailed analysis of the Allied diplomatic and military effort against Hitler, reached substantially the same conclusions as Baldwin. Roosevelt and his advisers, both writers maintained, had subordinated all political and postwar issues to the goal of winning a complete military victory over the Axis powers as rapidly as possible, and had thereby lost the peace to Stalin. The insistence on a cross-Channel military strategy and the refusal to agree to Churchill's plan for an invasion of the Balkans had guaranteed the Red Army's occupation and control of eastern Europe. The Americans had compounded this error at the Yalta Conference by agreeing to a division of Germany without guaranteed access rights to Berlin, and by vetoing a few months later Churchill's pleas for an advance on that city as well as on Vienna and Prague in the wake of the German collapse. In the Far East they had shown similar stupidity by making massive concessions for an unnecessary Soviet entry into the war against Japan, by insisting on Tokyo's unconditional surrender, and by dropping two atomic bombs on a country that would later be needed to check Soviet expansion.[6]

Some of the points raised by Baldwin and Wilmot bore a striking similarity to those emphasized by Chamberlin. Unlike the anti-interventionists, however, these writers did not appear to question the reality of the threats posed by Germany and Japan or the need to go to war.[7] They also differed from Chamberlin and his associates in the degree of blame they attributed to Roosevelt for the failures of American diplomacy. Political naivete, they argued, had been a severe weakness not only of the president, but of all branches of government and of the American people during World War II. Indeed, Wilmot claimed that such naivete, as exhibited in the total victory concept, in an idealistic vision of the postwar world, and in the intense American suspicion of British colonialism throughout the war, was largely the result of almost two hundred years of American immaturity in dealing with international affairs.[8]

The anti-interventionists, on the other hand, remained furious at

Roosevelt because of his supposed duplicity before Pearl Harbor, and seemed determined to make him and his close adviser Harry Hopkins the scapegoats for all the failures of American diplomacy. This involved them in some serious contradictions. How Roosevelt could have been so deviously clever from 1937 through 1941 and then become so naively stupid regarding Stalin and the war from 1942 to 1945 remained unexplained save for Chamberlin's comment that the president had never realized the menace posed by communism. Equally illogical was the attack on Roosevelt for being too idealistic and naive in his postwar plans and behavior toward Stalin on the one hand, and for cynically betraying those very ideals in the power politics of Yalta on the other.

Despite these contradictions, the anti-interventinist assault on Roosevelt's wartime diplomacy gained numerous adherents, and by 1952 had become an extremely powerful and emotional issue in American politics. A public paranoia, engendered by Russia's explosion of the atomic bomb, Mao's victory in China, the Korean War, and revelations regarding wartime communist spy rings in the government, led to increasing support for this assault. It also led to questions which went beyond the Roosevelt administration's lack of wisdom, and into the area of its very loyalty. Beneath the naivete and stupidity of giving away half of the globe to Stalin, many now argued, lay a massive conspiracy of communist agents which reached into the State Department and perhaps into the White House itself.[9]

Such charges of treason were enunciated not only by politicians like Senator McCarthy of Wisconsin, but also by historians. George Crocker explained away the contradiction of the duplicitous Roosevelt of 1937-1941 and the naive president of 1942-1945 by arguing that the naivete was simply a mask for a deliberate, secret policy of helping expand communist Russian power, a policy which had dominated the president's actions as far back as 1933.[10] Anthony Kubek alleged that communist spies and fellow-travellers in government had duped the gullible president and controlled American policy so that it aided in Mao's victory over Chiang.[11]

Both Roosevelt's supporters and numerous influential realist historians of the postwar era responded by claiming that such cries of betrayal and treason were, in the words of Forrest C. Pogue, "manifestations of national immaturity"[12] as well as a refusal to look at the facts within their historical context. That context, they argued, had been dominated not by the cold war, but by the need to maintain the Grand Alliance in order to defeat the Axis and by the new reality of Soviet power which was an inevitable outcome of the war. The real "great mistake" of the West, George F. Kennan pointed out in 1951, had been to allow the totalitarian dictatorships to accumulate so much power that the aid of one would be necessary to defeat the other. That mistake had been made long before World War II began, and had in effect made the conflict unwinnable. Most of Roosevelt's supposed blunders had been forced upon him by this fact, by the new reality of

Soviet power, by the need to keep the Grand Alliance together to defeat Hitler, and by the military realities of the war.[13]

These themes were most clearly enunciated in *The Meaning of Yalta*, a 1956 collection of essays written by historians John Snell, Forrest Pogue, Charles Delzell, and George Lensen. Using the recently declassified and published American records of the by then notorious Crimean conference, these writers attempted to analyze the meeting within the context of its time, and to dispel the myths which had arisen in the ensuing decade.[14] By February 1945, they argued, Soviet military power had already given Stalin physical control of eastern Europe as well as potential control over large areas of the Far East. Furthermore, Russian military assistance was still desperately needed by Britain and the United States, who were at that moment near the bottom of their manpower pool. Given this situation, Pogue contended, Western concessions to Stalin were minimal, unless one wished to ignore public opinion and try to make peace with the Axis while starting a war with Russia. The fact that Stalin had later broken the Yalta accords, and the fact that those accords could indeed be criticized as a violation of Roosevelt's moral principles, did not negate the additional fact that from a realistic point of view these concessions were the best course the West could have taken.[15]

Aside from *The Meaning of Yalta*, however, most defenses of American diplomacy during the war exhibited an odd duality, for many of the writers agreed with the charges of naivete levelled by the Baldwins and Wilmots if not with those levelled by writers like Chamberlin. Indeed, such charges of naivete were part of the general realist critique of American foreign policy. They were also a key component in the traditional self-perception held by most Americans, a self-perception based on the idea that their relative youth and lack of international experience made them more gullible than the worldly Europeans. Equally, if not more importantly, most of Roosevelt's defenders had by the 1950s become cold warriors themselves, and were therefore incapable almost by definition of supporting the cooperative approach the president had attempted with the Russians. In the process of defending American World War II diplomacy against its extreme critics, they wound up attacking it on some of the same grounds those critics had used.

This tendency was visible as early as 1947 when William Langer, who had been given special access to government files and who was in the process of writing a detailed history of administration policies from 1937 through 1941, published an article that defended most of the president's actions from 1942 to 1945 on the basis of the need to keep the Grand Alliance together to win the war. Langer, however, also criticized Roosevelt for placing too much faith in a postwar international organization, for vastly overrating both the danger of a separate Russo-German peace and his personal ability to influence Stalin, and for giving away too much in his efforts to placate the Soviet leader. American diplomacy, Langer concluded, had clearly deteriorated in quality after Pearl Harbor.[16] Kennan expressed similar criticism although, overall, he defended Roosevelt's policies.[17]

This duality also emerged in the first, and in many ways still the best general history of the Grand Alliance, William H. McNeill's *America, Britain and Russia*. Although written before the release of much archival material, this volume was, nevertheless, a detailed, comprehensive, and brilliant history that placed the alliance in the context of world history while simultaneously explaining the conflicting aims, methods, world-views, and actions of each member. In the process, the author made clear that like most alliances, this one had been held together primarily by fear of a common enemy, and that its breakup might therefore have been the natural result of victory rather than the fault of anyone. What may have been truly unique about the coalition was not its collapse, McNeill contended, but its extraordinary success in maintaining itself by compromises so that the war could be won. Yalta demonstrated this ability to compromise successfully, and also revealed the new military balance of power.[18]

Yet Yalta also represented the ultimate failure of Roosevelt's wartime policies. The president had compromised his ideals and still had failed to win Stalin's support for what remained of them. Agreeing with other critics, McNeill assailed the president for his naive separation of military and political issues during the war, a separation which had been based upon an equally naive "great myth" of a new, idealistic world order at war's end. He also berated Roosevelt for not perceiving that Stalin worked from very different assumptions, that a wide and indeed unbridgeable gap separated their world-views, and that there was little common ground on which to build an effective compromise or a future world order.[19]

Similar criticisms emerged in a 1957 publication that was the closest thing to an "official" history of United States diplomacy during the war, Herbert Feis's *Churchill, Roosevelt, Stalin*. An adviser to the Departments of State and of War during World War II, Feis had been granted special access to government files and to private papers of key individuals in the Roosevelt administration. Earlier he had produced *The China Tangle*, a scholarly and solid retort to the extreme attacks on America's China policy during the war.[20]

In neither this work nor in *Churchill, Roosevelt, Stalin*, however, did Feis claim to be or behave as if he were an official apologist. To the contrary, he frequently criticized American policy in terms quite similar to McNeill, albeit with less emphasis on the inevitability of postwar conflict and more emphasis on both Stalin's responsibility for the breakdown of the alliance and the naive and mistaken assumptions which had dominated United States policy. In *China Tangle* he had implied that one of these assumptions had been the American belief that the Nationalists and Communists could peacefully reconcile their differences and form a democratic postwar government. Throughout the detailed narrative of *Churchill, Roosevelt, Stalin*, Feis implicitly berated Roosevelt for working under another mistaken assumption, that he could win Stalin over to his viewpoint through face-to-face conversations. Furthermore, Roosevelt failed to mesh military and political goals.[21] Samuel P. Huntington, in his 1957 *The Soldier and the State*, expanded this latter criticism. He attacked not the president and his civilian advisers (of whom he appeared to expect such naivete) but the Joint Chiefs of Staff who had forgotten their military training in agreeing to this military-political duality and who had thereby failed to provide the president with a realistic perspective.[22]

While rejecting extreme attacks on Roosevelt, these pivotal works of the 1950s were modified versions of the Baldwin-Wilmot themes regarding American naivete and inability to mesh political ends with military means. By the early 1960s, this view had become dominant. Indeed, many historians during the first part of the decade became even more critical of American diplomacy than their 1950s predecessors, and at times appeared to be approaching the extremist viewpoint. Anne Armstrong, for example, recognized the origins and importance of the formula, unconditional surrender, in the search for wartime unity. She nevertheless condemned it as a moralistic, inflexible concept which had prolonged the war and which was symptomatic of American emotionalism and separation of strategy from political goals.[23] In his 1963 *America's Failure in China*, Tang Tsou levelled similar criticisms at Roosevelt while refuting extremist attacks on him for "losing" China.[24]

This tendency to start out attacking Roosevelt's extreme critics and then wind up basically agreeing with them was most evident in Gaddis Smith's 1965 survey, *American Diplomacy During the Second World War*. In the preface, series editor Robert Divine emphasized the inaccuracy of the statement, "the United States always wins the war and loses the peace." In his introduction Smith made clear his intention to write not about the origins of the cold war, but about World War II diplomacy within the context of 1941-1945. Throughout the text, however, Smith wound up doing exactly what he had attempted not to do, and in the process he seemed to validate the very generalization Divine had attacked in the preface. Roosevelt's World War II diplomacy had been a dismal failure, Smith concluded, because he had placed military affairs before political ones, because he had too much faith in a postwar league of nations, and because his attempts to "charm" Stalin had been based upon naive "hopes and illusions" instead of reality. All he had succeeded in doing was convince the Soviet leader that the United States would not oppose postwar Soviet expansion.[25]

Smith's criticism of Roosevelt was so strong that one historian has labelled it neo-revisionist, and it indeed illuminated the extraordinary extent to which many historians had embraced Chamberlin's accusations in the process of denying them.[26] By the early 1960s a virtual consensus existed among historians on the major flaws which had characterized America's World War II diplomacy.

This consensus was related to the cold war consensus which by that time had come to dominate American politics. And, just as that political consensus was shattered by events during the 1960s, so the historical consensus was broken by the rise of new schools of interpretation. The new left revisionists were the most visible of these new interpreters, but they were by no means the only historians to question the basic assumptions of Roosevelt's critics. Equally important was a group of neo-realist or nationalist historians who began to argue that in actuality United States World War II diplomacy had been much more realistic than any of its critics cared to admit.[27]

This theme was first enunciated clearly and forcefully by John Snell in his 1963 interpretive survey, *Illusion and Necessity*. After comparing Allied with Axis diplomacy throughout the war years, Snell concluded that it had been Axis leaders rather than Roosevelt and his advisers who had acted on the basis of illusions instead of a realistic appraisal, and who had thereby lost the war. Picking up Kennan's 1951 argument, Snell pointed out that a new global balance of power based on the United States and the Soviet Union was inevitable if the Axis were to be defeated in World War II. Since nothing could change this fact, and since the American people were by no means prepared to follow their war against the Axis with a war against Russia, Roosevelt's admittedly illusory hope of postwar cooperation had been "virtually imposed by necessity."[28]

Snell went far beyond Kennan, however, to argue that Roosevelt's specific policies constituted a highly realistic and pragmatic attempt to mesh military means with political ends, and to maximize American national interests while reconciling Allied differences in order to keep the alliance together. The outstanding example of such realism was the unconditional surrender formula. It had been motivated, Snell maintained, not only by the need to maintain unity but also by the desire to postpone all territorial settlements until a future date when either Soviet confidence had been won or, if this proved impossible, when American armies had arrived in Europe and the Far East in sufficient force to strengthen Roosevelt's postwar position. This highly realistic "strategy of postponement" had enabled the president not only to keep public opinion and the alliance unified, but also to create the basis for postwar cooperation with Russia "while at the same time placing limits to Soviet expansion" in case such cooperation failed to materialize. The fact that this policy had succeeded was evidenced not only by the victory over the Axis, but also by the severe limits to Stalin's territorial gains; those gains were no greater than those Czar Nicholas II would have received in 1918 had he not been overthrown.[29]

The groundwork for Snell's arguments had been laid in a series of articles and books published in the late 1950s and early 1960s. As summarized in chief Army historian Kent R. Greenfield's *American Strategy in World War II: A Reconsideration*, these works challenged the traditional notion of political naivete by the president and his military advisers. They pointed out that Roosevelt's vision of world order had been based upon a realistic assessment of international relations, that he had clearly controlled his military advisers rather than vice versa and had overruled them on numerous occasions throughout the war for political reasons, and that they as well as he were aware of the need to make sure that military strategy was designed to achieve rather than ignore political goals.[30]

These assessments were reinforced in 1969 and 1970 with the publication of two major reinterpretations of Roosevelt which, while highly critical of the president, emphasized his realism and pragmatism. In *Roosevelt and World War II* Robert Divine challenged the traditional view of an idealistic Wilsonian who had been duped by Stalin. Labelling this view an ahistorical judgment "reflecting essentially a Cold War disenchantment with the results of World War II," Divine argued that in actuality it was the public and the historians who had been duped by Roosevelt's Wilsonian public statements as opposed to his private comments and actions throughout the war. Those comments and actions, Divine noted, revealed a man who believed in the concept of great power domination and who had attempted to avoid Wilson's idealistic mistakes.[31] While following a more traditional approach in assessing the president's ideas of world order in *Roosevelt: The Soldier of Freedom*, James MacGregor Burns also emphasized the pragmatism which had dominated Roosevelt's actions if not his goals.[32]

Divine and Burns admitted that Roosevelt's policy toward Russia had ended in failure and had been marred by some wishful thinking, but they found this failure to be the result of the very expediency which others had found lacking in the president's behavior. The strategy of postponement of both territorial issues and the cross-Channel assault had indeed enabled the Grand Alliance to stay together and achieve military victory. But it had intensely, and perhaps irrevocably, aroused Soviet suspicion of the West and thereby doomed Roosevelt's postwar hopes.[33] Admittedly, Stephen Ambrose argued in 1967, postwar Soviet cooperation might have been an impossibility no matter what the president had done, but the alternative to cooperation "was too grim to think about" while Roosevelt's untimely death meant that his approach "did not have a fair trial."[34]

These reassessments of Roosevelt and American diplomacy were often linked to highly critical reinterpretations of the supposed Great Realist of the western powers, Winston Churchill. Building upon official United States and British military histories, American historians like Stephen Ambrose, Trumbull Higgins, and Raymond O'Connor attacked the notion that British strategy and policy had been motivated by a perceptive and realistic fear of postwar Soviet expansion. They emphasized instead the incorrect and indeed irrational factors which had motivated the British prime minister and his staff.[35] Some of those factors, Ambrose admitted, reflected a realistic attempt by the British to raise their power and prestige at the expense of the Soviet Union, but such goals were by no means identical with American interests despite the unprecedented Anglo-American collaboration during the war. Indeed, Britain actually needed a Soviet-American conflict to retain its position as a great power.[36] Even if one were to admit that a conflict with Russia was inevitable, O'Connor concluded, Churchill's military and political approach was unsound in comparison with the American grand strategy of delay while building up massive strength in Europe and the Far East. If followed, the British approach would have resulted in Soviet acquisition, by both war and Allied agreement, of even more territory than Stalin actually received.[37]

A few of these conclusions were shared by a second school of interpretation to emerge from the 1960s, the so-called new left. Throughout the 1940s and 1950s, a leftist critique had been noticeably missing from the debate over U.S. World War II diplomacy. Some leftist historians who could have provided such a critique, most notably the World War I revisionists, had been, in the words of one historian, "so obsessed by their hatred of Roosevelt" that they had been willing to join forces with the right and endorse "almost any attack on the President's reputation."[38] Others had been silenced by the cold war and the ensuing "great fear."

During the early 1960s, however, a leftist critique of United States diplomacy during World War II, and indeed during all of American history, began to emerge. In 1961 Wilsonian historian D. F. Fleming accused President Truman of having reversed Roosevelt's cooperative policy towards the Russians and in effect of having initiated the cold war.[39] And in a series of works published in the early 1960s, most prominently in *The Tragedy of American Diplomacy*, William Appleman Williams emphasized a neo-Beardian model of Open Door marketplace expansion as the primary factor in twentieth-century United States foreign policy. Applying this concept to the World War II years, Williams argued that American policymakers had been anything but naive from 1941 through 1945. Driven by a "nightmare of depression" at war's end and a "vision of omnipotence" by which military victory would inaugurate an American Century, they had systematically set about to create a worldwide postwar Open Door for American exports even while the war was raging. This effort had involved them in sharp conflict with their allies. They had attempted to dismantle the British Empire and its preferential trading system. They had practiced a policy of military and political postponement with the Soviet Union in order to maximize the postwar American bargaining position. They then had attempted to keep the door open in eastern Europe and to deny the Soviets' legitimate security needs through economic and military coercion.[40]

During the mid and late 1960s, a host of historians began to analyze the issues raised by these early revisionists. In *Economic Aspects of New Deal Diplomacy* and *Architects of Illusion*, for example, Lloyd Gardner used a modified Open Door approach to reinterpret the economic diplomacy and the political leadership of the 1930s and 1940s.[41] In *Atomic Diplomacy*, Gar Alperovitz attacked the traditional interpretation enunciated by Feis in *Japan Subdued* by maintaining that the decision to drop the first atomic bomb had been based not on a desire to end the war as quickly as possible, but on a determination to use the weapon as diplomatic blackmail against the Soviet Union.[42] In *Yalta*, Diane Shaver Clemens directly challenged the great symbol of Roosevelt's supposed appeasement by concluding that Stalin had made the bulk of the concessions at the conference and that Truman rather than the Soviet leader had later broken the accords.[43]

The most comprehensive of these revisionist critiques was Gabriel Kolko's *The Politics of War*, a massive reinterpretation which challenged virtually every traditional assumption regarding Allied diplomacy from 1943 through 1945. American wartime policy, Kolko maintained, had consisted of a conscious and highly aggressive effort to make the world safe for postwar capitalist expansion. This effort had led American policymakers, first, to define as enemies the British colonial empire, the Soviet Union, and, most importantly, the indigenous Left which had arisen in numerous countries to combat Axis occupation, and, secondly, to attempt to overcome these forces. The Allied leader who was really guilty of appeasement was not Roosevelt, whom Kolko portrayed as relatively unimportant in the formulation of American policy, but the highly conservative Stalin who proved consistently willing to sell out the Left in return for a small piece of the American-dominated postwar world. Ironically, however, the Americans considered his requested piece much too large, blamed him for the activities of the indigenous Left, and cut short their attack on the British empire in order to defeat this more pressing menace. The result was the cold war.[44]

This revisionist reassessment was catalyzed by the emerging events of the cold war, most noticeably those in Southeast Asia. In light of the inability of traditional cold war historiography to account for American actions in Vietnam, numerous historians began to revise their analyses of the origins of Soviet-American conflict. Once again, discussion of this issue led to a reinterpretation of World War II events. Publication during the 1960s of government records for the war years, most notably State Department documents in the *Foreign Relations* series, provided these historians with substantial new evidence for the revisionist conclusions they were reaching.[45]

Although these revisionist works raised a storm of controversy and cries of distortion of the evidence, the new left school continued to grow. Its members, however, soon showed themselves to be in profound disagreement on many issues. While agreeing that the United States employed atomic diplomacy against the Soviets, for example, many revisionists did not accept Alperovitz's assumption that Roosevelt had followed a cooperative policy toward the Soviet Union which Truman had reversed.[46] Kolko went a step further and denied the existence of *any* atomic diplomacy, even though he condemned the United States for highly aggressive behavior on virtually every other wartime issue.[47] Clemens in turn argued that Kolko's *Politics of War* had been as inaccurate as all the traditional accounts of the Yalta Conference, and that former Secretary of State Stettinius had been correct in 1949 when he wrote that Stalin had made most of the concessions.[48] That Clemens agreed with Stettinius was not any more confusing than the fact that Kolko agreed in effect with Herbert Feis on the atomic bomb while Williams payed homage to Charles Beard, whose last works had formed the basis for the right-wing assault of the late 1940s and early 1950s. Politics, it appeared, was not the only profession that made for strange bedfellows.

Indeed, like progressivism, the term new left revisionism had come to encompass so many diverse theories, approaches and individuals as to make it an almost meaningless label. While Williams's Open Door approach theoretically provided a general framework of analysis, that framework proved to be so broad that its numerous adherents could either apply a rigid economic determinism or virtually ignore economics and economic issues and concentrate instead on vaguely related political beliefs and actions. They could also reach diametrically opposite conclusions on the same event, issue, or individual. By the early 1970s all they really shared, aside from a host of critics, was a belief that at some time during World War II, and for some reason, the United States had been diplomatically aggressive and therefore was at least partially to blame for the ensuing cold war.

To their critics, however, the revisionists were united by much more: by the general incorrectness of their interpretations; by their narrow economic determinism; by their misuse and outright distortion of facts; and by their convenience as foils for a host of books, articles, professional papers, and doctoral dissertations. In 1973 Robert Maddox summarized and amplified these attacks in an article which labelled *Atomic Diplomacy* "creative writing," and in a book-length study which accused Alperovitz and six other major revisionists of gross distortion and misuse of the historical evidence.[49]

While the ensuing debates between revisionists and their critics moved from scholarly periodicals into the pages of *The New York Times*[50] and other popular journals, American World War II historiography was itself moving beyond such polarized confrontations into a new era of detailed analysis and attempted synthesis. This trend, evident in cold war historiography by the early 1970s, affected World War II interpretations soon thereafter. Increasingly, historians began to recognize that they shared a set of conclusions even if they could not agree on their meaning. Revisionists and neorealists could agree, for example, that American policy during the war had been grounded in the national interest, even though they disagreed as to whether this fact had led to a justifiable and commendable policy or one which was imperialistic and immoral. Both groups could further agree with the more traditional interpreters that United States policy had been universalistic as compared with British and Soviet policy. Again, however, disagreement remained as to whether such universalism constituted naive idealism, ultimate realism, or worldwide imperialism.[51]

As the decade progressed, the shared conclusions appeared more important than the divergent interpretations. This may have been partially the result of the calmer political environment which followed Watergate and the end of the Vietnam War. Equally if not more important were two other factors: the rise of a new generation of historians who attempted to synthesize the interpretations of the 1960s with the more traditional approaches; and a massive declassification of World War II archival material. The result in the 1970s was an outpouring of detailed studies on specific aspects of American World War II diplomacy and the beginnings of a new consensus.

While it is still too soon to make definitive statements regarding this new generation of studies, certain trends are already evident. Because of the recent availability of military as well as diplomatic records, numerous historians have reexamined highly controversial wartime issues in which political and military factors were inextricably interwoven. Aid to Russia, the second front controversy, the Darlan affair, the atomic bomb decision, and Anglo-American arguments over the direction of the war and the future of European colonies, to name but a few such issues, have all been subjects for recent studies which use British and American military records to substantially revise traditional interpretations and attempt new syntheses.[52]

Another trend is toward a large number of specialized works on American diplomacy toward specific countries during the war. Some such bilateral studies had appeared during the 1950s as relations with individual nations became highly visible issues in the cold war and domestic politics. Russo- and Sino-American relations obviously constituted two such issues. When wartime Free French leader Charles de Gaulle reassumed power and removed his country from NATO in the 1960s, Franco-American relations became a third.[53] In the 1970s, the large number of studies on United States wartime policy toward Indochina showed a continuation of this tendency to look to World War II for the roots of present-day problems.[54] However, the decade also witnessed a flood of specialized studies on United States relations with countries which were in no way major issues in contemporary U.S. policy.[55] Again, the new availability of archival material appears to have played a significant role in this trend.

The type of excellent synthesis which could result from these trends became clear in 1975 when Martin Sherwin's highly acclaimed *A World Destroyed* and a series of articles by Barton Bernstein revealed a new consensus on the issue of the atomic bomb. After extensive research in newly declassified British and American records, both historians concluded that the United States had indeed attempted atomic diplomacy against the Soviet Union in bombing Hiroshima. Unlike Alperovitz, however, they pointed out that this had been a secondary albeit complementary motive to ending the war, that it had always been a key component in Roosevelt's atomic energy policy and his decision to keep the bomb an Anglo-American monopoly, and that Truman had therefore in no way reversed Roosevelt's policies toward the Soviet Union.[56]

Similar syntheses emerged during the 1970s on a host of specific World War II issues. But many of these individual syntheses reached differing conclusions on general issues, making a broader synthesis quite difficult. Furthermore, major disagreements still remained on numerous points. For example, while generally praising John Gaddis's 1972 study on wartime and immediate postwar origins of the cold war, Ralph Levering took issue with Gaddis's contention that public opinion limited the policymakers' options; instead he emphasized the degree to which those policymakers were able to shape opinion during the war.[57] And although George Herring and Thomas Paterson individually rejected previous explanations regarding America's policy of wartime and postwar aid to the Soviet Union, their respective syntheses were quite different.[58] Similar disagreements marked historical discussions of Anglo-American strategy, the influence of government agencies in the formulation of United States policies, and the dominant ideas which stood behind the words of highly secretive Allied leaders like Roosevelt and Stalin.

The gap which continues to separate World War II historians and the problems which plague any effort to develop a consensus on American World War II diplomacy in general, was revealed with the publication of one of the most far-reaching and impressive syntheses to date, Christopher Thorne's *Allies of a Kind: The United States, Britain and the War Against Japan, 1941-1945*. Relying upon extensive and impressive research in archives and manuscript collections as well as on published primary and secondary works, Thorne has written what is without any doubt the most thorough, detailed, and penetrating history of the Allied war effort in the Pacific and Far East. In his attempt to be as comprehensive and eclectic as possible, however, he has qualified his generalizations so heavily as to rob them of much impact. Consistently trying to combine old with new interpretations, he has concluded that: the Anglo-American wartime alliance was unprecedented in its degree of cooperation but widespread suspicion still influenced each country tremendously; this suspicion was based largely upon ignorance but also upon very real differences in national aims and methods; and although American policy was in most cases neither naive nor purely military, it was nevertheless ambiguous and confused.[59]

Continuing historical disagreements are also obvious by comparing outstanding syntheses by Robert Dallek on Roosevelt and by Vojtech Mastny on Soviet foreign policy during the war. Expanding upon the defenses of Roosevelt which appeared during the 1960s, Dallek has concluded that he was a farsighted, realistic statesman who deserves much higher marks for his wartime diplomacy than even Divine and Burns were willing to give him ten years ago. Mastny, however, has attacked Roosevelt for not making his intentions clear to Stalin throughout the war, and has concluded that all three major Allied leaders were poor diplomats. The two historians are able to agree that postwar Soviet foreign policy was virtually predetermined and that no actions by Roosevelt, including a 1942 second front, could have broken down Soviet suspicion, but their agreement on this point ironically conflicts with many recent interpretations of the origins of the cold war.[60]

Continued research will probably clarify some of the remaining controversies regarding American World War II diplomacy, but it is unlikely that many of them will be completely settled. Despite the extraordinary wealth of evidence now available, the best of the new histories have been forced into educated guesses and disagreements on a host of issues. This is partially due to the incompleteness of the documentary record. Roosevelt's refusal to commit his innermost thoughts to paper or to any of his advisers, for example, has stymied historians (and in all likelihood will continue to do so) and led to different conclusions. Furthermore, documents simply do not speak for themselves. History is a matter of interpreting as well as collecting data, and interpretations are in many ways products of their times.

This fact remains as true today as it was in the past. The impact of the cold war on World War II historiography may not appear as great as it did during the 1950s and 1960s, but that is because the conflict itself is more uncertain and nonideological than it was in the past. Just as the interpretations of the 1950s reflected the cold war consensus and those of the 1960s reflected the breakdown of that consensus, so recent interpretations reflect the more balanced and polycentric approach of the United States to Soviet-American relations in the 1970s. As long as the victors of World War II continue to play a major role in international affairs, the state of their relations will continue to have a major impact on interpretations of United States World War II diplomacy.

Notes

1. The best introduction to these differing interpretations is in Robert Divine, ed., *Causes and Consequences of World War II* (Chicago: Quadrangle Books, 1969), pp. 3-30. *See also* Thomas M. Leonard, "The United States and World War II: Conflicting Views of Diplomacy," *Towson State Journal of International Affairs* 7 (Fall 1972): 25-30 and the introductions to the numerous "conflicting interpretations" collections on Franklin Roosevelt and specific World War II issues.

2. Charles A. Beard, *President Roosevelt and the Coming of War, 1941: A Case Study in Appearances and Realities* (New Haven: Yale University Press, 1948). *See also* Wayne S. Cole, "American Entry into World War II: An Historiographical Appraisal," *Mississippi Valley Historical Review* 43 (March 1957): 606-07 and Athan G. Theoharis, *The Yalta Myths: An Issue in U.S. Politics, 1945-1955* (Columbia: University of Missouri Press, 1970). To avoid confusion with the new left revisionists of the 1960s, these early revisionists will be referred to as anti-interventionists.

3. William Henry Chamberlin, *America's Second Crusade* (Chicago: Henry Regnery Co., 1950), quote from p. viii. *See also* Harry Elmer Barnes, ed., *Perpetual War for Perpetual Peace* (Caldwell, Idaho: Caxton, 1953).

4. William C. Bullitt, "How We Won the War and Lost the Peace," *Life* 25 (30 August 1948): 82-97. *See also* John R. Deane, *The Strange Alliance: The Story of Our Efforts at Wartime Cooperation with Russia* (New York: Viking Press, 1947).

5. Hanson W. Baldwin, *Great Mistakes of the War* (New York: Harper & Brothers, 1950), p. 24.

6. Ibid.; Chester Wilmot, *The Struggle for Europe* (New York: Harper & Brothers, 1952).

7. Wilmot did note, however, that Stalin "succeeded in obtaining from Roosevelt and Churchill what he had failed to obtain from Hitler," that he became Hitler's "heir" in Europe, and that with Allied victory in 1945 the "struggle for Europe . . . had merely entered on a new phase with a new protagonist, more dangerous perhaps than the old because less reckless and more calculating" (Ibid., pp. 12, 708).

8. Ibid., pp. 714-15.

9. *See* Theoharis, *Yalta Myths.*

10. George N. Crocker, *Roosevelt's Roads to Russia* (Chicago: Henry Regnery Co., 1959).

11. Anthony Kubek, *How the Far East Was Lost* (Chicago: Henry Regnery Co., 1963).

12. Forrest C. Pogue, "Yalta in Retrospect," in John L. Snell, ed., *The Meaning of Yalta: Big Three Diplomacy and the New Balance of Power* (Baton Rouge: Louisiana State University Press, 1956).

13. George F. Kennan, *American Diplomacy, 1900-1950* (Chicago: University of Chicago Press, 1951).

14. U.S., Department of State, *Foreign Relations of the United States: The Conferences at Malta and Yalta, 1945* (Washington, D.C.: Government Printing Office, 1955).

15. Snell, ed., *Meaning of Yalta.*

16. William L. Langer, "Turning Points of the War: Political Problems of a Coalition," *Foreign Affairs* 26 (October 1947): 73-89.

17. Kennan, *American Diplomacy*, pp. 66-76.

18. William Hardy McNeill, *America, Britain and Russia: Their Cooperation and Conflict, 1941-1946, Survey of International Affairs, 1939-1946* (London: Oxford University Press, 1953).

19. Ibid., esp. pp. 564-66, 748-68.

20. Herbert Feis, *The China Tangle: The American Effort in China from Pearl Harbor to the Marshall Mission* (Princeton: Princeton University Press, 1953) and *Churchill, Roosevelt, Stalin: The War They Waged and the Peace They Sought* (Princeton: Princeton University Press, 1957).

21. Ibid.

22. Samuel P. Huntington, *The Soldier and the State: The Theory and Politics of Civil-Military Relationships* (New York: Vintage Books, 1957).

23. Anne Armstrong, *Unconditional Surrender: The Impact of the Casablanca Policy Upon World War II* (New Brunswick, N.J.: Rutgers University Press, 1961).

24. Tang Tsou, *America's Failure in China, 1941-1950* (Chicago: University of Chicago Press, 1963).

25. Gaddis Smith, *American Diplomacy During the Second World War, 1941-1945* (New York: John Wiley & Sons, 1965).

26. Leonard, "The United States and World War II," pp. 27-28.

27. Jerald A. Combs, ed., *Nationalist, Realist and Radical: Three Views of American Diplomacy* (New York: Harper & Row, 1972), argues that defenders of U.S. foreign policy, the so-called nationalists, believe the country's leaders have combined realistic self-interest with an idealism which is good for the world. The historians discussed below could fit into such a category, but this author believes that neo-realist describes their approach and affinities better than nationalist.

28. John L. Snell, *Illusion and Necessity: The Diplomacy of Global War, 1939-1945* (Boston: Houghton Mifflin Co., 1963), p. 212.

29. Ibid., pp. 116, 137-43, 209-16. Raymond G. O'Connor's *Diplomacy for Victory: FDR and Unconditional Surrender* (New York: W. W. Norton & Co., 1971) analyzes unconditional surrender in similar terms, and contains a series of historiographical analyses of the formula and related issues in the footnotes and bibliography.

30. Snell's arguments draw heavily, but not exclusively, on volumes written by government historians in the massive *U.S. Army in World War II* series. *See* Kent R. Greenfield, *American Strategy in World War II: A Reconsideration* (Baltimore: Johns Hopkins Press, 1963), esp. pp. 49-84. *See also* Kent R. Greenfield, ed., *Command Decisions* (Washington, D.C.: Government Printing Office, 1960); William R. Emerson, "FDR as Commander-in-Chief" in Ernest May, ed., *The Ultimate Decision: The President as Commander-in-Chief* (New York: George Braziller, 1960); Maurice Matloff, "Franklin Delano Roosevelt as War Leader," in Harry L. Coles, ed., *Total War and Cold War: Problems in Civilian Control of the Military* (Columbus: Ohio State University Press, 1962); Willard Range, *Franklin D. Roosevelt's World Order* (Athens: University of Georgia Press, 1959); and John L. Snell, *Wartime Origins of the East-West Dilemma Over Germany* (New Orleans: L. G. Hauser, 1959).

31. Robert Divine, *Roosevelt and World War II* (Baltimore: Johns Hopkins Press, 1969).

32. James MacGregor Burns, *Roosevelt: The Soldier of Freedom, 1940-1945* (New York: Harcourt Brace Jovanovich, 1970). *See also* Robert Dallek, "Franklin Roosevelt as World Leader," *American Historical Review* 76 (December 1971): 1503-13.

33. Divine, *Roosevelt and World War II*, pp. 72-98; Burns, *Roosevelt*, p. 608.

34. Stephen E. Ambrose, *Eisenhower and Berlin: The Decision to Halt at the Elbe, 1945* (New York: W. W. Norton & Co., 1967).

35. Ibid.; Trumbull Higgins, *Soft Underbelly: The Anglo-American Controversy Over the Italian Campaign, 1943-1945* (New York: Macmillan Co., 1968); O'Connor, *Diplomacy for Victory*. *See also* Higgins, *Winston Churchill and the Second Front, 1940-1943* (New York: Oxford University Press, 1957).

36. Ambrose, *Eisenhower and Berlin*, p. 58.

37. O'Connor, *Diplomacy for Victory*, pp. 64-67, 103-4.

38. Warren F. Kimball, ed., *Franklin D. Roosevelt and the World Crisis, 1937-1945* (Lexington, Mass.: D. C. Heath & Co., 1973), p. xvii.

39. Denna F. Fleming, *The Cold War and Its Origins, 1917-1960*, 2 vols. (New York: Doubleday & Co., 1961).

40. William Appleman Williams, *The Tragedy of American Diplomacy* (enlarged ed., rev., New York: Delta, 1962). The original edition was published in 1959. *See also* Williams, *The Contours of American History* (Chicago: Quadrangle Books, 1961) and *The Great Evasion* (Chicago: Quadrangle Books, 1964).

41. Lloyd C. Gardner, *Economic Aspects of New Deal Diplomacy* (Madison: University of Wisconsin Press, 1964) and *Architects of Illusion: Men and Ideas in American Foreign Policy, 1941-1949* (Chicago: Quadrangle Books, 1970).

42. Gar Alperovitz, *Atomic Diplomacy: Hiroshima and Potsdam* (New York: Simon and Schuster, 1965); Herbert Feis, *Japan Subdued: The Atomic Bomb and the End of the War in the Far East* (Princeton: Princeton University Press, 1961). British physicist P. M. S. Blackett had first enunciated this theme of atomic diplomacy in his *Fear, War and the Bomb: Military and Political Consequences of Atomic Energy* (New York: McGraw-Hill, 1949).

43. Diane Shaver Clemens, *Yalta* (New York: Oxford University Press, 1970).

44. Gabriel Kolko, *The Politics of War: The World and United States Foreign Policy, 1943-1945* (New York: Random House, 1968).

45. Over thirty yearly and special conference volumes of *Foreign Relations* for the years 1941-1945 were published during the 1960s.

46. *See*, for example, Williams, *Tragedy*, pp. 204-24.

47. Kolko, *Politics of War*, pp. 555-67.

48. Clemens, *Yalta*, pp. 268, 274-79.

49. Robert J. Maddox, "Atomic Diplomacy: A Study in Creative Writing," *Journal of American History* 59 (March 1973): 925-34 and *The New Left and the Origins of the Cold War* (Princeton: Princeton University Press, 1973).

50. *See New York Times Book Review*, 17 June 1973, pp. 6-10.

51. In *Origins of the Cold War* (Waltham, Mass.: Ginn-Blaisdell, 1970) Lloyd C. Gardner, Arthur Schlesinger, Jr., and Hans Morgenthau discovered common

ground despite their disagreements. Gardner's 1970 *Architects of Illusion* was an attempt at synthesis from the revisionist point of view, while John L. Gaddis's *The United States and the Origins of the Cold War, 1941-1947* (New York: Columbia University Press, 1972) synthesized many revisionist findings regarding World War II diplomacy into a neotraditionalist explanation of the conflict. For the most recent revisionist work, *see* Leonard P. Liggio and James J. Martin, *Watershed of Empire: Essays on New Deal Foreign Policy* (Colorado Springs: Ralph Myles, 1976).

52. *See*, for example, Richard C. Lukas, *Eagles East: The Army Air Forces and the Soviet Union, 1941-1945* (Tallahassee: Florida State University Press, 1970); Richard W. Steele, *The First Offensive, 1942: Roosevelt, Marshall and the Making of American Strategy* (Bloomington, Ind.: Indiana University Press, 1973); Arthur L. Funk, *The Politics of TORCH: The Allied Landings and the Algiers Putsch, 1942* (Lawrence: University Press of Kansas, 1974); Mark A. Stoler, *The Politics of the Second Front: American Military Planning and Diplomacy in Coalition Warfare, 1941-1943* (Westport, Conn.: Greenwood Press, 1977); William Roger Louis, *Imperialism at Bay: The United States and the Decolonization of the British Empire, 1941-1945* (New York: Oxford University Press, 1978); and works cited below in Notes 56, 58, 59. *See also* Robert Beitzell, *The Uneasy Alliance: America, Britain and Russia, 1941-1943* (New York: Alfred A. Knopf, 1972) for a reexamination based on published sources.

53. Dorothy S. White, *Seeds of Discord: de Gaulle, Free France and the Allies* (Syracuse: Syracuse University Press, 1964) and Milton Viorst, *Hostile Allies: FDR and Charles de Gaulle* (New York: Macmillan Co., 1965). Other major bilateral studies during the 1945-1970 era include William L. Langer's semiofficial *Our Vichy Gamble* (New York: Alfred A. Knopf, 1947); Edward J. Rozek, *Allied Wartime Diplomacy: A Pattern in Poland* (New York: John Wiley & Sons, 1958); and works cited above in notes 11, 20, 24.

54. Edward R. Drachman, *United States Policy Toward Vietnam, 1940-1945* (Rutherford, N.J.: Fairleigh Dickinson University Press, 1970); Gary R. Hess, "Roosevelt and Indochina," *Journal of American History* 59 (September 1972): 353-68; Walter LaFeber, "Roosevelt, Churchill and Indochina, 1942-1945," *American Historical Review* 80 (December 1975): 1277-95; Christopher Thorne, "Indochina and Anglo-American Relations, 1942-1945," *Pacific Historical Review* 45 (February 1976): 73-96.

55. *See*, for example, Walter R. Roberts, *Tito, Mihailovic and the Allies, 1941-1945* (New Brunswick, N.J.: Rutgers University Press, 1973); Roger J. Bell, *Unequal Allies: Australian-American Relations and the Pacific War* (Melbourne: Melbourne University Press, 1977); Richard C. Lukas, *The Strange Allies: The United States and Poland, 1941-1945* (Knoxville, Tenn.: University of Tennessee Press, 1978); and James J. Dougherty, *The Politics of Wartime Aid: American Economic Assistance to France and French West Africa, 1940-1946* (Westport, Conn.: Greenwood Press, 1978). Recent articles and dissertations too numerous to mention have examined U.S. relations with Portugal, the Vatican, the Latin American states, Turkey, and other minor powers.

56. Martin J. Sherwin, *A World Destroyed: The Atomic Bomb and the Grand Alliance* (New York: Random House, 1975). Barton J. Bernstein summarizes his

numerous articles and reprints two of them in his *The Atomic Bomb: The Critical Issues* (Boston: Little, Brown & Co., 1976). *See also* Brian J. Villa, "The U.S. Army, Unconditional Surrender, and the Potsdam Proclamation," *Journal of American History* 63 (June 1976): 66-92 and "The Atomic Bomb and the Normandy Invasion," *Perspectives in American History* 11 (1977-78): 463-502. For a recent neotraditional approach, *see* Lisle Rose, *After Yalta* (New York: Charles Scribner's Sons, 1973) and *Dubious Victory: The United States and the End of World War II* (Kent, Ohio: Kent State University Press, 1973).

57. Gaddis, *The United States and the Origins of the Cold War*; Ralph B. Levering, *American Opinion and the Russian Alliance, 1939-1945* (Chapel Hill: University of North Carolina Press, 1976).

58. George C. Herring, *Aid to Russia, 1941-1946: Strategy, Diplomacy, the Origins of the Cold War* (New York: Columbia University Press, 1973) and Thomas G. Paterson, *Soviet-American Confrontation: Postwar Reconstruction and the Origins of the Cold War* (Baltimore: Johns Hopkins Press, 1973). *See also* their articles in the *Journal of American History* 56 (June 1969): 70-114.

59. Christopher Thorne, *Allies of a Kind: The United States, Britain and the War Against Japan, 1941-1945* (New York: Oxford University Press, 1978).

60. Robert Dallek, *Franklin D. Roosevelt and American Foreign Policy, 1932-1945* (New York: Oxford University Press, 1979); Vojtech Mastny, *Russia's Road to the Cold War: Diplomacy, Warfare, and the Politics of Communism, 1941-1945* (New York: Columbia University Press, 1979).

11 ______ Historians and Cold War Origins: The New Consensus

J. SAMUEL WALKER

No topic in American diplomatic history in the past decade has inspired as much literature or provoked as much acrimony as the origins of the cold war. The revisionist challenge to traditional interpretations shattered the consensus that had dominated historical writing on the cold war in the 1950s and early 1960s. The ensuing controversy often resembled a political debate more than an academic one as partisans on opposing sides of the issue exchanged polemics. But it also aroused interest and generated research on a wide variety of questions. In recent years, a vast body of writing, based on extensive research in newly opened sources, has produced a new cold war consensus. The new consensus draws from both traditional and revisionist interpretations to present a more balanced explanation of the beginning of the cold war. The defusing of the passions of the debate and the emergence of broad agreement on many key issues need not consign cold war scholarship to bland, bloodless eclecticism, however, because important questions remain unanswered.

The prevailing consensus in cold war literature of the 1950s and early 1960s cited Soviet aggression and expansion as the fundamental cause of postwar tensions. But within that general traditionalist framework, scholars offered divergent opinions about the nature of the Soviet threat and the appropriateness of the American response. A single "orthodox" explanation of the cold war never existed in the period; writing divided among three different schools of interpretation. One group consisted of conservatives who condemned Presidents Roosevelt and Truman for failing to recognize and take decisive action to stop the Soviet drive for world conquest. Roosevelt, they alleged, surrendered eastern Europe and China to Joseph Stalin at Yalta, while Truman was too conciliatory and irresolute in dealing subsequently with the communist menace. The conservative interpretation of the cold war received little support in academic circles, but it seemed a plausible explanation to large numbers of Americans who believed that the United States was losing its struggle with international communism. In that sense, it was an accurate reflection of widespread frustration with United States foreign policy in the early 1950s.[1]

In contrast to the right-wing critics, a liberal school of interpreters defended and applauded America's cold war policies. The liberals, like the conservatives, viewed the Soviet Union as driven by communist ideology to seek unlimited expansion. They denied, however, that Roosevelt had sold out at Yalta and praised Truman for a firm but restrained manner of dealing with Russia. The liberals identified Soviet aggression and residual isolationism in the United States as the two major problems confronting American policymakers. They hailed the Truman Doctrine, therefore, as a bold initiative that not only thwarted Soviet expansion but also marked the final triumph over isolationism. The liberal interpretation, though not simply a product of "court historians," coincided with official versions of the origins of the cold war. It contained little that Harry Truman or Dean Acheson could have found objectionable.[2]

A much more critical perspective on United States cold war policies was provided by a group of writers known as realists. They also attributed the origins of the cold war to Soviet transgressions, but they strongly disapproved of the way the United States responded. Realists argued that the basic flaw in twentieth-century American foreign policy was the tendency to act according to moralistic and idealistic precepts that ignored the realities of power. Excessive moralism and vacuous universalism led the United States to make commitments that transcended its capabilities and disregarded its national interest. The Truman Doctrine offered a prime example of the worst aspects of America's diplomatic tradition. Although the realists believed that aid to Greece was necessary to preserve the European balance of power and protect legitimate American interests in the Mediterranean, they condemned Truman for undertaking an ideological crusade to uphold freedom throughout the world. "Thus the Truman Doctrine," wrote Hans J. Morgenthau, "transformed a concrete interest of the United States in a geographically defined part of the world into a moral principle of worldwide validity, to be applied regardless of the limits of American interest and American power."[3]

Many realists, unlike the conservatives and liberals, deemphasized communist ideology as the basis of Soviet expansion. Morgenthau and Louis J. Halle, for example, contended that Stalin's foreign policy was an effort to carry out traditional Russian objectives rather than an attempt to incite world revolution. Stalin sought limited goals, and the challenge he posed was an outgrowth of Russian imperialism, not Marxist ideology. George F. Kennan partially dissented from that view by stressing ideology as the fundamental reason for intense Soviet hostility toward the West and by asserting that a "complete sweep of dominant Soviet influence over Europe and Asia . . . was Stalin's initial postwar hope." But he too argued that Soviet foreign policy was flexible and that its power, not its ideology, threatened American national interests.[4]

The realists shared a sense of fatalism about the origins of the cold war. Halle articulated that tendency most clearly by comparing America and Russia to a scorpion and tarantula in a bottle, locked "in a situation of irreducible dilemma." A historical tradition of insecurity and suspicion of the West compelled the Soviets to expand, and the Wilsonian legacy caused the United States to react as it did. The result was a tragic but inevitable conflict. Kennan considered the cold war unavoidable because of the implacable hostility of Soviet leaders and their need to cite foreign enemies as the reason for perpetuating their absolute authority over the Russian people. In general, the realists concurred in depicting the cold war as an inevitable result of World War II. Although they suggested that tensions could have been reduced significantly if the United States had recognized a Soviet sphere of influence in eastern Europe, they believed that American diplomatic tradition precluded that possibility.[5]

The realist view, which was probably the most influential and certainly the most sophisticated of the traditional interpretations of the cold war, was highly critical of many American policies, but it did not question the conventional idea that Soviet actions triggered the cold war. A few writers in the 1950s and early 1960s did argue that the United States at least shared responsibility for postwar tensions, but their efforts made little impression on the prevailing consensus. Not until the mid-1960s did revisionist studies begin to generate serious debate about the origins of the cold war. The most consequential challenge to traditional interpretations was Gar Alperovitz's contention that the United States had dropped atomic bombs on Japan not because of military necessity but to impress the Russians and make them more tractable in eastern Europe. Although it received far less attention than Alperovitz's book, David Horowitz published at about the same time a general indictment of United States policies throughout the cold war era. Horowitz, like Alperovitz, argued that Truman reversed Roosevelt's conciliatory position toward Russia immediately after taking office. The United States severed the wartime alliance, initiated the cold war, and failed to recognize that much of Stalin's expansionist drive was an effort to secure his borders.[6]

Much of the Alperovitz and Horowitz critiques was not particularly new. Others had previously asserted that the United States had used the atomic bomb more for political than military reasons, and Horowitz's analysis followed along the same basic lines as D. F. Fleming's 1961 book, *The Cold War and Its Origins*. The timing as much as the content of their books explained why Alperovitz and eventually Horowitz had more impact on cold war historiography than earlier revisionists. A new generation of scholars came of age in the mid-1960s. It was natural that younger writers whose memories of brinksmanship and bomb shelters were more vivid than of World War II and its aftermath would have a new perspective on the cold war. Although neither the Alperovitz nor the Horowitz book approached being definitive—Alperovitz admitted that his conclusions were tentative and Horowitz based his polemic on sparse research—both raised questions that older scholars had not seriously considered. It was inevitable that a body of revisionist writing on the cold war would appear, as had occurred in interpretations of other major events in American diplomatic history.[7]

The Vietnam conflict gave additional impetus to cold war revisionism. The war did not precipitate the rise of revisionism, which was underway before Southeast Asia became a major issue. But Vietnam made the beginning of the cold war a much more urgent and controversial subject than it might otherwise have been and enhanced the credibility of revisionist arguments. As Ronald Steel observed in 1971: "To reject the war in Vietnam is to question the basic assumptions on which American foreign policy rests. It is to ask not only whether the prevalent conception of the cold war might now be wrong, but whether it was ever right." The passions aroused by the war and its impact on college campuses intensified the debate over that question to a point where scholarly restraint and tolerance for opposing opinions were often conspicuously lacking.[8]

In a remark that foreshadowed the tone of the emerging controversy, Arthur M. Schlesinger, Jr., wrote in October 1966: "Surely the time has come to blow the whistle before the current outburst of revisionism regarding the origins of the cold war goes much further." A year later, in an article published in *Foreign Affairs*, he regretted that he had remonstrated "somewhat intemperately" and affirmed that revisionism remained "an essential part of the process by which history . . . enlarges its perspectives and enriches its insights." Schlesinger then offered an analysis of the cold war that combined elements of the liberal and realist views while countering revisionist opinions. He submitted that a fundamental conflict between the American commitment to universalism (which he regarded more sympathetically than the realists) and Stalin's insistence on a Soviet sphere of influence in eastern Europe led to the cold war. Stalin misinterpreted American protests against his policies in eastern Europe as an effort to undermine Russian security, and the United States misread Stalin's intentions by assuming he planned to expand into western Europe. Schlesinger further argued that communist ideology, Soviet totalitarianism, and Stalin's personal paranoia made postwar cooperation between the United States and the Soviet Union impossible. Like Kennan, he contended that American acts of friendship and generosity could not have overcome

Stalin's suspicion or changed Soviet policy, and that revisionists erred in believing otherwise.[9]

Schlesinger's article, if such were his intention, was no more effective than his earlier appeal in whistling revisionism to a halt. Revisionist scholars rejected his assumption that a more conciliatory American posture would not have reduced postwar tensions and questioned his premise that Stalin's personality and communist ideology guaranteed Soviet intransigence in the early cold war period.[10] They claimed that American actions, at least as much as Soviet ones, provoked the cold war. Yet for the most part the early revisionists had not provided an adequate explanation of why the United States took a hostile position toward Russia. Only William Appleman Williams in *The Tragedy of American Diplomacy* had offered a comprehensive view that placed American cold war policies in a broad historical context. He contended that the driving force behind twentieth-century United States foreign policy was overseas economic expansion. Business and political leaders agreed that American domestic prosperity depended on the availability of foreign markets and they focused their attention on maintaining an Open Door for trade opportunities throughout the world. American insistence on preserving the Open Door clashed with Stalin's primary objectives after World War II, because he did not welcome the prospect of United States economic penetration in areas he regarded as vital to Soviet security. Thus, in Williams's opinion, America's aggressive economic expansion, supported by its predominant power, initiated postwar tensions. When *The Tragedy of American Diplomacy* first appeared in 1959, it exerted little perceptible influence on cold war historiography. By the end of the 1960s, however, Williams's analysis had emerged as the nucleus of a burgeoning body of revisionist literature. Stressing foreign economic expansion as the central impulse in American diplomacy, Walter LaFeber, Lloyd C. Gardner, Barton J. Bernstein, Stephen E. Ambrose, and Joyce and Gabriel Kolko published major studies that advanced what was by then referred to as the new left interpretation of the cold war.[11]

Despite disagreements among themselves on some issues and variations in tone and emphasis, new left scholars concurred on many key points that contrasted with the realist and liberal interpretations. The most fundamental and obvious distinction was the revisionist contention that the United States, not Russia, was primarily responsible for the cold war. They argued that America's overwhelming power and its concerted effort to shape the postwar world created friction with the Soviet Union. Few new left historians—the Kolkos were a notable exception—found the United States solely to blame for postwar tensions. But their analyses of American policies differed sharply from the traditional view that the country had responded defensively to Soviet thrusts. According to Gardner, for example, the United States determined "the *way* in which the Cold War developed, at least," because "it had much greater opportunity and far more options to influence the course of events than the Soviet Union."[12]

New left writers also departed from traditional interpretations by emphasizing economic factors as the basis of American diplomacy. Some revisionists, such as Diane Shaver Clemens and Athan Theoharis, focused on the personalities and visceral anticommunism of American leaders rather than on economic considerations in explaining United States hostility toward Russia.[13] But most, dissenting from the realist argument that moralistic and legalistic precepts were the fundamental motivating forces in American foreign policy, stressed America's commitment to Open Door expansion as the key to its cold war position. New left scholars, as Barton J. Bernstein and Robert W. Tucker pointed out, disagreed among themselves on the relationship between America's economy and its foreign policy. The most extreme revisionists, represented by the Kolkos, considered overseas economic expansion as essential for the functioning of the capitalist system and, therefore, unalterable as long as capitalism survived. The more moderate position, most clearly outlined by Williams, held that American leaders mistakenly believed that foreign markets were critical for domestic prosperity and, therefore, a change in attitudes could modify the Open Door ideology. A similar dichotomy existed in how the new left viewed American idealism. Williams and most other revisionists regretted that United States economic activity abroad subverted the nation's ideal of self-determination and genuine concern for the well-being of other peoples. The Kolkos, on the other hand, refused to take idealistic pronouncements of American policymakers seriously. Those differences, however, were less striking than the contrast between the broad agreement among new left historians on the primacy of economic concerns and traditional interpretations that largely ignored economic aspects of American foreign policy.[14]

The new left interpretation presented an image of American leaders that markedly diverged from that provided by the realists. Realists credited Truman and his chief advisors with good intentions, but portrayed United States policies as drifting, misguided, and innocent of the realities of power politics. Revisionists, however, depicted American policymakers as purposeful, calculating, and effective in promoting Open Door expansion. They credited United States leaders with being competent in carrying out lamentable objectives. Revisionists played down the importance of chance and accident in determining national actions. "Whereas a conventional historiography emphasizes the role of the unforeseen, the contingent, and the inadvertent," commented Robert Tucker, "a radical historiography leaves very little scope to these factors."[15]

New left writers viewed Stalin's leadership in quite different terms than liberals and some realists. They described him as tentative, cautious, and flexible and agreed with realists such as Morgenthau and Halle that his goals were limited. Revisionists denied the assertion that Stalin was paranoid; Williams, for example, argued that American policymakers did not deal with him as though he were demented and that Stalin had ample rational reasons for suspecting United States hostility. In new left analyses, American policies after the war shattered Stalin's hope for cooperation with the West, prompting him to consolidate his hold on eastern Europe and reluctantly adopt an antagonistic position toward the United States.[16]

Unlike the realists, most revisionists did not regard the cold war as inevitable. "To see the Cold War as a struggle between two scorpions in a bottle," commented Gardner, "reduces history to a cast of witless characters." New left historians generally maintained that a more conciliatory position on a number of crucial issues could have significantly altered the course of postwar events. If the United States had been more accommodating by sharing information on atomic energy, offering the Soviets economic assistance for reconstruction, accepting a Russian sphere of influence in eastern Europe, and recognizing legitimate Soviet security concerns, the cold war, or at least the worst aspects of it, could have been averted. From the new left frame of reference, those policies would have required the United States to compromise substantially its commitment to worldwide economic expansion. Therefore, only those revisionists who thought that American capitalism was flexible enough to modify its adherence to the Open Door system could argue that the cold war was preventable. As Christopher Lasch pointed out, scholars who believed that the imperatives of capitalism required American leaders to act as they did to protect the nation's economic interests necessarily affirmed the inevitability of the cold war. "According to a certain type of revisionism," he wrote, "American policy has all the rigidity the orthodox historians attribute to the U.S.S.R., and this inflexibility made the cold war inevitable." Most revisionists eschewed such a stance, however, and insisted that the Truman administration had the means and the opportunity, but lacked the will or the wisdom, to get along with Russia after the war.[17]

The growing volume and impact of revisionist literature provoked a spirited reaction from traditionalist-minded scholars. Some dismissed the new left interpretation as thoroughly deficient. John W. Spanier thought it made the cold war "into a fairy tale," Adam B. Ulam declared that "as history this revisionism is fallacious," and Robert H. Ferrell asserted in 1972 "that the revisionists have not proved a single one of their points."[18] Others compared cold war critics to revisionists of previous conflicts in American history and suggested that the new left would have no more lasting influence than their predecessors.[19] Some writers, however, while questioning revisionist assumptions and conclusions, took their arguments seriously. For example, Robert Tucker, who published an extended and sophisticated commentary on "radical left" historians, was sharply critical of their emphasis on economic expansion as the determinant of U.S. diplomacy and their supposition that a socialist United States would carry out a more benign foreign policy than capitalist America. But he also maintained that revisionism was more than a passing fad and had made important contributions to understanding the conduct of American foreign policy.[20]

There were no such concessions in the most controversial assessment of the revisionist interpretation, Robert James Maddox's *The New Left and the Origins of the Cold War*. Rather than contesting the revisionists on the basis of their arguments, Maddox attacked them on their use of sources. After checking the footnotes of books by seven leading revisionists—Williams, Fleming, Horowitz, Kolko, Alperovitz, Clemens, and Gardner—he accused all of deliberately distorting the evidence. "Perhaps," he wrote, "the New Left view of American foreign policy during and after World War II can *only* be sustained by doing violence to the historical record?" Maddox left little doubt that his answer to that question was affirmative. His book and the response to it highlighted the choleric tone that was so typical of the cold war controversy. The authors of the books examined retorted angrily. Many traditionalists felt gratified and vindicated while many revisionists attacked Maddox with the same harshness that infused his book. Those who stood somewhere between the two positions often were saddened by the spectacle. Warren F. Kimball, for example, found the bitterness of the debate more disturbing than the charges in Maddox's book. "It is not hypocritical to disagree with someone in a gentle, courteous manner," he observed. "Granted, it is far easier and much more fun to be vitriolic and sarcastic, but such writing hardly qualifies as a dispassionate search for truth; rather it merely polarizes the argument."[21]

The vituperative tone of the dispute over cold war origins obscured the fact that the revisionist and realist (though not the liberal) positions were not totally irreconcilable. Although a balanced synthesis drawing on both interpretations was theoretically possible, the pattern of mutual recrimination made it difficult for scholars on one side of the debate to recognize virtues in the opposing view. A dearth of sources also contributed to polarization. Before the early 1970s, only a relatively few official records and personal papers were available to cold war historians, who had to rely on scattered sources that failed even to approach giving a full account of the early postwar period. It was easy for scholars to interpret the limited evidence according to their own predilections and difficult for others to refute their arguments convincingly. Therefore, much of the cold war debate was an intemperate exchange of biases for which there seemed no middle ground. The opening of new sources did not eliminate that problem, of course, but it did provide a more complete picture of American policies and allowed for a more sophisticated and judicious explanation of the historical context in which they were formulated. It was no accident that the beginning of a new phase of cold war scholarship, characterized by a more restrained tone and more balanced interpretation, coincided with the availability of a growing body of fresh evidence. In fact, Maddox's book was something of an atavism the day it was published, because a trend toward moderation and eclecticism was already under way.

The most prominent example of the emerging trend was John Lewis Gaddis's 1972 study, *The United States and the Origins of the Cold War, 1941-1947.* Drawing on many recently opened sources, Gaddis stressed the fundamental continuity of Roosevelt's and Truman's foreign-policy aims and their incompatibility with Stalin's primary objectives. Truman sincerely wanted to continue his predecessor's conciliatory policies toward Russia, but by the early months of 1946 he and his advisors had reluctantly concluded that the only way to preserve world peace and American security was to adopt a posture of firmness. Gaddis agreed with the revisionists that domestic factors significantly influenced the Truman administration's diplomatic stance and that the United States had attempted to use economic pressure to extract political concessions from the Soviets. But he contended that other domestic concerns, particularly public opinion and congressional attitudes, played a much more important role in shaping Truman's decisions than did economic considerations.

In assessing responsibility for the development of the cold war, Gaddis took a moderate position that was slightly right of center. He denied the new left argument that more accommodating American policies toward eastern Europe, economic assistance for Russia, or sharing atomic information were feasible options for United States leaders because of adamant public and congressional opposition. He concurred, however, with revisionists who viewed the cold war as avoidable, though he did so on abstract philosophical grounds rather than citing specific actions that might have changed the course of postwar events. Gaddis maintained that neither the United States nor the Soviet Union was solely at fault for the cold war, but he concluded that Stalin was more to blame because he was free of the domestic constraints that so limited the alternatives available to Truman. Many traditionalists hailed Gaddis's book as an effective antidote to revisionism. But his measured tone, balanced interpretation, and emphasis on the complexities of postwar issues were more an indication of the direction in which cold war scholarship was moving than a vindication of rigid traditionalism.[22]

The trend toward eclecticism so apparent in Gaddis's book was also evident in major studies published in 1973 by George C. Herring, Jr., and Thomas G. Paterson. Both provided richly detailed and thoroughly researched examinations of the central question raised by new left scholars—the role of economic motives in American cold war policies. Herring investigated American lend-lease assistance to Russia during and after World War II. He agreed with many revisionists that Truman's abrupt termination of lend-lease in May 1945 and later failure to extend credit to Russia contributed to the onset of the cold war by reinforcing Soviet suspicion of the West. But Herring attributed those policies to bureaucratic ineptness, bad planning, and domestic pressures rather than a deliberate attempt to extort concessions from the Soviet Union. He denied that more generous American actions would have significantly allayed Stalin's distrust or won his gratitude. The cold war, he believed, evolved from "the depth of the issues that divided the two allies," and was to some degree and in some form, unavoidable. Herring, like Gaddis, took a moderately right-of-center position and assigned the United States partial responsibility for the cold war. He incorporated some revisionist arguments in his book but rejected their overall view of an aggressive United States using its economic power to coerce the Soviet Union.[23]

Paterson was much more critical of American actions than was Herring, but he too offered an evenhanded analysis that affirmed some elements of the new left interpretation while questioning others. He echoed a revisionist theme by asserting that American policy was "not accidental or aimless: rather it was self-consciously expansionist." A crucial part of that expansionism was economic, and, in contrast to Herring, Paterson argued that premeditated American efforts to use economic power to pressure the Soviets were an important cause of the cold war. Unlike many new left scholars, however, he emphasized that factors other than economic considerations also played a key role in United States cold war diplomacy. He did not depict American economic concerns as inherently pernicious, and viewed United States economic pressure as a tactical effort to influence Soviet behavior in eastern Europe rather than an attempt to secure markets and guarantee an open world for trade opportunities. Paterson contended that the Soviets did not adamantly oppose American trade expansion and that the Truman administration undercut its own economic objectives by sharply reducing commerce with and withholding economic assistance from Russia and eastern Europe. He denied that the cold war was inevitable, because "Washington was free to make different choices or, at the very least, to pursue its reconstruction plans less coercively." Paterson's left-of-center interpretation condemned American cold war policies much more severely than Gaddis or Herring, but his tone and perspective were in keeping with the trend toward moderation and recognition of the complexities of the cold war.[24]

The availability of new sources and the continuing debate over cold war origins inspired investigations of a broad range of specific issues. Most of them necessarily concentrated on American policies and perceptions because that was what the documents revealed. But within the constraints imposed by the evidence, a vast body of literature provided new insights and deeper understanding into the Truman administration's response to postwar crises. Those studies, though frequently disagreeing with one another on particulars, generally conformed with the trend toward eclecticism that narrowed the cleavage between the realist and new left views. Many offered fresh ideas and original analyses, but most fell within the broad perimeters defined by the basic interpretations.

Considerable attention focused on American policies toward eastern Europe. Although realists and revisionists had agreed that the Truman administration should have conceded Stalin a sphere of influence in eastern Europe, they sharply differed on other points. Realists regarded Stalin's violation of the Yalta accords in eastern Europe as the basic cause of the cold war, and maintained that American opposition, which was largely rhetorical, stemmed from its commitment to the ideal of self-determination. Revisionists argued that the United States attempted to undermine Soviet control of eastern Europe through economic coercion and atomic diplomacy to promote Open Door expansion. They stressed that Stalin had no preconceived plan for dealing with eastern Europe and gradually tightened his hold on all the countries in that area in response to American pressure.

Studies of the United States stance in eastern Europe that appeared in the mid-1970s did not accept either realist or new left arguments in their pure form but stood somewhere between the two positions. Lynn Etheridge Davis supported much of the realist view by emphasizing the principles of the Atlantic Charter rather than economic concerns as the guiding force in American policies. But she suggested that the United States shared responsibility for the beginning of the cold war because its protests against Soviet behavior aroused Stalin's fears and prompted him to extend his domination of eastern Europe. Geir Lundestad agreed with revisionists that Stalin took a flexible position toward eastern Europe and that the United States did apply some pressure on him. But like the realists, he deemphasized economic motives as the basis of American diplomacy and regarded postwar tensions as unavoidable.[25] In an examination of United States policies toward Czechoslovakia, Mark S. Steinitz contended that America's fundamental goal of self-determination was undermined by its own "inflexible economic diplomacy" as well as by Soviet machinations. Without discounting Russian accountability, Stephen A. Garrett cited misperceptions by American policymakers of the situation in eastern Europe as contributing to cold war tensions. Hugh De Santis considered psychological and bureaucratic factors in describing divergent American responses to the situation in eastern Europe. He asserted that American diplomats stationed there concluded that America and Russia were locked in an ideological struggle long before desk officers at the State Department, who continued to hope for cooperation between the two nations until early 1946, reached that conclusion.[26]

There was wide agreement among postrevisionist studies of the American stance toward eastern Europe that the United States lacked a coherent policy, and that other than lodging verbal protests, did little to challenge Soviet domination of the region. Bennett Kovrig and Walter Ullmann, taking a conservative position that seemed curiously anachronistic in the 1970s, asserted that more decisive American actions might have prevented Soviet subjugation of eastern European nations. Lundestad maintained that American leaders did not view eastern Europe as an area of vital concern and vacillated between promoting universalist principles and accepting a Soviet sphere of influence. The result was a "non-policy" in eastern Europe. Hugh B. Hammett claimed that Roosevelt's failure to define his goals and make them clear to Stalin and the American people led to misunderstandings after the war. Davis indicted American officials for neglecting to give much thought to how Atlantic Charter principles could be implemented and how efforts to do so might affect United States relations with Russia. Eduard M. Mark found American policies more calculated than other postrevisionist scholars. He maintained that the Truman administration was willing to accept a Soviet sphere of influence in eastern Europe as long as it was "open" but objected to the "exclusive" spheres that Stalin established.[27]

If the Truman administration largely acquiesced in Soviet control of eastern Europe, then the explanation of why the United States adopted a firm posture toward Russia must be found elsewhere. A number of scholars stressed United States-Soviet conflict in the Near East as the key to the origins of America's containment policies. In the realist view, Stalin's thrusts into Iran, Turkey, and Greece were aggressive and provocative, and, unlike eastern Europe, could not be justified as defensive measures. The United States took decisive action to protect legitimate national interests. Revisionists argued that American economic expansion in the Near East was a basic source of tension. They depicted Stalin's aims in Iran and Turkey as limited and reasonable and his role in the Greek revolution as virtually nonexistent. Therefore, a strong American reaction was necessary only to uphold economic interests.[28]

In recent writing on the United States and the Near East, some scholars adhered closely to one or the other side of the debate. Eduard M. Mark followed the new left interpretation by describing Russian intervention in Iran as a response to American economic activities that seemed to endanger Soviet oil supplies. David S. McLellan affirmed the realist position by contending that Soviet pressure in Iran and Turkey demonstrated its lack of respect for the sovereignty of its neighbors and imperiled the world balance of power. American leaders interpreted Soviet actions as an indication of unlimited ambitions and reacted accordingly.[29]

Other writers combined elements of the realist and revisionist views. Gary R. Hess attributed Soviet activities in Iran to their concern for national security and prestige. Although their methods were heavy-handed, the United States overreacted and unnecessarily intensified cold war tensions and mutual misunderstandings. In studies of the civil war in Greece, John O. Iatrides and D. George Kousoulas characterized the Greek Communists as acting independently of Stalin, who abided by his promise to Winston Churchill not to interfere in that country. Iatrides, however, concluded that if the Greek Communists had triumphed, they probably would have become "Stalin's helpless wards." Kousoulas asserted that the situation in Greece suggested that Stalin put national interests ahead of revolutionary ones, and that he did not direct a coordinated international communist movement. But he also argued that the United States reacted responsibly to what appeared to be serious provocation. In a comprehensive and thoroughly researched study of the internal situations in and American policies toward Iran, Turkey, and Greece, Bruce R. Kuniholm elaborated on previous scholarship. He maintained that before the Truman Doctrine, "containment in the Near East was a realistic and pragmatic" response to Soviet activities. But he agreed with Iatrides and Kousoulas in their description of Stalin's role in the Greek revolution. He also suggested that the "public rationalization" of containment and the universalization of policies that appeared to succeed in the Near East seriously impaired the vision and restricted the alternatives of American policymakers in dealing with subsequent crises.[30]

Another flashpoint of the cold war, Germany, has been the subject of several comprehensive studies reflecting various perspectives. Bruce Kuklick took a revisionist position by asserting that the American commitment to economic expansion caused conflict with the Soviet Union and led to the division of Germany. The United States was determined to ensure German recovery because it was essential to the economic revival of Europe and, therefore, vital to American economic interests. In Kuklick's opinion, the Truman administration's resistance to Soviet claims for reparations that would impede German recovery and its efforts to unify Germany under American control played a major role in generating postwar tensions. John Gimbel dissented from both the new left interpretation and the traditionalist view that Soviet ambitions and intransigence destroyed four-power cooperation in occupied Germany. Unlike traditionalists, he insisted that French rather than Russian obstructions undermined the Potsdam agreements and that the Soviet stance toward Germany was flexible and pragmatic. The State Department, however, "leveled its guns on the Russians" and ignored French obstinance to secure congressional approval of the Marshall Plan. In contrast to revisionists, Gimbel denied that American policies in Germany were either consistent or carefully planned. He attributed them instead to a "series of pragmatic bureaucratic decisions and compromises" that attempted to reconcile the views and demands of the State Department, United States Army occupation authorities, the nations of western Europe, Congress, and the American people.[31]

John H. Backer agreed with Gimbel that the United States lacked a single-minded approach in Germany and described United States actions as a series of incremental decisions that eventually defined the American position. Although he rejected the revisionists' emphasis on economic expansion as the basis of American policies, he accepted their view that Soviet demands were reasonable and negotiable. In an analysis of the origins of the Marshall Plan, Scott Jackson maintained that Gimbel's emphasis on bureaucratic rivalries and American concern over German questions as the basic catalysts for the plan provided only a partial explanation. He contended that strategic and security interests and economic considerations played a more central role in the formulation of the European recovery program. Although Gimbel, Backer, and Jackson all took eclectic positions, their studies illustrated that within that general framework, there was ample allowance for differing emphases and viewpoints.[32]

Much cold war scholarship focused more on the domestic roots of United States foreign policy than on interactions between America and Russia. The role of public opinion inspired considerable debate but remained an elusive subject. Several writers disputed the argument, most clearly set forth by John Lewis Gaddis, that public and congressional attitudes sharply limited the foreign-policy options available to American leaders. In a theoretical analysis published before Gaddis's book, Bernard C. Cohen suggested that the public was generally uninformed about foreign affairs and usually could be persuaded to endorse the government's course of action without great difficulty. Walter LaFeber and Thomas Paterson accepted that line of reasoning and asserted that the Truman administration molded, not followed, public and congressional opinion in the early cold war period. Peter H. Irons concluded that Polish-Americans, despite strenuous lobbying, exerted little effective influence on Roosevelt's and Truman's policies toward Poland. Michael Leigh took a middle position on the issue by agreeing that Truman manipulated public opinion to an extent. But he added that "the need to mobilize consent is itself witness to the constraint that national leaders perceive as inhering in the mass public."[33]

Scholars also differed on how the American people regarded Russia immediately after World War II. Richard M. Freeland and Athan Theoharis, for example, maintained that most Americans were kindly disposed toward their wartime ally and hopeful of continuing cooperation between the United States and the Soviet Union. Ralph B. Levering and Gary J. Buckley, on the other hand, contended that a legacy of suspicion and animosity toward the Soviets lingered throughout the war and that public gratitude for Russian contributions to defeating Germany quickly dissipated. Despite their disagreements on other matters, many writers concurred in depicting the enunciation of the Truman Doctrine as a public relations effort that backfired. Gaddis, for example, argued that the effect of Truman's speech was "to imprison American diplomacy in an ideological straitjacket." Freeland and Theoharis condemned it even more harshly. Both viewed the Truman Doctrine as a crucial element in a series of anticommunist activities that destroyed public goodwill toward Russia and laid the foundations for McCarthyism.[34]

Other domestic influences, related to but separate from public opinion, received less attention. Although scholars frequently cited the impact of Congress on the administration's diplomatic position, they did not undertake detailed examinations of the pressures, impulses, and traditions that defined its role in the cold war era. In a brief look at the subject, John T. Rourke concluded that Congressmen's views on foreign policy were parochial and their impact was unconstructive. The need remains for closer scrutiny of the institutional functions of Congress and the ideas and influence of its individual members.[35] A number of writers investigated the societal roots of American diplomacy. They denied that the public or the Congress had any significant input and attributed United States foreign policy to the decisions of a group of elites. They did not, however, fully agree on who the elites were or where they came from. G. William Domhoff emphasized their social and educational background while Gabriel Kolko argued that they represented "dominant business circles and their law firms." Richard J. Barnet denounced the power of the "national security bureaucracy" and John C. Donovan identified a "policy elite" drawn from leading financial institutions, law firms, corporations, and universities.[36] All of those studies reflected a revisionist perspective and none was definitive, but they raised intriguing questions that deserve careful examination. A few scholars focused on the intellectual foundations of American cold war diplomacy. Donovan stressed the "mind-set" of the policy elite, based largely on its "obsessive fear of communist expansion" and "voracious hunger for foreign markets." Les K. Adler and Thomas G. Paterson traced the transfer of fear and hatred of Nazi Germany to the Soviet Union by American leaders and the public. Ernest R. May described how the Truman administration applied the "lessons" of the 1930s in adopting a policy of firmness toward Russia after the war. Biographies of individuals also shed light on intellectual trends, but the subject requires further study.[37]

The relationship between military considerations and foreign policy has generated growing interest among cold war scholars. The controversy over the use of the atomic bomb inspired several detailed studies that have achieved a broad consensus. Martin J. Sherwin, Barton J. Bernstein, and Lisle A. Rose agreed that the United States dropped the bomb primarily to hasten the war's end. Sherwin and Bernstein argued that American leaders viewed the weapon as a means of winning concessions from Stalin, though that was a distinctly secondary goal. Rose, Bernstein, and Gregg F. Herken also concurred that the Truman administration attempted to take advantage of its atomic monopoly to secure diplomatic objectives. Atomic diplomacy not only proved futile, but it escalated cold war tensions and diminished the already slight possibility of United States-Soviet cooperation on international control of atomic energy. The consensus on the role of the bomb in the cold war combined the traditional view that the United States had no ulterior motives in using it against Japan with the revisionist assertion that its inclusion in America's diplomatic arsenal helped cause the cold war.[38]

The increasing availability of military documents stimulated research on the role of the armed services in the cold war. Historians approached the subject in a variety of ways. In a study of the Joint Chiefs of Staff, Walter S. Poole asserted that aggressive Soviet expansion transformed the chiefs' position from conciliation to a conviction that Stalin sought world domination and that peaceful coexistence was impossible. Lawrence S. Wittner, by contrast, contended that the Office of Strategic Services in the spring of 1945 expressed deep concern about Soviet activities and formulated an early rationale for a policy of containment. Other writers emphasized that a systematic attempt to coordinate strategy and diplomacy occurred for the first time in the cold war period. Jonathan Knight demonstrated how Secretary of the Navy Forrestal promoted "casual" visits by American ships to Mediterranean ports to uphold United States interests and guarantee an important role for the navy in combating communism.[39] Thomas H. Etzold and John Lewis Gaddis compiled a volume of original documents to show that containment was a product of the effort "to integrate political and military considerations in national security planning." In an introductory essay, Etzold described the origins and functions of the agencies created to carry out that task. He concluded that the National Security Council and the Policy Planning Staff of the State Department performed more effectively than the Joint Chiefs or the Central Intelligence Agency. Alfred D. Sander, however, maintained that Truman made little use of the National Security Council until after the Korean War began. Although many key documents have opened too recently to be incorporated into cold war studies, the prospects are promising that they will add an exciting new dimension to the historiography of the period.[40]

Many important contributions to cold war scholarship have appeared in biographies of major, and in some cases, minor figures. The rise of revisionism inspired many scholars to examine the careers of critics of American cold war policies. The most prominent opponent of Truman's diplomacy, Henry A. Wallace, commanded considerable attention. Although Edward L. and Frederick H. Schapsmeier took a traditional view by depicting Wallace's stand as naive and misguided, others regarded him more sympathetically. Norman D. Markowitz compared him favorably with cold war liberals, though he criticized Wallace for failing to recognize the defects inherent in American capitalism. Richard J. Walton hailed Wallace as a remarkably prescient observer whose ideas, had they been followed, could have prevented the cold war. J. Samuel Walker argued that Wallace offered a restrained and sensible critique of United States foreign policy in the early cold war period, and despite flaws in his position, deserved better treatment and a fairer hearing than he received.[41]

Other less conspicuous dissenters often fared better in the hands of historians than they had with their contemporaries. Wallace's running mate in his 1948 presidential campaign, Glen H. Taylor, Senator from Idaho, was the subject of an admiring biography by F. Ross Peterson. A number of critics who attacked United States foreign policy from various perspectives, including Wallace, Taylor, Walter Lippmann, James Paul Warburg, Claude Pepper, Robert A. Taft, and I. F. Stone, were portrayed favorably in a collection of essays edited by Thomas G. Paterson. Ronald Radosh sought to rehabilitate a group of conservative spokesmen by stressing their opposition to American globalism.[42] James T. Patterson provided a sympathetic portrait of Robert A. Taft, though he was less impressed with Taft's views than was Radosh. Two obscure conservatives, Lawrence Dennis, an avowed fascist, and James P. Kem, Senator from Missouri, also won praise from scholars for the objections they voiced to American cold war policies.[43]

Key figures in the Truman administration also were the subjects of biographies. Although a full scholarly treatment of Truman's career has yet to appear, John Lewis Gaddis and Richard S. Kirkendall contributed brief, appreciative accounts. Wilson D. Miscamble, in a study of Truman's prepresidential views on foreign policy, emphasized his fear that the country would retreat to isolationism and his guarded hope for cooperation with the Soviet Union after the war.[44] David S. McLellan and Gaddis Smith provided sympathetic portraits of Dean Acheson that described his concern that Soviet expansion would undermine the world balance of power and threaten American strategic interests. George T. Mazuzan traced the American ambassador to the United Nations Warren R. Austin's gradual disillusionment with the Soviet Union and showed how little his appeals for collective security through the United Nations influenced the administration.[45]

Scholars studied and debated the ideas of George F. Kennan more than any other administration official. C. Ben Wright disputed Kennan's claims that his original concept of containment had been distorted and militarized. Wright contended that Kennan made a substantial contribution "to the Cold War mentality" because his writings envisioned the use of military power in many parts of the world to stop communism. Kennan angrily denied Wright's assertions. He received support from John L. Gaddis, who argued that Kennan's containment theory had always stressed the limits of American power and deemphasized the value of military intervention. Gaddis's article, in turn, brought sharp rejoinders from Eduard Mark, Michael H. Hunt, and John W. Coogan. The exchange of opinions about Kennan's views left the question unresolved and in need of further investigation.[46] Many other key figures in the early cold war era have not received adequate scholarly attention. Although would-be biographers in some cases must await the opening of personal papers, cold war historiography can be greatly enriched by current and comprehensive studies of Truman, Edward R. Stettinius, James F. Byrnes, Averell Harriman, Charles Bohlen, Robert Lovett, Joseph Davies, Arthur H. Vandenberg, George C. Marshall, Tom Connally, William L. Clayton, Robert P. Patterson, and Walter Bedell Smith. As is usually the case in biographies, most cold war scholars sympathized with the positions espoused by their subjects. At the same time, few were uncritical admirers of their protagonists, and, in general, biographies of cold war personalities reflected the trend toward moderation and eclecticism that characterized writing on the Truman period after the early 1970s.

Although analyses of Stalin's foreign policy are inherently precarious, a few recent books on the topic made notable contributions to cold war historiography. In an examination of the major components of Soviet diplomacy, Morton Schwartz argued that Stalin's weakness relative to the United States made him cautious, though he launched a rhetorical offensive in hopes that harsh words would disguise his vulnerability. In general, Stalin acted "tough but restrained, belligerent but cautious, assertive but not adventurous." Schwartz also insisted, however, that ideology was an important motivating factor in Soviet diplomacy and a major cause of the outbreak of the cold war. Like Schwartz, Adam B. Ulam regarded Stalin's political power as absolute. In most ways, Ulam's portrait of Stalin conformed with the traditionalist image. He depicted the Soviet leader as cunning, ruthless, suspicious, and unapproachable. In return for giving in on minor points at Teheran and Yalta, the wily dictator secured major concessions from the West. Ulam maintained that winning Stalin's respect, not trying to allay his distrust, was the proper way to deal with him. In certain respects, however, Ulam's analysis was compatible with revisionist arguments. He viewed Stalin's primary goal in eastern Europe as being the establishment of friendly governments, though not necessarily communist ones. He contended that Stalin asserted complete control over Russia's neighbors in response to American policies, particularly the Marshall Plan. Ulam denied that Stalin was paranoid, at least until about 1947.[47]

In a study of Stalin's wartime diplomacy, Vojtech Mastny disputed revisionist views even more sharply than Ulam. He argued that during the war Stalin planned to expand into eastern Europe and beyond and that his ambitions were tempered only by his fear of inciting a strong reaction from the West by going too far. The United States and Britain blundered by not firmly opposing Stalin's actions much earlier than they did. William O. McCagg provided a different picture of Stalin's foreign policy by emphasizing how domestic concerns shaped it. He contended that during the war, Stalin lost some of his political control to military leaders and industrial managers. In an effort to regain that power, he moved to revive the Communist party, which necessitated a renewed rhetorical emphasis on ideology. Stalin realized that this would cause misunderstandings with the West, but he declined to make his limited foreign-policy ambitions clear in order to carry out his domestic priorities. Both the Mastny and McCagg books were scrupulously researched and richly documented. Their focus and analysis were dissimilar; McCagg, for example, regarded Stalin as less belligerent and ambitious than did Mastny. Both were important works, though at present their impact on cold war historiography is difficult to predict.[48]

In the late 1970s, three major comprehensive studies of the early cold war were published. Each was balanced and moderate in interpretation and drew on the work of scholars during the previous decade. Robert J. Donovan's *Conflict and Crisis: The Presidency of Harry S. Truman, 1945-1948* was more anecdotal than analytical and reflected the author's journalistic background. But it was a serious book that indicated that revisionist arguments had influenced even quasi-popular writing on the cold war. Though clearly sympathetic to Truman, Donovan was neither reverential nor uncritical. He chided Truman, for example, for failing to consider that Soviet expansion in eastern Europe might have been an outgrowth of national insecurity and for "his tendency to exaggerate Soviet motives." He agreed with scholars who contended that administration officials hoped that increased diplomatic leverage would be a valuable by-product of using the atomic bomb. In discussing the 1946 Iranian crisis, Donovan faulted Truman and Byrnes for not "allowing for the possibility that Stalin's actions may have been essentially defensive." Those and other reproachful comments hardly qualified Donovan's book as a revisionist tract. But it was much more evenhanded than fellow reporter Cabell Phillips's 1966 acclamatory account of the Truman administration, which also had been directed at a general audience.[49]

Donovan's book, despite its lively style and considerable merit, failed to provide much original analysis and arrived at conclusions that carried eclecticism to the point of blandness. A more creative and stimulating examination of Truman's diplomacy was Daniel Yergin's *Shattered Peace.* Yergin described a fundamental dichotomy in how American leaders viewed the Soviet Union. State Department officials, including William Bullitt, Loy Henderson, George Kennan, Charles Bohlen, and others, adhered to the

"Riga axioms," which held that Soviet foreign policy followed ideological dictates and plotted world revolution and unlimited expansion. The United States could deal with the Soviets only by being firm and wary. Other American leaders, including Roosevelt and Harry Hopkins, espoused the "Yalta axioms," which assumed that Stalin sought traditional Russian diplomatic goals and could be approached as a "realistic, rational statesman." They believed that the United States could and must win Stalin's trust and lay the foundations for civil if not harmonious relations after the war. After Truman took office, he took a position between the two axioms. Gradually, however, he lost patience with Russia, partly because of his own convictions and partly because of the influence of his advisors, Congress, and public opinion. By the summer of 1946, the Riga axioms had clearly triumphed as government officials and most Americans came to view the Soviet Union as an ideological foe with unlimited ambitions. At that point, the United States ceased trying to resolve its differences with the Soviets through diplomacy and began building a formidable military arsenal.[50]

Yergin synthesized much existing scholarship and contributed new insights of his own, such as his emphasis on the competing axioms, his discussion of how bureaucratic rivalries within the military added to the growing fear of Russia, and his explanation of the rise of the "gospel of national security." On issues that divided traditionalists and revisionists, his analysis was thoroughly eclectic. He criticized many American policies and perceptions, for example, but also depicted them as understandable, though unfortunate, responses to Soviet activities. Yergin acknowledged the presence of economic considerations in United States foreign policy, but found other motives, such as Wilsonian principles and strategic concerns, more important. He suggested that a cold war in some form was inevitable, but argued that by not following the Yalta axioms, the United States "not only helped to make the division sharper than it might otherwise have been, but also made the Soviet-American confrontation more highly militarized and much more costly and dangerous." *Shattered Peace* received many rave notices, but it also inspired some sharp attacks. Carolyn Eisenberg thought its basic premises were flawed because they rested "upon the indefensible refusal to acknowledge the American stake in the maintenance of a liberal capitalist international order." Daniel F. Harrington denied that either Kennan or Bohlen believed in the Riga axioms as outlined by Yergin, since neither viewed the Soviets as primarily motivated by ideology or a quest for world domination.[51]

In the most recent general study of the origins of the cold war, Thomas G. Paterson attributed the growth of Soviet-American tensions to the frictions inherent in the postwar situation, the varying needs and ideologies of the two countries, and the diplomatic tactics employed by their leaders.

While pointing out that any international system is "conflict-ridden," he argued that the power vacuums, economic dislocations, and political upheavals caused by the war intensified differences between the United States and Russia. Paterson cited both American and Soviet policies as responsible for creating dissension. Each nation sought to establish spheres of influence, and viewed the activities of the other as an effort to threaten its own sphere and undermine its interests. The vital concerns of both nations, he maintained, derived from a complex mixture of ideological, political, economic, strategic, and historical factors that generated tensions and escalated mutual misapprehensions. In addition, the personalities and tactics of American and Soviet officials contributed to an atmosphere of distrust and discord. Although Truman sought the same fundamental goals as Roosevelt, his brash, abrasive, and impatient manner of conducting diplomacy offended the Soviets. On the other hand, Americans generally found Soviet leaders to be "rude, untrustworthy, excessively suspicious, devious, unreceptive to gestures of kindness, and too dependent upon direct instructions from the Kremlin." Paterson's book, like Yergin's, incorporated the opinions and perspectives of a wide range of previous studies to produce an original analysis. Both works featured an eclectic approach and a balanced interpretation that was characteristic of postrevisionist cold war scholarship.[52]

By the late 1970s a broad consensus, amalgamating elements of the realist and revisionist interpretations, had emerged on the basic questions that had divided the two viewpoints. First and most obviously, nearly all cold war scholars agreed that America and Russia shared responsibility for the onset of the cold war in approximately equal proportions. Some found the United States slightly more culpable while others allocated a somewhat greater share of the blame to the Soviet Union. But the idea that either the United States or Russia was exclusively or chiefly accountable for the development of tensions gave way to a middle position. Assigning responsibility was a central focus of writing on the cold war, and the shift to an even-handed assessment was a major historiographical milestone that testified to the impact of the new left. Furthermore, recent studies generally regarded a cold war in some form as inevitable, but also maintained that United States policies exacerbated the situation and made the American-Soviet rivalry more intense than it otherwise would have been. The argument that even if the postwar conflict were unavoidable it could have been less bitter blended the fatalism of the realists with the new left conviction that the cold war was largely preventable.

Revisionists and many realists had always concurred in viewing Stalin's foreign-policy objectives as limited and motivated more by Soviet national concerns than by ideological commitments. That premise remained prevalent in postrevisionist literature, along with a number of corollaries that followed from it. Most scholars, without depicting Stalin's aims as perfectly benign, contended that the United States misperceived and overreacted to the Soviet threat. As a result, the Truman administration took actions that it saw as defensive, but that appeared aggressive to the Soviets. Growing misunderstanding and failure to communicate effectively escalated tensions and exaggerated differences. One consequence was that Stalin consolidated his hold on eastern Europe by assuming control in nations where he had permitted some autonomy immediately after the war. For the most part, recent writing on the cold war has described a pattern of challenge and response, action and reaction by both countries rather than a case of one side responding to the aggressive expansion of the other.

The trend toward eclecticism was also evident in the partial acceptance in recent works of two major components of the new left position. Few postrevisionist scholars endorsed the thesis that economic considerations were the fundamental motivating forces in United States diplomacy or the basic cause of conflict with the Soviet Union. Many did agree, however, that the United States tried to use economic pressure to modify Soviet behavior and that economic concerns were a part of the complex mixture of factors that activated American foreign policy. Similarly, most recent studies of the cold war did not confirm the new left image of United States policymakers implementing coherent, well-planned diplomatic objectives. They have, on the other hand, generally shown that American leaders, in dealing with day-to-day pressures and problems, were neither naive nor overly idealistic in their responses.

Within the consensus that has materialized on the origins of the cold war, differences still exist on many specific issues. All of the points on which scholars generally, though not unanimously, agree are subject to further reassessment and reinterpretation, especially as more sources become available. The new cold war consensus, though based on a much larger body of evidence than the old one, remains provisional.

The existing agreement on a number of controversial questions should not obscure the fact that more research is needed on many important and potentially exciting topics. The impact of public opinion on American policymakers merits further attention. Although the sources are limited and polls have been closely scrutinized, detailed study of the ideas and influence of business, ethnic, and religious groups, the press, and geographical sections of the country would be instructive. If, as some historians suggest, a widespread feeling of animosity toward Russia carried into the cold war, then the argument that the Truman administration marshaled public opinion to endorse a vigorous anti-Soviet posture needs to be critically reexamined. On the other hand, the assertion that public attitudes helped influence American officials to take a firm stand cannot be confirmed without looking carefully at the views of various interest groups and sectors of the population.

Much more work should be done on the social and intellectual roots of United States foreign policy. Analyzing the societal bases would benefit from new approaches, such as group biography, and employing computer technology to discern both common and unique traits among American leaders. Intellectual foundations could also be surveyed through group biographies, as well as through individual biographies and perhaps judicious use of psychological insights. More detailed research is needed on the role of Congress in the cold war, by examining both its institutional functions and its individual members. In general, biographies should be written on many administration officials and diplomats as well as senators and congressmen.

Other subjects invite further study. Most historians agree that the United States adopted a firm policy toward Russia in the spring or summer of 1946, but the question of exactly what that policy entailed is unresolved. Truman vehemently denied to Henry Wallace in September 1946 that he was committed to a get-tough position, partly because he wanted to placate Wallace but perhaps also because he did not view his own stance as unaccommodating. John L. Gaddis and Lisle A. Rose have suggested that even after the Truman Doctrine, American leaders recognized their limited resources and refrained from undertaking a worldwide anticommunist crusade. Not until the Korean War did they conclude that the Soviet Union was motivated primarily by unrestrained ideological objectives, and at that point, containment became universalized.[53] The question of how administration officials perceived their own and Soviet policies and how they transferred those perceptions into action deserves more attention.

Additional research on the role of the military in the formulation of United States foreign policy will doubtlessly shed light on that issue and generally enhance understanding of American cold war diplomacy. Administrative histories of the State and Defense Departments and subsidiary bodies such as the Policy Planning Staff and the Joint Chiefs would also be helpful. They could provide a clearer picture of the disputes within and between key policy agencies and how bureaucratic pressures and rivalries influenced foreign policy. Finally, more cross-cultural studies of the ways in which the United States interacted with leaders, responded to social movements, and dealt with political complexities in foreign countries are needed. Bruce R. Kuniholm, Walter Ullmann, and John Iatrides have provided models for that kind of analysis, which should be extended to all nations that were focal points in the evolution of the cold war.

Addressing the outstanding questions on the origins and development of the cold war will help guarantee that the subject will remain as lively and absorbing as it has been since the growth of revisionism. At the same time, scholars can hope that the continuing debate will be carried on with the tolerant spirit and moderate tone that has typified most recent writing on the cold war.

Notes

1. *See*, for example, William Henry Chamberlin, *America's Second Crusade* (Chicago: Henry Regnery Co., 1950); Ellis M. Zacharias, *Behind Closed Doors: The Secret History of the Cold War* (New York: G. P. Putnam's Sons, 1950); James Burnham, *Containment or Liberation: An Inquiry into the Aims of United States Foreign Policy* (New York: John Day, 1952). For an informed discussion of the conservative view, *see* Robert W. Sellen, "Origins of the Cold War: An Historiographical Survey," *West Georgia Studies in the Social Sciences* 9 (June 1970): 57-98.

2. Examples include Herbert Feis, *Churchill, Roosevelt, Stalin: The War They Waged and the Peace They Sought* (Princeton: Princeton University Press, 1957) and *Between War and Peace: The Potsdam Conference* (Princeton: Princeton University Press, 1960); Joseph M. Jones, *The Fifteen Weeks* (New York: Viking Press, 1955); Eric F. Goldman, *The Crucial Decade—And After* (New York: Alfred A. Knopf, 1960); Herbert Druks, *Harry S Truman and the Russians, 1945-1953* (New York: Robert Speller and Sons, 1966).

3. Hans J. Morgenthau, *In Defense of the National Interest: A Critical Examination of American Foreign Policy* (New York: Alfred A. Knopf, 1951), p. 116. For other statements of the realist position, *see* George F. Kennan, *American Diplomacy, 1900-1950* (Chicago: University of Chicago Press, 1951) and *Realities of American Foreign Policy* (Princeton: Princeton University Press, 1954); Norman A. Graebner, *Cold War Diplomacy: American Foreign Policy, 1945-1960* (Princeton: D. Van Nostrand Co., 1962); Louis J. Halle, *The Cold War as History* (New York: Harper & Row, 1967). John W. Spanier, *American Foreign Policy since World War II* (New York: Frederick A. Praeger, 1960) combined elements of the realist and liberal interpretations.

4. Morgenthau, *In Defense of the National Interest*, pp. 75-81, 97-99; Halle, *Cold War as History*, pp. 10-12, 86; Kennan, *Realities of American Foreign Policy*, pp. 69-76.

5. Morgenthau, *In Defense of the National Interest*, pp. 39, 108-9; Halle, *Cold War as History*, pp. xiii, 50-51; Kennan, *American Diplomacy*, pp. 113-14; Graebner, *Cold War Diplomacy*, pp. 15-23. Charles E. Neu, "The Changing Interpretive Structure of American Foreign Policy," in John Braeman, Robert H. Bremner, and David Brody, eds., *Twentieth Century American Foreign Policy* (Columbus: Ohio State University Press, 1971) found fatalism symptomatic of much writing in U.S. diplomatic history in the 1950s. But among cold war scholars it was most prevalent in the realist interpretation.

6. Gar Alperovitz, *Atomic Diplomacy: Hiroshima and Potsdam* (New York: Simon and Schuster, 1965); David Horowitz, *The Free World Colossus: A Critique of American Foreign Policy in the Cold War* (New York: Hill & Wang, 1965). Earlier accounts dissenting from standard interpretations included Carl Marzani, *We Can Be Friends* (New York: Topical Books, 1952); Frederick L. Schuman, *Russia since 1917: Four Decades of Soviet Politics* (New York: Alfred A. Knopf, 1957); William Appleman Williams, *American-Russian Relations, 1781-1947* (New York: Rinehart and Co., 1952) and *The Tragedy of American Diplomacy* (Cleveland: World Publishing Co., 1959); D. F. Fleming, *The Cold War and Its Origins* (Garden City: Doubleday & Co., 1961).

7. Williams, *Tragedy*, Fleming, *Cold War*, and P. M. S. Blackett, *Military and Political Consequences of Atomic Energy* (London: Turnstile Press, 1948), for example, had suggested the outlines of Alperovitz's argument. For comments on the rise of revisionism from contrasting points of view, see the essays by Robert H. Ferrell and Lloyd C. Gardner in Richard S. Kirkendall, ed., *The Truman Period as a Research Field: A Reappraisal, 1972* (Columbia: University of Missouri Press, 1974).

8. Ronald Steel, "Did Anyone Start the Cold War?" *New York Review of Books* 17 (2 September 1971): 23.

9. Arthur M. Schlesinger, Jr., Letter to the Editors, *New York Review of Books* 7 (20 October 1966): 37; and "Origins of the Cold War," *Foreign Affairs* 46 (October 1967): 22-52.

10. For critiques of Schlesinger's article from a revisionist perspective, *see* Christopher Lasch, "The Cold War, Revisited and Re-visioned," *New York Times Magazine*, 14 January 1968, p. 59, and William Appleman Williams, "The Cold War Revisionists," *Nation* 205 (13 November 1967): 492-95. Commenting from a realist point of view, Hans J. Morgenthau reproached Schlesinger for depicting U.S. universalism in a favorable light and exaggerating Stalin's paranoia as a cause of the cold war. *See* Lloyd C. Gardner, Arthur M. Schlesinger, Jr., and Hans J. Morgenthau, *Origins of the Cold War* (Lexington, Mass.: Ginn and Co., 1970).

11. Walter LaFeber, *America, Russia, and the Cold War* (New York: John Wiley & Sons, 1967); Lloyd C. Gardner, *Architects of Illusion: Men and Ideas in American Foreign Policy, 1941-1949* (Chicago: Quadrangle Books, 1970); Barton J. Bernstein, "American Foreign Policy and the Origins of the Cold War," in Barton J. Bernstein, ed., *Politics and Policies of the Truman Administration* (Chicago: Quadrangle Books, 1970); Stephen E. Ambrose, *Rise to Globalism: American Foreign Policy, 1938-1970* (Baltimore: Penguin Books, 1971); Joyce and Gabriel Kolko, *The Limits of Power: The World and United States Foreign Policy, 1945-1954* (New York: Harper & Row, 1972). In discussing writing on the cold war after the mid-1960s, I use the terms "new left" and "revisionism" interchangeably because I find no meaningful distinction between them. There were, of course, important differences among scholars who criticized U.S. policies from a left-of-center perspective, but there was not a discrete school of "revisionists" who stood apart from the "new left" school.

12. Gardner, *Architects of Illusion*, p. 317.

13. Diane Shaver Clemens, *Yalta* (New York: Oxford University Press, 1970); Athan Theoharis, "Roosevelt and Truman on Yalta: The Origins of the Cold War," *Political Science Quarterly* 87 (June 1972): 210-41. Theoharis stressed a sharp break between Roosevelt's policy of conciliation and Truman's firmness toward Russia. Clemens was not so certain that Roosevelt's stance, had he lived, would have differed much from Truman's.

14. Barton J. Bernstein, "Commentary," in Kirkendall, *Truman Period*, pp. 163-66; Robert W. Tucker, *The Radical Left and American Foreign Policy* (Baltimore: Johns Hopkins Press, 1971), pp. 13-17. Tucker cited differences between Kolko and Williams but concluded that their similarities were more significant.

15. Tucker, *Radical Left*, p. 28.

16. Williams, "Cold War Revisionists," pp. 493-95.

17. Gardner, *Architects of Illusion*, p. xi; Lasch, "The Cold War, Revisited and

Re-visioned," p. 59. For a general description of the new left position by one of its leading spokesmen, *see* Walter LaFeber, "War: Cold," in James V. Compton, ed., *America and the Origins of the Cold War* (Boston: Houghton Mifflin Co., 1972). The article was originally published in the October 1968 issue of the *Cornell Alumni News*.

18. John W. Spanier, "The Choices We Did Not Have," in Charles Gati, ed., *Caging the Bear: Containment and the Cold War* (Indianapolis: Bobbs-Merrill Co., 1974); Adam Ulam, "Re-reading the Cold War," *Interplay* 2 (March 1969): 53; Ferrell, "Truman Foreign Policy: A Traditionalist View," in Kirkendall, *Truman Period*, p. 45.

19. *See*, for example, Schlesinger, "Origins of the Cold War," p. 23; and Joseph M. Siracusa, *New Left Diplomatic Histories and Historians: The American Revisionists* (Port Washington, N.Y.: Kennikat Press, 1973), p. 114.

20. Tucker, *Radical Left*, chaps. 3-4. For other thoughtful and tempered critiques, *see* Charles S. Maier, "Revisionism and the Interpretation of Cold War Origins," *Perspectives in American History* 4 (1970): 313-47; Daniel M. Smith, "The New Left and the Cold War," *Denver Quarterly* 4 (Winter 1970): 78-88; J. L. Richardson, "Cold War Revisionism: A Critique," *World Politics* 24 (July 1972): 579-612. For assessments that faulted aspects of revisionist writing but were sympathetic to many of its arguments, *see* David S. Patterson, "Recent Literature on Cold War Origins: An Essay Review," *Wisconsin Magazine of History* 55 (Summer 1972): 320-29; and Stanley Hoffman, "Revisionism Revisited," in Lynn H. Miller and Ronald W. Pruessen, eds., *Reflections on the Cold War* (Philadelphia: Temple University Press, 1974).

21. Robert James Maddox, *The New Left and the Origins of the Cold War* (Princeton: Princeton University Press, 1973); *New York Times Book Review*, 17 June 1973, pp. 6-10; Warren F. Kimball, "The Cold War Warmed Over," *American Historical Review* 79 (October 1974): 1119-36. Edward S. Shapiro surveyed the reaction to Maddox's book in "Responsibility for the Cold War: A Bibliographical Review," *Intercollegiate Review* 12 (Winter 1976-1977): 113-20.

22. John Lewis Gaddis, *The United States and the Origins of the Cold War, 1941-1947* (New York: Columbia University Press, 1972); Kimball, "Cold War Warmed Over," pp. 1123-24.

23. George C. Herring, Jr., *Aid to Russia, 1941-1946: Strategy, Diplomacy, the Origins of the Cold War* (New York: Columbia University Press, 1973). For an earlier statement of Herring's views, *see* "Lend-Lease to Russia and the Origins of the Cold War, 1944-1945," *Journal of American History* 56 (June 1969): 93-114, which was less sympathetic to revisionist ideas than his book.

24. Thomas G. Paterson, *Soviet-American Confrontation: Postwar Reconstruction and the Origins of the Cold War* (Baltimore: Johns Hopkins Press, 1973).

25. Lynn Etheridge Davis, *The Cold War Begins: Soviet-American Conflict over Eastern Europe* (Princeton: Princeton University Press, 1974); Geir Lundestad, *The American Non-Policy Towards Eastern Europe, 1943-1947* (New York: Humanities Press, 1975).

26. Mark S. Steinitz, "United States Economic Assistance Policy Toward Czechoslovakia, 1946-1948," *Maryland Historian* 7 (Fall 1976): 21-46; Stephen A. Garrett, "Images and Foreign Policy: The United States, Eastern Europe, and the Begin-

nings of the Cold War," *World Affairs* 138 (Spring 1976): 288-308; Hugh De Santis, "Conflicting Images of the U.S.S.R.: American Career Diplomats and the Balkans, 1944-1946," *Political Science Quarterly* 94 (Fall 1979): 475-94.

27. Davis, *Cold War Begins*; Lundestad, *American Non-Policy*; Bennett Kovrig, *The Myth of Liberation: East-Central Europe in U.S. Diplomacy and Politics since 1941* (Baltimore: Johns Hopkins Press, 1973); Walter Ullmann, *The United States in Prague, 1945-1948* (New York: Columbia University Press, 1978); Hugh B. Hammett, "America's Non-Policy in Eastern Europe and the Origins of the Cold War," *Survey* 19 (Autumn 1973): 144-62; Eduard Mark, "Charles E. Bohlen and the Acceptable Limits of Soviet Hegemony in Eastern Europe: A Memorandum of 18 October 1945," *Diplomatic History* 3 (Spring 1979): 201-13. *See also* Richard Lukas, *The Strange Allies: The United States and Poland, 1941-1945* (Knoxville: University of Tennessee Press, 1978).

28. For useful reviews of the literature on Iran, *see* Justus D. Doenecke, "Revisionists, Oil, and Cold War Diplomacy," *Iranian Studies* 3 (Winter 1970): 23-33 and "Iran's Role in Cold War Revisionism," *Iranian Studies* 5 (Spring-Summer 1972): 96-111.

29. Eduard M. Mark, "Allied Relations in Iran, 1941-1947: The Origins of a Cold War Crisis," *Wisconsin Magazine of History* 59 (Autumn 1975): 51-63; David S. McLellan, "Who Fathered Containment: A Discussion," *International Studies Quarterly* 17 (June 1973): 205-26.

30. Gary R. Hess, "The Iranian Crisis of 1945-46 and the Origins of the Cold War," *Political Science Quarterly* 89 (March 1974): 117-46; John O. Iatrides, *Revolt in Athens: The Greek Communist "Second Round," 1944-1945* (Princeton: Princeton University Press, 1972); D. George Kousoulas, "The Truman Doctrine and the Stalin-Tito Rift: A Reappraisal," *South Atlantic Quarterly* 72 (Summer 1973): 427-39; Bruce R. Kuniholm, *The Origins of the Cold War in the Near East: Great Power Conflict and Diplomacy in Iran, Turkey, and Greece* (Princeton: Princeton University Press, 1980).

31. Bruce Kuklick, *American Policy and the Division of Germany: The Clash over Reparations* (Ithaca: Cornell University Press, 1972); John Gimbel, *The American Occupation of Germany: Politics and the Military, 1945-1949* (Stanford: Stanford University Press, 1968) and *The Origins of the Marshall Plan* (Stanford: Stanford University Press, 1976).

32. John H. Backer, *The Decision to Divide Germany: American Foreign Policy in Transition* (Durham: Duke University Press, 1978); Scott Jackson, "Prologue to the Marshall Plan: The Origins of the American Commitment for a European Recovery Program," *Journal of American History* 65 (March 1979): 1043-68.

33. Bernard C. Cohen, "The Relationship Between Public Opinion and Foreign Policy Maker," in Melvin Small, ed., *Public Opinion and Historians: Interdisciplinary Perspectives* (Detroit: Wayne State University Press, 1970); Walter LaFeber, "American Policy Makers, Public Opinion, and the Outbreak of the Cold War, 1945-1950," in Yonosuke Nagai and Akira Iriye, eds., *The Origins of the Cold War in Asia* (New York: Columbia University Press, 1977); Thomas G. Paterson, "Presidential Foreign Policy, Public Opinion, and Congress: The Truman Years," *Diplomatic History* 3 (Winter 1979): 1-18; Peter H. Irons, "The Test Is Poland: Polish-Americans and the Origins of the Cold War," *Polish American Studies* 30

(Autumn 1973): 5-63; Michael Leigh, *Mobilizing Consent: Public Opinion and American Foreign Policy, 1937-1947* (Westport, Conn.: Greenwood Press, 1976).

34. Athan Theoharis, *Seeds of Repression: Harry S. Truman and the Origins of McCarthyism* (Chicago: Quadrangle Books, 1971); Richard M. Freeland, *The Truman Doctrine and the Origins of McCarthyism* (New York: Alfred A. Knopf, 1972); Ralph B. Levering, *The Public and American Foreign Policy, 1918-1978* (New York: William Morrow and Co., 1978); Gary J. Buckley, "American Public Opinion and the Origins of the Cold War: A Speculative Reassessment," *Mid-America* 60 (January 1978): 35-42; Gaddis, *United States and Cold War*, p. 352.

35. John T. Rourke, "Congress and the Cold War," *World Affairs* 139 (Spring 1977): 259-77.

36. G. William Domhoff, "Who Made American Foreign Policy, 1945-1963?" in David Horowitz, ed., *Corporations and the Cold War* (New York: Monthly Review Press, 1969); Gabriel Kolko, *The Roots of American Foreign Policy* (Boston: Beacon Press, 1969); Richard J. Barnet, *Roots of War* (New York: Atheneum, 1972); John C. Donovan, *The Cold Warriors: A Policy-Making Elite* (Lexington, Mass.: D. C. Heath & Co., 1974). *See also* Thomas A. Krueger, "The Social Origins of Recent American Foreign Policy," *Journal of Social History* 7 (Fall 1973): 93-101.

37. Donovan, *Cold Warriors*, p. 285; Les K. Adler and Thomas G. Paterson, "Red Fascism: The Merger of Nazi Germany and Soviet Russia in the American Image of Totalitarianism, 1930s-1950s," *American Historical Review* 75 (April 1970): 1046-64; Ernest R. May, *"Lessons" of the Past: The Use and Misuse of History in American Foreign Policy* (New York: Oxford University Press, 1973).

38. Martin J. Sherwin, *A World Destroyed: The Atomic Bomb and the Grand Alliance* (New York: Alfred A. Knopf, 1975); Lisle A. Rose, *After Yalta: America and the Origins of the Cold War* (New York: Charles Scribner's Sons, 1973); Barton J. Bernstein, "Roosevelt, Truman, and the Atomic Bomb, 1941-1945: A Reinterpretation," *Political Science Quarterly* 90 (Spring 1975): 23-69; Gregg F. Herken, "Atomic Diplomacy Reversed and Revised," in Barton J. Bernstein, ed., *The Atomic Bomb: The Critical Issues* (Boston: Little, Brown & Co., 1976).

39. Walter S. Poole, "From Conciliation to Containment: The Joint Chiefs of Staff and the Coming of the Cold War, 1945-1946," *Military Affairs* 42 (February 1978): 12-16; Lawrence S. Wittner, "When CIA Hearts Were Young and Gay: Planning the Cold War (Spring, 1945)," *Peace and Change* 5 (Fall 1978): 70-76; Jonathan Knight, "American Statecraft and the 1946 Black Sea Straits Controversy," *Political Science Quarterly* 90 (Fall 1975): 451-75.

40. Thomas H. Etzold and John Lewis Gaddis, *Containment: Documents on American Policy and Strategy, 1945-1950* (New York: Columbia University Press, 1978); Alfred D. Sander, "Truman and the National Security Council, 1945-1947," *Journal of American History* 59 (September 1972): 369-88. For an early study of Truman and the military that suffered from a lack of sources, *see* Richard F. Haynes, *The Awesome Power: Harry S. Truman as Commander-in-Chief* (Baton Rouge: Louisiana State University Press, 1973).

41. Edward L. and Frederick H. Schapsmeier, *Prophet in Politics: Henry A. Wallace and the War Years, 1940-1965* (Ames: Iowa State University Press, 1970); Norman D. Markowitz, *The Rise and Fall of the People's Century: Henry A.*

Wallace and American Liberalism, 1941-1948 (New York: Free Press, 1973); Richard J. Walton, *Henry Wallace, Harry Truman, and the Cold War* (New York: Viking Press, 1976); J. Samuel Walker, *Henry A. Wallace and American Foreign Policy* (Westport, Conn.: Greenwood Press, 1976).

42. F. Ross Peterson, *Prophet Without Honor: Glen H. Taylor and the Fight for American Liberalism* (Lexington: University Press of Kentucky, 1974); Thomas G. Paterson, ed., *Cold War Critics: Alternatives to American Foreign Policy in the Truman Years* (Chicago: Quadrangle Books, 1971); Ronald Radosh, *Prophets on the Right* (New York: Simon and Schuster, 1975).

43. James T. Patterson, *Mr. Republican: A Biography of Robert A. Taft* (Boston: Houghton Mifflin Co., 1972); Justus Doenecke, "Lawrence Dennis: Revisionist of the Cold War," *Wisconsin Magazine of History* 55 (Summer 1972): 275-86; Mary W. Atwell, "A Conservative Response to the Cold War: Senator James P. Kem and Foreign Aid," *Capitol Studies* 4 (Fall 1976): 53-65.

44. John Lewis Gaddis, "Harry S. Truman and the Origins of Containment," in Frank J. Merli and Theodore A. Wilson, eds., *Makers of American Diplomacy: From Theodore Roosevelt to Henry Kissinger* (New York: Charles Scribner's Sons, 1974); Richard S. Kirkendall, "Harry Truman," in Morton Borden, ed., *America's Eleven Greatest Presidents* (Chicago: Rand McNally and Co., 1971); Wilson D. Miscamble, "The Evolution of an Internationalist: Harry S. Truman and American Foreign Policy," *Australian Journal of Politics and History* 23 (August 1977): 268-83.

45. David S. McLellan, *Dean Acheson: The State Department Years* (New York: Dodd, Mead, & Co., 1976); Gaddis Smith, *Dean Acheson* (New York: Cooper Square Publishers, 1972); George T. Mazuzan, *Warren R. Austin at the U.N., 1946-1953* (Kent: Kent State University Press, 1977).

46. C. Ben Wright, "Mr. 'X' and Containment," and George F. Kennan, Reply, *Slavic Review* 35 (March 1976): 1-36; John Lewis Gaddis, "Containment: A Reassessment," *Foreign Affairs* 55 (July 1977): 873-87; Eduard M. Mark, "The Question of Containment: A Reply to John Lewis Gaddis," *Foreign Affairs* 56 (January 1978): 430-40; John W. Coogan and Michael H. Hunt, "Kennan and Containment: A Comment," *Society for Historians of American Foreign Relations Newsletter* 9 (March 1978). Other noteworthy studies of Kennan included John W. Coffey, "George Kennan and the Ambiguities of Realism," *South Atlantic Quarterly* 73 (Spring 1974): 184-98, and Thomas G. Paterson, "The Search for Meaning: George F. Kennan and American Foreign Policy," in Merli and Wilson, eds., *Makers of American Diplomacy.*

47. Morton Schwartz, *The "Motive Forces" of Soviet Foreign Policy: A Reappraisal* (Denver: University of Denver Monograph Series in World Affairs, 1971); Adam B. Ulam, *Stalin: The Man and His Era* (New York: Viking Press, 1973).

48. Vojtech Mastny, *Russia's Road to the Cold War* (New York: Columbia University Press, 1979); William O. McCagg, Jr., *Stalin Embattled, 1943-1948* (Detroit: Wayne State University Press, 1978).

49. Robert J. Donovan, *Conflict and Crisis: The Presidency of Harry S. Truman, 1945-1948* (New York: W. W. Norton & Co., 1977); Cabell Phillips, *The Truman Presidency: The History of a Triumphant Succession* (New York: Macmillan Co., 1966).

50. Daniel Yergin, *Shattered Peace: The Origins of the Cold War and the National Security State* (Boston: Houghton Mifflin Co., 1977).

51. Ibid.; Carolyn Eisenberg, "Reflections on a Toothless Revisionism," *Diplomatic History* (Summer 1978): 295-305; Daniel F. Harrington, "Kennan, Bohlen, and the Riga Axioms," *Diplomatic History* 2 (Fall 1978): 423-37.

52. Thomas G. Paterson, *On Every Front: The Making of the Cold War* (New York: W. W. Norton & Co., 1979).

53. John Lewis Gaddis, "Was the Truman Doctrine a Real Turning Point?" *Foreign Affairs* 52 (January 1974): 386-402; Lisle A. Rose, *The Long Shadow: Reflections on the Second World War Era* (Westport, Conn.: Greenwood Press, 1978).

12 ______ United States Relations with Asia in the Twentieth Century: Retrospect and Prospect

ROBERT J. McMAHON

Few subjects have proved more intriguing to historians of American foreign policy than the stormy relationship between the United States and Asia during the present century. And there are few areas in which diplomatic historians have disagreed as vehemently or as fundamentally as they have in their various efforts to explain the nature of that relationship. This attraction, and this controversy, is hardly surprising. Indeed, even the barest outline of the sweeping events encompassed within this time frame reveals some of the most profound and far-reaching developments of the modern era: the Chinese revolt against Western hegemony and the eventual consolidation and unification of China under a communist regime; the emergence of Japan as a global power, its doomed efforts to establish a modern Asian empire, and its subsequent reemergence after the Pacific war as one of the world's preeminent commercial powers; the rise of indigenous nationalist movements in South and Southeast Asia and the corresponding disintegration of the Western colonial system, replaced in the postwar period by independent nationalist regimes in virtually all of the former colonial areas. Washington's attempts to influence these momentous developments, as well as its varying efforts to adapt to such profound changes, have long been subjects of intense scholarly debate.

This chapter is divided into several sections. The first section surveys the major historical schools of thought regarding the overall nature of America's encounter with Asia, focusing primarily on conceptual studies and works which consider American-Asian relations in a broad framework or over a long period of time. The following section concentrates more specifically on writings concerning American relations with East Asia in the 1900-1919 period, while the next section analyzes the historical literature for 1919-1945. The fourth section takes a brief look at the relatively limited literature concerning American relations with South and Southeast Asia prior to 1945, an area which until recently was consigned to the periphery by scholars and diplomats alike. The final section surveys historical studies of the turbulent period in United States-Asian relations since World War II.

The traditional view of American-East Asian relations was set forth by A. Whitney Griswold in his influential volume, *The Far Eastern Policy of the United States.*[2] Building on the work of Tyler Dennett, Griswold emphasized the continuity of American policy in the Far East during the first four decades of the twentieth century.[3] United States policy, he argued, had two complementary objectives: the maintenance of the Open Door policy and the preservation of China's integrity. These goals were first articulated during the McKinley administration by Secretary of State Hay in a determined effort to protect American commercial interests in China; each succeeding administration adopted the same objectives, convinced that vital American interests were at stake in the Far East and that the United States had made an irrevocable commitment there. The aims of American policy remained static, although different administrations pursued those aims with varying degrees of intensity, resulting, in Griswold's view, in a cyclical pattern of advance and retreat. To Griswold, this traditional American Far Eastern policy was based on false premises. The United States, he insisted, never had a significant economic stake in East Asia; on the contrary, the fabled China market was merely an illusion. Neither was the preservation of China's integrity a vital American interest; by pursuing such an illusory goal the United States only endangered the territorial integrity of its own colonial possessions in the Pacific, raised false hopes among Chinese nationalists, and risked entanglement in European politics "via the back door of eastern Asia." In short, the United States had consistently misunderstood the true proportions of its interests in the Pacific.

George F. Kennan's equally influential work, *American Diplomacy, 1900-1950,* shared many of Griswold's major assumptions.[4] A proponent of the realist approach to the study of American foreign relations, the former diplomat eloquently argued that United States policy in East Asia during the first half of the twentieth century was based on lofty moral and legal precepts which disguised the true nature of American interests. Agreeing with Griswold that the maintenance of the Open Door and the preservation of the territorial and administrative integrity of China remained the chief American objectives in the Far East from administration to administration, Kennan maintained that "these terms were not clear and precise ones which could usefully be made the basis of a foreign policy." Kennan also faulted American policymakers for their chronic inability to implement these principles. American officials, he noted, generally proved reluctant to translate high principles into substantive, negotiable diplomatic arrangements, a pattern which in the case of United States-Japanese relations prior to Pearl Harbor reached tragic dimensions. Viewing the power constellation in East Asia from the standpoint of 1951, Kennan noted ironically that the United States had actually attained its traditional objectives in the area—Western influence had been effectively removed from China while the Japanese had completely withdrawn from Manchuria—and yet, with communist regimes in power in Peking and Pyongyang, Washington's security was more gravely threatened than ever before. The present course of events could only have been altered, Kennan suggested, "by an American policy based consistently, over a long period of time, on a recognition of power realities in the Orient as a factor worthy of our serious respect, and directed toward the stability and quietness as well as the legal and moral tidiness of the situation there."[5]

Taking their cue from Kennan, most studies of American foreign policy written during the 1950s and early 1960s adopted a realist framework to explain the failures of United States diplomacy. The proposition, popularized by Griswold and Kennan, that American leaders consistently overvalued the importance of the Pacific region to American security gained wide currency. Robert E. Osgood's seminal work, *Ideals and Self-Interest in America's Foreign Relations*, placed this thesis in a broad historical perspective.[6] Insisting that the endemic mistakes and misperceptions of American diplomats stemmed from an unwillingness to base policy on a firm foundation of realism, he suggested that "Americans acted upon the basis of expectations that could not be fulfilled, undertook commitments they would not honor, plunged themselves into bewilderment and disillusionment and drifted about aimlessly, without chart or compass, upon the strange currents of international politics."[7] William L. Neumann applied these ideas more specifically to Asia in a 1957 essay.[8] He stressed that American interests in that area remained ambiguous throughout the twentieth century and that United States officials consistently failed to clarify which interests, if any, were vital enough to justify war. Paul H. Clyde's interpretive overview of America's East Asian policy was even more critical.[9] Washington's record in Asia, he suggested, was nothing short of a "disaster" and a "calamity." The historian reflecting on a century of American experience in Asia, Clyde suggested, "is inclined at first to throw up his hand and exclaim, 'This is impossible, unbelievable. No people could produce so fantastic a saga of ineptitude.' "[10] Yet he insisted that the evidence to support such a view was inescapable, a state of affairs which he attributed to a foolish reliance on moral principles and moral force in the conduct of American foreign relations. Neumann's brief survey of United States-

Japanese relations, *American Encounters Japan: From Perry to MacArthur*, added further weight to the realist critique.[11] In its relations with Tokyo, he asserted, Washington failed to recognize and work within the limits of power to achieve the achievable; instead, it overextended itself, pursuing national interests and policies which were incompatible with existent national strength.

The publication in 1959 of William Appleman Williams's landmark study, *The Tragedy of American Diplomacy*, posed a major challenge to both the traditionalist and realist interpretations.[12] In this study, which in effect gave birth to the revisionist interpretation of American foreign policy, he emphasized the domestic roots of that policy, arguing that ever since the 1890s there had been a virtual consensus among American ruling elites that domestic prosperity was directly dependent upon economic expansion overseas. The Open Door policy—according to Williams a brilliant tactic for achieving the objective of economic expansion—was the keynote of American policy toward East Asia and elsewhere from the McKinley administration onward. By promoting equality of commercial opportunity, American leaders, confident of their nation's economic prowess, believed that they could eventually achieve commercial supremacy in Asia. Stressing the continuity in policy throughout the various Republican and Democratic administrations, Williams accused American policymakers of a continual failure to appreciate the transforming nature of revolutionary nationalism in Asia. Washington's staunch opposition to nationalist movements there and throughout the Third World was to Williams one of the greatest blunders—and tragedies—of American foreign relations.

Williams's probing work both anticipated and influenced the searching reexamination of American foreign relations undertaken by scholars and activists alike in the 1960s. As the wrenching conflict in Vietnam led in turn to widespread political upheaval and social turmoil at home, critics of American involvement there asked penetrating new questions about the history of United States-Asian relations in an effort to place America's commitment in Southeast Asia in its historical context. Many of these critics borrowed insights from Williams and eagerly sought to extend his interpretive structure. As a result, more radical views about the history of American-Asian relations gained a degree of respectability in both academic and nonacademic quarters. By the end of the decade a substantial body of scholarship had emerged to challenge traditional notions about American foreign relations. While often shrill in tone and sometimes unabashedly present-minded in its criticism, this revisionist scholarship unquestionably infused new life into the debate over American policy in Asia and throughout the world. The work of historians such as Walter LaFeber, Lloyd Gardner, Gabriel Kolko, and Robert Freeman Smith, to mention a few representatives of the new left school, suggested fundamental new approaches to the study of American diplomacy, and began a debate over the nature of American policy. In their introduction to *America's Asia: Dissenting Essays on Asian-American Relations*,[13] a collection of radical critiques of United States policy that attests to the strong impact of these views, Edward Friedman and Mark Selden asserted: "As the studies in this book make plain, Vietnam is no aberration. It is an integral if extremely costly link in the chain of creating and maintaining an Asian *Pax Americana*."[14]

An alternative framework for understanding American-East Asian relations has been advanced in the refreshingly original work of Akira Iriye, one of the most prolific and influential authorities writing on the subject. In his first two major works, *After Imperialism*[15] and *Across the Pacific*,[16] Iriye made several major contributions to the study of American-East Asian relations, contributions which have been refined and elaborated upon in his subsequent work. Strongly influenced by concepts derived from the social sciences, he views international relations as a system and each individual nation as an actor within that system. American actions in the Pacific, according to this systemic or structuralist approach, cannot be understood within a vacuum; instead, they must be seen within their larger international context. In *After Imperialism*, his study of Far Eastern diplomacy during the 1921-1931 period, Iriye skillfully analyzed the policies pursued by each of the major parties involved in the area—China, Japan, the United States, and the Soviet Union—using, where possible, the diplomatic records of each country to substantiate his central argument that those policies were conditioned primarily by changes in the international order itself. Iriye's use and advocacy of the multiarchival approach in many ways represented a methodological breakthrough for students of American-East Asian affairs; by stressing the importance of multiarchival research and, as a corollary, urging American diplomatic historians to learn Asian languages, Iriye helped break down the traditional parochialism of the field. His work thus sought to move the United States off center stage in studies of Far Eastern diplomacy, a useful corrective to many of the standard accounts of the subject. In his later work he has stressed the important role which mutual images have played in influencing relations between the United States, China, and Japan, introducing yet another relatively neglected factor into the diplomatic equation.

The 1970s have been marked by an increasing degree of fragmentation in the field of American diplomatic history, a development which has had a particularly telling impact on studies of American-East Asian affairs. While some historians continue to be affected deeply by realist assumptions, others, convinced of the general validity of the new left framework, seek to add subtleties and complexities to the revisionist arguments. Warren Cohen's overview of United States-Chinese relations and Charles E. Neu's survey of United States-Japanese relations, both of which apply realist concepts in a sophisticated manner, clearly attest to the resiliency of that approach.[17] At the same time, the challenging essays contained in Mark Selden's *Remaking Asia* extend the dimensions of the revisionist critique.[18] Amid the continuing clash of realist and revisionist views, other historians have eagerly sought to use multiarchival research to bring greater insight to the study of United States relations with Asia. The recent studies of Christopher Thorne, Stephen Pelz, and William Roger Louis are outstanding examples of the new perspectives which can be brought to bear by historians in the latter category.[19] Other historians have borrowed selectively from these competing approaches, fashioning syntheses in their own manner. The recent overviews of United States-Asian relations by Richard W. Van Alstyne and Robert Hart ably reflect this eclectic approach.[20]

American policy toward East Asia from 1900 to 1919 is viewed by most historians, regardless of their perspective, as an abject failure. However, many see the skillful and realistic diplomacy of the Theodore Roosevelt administration as a significant exception to this rule. This favorable interpretation of Roosevelt's Asian policy was first set forth by Thomas A. Bailey and Howard K. Beale and has been generally substantiated and elaborated upon in the more recent studies by Raymond A. Esthus, Charles E. Neu, Eugene P. Trani, and Warren I. Cohen.[21] The two most thoroughly researched monographs on Roosevelt's East Asian diplomacy, those of Esthus and of Neu, argue that the president correctly viewed the Far East as an area of peripheral concern to the United States. They point out that his refusal to adopt a vigorous policy in the Pacific was based upon a perceptive estimate of United States interests in the region, as well as upon an acute awareness of the relationship between diplomacy and public opinion. According to Neu, Roosevelt's decision to seek an accommodation with Japan on the key questions of Manchuria and racial discrimination against Japanese laborers in the United States was a policy which in the context of its era was "shrewd, skillful, and responsible." In short, his Far Eastern policy was "a largely successful policy based upon political realities at home and in the Far East and upon a firm belief that friendship with Japan was essential to preserve American interests in the Pacific."[22] Esthus similarly contends that Roosevelt and his secretary of state, Elihu Root, could leave office with the assurance that they "had resolved the difficulties with Japan as well as was possible under the limitations reality imposed upon them."[23] Cohen, who has studied the problem through the lens of China, lends support to that view. While strongly disagreeing with Beale's assertion that Roosevelt was antagonistic to Chinese nationalism, he points out that the president was correct in his belief that the interests of the United States could not be served by aligning the United States with China in such a way as to offend Japan, the dominant force in the region.[24]

The Far Eastern initiatives of William Howard Taft and Philander C. Knox, Taft's secretary of state and the principal architect of his foreign policy, have been treated far more severely by historians. The Taft administration pursued an active policy in East Asia, seeking, in its two chief initiatives, to include American financiers in the China consortium and to neutralize Manchuria's railroads. These efforts, which have been derisively labelled dollar diplomacy by many historians, have generally been viewed as a reversal of Roosevelt's priorities in the area and as such have been roundly criticized. Charles Vevier indicted the Taft administration for pursuing narrowly conceived policies aimed only at enriching certain business groups in the United States.[25] Other critics have been less harsh, but the general contention that Taft failed to perceive the true nature of American interests in East Asia—as had his predecessor—has been reinforced in much of the recent literature. Charles Neu, for instance, claims that Taft reversed Roosevelt's policy, thereby engendering a steady deterioration in United States-Japanese relations.[26] Likewise, Warren Cohen suggests that Taft and Knox foolishly sought to align the United States with China's aspirations, regardless of Japanese opposition—a policy which served the interests of neither China nor the United States.[27] Akira Iriye, writing from a somewhat different perspective, chides the Taft administration for beginning an American tradition of moralistic diplomacy in Asia.[28] Walter and Marie Scholes, in their carefully researched account of Taft's foreign policy, generally echo these earlier views.[29] In common with these various critics is the view that the Taft administration, whether acting out of economic or moralistic motives or a combination thereof, greatly exaggerated America's stake in the Pacific region, and once having made that fundamental mistake compounded it by pursuing illusory goals in China while risking the alienation of Japan, the area's only world power. A greater violation of the hallowed principles of *realpolitik*, according to this school of thought, is scarcely imaginable.

These studies of the Far Eastern policies of Roosevelt and Taft, while often differing considerably in emphasis and interpretation, share many assumptions about American diplomacy. Each of these studies is written primarily in a realist mode; each evaluates American policy with reference to the time-honored concepts of the international balance of power. Within this conceptual framework, Roosevelt, who correctly gauged the limited nature of United States interests in the area and conducted his diplomacy accordingly, is generally considered to be a successful statesman, while Taft, who recklessly departed from his mentor's East Asian policy, is usually viewed as a bumbling and inept leader. Unlike the work of Williams and the revisionists, these studies do not concentrate upon the economic wellsprings of American foreign policy, nor do they probe very deeply into the real meaning of that ambiguous and rarely defined term "national interest." In short, these works are dominated by a concern with the traditional questions of diplomatic history: Did American actions contribute to a furtherance of the national interests, understood, at least implicitly, to mean a strengthening of the international and regional balances of power? Were the tactics consistent with the objectives sought?

The first major studies of Woodrow Wilson's East Asian policy framed similar questions. These appraisals, notably Tien-yi Li's *Woodrow Wilson's China Policy*,[30] Russell H. Fifield's *Woodrow Wilson and the Far East*,[31] and Roy W. Curry's, *Woodrow Wilson and Far Eastern Policy*,[32] while varying in their assessments of Wilsonian diplomacy, accept the basic tenets of the realist school of thought. Curry's book, probably the most thoughtful and comprehensive of these studies, offers a generally favorable appraisal of Wilson's policies toward the Far East. He contends that Wilson followed traditional American policy in the Pacific—namely, maintenance of the Open Door and preservation of China's territorial and political sovereignty. The president's championship of Chinese sovereignty, Curry suggests, proceeded from a recognition that it was in the American national interest to preserve the Asian power balance; Wilson believed it vital that this balance not be too severely jeopardized by Japan's advances during World War I. By actively thrusting the United States into the struggle to maintain the balance of power in the region, Wilson created an important precedent; he set the pace for foreign opposition to Japanese expansion while helping to keep policy options open. Emphasizing the relative insignificance of East Asian affairs to the United States during the early years of the twentieth century, Curry praises Wilson for recognizing this reality and scrupulously avoiding, accordingly, any thought of using force to achieve American objectives.

Other students of Wilson's diplomatic maneuverings in the Far East find the president's staunch opposition to Japanese ambitions and support for Chinese sovereignty to be a far less admirable application of *realpolitik* than Curry postulated. Burton F. Beers, for example, argues in his study of Robert Lansing that Wilson overturned several of his secretary of state's efforts to reach an accommodation with Tokyo.[33] Lansing had urged Wilson to recognize Japan's "special interests" in Shantung, eastern Inner Mongolia, and southern Manchuria in return for a firm Japanese commitment to honor the Open Door elsewhere in China and to accept American terms for settling the troublesome immigration and land tenure issues. The secretary held that this quid pro quo would only grant formal recognition to the existing state of affairs and if it worked would benefit both the United States and China. In Beers's view, Lansing's proposal, which Wilson ultimately rejected, could well have protected America's economic interests while limiting its political commitment; moreover, it "might well have opened the way for substantial American accomplishments in East Asia."[34] In his overview of American-Japanese relations, Charles Neu similarly characterizes the Wilson administration as a period of lost opportunities.[35] Wilson's China policy has also been vigorously criticized by other scholars. Arthur S. Link, Wilson's chief biographer, has pointed out that the president's policies vis-à-vis China, no matter how well intentioned, actually worked to that nation's detriment, a view which the works of Warren Cohen and Tien-yi Li strongly support.[36]

The work of William Appleman Williams and the revisionist school offers a strikingly different conceptual framework for understanding both the formulation and implementation of America's East Asian policy during the first two decades of the twentieth century. According to that school of thought, American actions in the Pacific cannot be understood without an appreciation of the ideology which was implicitly accepted by virtually all American policymakers throughout this period.[37] N. Gordon Levin's award-winning book, *Woodrow Wilson and World Politics*, builds upon this perspective in its sophisticated analysis of Wilsonian diplomacy.[38] The ultimate Wilsonian goal, in Levin's words, "may be defined as the attainment of a peaceful liberal capitalist world order under international law, safe both from traditional imperialism and revolutionary socialism, within whose stable liberal confines a missionary America could find moral and economic preeminence."[39] In East Asia, the Wilson administration sought to achieve this objective by convincing moderate Japanese statesmen that their nation's true political and economic interests lay in cooperation with the Western powers through the League of Nations and the financial consortium in China. This cooperation would then guarantee China's political and territorial integrity while ensuring peaceful access to commercial opportunities in China for all the great powers. Wilson's fundamental goal in East Asia was thus his effort to turn Tokyo away from the path of militant nationalism and induce it to join instead the American-led liberal-internationalist struggle against war and revolution in Asia.

Another work written from a broadly conceived revisionist perspective is Jerry Israel's *Progressivism and the Open Door*, an effort to link the reform movement at home with American actions abroad.[40] He also believes that idealism and self-interest were not mutually exclusive motivations for America's China policy; on the contrary, he sees the two as inseparable. Those who dismiss altruism, reform, or ideology as sheer rationalization and camouflage, Israel contends, and likewise those who insist that religious, humanitarian, and ideological motives transcend mere material ones, are only seeing part of the picture. In actuality, missionaries and businessmen, Red Cross relief workers and Wall Street bankers, all brought differing perceptions, goals, tactics, and conflicts to any particular Open Door project in China; yet the eventual shape of that project emerged not from any single motive, personality, or goal, but from the combined energies of all concerned. He concludes that the Open Door in action "was neither a heartless, calculated exploitation, nor a foolish naive crusade." It was instead an outgrowth of a foreign policy which from its inception functioned "to preserve, protect, and expand a progressive, business, and Christian society. Reforming cultures, making profits, and saving souls were not incompatible goals, or so it was felt. Rather, each activity worked, sometimes consciously, sometimes not, to the other's advantage."[41]

In recent years, historians have asked new questions about American involvement in East Asia in the period 1900-1919. One such question concerns the actual functioning or implementation of the Open Door policy in China, a topic skillfully explored in Israel's book. Noel Pugach's "Making the Open Door Work," suggests that Wilson's appointment of Paul Reinsch as minister to China underscored his intention to foster overseas expansion.[42] Pugach believes that Reinsch failed in his mission, however, because the American business community remained too divided, timid, and backward to meet the challenge of the political and economic situation in the Far East. Similarly, studies by Helen Dodson Kahn and by Harry N. Scheiber have considered the role of Willard Straight, the diplomat, businessman, and promoter who vigorously sought to encourage the deepening of American-Chinese commercial ties.[43] Michael H. Hunt, while convincingly arguing that Straight's role in China has been greatly exaggerated by historians, details many of the impediments to the implementation of the Open Door.[44]

Crucial to a proper understanding of the actual functioning of the Open Door is an appreciation of the role which private American business and financial groups played in the development of commercial relations with China. Historians have only recently begun to expand the pioneering work of Paul H. Clyde and Harry Kirwin.[45] William R. Braisted's "China, the United States Navy, and the Bethlehem Steel Company" effectively uses the case study approach to show how the United States government exerted its diplomatic muscle to benefit at least one American corporation interested in securing a foothold in the fabled China market.[46] Noel Pugach's "Standard Oil and Petroleum Development in Early Republican China" also demonstrates Washington's interest in supporting an American corporation's attempts to capture part of the China market.[47] This particular effort failed miserably; the backwardness and instability of China, foreign competition, inadequate government backing, and the inefficiency and ill-preparedness of American business itself all combined to thwart Standard Oil's initiative. This incident, Pugach claims, adds another dimension to our understanding of the general failure by the United States to make the Open Door in China work. In "Anglo-American Aircraft Competition and the China Arms Embargo, 1919-1921," Pugach probes the conflict between

Washington's policy of fostering cooperation among the major powers in East Asia and its contradictory interest in promoting the interests of individual American firms.[48]

Michael Hunt closely examines the activities of American firms in China, and he finds that while the China market was not vast it was not impenetrable either.[49] He suggests that the United States government was largely inactive as a promoter of American business in China, but adds that its inactivity "should not overshadow the importance of the structure of unequal treaties within which American firms operated and from which they derived ample benefit."[50] He concludes that while the realists overemphasize the difficulties of the China market, the revisionists slight the issue of economic performance and place too much stress on the significance of business-government cooperation.

Another central issue of increasing importance in recent historical studies is the relationship between America's East Asian policy and its discriminatory immigration laws aimed at orientals. Delber L. McKee's *Chinese Exclusion Versus the Open Door Policy* analyzes the role of this exclusionary legislation.[51] Stressing the contradictions between the Open Door and the exclusion laws, he wryly observes that a merchant, as one Chinese official put it, could hardly sell goods to a man he was insulting. McKee finds that racial exclusion undermined the Open Door policy and served as a major barrier to the extension of commercial and cultural ties with China. The adverse effect which racial exclusion legislation had on United States-Japanese relations has been well documented in works by Thomas Bailey and Roger V. Daniels.[52] Kell F. Mitchell's "Diplomacy and Prejudice"[53] and Paul Gordon Lauren's "Human Rights in History"[54] similarly scrutinize the effects of racial prejudice on American-East Asian relations, while Akira Iriye's work has explored this theme in considerable depth. The often critical nature of the interrelationship between diplomacy and racism, or ethnocentrism, will surely continue to attract the attention of historians.

In moving toward a deeper understanding of the functioning of the Open Door, the role of private business and financial groups, and the influence of racial factors on policy, historians have added to our knowledge of this formative period. Much of this work, however, is only preliminary, and future studies will hopefully expand its boundaries. Another fruitful area for historical inquiry might be the significance of Asia to the United States in terms of objective reality and the subjective perceptions of policymakers. The differing judgments of realist and revisionist historians on this crucial question must be evaluated in the light of further archival research. The term national interest, moreover, must be used with a greater degree of precision. Other possible avenues for future researchers are suggested by Michael Hunt's innovative study, *Frontier Defense and the Open Door*. His integration of multiarchival research with provocative insights about the unusual encounter of two alien cultures makes for fascinating reading and sets a model for future work.

The diplomacy of the 1920s poses a very different set of problems for the historian. "The decade of the twenties challenges the historian," Akira Iriye observed, "because of the absence of easily recognizable international crises such as wars and overt aggression that have characterized all other decades of the twentieth century. There were more subtle crises in the 1920s, and to identify and analyze them is to go a long way toward comprehending the complex nature of American-East Asian relations."[55] While most historians, aware of these problems, have carefully avoided broad interpretive studies of Washington's Far Eastern policy during this elusive period, Williams and Iriye have been notable exceptions. In "China and Japan: A Challenge and a Choice of the 1920's," Williams suggested that Washington's failure to come to grips with the force of revolutionary nationalism in China is the key to understanding American diplomatic errors in East Asia.[56] United States policy consistently sought to bolster the status quo in the Pacific, and correspondingly failed to adapt to the rapid and profound transformation which was taking place in China. "By declining to support effectively the rising nationalism of China," Williams emphasizes, "American private and official leaders made it clear in Tokyo that Japan could risk a more overt penetration of Manchuria." Iriye's *After Imperialism*, while agreeing that the United States grievously underestimated the force of Chinese nationalism, offers a different interpretive scaffolding. He sees American leaders, in the wake of the destructive impact of World War I, engaging in bold efforts to help construct a new international order in East Asia. In his view, these efforts, which were largely unsuccessful, are more easily comprehended when viewed from the perspective of the weaknesses of the international system itself than from the narrower focus of internal domestic influence on policy.

A consideration of two particular issues is crucial for students of United States-East Asian relations during the 1920s: the Washington conference of 1921-1922 and the American response to Chinese nationalism. While Williams sees the Washington conference as the keynote of American efforts to contain revolutionary nationalism in East Asia, Iriye views it as an imaginative, if flawed, effort to build a new structure for the peaceful conduct of international relations in the Far East. The most recent full-length treatment of the American role at the conference, Thomas H. Buckley's solidly researched *The United States and the Washington Conference, 1921-1922*, offers a neorealist interpretation.[57] Viewing the conference as a notable success for American diplomacy, he stresses that the United States sought and achieved limited goals through practical negotiation. American accomplishments were considerable: the elimination of a naval arms race which could threaten United States interests in the Pacific; a formal acceptance by the powers of the Open Door; and an end to the Anglo-Japanese alliance. While admitting that the United States in effect relegated the China problem to a secondary position, Buckley sees this as a realistic move since the defense of China's territorial and administrative integrity was not within reach of American power. American statesmen wisely realized that American interests in the Far East were not of sufficient consequence to rank as vital interests; accordingly, Buckley suggests that "with the achievement of limited objectives the American delegation took a necessary first step toward a Pacific and Far East policy based on a realistic assessment of American interests."[58]

Several recent studies have contributed to a balanced evaluation of the Washington conference. In discussing American friendship for China at the conference, Noel Pugach argues that the United States effected a disposition of the tangled Shantung question, which was markedly favorable to Chinese interests.[59] Drawing heavily upon British as well as American archival sources, he asserts that the Shantung settlement was at least a partial victory for China because it made progress in eliminating the spheres of influence and removing the Japanese from Chinese soil. Moreover, like many of the other Far Eastern arrangements at the conference, it gave China the potential to recover certain aspects of its sovereignty. American policy toward China, Pugach contends, was rooted in self-interest as well as idealism. Continued Chinese confidence, many high-ranking American diplomats were convinced, would enable the United States to assert economic and political primacy in Asia, would encourage the development of democracy and modernization in China, and would contain Japanese and European aggression. Robert H.van Meter, Jr.'s "The Washington Conference of 1921-22: A New Look," explores a largely ignored aspect of the conference.[60] Arguing that it had a European as well as an Asian dimension, he emphasizes that Secretary of Commerce Hoover and other top administration figures were convinced that international disarmament would encourage financial stabilization and economic recovery in Europe, a development which would in turn help restore prosperity to the United States by stimulating overseas demand for surplus American products. Roger Dingman, in *Power in the Pacific*, makes effective use of the multiarchival approach to add another dimension to the study of the Washington conference.[61] Exploring thoroughly the archival records of Japan and Great Britain as well as those of the United States, he concludes that politics within the capitals of the three major naval nations, far more than international relations among them, determined the character and assured the success of the first strategic arms limitation agreement in modern times. Stressing internal bureaucratic imperatives—a methodological approach pioneered by social scientists—Dingman sees the men responsible for the

Washington conference as men of power trying simply to retain their hold on it. Concluding a naval arms-limitation agreement at Washington appeared to them as one effective means.

The nature of the American response to Chinese nationalism during the 1920s looms as an equally significant and controversial historiographical question. Dorothy Borg, in her path-breaking study *American Policy and the Chinese Revolution, 1925-1928*, praised the China policy of the Coolidge administration, which she says actively sought to help that struggling nation achieve national sovereignty.[62] Secretary of State Kellogg's policy "was both bold and imaginative in intent and his ideas were considerably in advance of his time."[63] Other historians have taken sharp exception to the view that the United States was at all sympathetic to an emerging Chinese nationalism. Both Williams and Iriye contend that in the 1920s the United States squandered an ideal opportunity to help shape the future course of China's national development. This interpretation is substantiated by Brian T. George in "The State Department and Sun Yat-sen."[64] He believes that American officials did not reject Sun's overtures to the United States on account of his "fuzzy idealism" as some historians have suggested; rather, the prime considerations from Washington's perspective were the destabilizing effects on China of his activities and the problems these raised for the successful implementation of the Open Door policy. Acknowledging his intellectual debt to Williams, George insists that American policymakers failed to comprehend the revolutionary process in which China was engaged and instead aligned itself with the reactionary elements in Chinese politics, a strategy which he categorizes as classically counterrevolutionary as well as self-defeating. Warren Cohen's view of America's China policy during this period is somewhat less critical. He argues that Sun cannot fairly be considered the personification of Chinese nationalism in the 1920s and thus Washington's failure to come to terms with his movement was hardly apocalyptic. Indeed, the succeeding years offered ample opportunities for constructive action on the part of American officials. Still, Cohen considers the United States response to Chinese nationalism between the Washington conference and the Northern Expedition to be inadequate and unsatisfactory; the United States insensitively clung to its privileges under the unequal treaties, a position which he attributes to sterile legalism.[65]

The relative quietude of the 1920s was abruptly shattered by the Mukden incident of 1931—the beginning of outright Japanese aggression in China. Historians have long been divided on the American response to Tokyo's aggressive actions, focusing particularly upon the critical role played by Secretary of State Stimson. To Kennan, Stimson's famous nonrecognition doctrine was typical of the moralistic-legalistic tradition of American policy and was a wholly inadequate response to an explosive situation. Taking their cue from the diplomat-scholar, historians such as Robert Ferrell, Richard Current, and Armin Rappaport, all properly schooled in the tenets of *realpolitik*, similarly chide Stimson for eschewing balance-of-power diplomacy in favor of a narrow and counterproductive stance of moral condemnation.[66] Rappaport asserts that the secretary had his moral sensibilities outraged by Japanese actions in Manchuria and accordingly "elected to give vent to his ire by brandishing the pistol, which, unhappily, was not loaded, thereby transgressing the cardinal maxim of the statesman and placing his country in jeopardy." By allowing emotion and morality to guide his conduct rather than careful calculation and circumspection, he achieved nothing.[67]

A more balanced evaluation of Stimson's response to the Manchurian crisis is set forth in Christopher Thorne's study, *The Limits of Foreign Policy*.[68] Placing American policy in its broader context, he decries the false dichotomy between realism and idealism in American foreign policy advanced by many diplomatic historians. While acknowledging that Stimson's nonrecognition doctrine did little either to hinder Japan or help China, he emphasizes throughout his narrative that without high risk and considerable expenditure there was little that the United States, Great Britain, or France, either singly or even together, could have done to compel Japan to surrender its gains in Manchuria. He suggests, moreover, that London's economic stake in East Asia was too great and Washington's too small to risk challenging Japan's decided military superiority in the region. Tightly argued and based solidly on the diplomatic records of several nations, Thorne's impressive book sets high standards for all diplomatic historians.

The Roosevelt administration, according to historians such as Dorothy Borg, steered American Far Eastern policy away from the direction pursued by Stimson. In her influential monograph, *The United States and the Far Eastern Crisis of 1933-1938*, Borg states that from its inception the Roosevelt administration reasoned that the primary objective of the United States in East Asia for the foreseeable future would be to avoid any conflict with Japan, an objective which could best be achieved by a strict adherence to a strategy of inaction.[69] Unlike some earlier studies which saw traditional American amity for China exerting a deep influence on United States policy, she painstakingly details a sorry record of veritable American indifference to China's fate throughout this period. "The degree of passivity which the United States government maintained is the feature of our record in the Far East in the mid-1930's that is most likely to seem astonishing in retrospect."[70] Only after full-scale warfare between Japan and China broke out in 1937 did the Roosevelt administration begin to change its policy, and this shift, she contends, was due to the fact that both Franklin D. Roosevelt and his secretary of state, Cordell Hull, became convinced that the Sino-Japanese conflict involved broader issues intimately affecting the entire international community—namely, that warfare in the Far East might in turn precipitate a concerted effort on the part of the Axis powers to overwhelm the Western democracies. In short, Roosevelt's appeasement of Japan ended only when the president, in Warren Cohen's words, "became convinced that Japan's ties with Nazi Germany augmented the German threat to U.S. security."[71]

The view that American policy toward Japan prior to Pearl Harbor is best understood within an international rather than an East Asian context is firmly supported by much of the traditional historical literature concerning the coming of World War II. The early accounts by Herbert Feis, William L. Langer and S. Everett Gleason, all of which are generally favorable to American policy, are written from this viewpoint.[72] Even those works which vigorously attack the Roosevelt administration for using Japan as a back door to intervention in Europe share the assumption that the international context is critical for understanding the origins of the Pacific war.[73] Paul Schroeder's provocative, realist critique of American policy similarly emphasizes the important interconnection between European and Asian developments, contending that once Japan joined the Axis alliance the United States could no longer isolate German from Japanese aggression. Indeed, he points out, from that point forward American officials increasingly viewed fascist aggression on the part of either Germany, Italy, or Japan as a unified international movement.[74] Bruce Russett's idiosyncratic look at American involvement in World War II proceeds from the same point of view. American intervention in the Pacific, he insists, was based on a grave misperception of United States interests by an administration which saw a false relationship between events in Asia and Europe.[75]

The revisionist scholarship of William Appleman Williams, Lloyd Gardner, and Robert Freeman Smith presents a different interpretation of the role which East Asian developments played in the American entry into World War II. To these historians, American insistence on the maintenance of the Open Door in East Asia was a root cause of the conflict. As Williams baldly states: "The United States finally went to war to preserve the Open Door in Asia."[76] Japan's blatant violation of Open Door principles, in this view, constituted a direct threat to American national security—at least in the minds of key American policymakers. Regardless of developments in Europe, then, the war with Japan might well have taken place. The very act of asserting an American frontier in Asia, Smith argues, placed the United States in direct conflict with an equally assertive and expansionist Asian power; and as it became increasingly clear that Tokyo's interests could not be accommodated within a framework acceptable to the United States, war became virtually inevitable.[77]

In recent years historians have pursued a variety of approaches in their efforts to gain new and richer perspectives on the road to Pearl Harbor. The publication in 1973 of *Pearl Harbor as History*, a stimulating collection of original essays on American-Japanese relations by leading scholars from the two countries, in many ways represented an historiographical watershed.[78] The essays used both comparative and institutional approaches to shed greater light on the 1931-1941 period in United States-Japanese relations. The collection provided new insights into the period and suggested new areas of inquiry. Other historians have explored these comparative and institutional factors in greater depth. A model study of the comparative-institutional approach, Stephen Pelz's *Race to Pearl Harbor*, provides a penetrating examination of the breakdown of naval arms limitation in the 1930s, analyzing the relationship between that breakdown and the onset of war.[79] After carefully examining the rich archival material in the United States, Great Britain, and Japan, he recommends that much greater emphasis be placed on the role and influence of the navy as well as other bureaucracies. Studies by James H. Herzog, Jonathan G. Utley, and John M. Haight, Jr. have similarly taken a close look at the role of the United States Navy in the period prior to Pearl Harbor, and, like Pelz, have suggested the need for studying bureaucracies themselves in order to gain a greater understanding of the policymaking process.[80] Different avenues of exploration have been suggested by Robert J. C. Butow and Irvine Anderson, Jr. in their careful scrutinies of the influence of nongovernmental and nonpolitical groups in the events leading up to the Pacific war.[81] These works reflect the complexities involved in attempting to gain a truer appreciation of the multitude of forces involved in the road to conflict; they have, moreover, shifted historical study away from simplistic moral categories and toward more subtle and sophisticated analyses.

Historical assessments of World War II diplomacy have varied as fundamentally as those concerned with the war's origins. The first stage of historiography concerning this topic, ably represented in works by Herbert Feis, William H. McNeill, John L. Snell, and Gaddis Smith, tended to defend American wartime policy while searching, in many cases, for a justification of subsequent United States actions in the cold war confrontation with the Soviet Union.[82] Gabriel Kolko's important study, *The Politics of War*, suggested a radically different interpretation of Washington's wartime policy.[83] He boldly argued that the chief political concerns of the United States throughout the war were to help create a stable world order safe for an American-led world capitalism and to crush all elements, especially the Left, which posed a threat to such a world order. Following Kolko's lead, other revisionist historians analyzed wartime diplomacy in a similar light, setting down a radically different framework for understanding both the war and subsequent cold war. Two recently published works, Christopher Thorne's *Allies of a Kind*, which focuses primarily on the Anglo-American alliance, and William Roger Louis's *Imperialism at Bay*, which analyzes the colonial issue, suggest the beginning of a third wave of historical scholarship on World War II diplomacy.[84] These superb studies, based on broad and incisive research in the rich diplomatic sources of several countries, raise many questions about the motivations of wartime diplomacy. Rejecting the economic interpretation of the revisionists as too narrowly conceived, they stress instead the subtle and complex interplay among a multiplicity of factors influencing international relations. At the same time, both works emphasize the political aspects of wartime diplomacy, detailing the sustained efforts of the United States to translate its enormous economic and military power into concrete political advantage in the postwar world.

Also reflective of this new wave of historical scholarship on the World War II period is Michael Schaller's *The U.S. Crusade in China, 1938-1945.*[85] Most previous work on this subject was dominated, in his view, by "a belief in the monolith of Sino-Soviet Communism, and an assumption that all revolution is a conspiracy." Clearly a product of the post-cold war era, Schaller's study raises quite different questions: why did the Koumintang's conservative nationalism appeal to American planners? what forces prejudiced Washington against the Chinese Communists? to what extent was the United States involved in the Chinese civil war? Blending deep archival research with a compelling writing style, he provides fresh and challenging answers to these important questions. Schaller concludes that United States efforts in China, if measured in terms of keeping Chiang Kai-shek in power, were "unrealistic, inappropriate, and probably doomed." On the other hand, he adds, if success for the United States meant keeping China unified, stable, and pro-American, then "not even the communist victory necessarily would have been a failure."[86] It was American preconceptions about China, however, and the inability of American policymakers to comprehend the revolutionary tide which was sweeping away the old China, which prevented any accommodation with the new China which was rapidly replacing it. In Schaller's view, the American reformist strategy which proved so costly to American policy goals in China would find its macabre fulfillment in Vietnam.

The study of United States relations with South Asia and Southeast Asia from 1900-1945 has until recently been virtually ignored by historians of American-Asian relations. Except for the dramatic events connected with the Spanish-American War and the accompanying annexation of the Philippines—a topic of intense scholarly debate—historians have largely overlooked United States interest in and policies toward the South Asia and Southeast Asian regions. In many ways, this lack of scholarly treatment is hardly surprising: it follows from the organization of the State Department itself during these years. United States relations with China, Japan, and Korea were handled by the Division of Far Eastern Affairs—the only Asian division in the department—whereas the remaining territories of Asia, predominantly colonial dependencies, fell under the jurisdiction of the Division of European Affairs. The distinction is extremely significant: in Washington's eyes, these areas were merely appendages of their respective European mother countries; there was thus no need to develop independent policies toward them. In comparison with the thunderous events unfolding in China and Japan during these years, moreover, British India, French Indochina, and the Dutch East Indies seemed placid. If regional stability was one of the overriding goals of United States policy, as many historians have argued, then it is logical to assume that the United States would have welcomed the order brought by European rule. The apparent lack of interest in the region is accordingly quite understandable.

Yet there are many significant aspects of United States policy toward the colonial areas of Asia which remain unanswered. The revisionist contention, for instance, that American policy was motivated largely by Washington's determination to secure an Open Door for American products and investments should be tested with reference to the colonial world. Was there a conflict between this aim and the apparently unquestioned acceptance of European colonial rule in South and Southeast Asia? If so, how was it manifested? Peter Mellish Reed's "Standard Oil in Indonesia,"[87] Joan Hoff Wilson's *American Business and Foreign Policy*, and Lloyd Gardner's *Economic Aspects of New Deal Diplomacy*[88] have addressed some of these matters, but their work represents a preliminary stage of historical inquiry. As Ernest R. May has pointed out, the United States economic stake in the colonial areas of Asia was considerable. American trade with Southeast Asia alone constituted one-quarter to one-third of all American trade with Asia during the period prior to Pearl Harbor, "and from 1900 onwards trade with Southeast Asia exceeded trade with China by a wide and increasing margin."[89] Future work in this field should certainly take account of the role which economic factors—especially the Open Door policy—played in affecting United States relations with South and Southeast Asia. The conflict—if there was any—between traditional American anticolonial ideas and incipient nationalist movements in these areas must also be examined in future studies before a deeper understanding of United States policy in Asia can be reached. While the studies of United States-Indian relations by Gary R. Hess, A. Guy Hope, and Alan Raucher represent significant contributions to an appreciation of this complex question, they are mere beginnings.[90] Likewise Russell Fifield's interpretive overview of American-Southeast Asian relations, an excellent introduction to the subject, must be supplemented by more detailed, monographic work.[91]

Perhaps the most glaring omission in studies of United States-Asian relations is the Philippines. In 1972 Peter W. Stanley published a comprehensive historiographical essay on United States-Philippine affairs which he appropriately entitled, "The Forgotten Philippines."[92] Indeed, as Ernest May has pointed out, "the history of American governance of that country has not been incorporated into the conventional framework for understanding American-East Asian relations."[93] Stanley's later and equally important study, *A Nation in the Making: The Philippines and the United States*, virtually stands alone in this field.[94] Making use of extensive research in both American and Philippine records, he finds the American impact on the islands to be immense. For the Filipinos American rule "has been a major determinant of political, social, cultural, and economic development. Possession of sovereignty—even a sovereignty markedly circumscribed in practical application—permitted Americans to affect Philippine life directly, whether by shooting revolutionaries, eradicating cholera, building roads, establishing curricula, defining political and economic structure, or sanctioning power relationships." American colonialism in the Philippines, Stanley concludes, became "an exemplar, a controlled experiment of sorts, for dealing with the lightly developed colonial and postcolonial parts of the world."[95] A fuller understanding of the American approach to development, liberal reform, and modernization can thus be gleaned by a close examination of the Philippine microcosm. Other studies of United States-Philippine relations, especially those by Theodore Friend and Gerald E. Wheeler, contribute significantly to an understanding of the Filipino-American encounter.[96] Much work, however, remains to be done. The contrasting evaluations of George E. Taylor and William J. Pomeroy—the former a sympathetic account of American policy by a liberal who sees the United States as a benevolent imperial power guiding the Filipinos toward independence and the latter a condemnatory assessment by a Marxist scholar who views United States actions as manipulative and exploitative—must be closely examined in the light of further historical research.[97]

The relations of the United States with Asia since 1945 have been a subject of controversy ever since the close of World War II. Although the unavailability of basic government and private manuscript sources has until recently precluded definitive scholarly work, historical and journalistic accounts of United States-Asian relations during this tumultuous period have proliferated nonetheless. Unfortunately, much of this effort has been infused with polemicism; in many cases the scholarly arena has been merely another forum for shrill political debate. Early accounts, written between the late-1940s and the mid-1960s, tended to reflect the cold war biases of the respective authors. These studies were generally of two distinct types: those which charged the United States with responsibility for "losing" China and failing to respond adequately to the communist challenge in Asia and those which, while often critical of certain aspects of American policy, generally defended Washington's response to postwar developments throughout

Asia. From the latter school of thought, which largely dominated the serious historical literature during these years, the following general picture emerges: the United States made some grievous mistakes in China, but the ultimate responsibility for the success of Mao Tse-tung lies with the Nationalist Chinese and not with Washington; the American occupation of Japan admirably succeeded in destroying the deep-rooted vestiges of militarism in Japanese society while at the same time it carefully steered Tokyo toward a peaceful, democratic, and capitalistic road; in the former colonial areas of South and Southeast Asia, the United States, in keeping with its anticolonial traditions, encouraged wherever possible the establishment of independent governments led by moderate nationalist leaders; and in Korea and later in Vietnam, the United States responded forthrightly to the communist challenge with its military and economic might, helping to stem the Soviet-directed tide.[98]

Revisionist historians, influenced strongly by the collapse of American policy in Vietnam in the 1960s, mounted a veritable full-scale assault on this liberal interpretive scaffolding. Dissenting radically from preconceptions about American diplomacy which had characterized earlier work, the revisionist school offered a contrary framework for understanding United States actions vis-à-vis Asia. American officials, they insisted, bore the major responsibility for the onset of the cold war in Asia as well as in Europe. The United States was just another imperial power intent upon advancing its own interests in Asia, especially economic ones. Indeed, they viewed the United States as a nation which tragically failed to understand the transforming dynamic of revolutionary nationalism, and instead falsely branded nationalism and revolution as threats to both world order and vital American security interests. While Williams has properly been called the intellectual forefather of this critical view, historians such as Walter LaFeber, Barton Bernstein, Gabriel Kolko, Thomas G. Paterson, and Stephen Ambrose have ably added substance to the outline sketched by Williams.[99] The revisionists, of course, have been no less free of political bias than earlier scholars; their search for an explanation of the origins of America's Vietnam debacle in the early postwar years has certainly pervaded much of their historical writing. Nonetheless, the probing questions raised by these historians about the nature of American foreign policy are fundamental ones which continue to influence much of the work on United States diplomacy in the postwar era.

Some studies have sought to move beyond this traditionalist-revisionist debate. Akira Iriye's suggestive work, *The Cold War in Asia*, belongs to this new wave.[100] While acknowledging the important contributions made by Joyce and Gabriel Kolko,[101] he insists that their work, and by implication that of other revisionists, is no less American-centered than the official and semiofficial cold war accounts of United States policy. It is time to create a new conceptual framework for comprehending contemporary history, Iriye asserts, and in his study he seeks to do this by looking at the larger picture in postwar Asia. As in many of his writings, he focuses upon the structure of international relations. Aware that the war had shattered the previous system of diplomatic relations in Asia, the United States, Iriye contends, sought to create a new international order in the postwar years, an ultimately unsuccessful effort which he labels "the Yalta system." Another approach is Lisle Rose's synthesis *The Roots of Tragedy*.[102] While sharply critical of United States policy toward what he terms the "great revolt" in Asia against Western influence, he downplays the role of economic factors in the formulation of American policy and emphasizes instead the importance of ethnocentric and racial attitudes. American actions in postwar Asia constituted "an inevitable tragedy given America's cast of mind. A country which in 1953 still denied its own black citizens their basic rights could not be expected to view the peoples of Asia—however repellent their current leadership—as potential equals in a worldwide search for lasting peace."[103]

These shifting historiographical trends are reflected in the literature concerning the United States response to the Chinese revolution. The famous China White Paper, published by the State Department just weeks before the proclamation of the People's Republic in October of 1949, officially attempted to absolve the United States of any responsibility for the Kuomintang defeat.[104] "The ominous result of the civil war in China was beyond the control of the government of the United States," concluded Secretary of State Dean Acheson in his introduction to the volume. "Nothing that this country did or could have done within the reasonable limits of its capabilities could have changed the result; nothing that was left undone by this country has contributed to it."[105] Not everyone, however, was convinced by the conclusions of this mammoth study; in fact, a junior senator from Wisconsin named Joseph McCarthy launched his vitriolic career largely on the thesis that Mao's success in China resulted from an unfortunate combination of American naivete and treason. Anthony Kubek's *How the Far East Was Lost* is one of a number of works which sought to lend scholarly credibility to that thesis.[106] A far more balanced account, Tang Tsou's *America's Failure in China* reflected the mainstream scholarly assessment of America's postwar China policy.[107] The United States did not "lose" China, in Tang's judgment, but it does bear at least limited responsibility for the ultimate collapse of the Chiang Kai-shek regime. By failing to tie its military aid to demands that the Nanking government curb its political corruption and instead create a more stable and popular alternative to communist rule, the Truman administration played its part in the nationalist denouement. Squarely within the realist tradition, Tang faults the United States for pursuing idealistic goals in China and never coming to grips with the true nature of its interests in that part of the world. "One could hardly find a more sobering example," he concludes, "of the tragic results produced by a policy of good intentions and high ideals which lacked the foundation of a correlative estimate of self-interest and which was not supported by military power equal to the noble tasks."[108]

The revisionist critique of American diplomacy coupled with the thaw in United States-Chinese relations in the 1970s has lent fresh perspectives to the study of American policy toward the Chinese revolution. Joyce and Gabriel Kolko view that policy as dominated by economic concerns. Washington was intent upon integrating China into "a liberalized, American-led world capitalism, a China that American capital could eventually penetrate and develop."[109] Lewis McCarroll Purifoy's study of the Truman administration's China policy, also written within a revisionist framework, similarly stresses the importance of economic factors and the traditions of the Open Door in conditioning the American response to the Chinese revolution.[110] Ernest May, on the other hand, stresses a series of factors influencing American policy, focusing particularly on the United States decision against active intervention.[111] Robert M. Blum's essay, "The Peiping Cable," takes a completely different tack.[112] Using new evidence, he suggests that the United States missed a golden opportunity in 1949 when it failed to respond to a secret request by Chinese Communist leader Chou En-lai for American economic assistance to help rebuild China. A potential opportunity to keep China unaligned in the cold war was thus inexcusably fumbled by United States officials, in Blum's view. The dramatic documents cited by Blum, released for the first time in the *Foreign Relations* series, and only after a long clearance controversy, raise many new and disturbing questions about the subsequent course of United States-Chinese relations.[113] In short, were the two decades of confrontation between the United States and China inevitable given the ideology of the Chinese Communists? Or does the United States bear a certain degree of responsibility for this period of hostility? An earlier article by Warren W. Tozer, drawing on different materials, similarly accuses Washington of pursuing a tragic policy "which forestalled any chance of developing relations with the People's Republic of China."[114] Much additional work on this subject must be undertaken before we can begin to answer critical questions concerning the initial encounter between the United States and the People's Republic of China. The vastly improved relations between Washington and Peking during the Nixon, Ford, and Carter administrations underscores the need to reconceptualize studies of this formative period.

The American occupation of Japan, far less controversial at the time than the explosive civil war in China, has consequently attracted far less scholarly attention. The traditional view that the occupation was an unqualified success for both the United States and Japan has only recently been challenged, and one can only hope that the recent availability of rich archival sources for the postwar period will encourage the kind of in-depth study that is sorely needed. This traditional interpretation, as well as the provocative contrary judgment of the Kolkos that the chief aim of American policy in postwar Japan was to reintegrate Japan into the American economic and strategic orbit, in part by bolstering the conservative Japanese ruling class, must be carefully evaluated in the light of these new materials. Stimulating essays by Lawrence S. Wittner and Howard Schoenberger, both written from a revisionist perspective, ask probing and important new questions about the occupation.[115] Akira Iriye's contribution, "Continuities in U.S.-Japanese Relations," raises additional questions. He suggests, in his refreshingly original manner, that the continuities in United States-Japanese relations far outweighed the discontinuities during the years of American occupation.[116] William Manchester's best-selling biography of Douglas MacArthur likewise sheds some new light on the period, although his lucid, anecdotal account is not entirely satisfactory to scholars.[117] Hopefully, other historians will extend the scope of these promising studies, for until more solid monographic work on American-Japanese relations in the postwar period has been completed it will be virtually impossible to draw larger conclusions about Washington's actions in the Pacific during this era.

That judgment is equally appropriate in the case of Korea. While the Korean War marked, in the view of many historians, the extension of the cold war to Asia, until recently very little research had been done on United States-Korean relations in the immediate postwar years. Traditional accounts, such as those by Robert T. Oliver, Glenn Paige, Gregory Henderson, and Soon Sung Cho, generally defend the American record in Korea, while accusing the Soviets of almost complete responsibility for the events leading to the war.[118] On the other end of the interpretive spectrum, the Kolkos see American policy as calculated and aggressive while insisting that the Kremlin's actions were primarily defensive. Less radical revisionists such as Walter LaFeber and Stephen Ambrose are not as strident, but still see Washington as in large part responsible for the onset of war in Korea. They also emphasize that the United States totally misperceived the nature of the conflict there and seriously overreacted to what was in fact a relatively limited threat to United States security.[119] A different interpretation of the war is set forth by Ernest May in his book *"Lessons" of the Past*.[120] Rejecting the rational-actor model favored by the revisionists, he stresses the importance of misperceptions and nonrational factors in the American decision for intervention. Recent interpretive essays by John Lewis Gaddis, Russell Buhite, and Stephen Pelz make use of newly released documents to add greater sophistication to the study of the Korean War, while pointing to numerous new directions for future scholars.[121] Gaddis's suggestion that the conflict was fought by the United States in such a way as to encourage rather than undermine Sino-Soviet cooperation certainly deserves further scrutiny. Buhite's concluding judgment about American policy, while not original, is equally provocative: "Korea," he insists, "was more the occasion for United States intervention than the reason for it."[122] Further work along these lines must continue if we are to gain a balanced appreciation of the origins and conduct of the Korean War, work which will be greatly spurred by the continuing declassification of crucial diplomatic records.

Washington's response to the independence movements which emerged in South and Southeast Asia in the postwar period has only recently begun to command the attention of scholars. The role which the United States played in the decolonization of vast areas of South and Southeast Asia requires careful and detailed examination, yet few scholars have addressed this important historical question. Gary Hess's *The United States Encounters India* is one notable exception, although the declassification of important government records in both the United States and Great Britain since its publication would certainly seem to justify further study. As yet, no detailed analysis of the United States response to independence movements in Indonesia, Burma, Malaya, or Ceylon has been published.[123] Inexplicably, American policy toward its own colony in Southeast Asia has also been largely neglected by historians. Washington's decision to grant independence to the Philippines in 1946 has been explained by some as a natural outgrowth of America's traditional anticolonialism, but the charge of other historians that a neocolonial relationship continued after independence must be carefully evaluated in the light of the documentary record. The successful counterinsurgency campaign against the Huk rebellion, in which the United States appears to have played a major role and which set such an important precedent for later actions in Vietnam, should be given in-depth study.

For obvious reasons, historians have been more attentive to Vietnam than to any other area of South or Southeast Asia. In recent years, scholars in search of the roots of the United States involvement there have painstakingly examined the initial American response to Indochinese developments in the 1940s. Edward Drachman, Gary Hess, Walter LaFeber, Christopher Thorne, and George C. Herring have all made significant contributions.[124] In general, they have found that Washington was unable to understand or adjust to the force of Vietnamese nationalism during this early period, which foreshadowed later problems. Further work must be undertaken, however, if we are to gain a deeper comprehension of the role which Vietnam and the other dependent areas of South and Southeast Asia played in the global planning of the United States during the cold war era. The interrelationship between Asian and European priorities in the postwar years requires particular attention, as does the relationship between the anticolonial ideals so often espoused by the United States and the policies Washington actually pursued toward colonial questions. While some stimulating general works, such as those by Russell Fifield and Evelyn Colbert, set forth adequate overviews of American policy in Southeast Asia, more monographic work must be undertaken.[125] The dearth of scholarly work on United States-South Asian relations is even more glaring, an unfortunate state of affairs which will hopefully be redressed in the near future.

This breathless—and unavoidably oversimplified—race through the secondary literature suggests a series of concluding thoughts about the historiography regarding United States-Asian relations. The historical debate concerning American policy toward Asia has been a rich one; in recent years, it has become one of the liveliest and most stimulating debates within the entire discipline of United States diplomatic history. The innovative work of the past decade has been especially significant and has in many ways greatly expanded the scope of the field. The proliferation of multiarchival work along with studies informed with bureaucratic and institutional methodology has had a deep and far-reaching impact. These studies, coupled with the searching questions raised by the revisionists about the very nature of the American diplomatic process and the conception of the national interests, have unquestionably infused new life and excitement into the study of American-Asian relations.

It is always tempting to view historical scholarship in a linear, evolutionary fashion: each generation builds upon the work of the previous generation, refining it, asking new questions, uncovering previously untapped source materials, and adding greater breadth and sophistication to its own analyses. Such a view could arguably be applied to the study of American-Asian relations over the past several decades. Although there would certainly be a substantial degree of truth and utility to such an interpretation, it would grievously oversimplify the complexities involved in attempting to comprehend the changing modes of historical scholarship, for, as Croce's much-quoted remark so aptly puts it, each generation must write its own history. Just as realist concepts and consensus history grew naturally out of the social and intellectual milieux of the 1950s, so too did the radical revisionist critique emerge logically from the turbulent 1960s. While the notion that one can often learn more about the period during which an author is writing than about the subject matter of his work is probably an overstatement, it is nonetheless suggestive of the intimate interaction between the scholarly process and the prevailing social and intellectual milieux. In evaluating the work of the 1970s, or any other period, such caveats must be borne in mind.

An additional factor to keep in mind when reviewing and evaluating the secondary literature concerning American-Asian relations is that different historians have approached the subject with entirely different interests and intentions. While the traditional concerns of American diplomatic historians have centered on the formulation and implementation of United States policy toward a particular area—the primary concern of this essay—other historians, concerned more with international relations as a whole or with the United States impact on another country or region, have framed very different questions. The work of an Asian area specialist, for instance, often deals with American policy as a secondary rather than a primary focus, and properly so. One might hope for a greater integration of these differing approaches, but it is unlikely to occur. Instead, the diplomatic historian—and especially one concerned with the interaction between the United States and Asia—should welcome a variety of interpretive and methodological approaches, believing that each, equally valid in its own way, will shed some light on the larger questions about the role and influence of the United States in the world community.

Notes

1. Neither doctoral dissertations nor unpublished papers are considered in this study. The reader is especially referred to the generally excellent historiographical essays contained in Ernest R. May and James C. Thomson, Jr., eds., *American-East Asian Relations: A Survey* (Cambridge, Mass.: Harvard University Press, 1972). This survey will apply the geographical term East Asia only to those areas which are located in the northeastern section of that continent: China, Japan, and Korea. The terms Southeast Asia and South Asia will follow common usage.

2. A. Whitney Griswold, *The Far Eastern Policy of the United States* (New York: Harcourt, Brace & World, 1938). Two stimulating reviews of his work are Robert H. Ferrell, "The Griswold Theory of Our Far Eastern Policy," in Dorothy Borg, comp., *Historians and American Far Eastern Policy* (New York: Columbia University East Asian Institute, 1966), and Dorothy Borg, "Two Historians of the Far Eastern Policy of the United States: Tyler Dennett and A. Whitney Griswold," in Dorothy Borg and Shumpei Okamoto, eds., *Pearl Harbor as History: Japanese-American Relations, 1931-1941* (New York: Columbia University Press, 1973).

3. Tyler Dennett, *Americans in Eastern Asia* (New York: Macmillan Co., 1922).

4. George F. Kennan, *American Diplomacy, 1900-1950* (New York: Mentor, 1951).

5. Ibid., p. 47.

6. Robert E. Osgood, *Ideals and Self-Interest in America's Foreign Relations* (Chicago: University of Chicago Press, 1953).

7. Ibid., pp. 430-31.

8. William L. Neumann, "Ambiguity and Ambivalence in Ideas of National Interest in Asia," in Alexander DeConde, ed., *Isolation and Security: Ideas and Interests in Twentieth-Century American Foreign Policy* (Durham: Duke University Press, 1957).

9. Paul H. Clyde, "Historical Reflections on American Relations with the Far East," *South Atlantic Quarterly* 61 (Autumn 1962): 437-49.

10. Ibid., p. 445.

11. William L. Neumann, *America Encounters Japan: From Perry to MacArthur* (Baltimore: Johns Hopkins Press, 1963).

12. William Appleman Williams, *The Tragedy of American Diplomacy* (New York: Delta Books, 1962).

13. Edward Friedman and Mark Selden, eds., *America's Asia: Dissenting Essays on Asian-American Relations* (New York: Vintage Books, 1971).

14. Ibid., p. xi.

15. Akira Iriye, *After Imperialism: The Search for a New Order in the Far East, 1921-1931* (Cambridge, Mass.: Harvard University Press, 1965).

16. Akira Iriye, *Across the Pacific: An Inner History of American-East Asian Relations* (New York: Harcourt, Brace, & World, 1967).

17. Warren I. Cohen, *America's Response to China: An Interpretive History of Sino-American Relations* (New York: John Wiley & Sons, 1971). *See also* his "From Contempt to Containment: Cycles in American Attitudes toward China," in John Braeman, Robert H. Bremner, and David Brody, eds., *Twentieth Century American Foreign Policy* (Columbus: Ohio State University Press, 1971). Charles E. Neu, *The Troubled Encounter: The United States and Japan* (New York: John Wiley & Sons, 1975).

18. Mark Selden, ed., *Remaking Asia: Essays on the American Uses of Power* (New York: Pantheon, 1974).

19. Christopher Thorne, *Allies of a Kind: The United States, Britain and the War Against Japan, 1941-1945* (London: Hamish Hamilton, 1978); William Roger Louis, *Imperialism at Bay: The United States and the Decolonization of the British Empire, 1941-1945* (New York: Oxford University Press, 1978); Stephen E. Pelz, *Race to Pearl Harbor: The Failure of the Second London Naval Conference and the Onset of World War II* (Cambridge, Mass.: Harvard University Press, 1974).

20. Richard W. Van Alstyne, *The United States and East Asia* (New York: W. W. Norton & Co., 1973); Robert A. Hart, *The Eccentric Tradition: American Diplomacy in the Far East* (New York: Charles Scribner's Sons, 1976).

21. Howard K. Beale, *Theodore Roosevelt and the Rise of America to World Power* (Baltimore: Johns Hopkins Press, 1956); Thomas A. Bailey, *Theodore Roosevelt and the Japanese-American Crises* (Stanford: Stanford University Press, 1934); Raymond A. Esthus, *Theodore Roosevelt and Japan* (Seattle: University of Washington Press, 1966); Charles E. Neu, *An Uncertain Friendship: Theodore Roosevelt and Japan, 1906-1909* (Cambridge, Mass.: Harvard University Press, 1967); Eugene P. Trani, *The Treaty of Portsmouth: An Adventure in American Diplomacy* (Lexington: University of Kentucky Press, 1969); Cohen, *America's Response to China.*

22. Neu, *An Uncertain Friendship*, p. 319.

23. Esthus, *Theodore Roosevelt and Japan*, p. 308.

24. Cohen, "From Contempt to Containment," pp. 515-17.

25. Charles Vevier, *The United States and China, 1906-1913: A Study of Finance and Diplomacy* (New Brunswick, N.J.: Rutgers University Press, 1955).

26. Charles E. Neu, "Theodore Roosevelt and American Involvement in the Far East, 1901-1909," *Pacific Historical Review* 35 (November 1966): 433-49.

27. Cohen, *America's Response to China*, pp. 77-84.

28. Iriye, *Across the Pacific*, p. 122.

29. Walter V. Scholes and Marie V. Scholes, *The Foreign Policies of the Taft Administration* (Columbia: University of Missouri Press, 1970).

30. Tien-yi Li, *Woodrow Wilson's China Policy, 1913-1917* (New York: Twayne, 1952).

31. Russell H. Fifield, *Woodrow Wilson and the Far East: The Diplomacy of the Shantung Question* (New York: Thomas Y. Crowell Co., 1952).

32. Roy Watson Curry, *Woodrow Wilson and Far Eastern Policy, 1913-1921* (New York: Bookman Associates, 1957).

33. Burton F. Beers, *Vain Endeavor: Robert Lansing's Attempts to End the American-Japanese Rivalry* (Durham: Duke University Press, 1962).

34. Ibid., p. 184.

35. Neu, *Troubled Encounter*, pp. 91-97.

36. Arthur S. Link, *Wilson* (Princeton: Princeton University Press, 1956), vol. 2, *The New Freedom*, p. 278.

37. Williams, *Tragedy of American Diplomacy*, pp. 67-83.

38. N. Gordon Levin, Jr., *Woodrow Wilson and World Politics: America's Response to War and Revolution* (New York: Oxford University Press, 1968).

39. Ibid., p. vii.

40. Jerry Israel, *Progressivism and the Open Door: America and China, 1905-1921* (Pittsburgh: University of Pittsburgh Press, 1971). *See also* Israel's earlier article, " 'For God, For China and For Yale'—The Open Door in Action," *American Historical Review* 75 (February 1970): 796-807.

41. Israel, " 'For God, For China and For Yale,' " p. 807.

42. Noel Pugach, "Making the Open Door Work: Paul S. Reinsch in China, 1913-1919," *Pacific Historical Review* 38 (May 1969): 157-75.

43. Helen Dodson Kahn, "Willard D. Straight and the Great Game of Empire," in Frank J. Merli and Theodore A. Wilson, eds., *Makers of American Diplomacy: From Theodore Roosevelt to Henry Kissinger* (New York: Charles Scribner's Sons, 1974); Harry N. Scheiber, "World War I as Entrepreneurial Opportunity: Willard Straight and the American International Corporation," *Political Science Quarterly* 84 (September 1969): 486-511.

44. Michael H. Hunt, *Frontier Defense and the Open Door: Manchuria in Chinese-American Relations, 1895-1911* (New Haven: Yale University Press, 1973).

45. Paul H. Clyde, "Railway Politics and the Open Door in China, 1916-1917," *American Journal of International Law* 25 (October 1931): 642-57 and "An Episode in American-Japanese Relations: The Manchurian Freight-Rate Controversy, 1914-1916," *Far Eastern Review* 26 (August-September 1930): 410-12; Harry W. Kirwin, "The Federal Telegraph Company: A Testing of the Open Door," *Pacific Historical Review* 22 (August 1953): 271-86.

46. William R. Braisted, "China, the United States Navy, and the Bethlehem Steel Company, 1909-1929," *Business History Review* 42 (Spring 1968): 50-66.

47. Noel Pugach, "Standard Oil and Petroleum Development in Early Republican China," *Business History Review* 65 (Winter 1971): 452-73.

48. Noel Pugach, "Anglo-American Aircraft Competition and the China Arms Embargo, 1919-1921," *Diplomatic History* 2 (Fall 1978): 351-71.

49. Michael H. Hunt, "Americans in the China Market: Economic Oppor-

tunities and Economic Nationalism, 1890s-1931," *Business History Review* 51 (Autumn 1977): 277-307.

50. Ibid., p. 306.

51. Delber L. McKee, *Chinese Exclusion Versus the Open Door Policy, 1900-1906: Clashes Over China Policy in the Roosevelt Era* (Detroit: Wayne State University Press, 1977).

52. Bailey, *Theodore Roosevelt and the Japanese-American Crises*; Roger Daniels, *The Politics of Prejudice: The Anti-Japanese Movement in California and the Struggle for Japanese Exclusion* (Berkeley: University of California Press, 1962).

53. Kell F. Mitchell, Jr., "Diplomacy and Prejudice: The Morris-Shidehara Negotiations, 1920-1921," *Pacific Historical Review* 34 (February 1970): 85-104.

54. Paul Gordon Lauren, "Human Rights in History: Diplomacy and Racial Equality at the Paris Peace Conference," *Diplomatic History* 2 (Summer 1978): 257-78. *See also* Robert McClellan, *Heathen Chinese: A Study of American Attitudes Toward China, 1890-1905* (Columbus: Ohio State University Press, 1970).

55. Akira Iriye, "1921-1931," in May and Thomson, eds., *American-East Asian Relations*, pp. 221-22.

56. William A. Williams, "China and Japan: A Challenge and a Choice of the 1920s," *Pacific Historical Review* 26 (August 1957): 259-79; Iriye, *After Imperialism*.

57. Thomas H. Buckley, *The United States and the Washington Conference, 1921-1922* (Knoxville: University of Tennessee Press, 1970).

58. Ibid.

59. Noel Pugach, "American Friendship for China and the Shantung Question at the Washington Conference," *Journal of American History* 64 (June 1977): 67-86.

60. Robert H. van Meter, Jr., "The Washington Conference of 1921-1922: A New Look," *Pacific Historical Review* 46 (November 1977): 603-24.

61. Roger Dingman, *Power in the Pacific: The Origins of Naval Disarmament, 1914-1922* (Chicago: University of Chicago Press, 1976).

62. Dorothy Borg, *American Policy and the Chinese Revolution, 1925-1928* (New York: American Institute of Pacific Relations, 1947).

63. Ibid., p. 431.

64. Brian T. George, "The State Department and Sun Yat-sen: American Policy and the Revolutionary Disintegration of China, 1920-1924," *Pacific Historical Review* 46 (August 1977): 387-408.

65. Cohen, *America's Response to China*, pp. 108-13.

66. Robert H. Ferrell, *American Diplomacy in the Great Depression: Hoover-Stimson Foreign Policy, 1929-1933* (New Haven: Yale University Press, 1957); Richard N. Current, *Secretary Stimson: A Study in Statecraft* (New Brunswick: Rutgers University Press, 1954); Armin Rappaport, *Henry L. Stimson and Japan* (Chicago: University of Chicago Press, 1963).

67. Rappaport, *Stimson and Japan*, p. 203.

68. Christopher Thorne, *The Limits of Foreign Policy: The West, the League and the Far Eastern Crisis of 1931-1933* (New York: G. P. Putnam's Sons, 1973).

69. Dorothy Borg, *The United States and the Far Eastern Crisis of 1933-1938* (Cambridge, Mass.: Harvard University Press, 1964).

70. Ibid., p. 544.

71. Cohen, "From Contempt to Containment," p. 540.

72. Herbert Feis, *The Road to Pearl Harbor* (Princeton: Princeton University Press, 1950); William L. Langer and S. Everett Gleason, *The Challenge to Isolation, 1937-1940* (New York: Harper & Brothers, 1952) and *The Undeclared War, 1940-1941* (New York: Harper & Brothers, 1953).

73. *See* especially Charles Tansill, *Back Door to War: The Roosevelt Foreign Policies, 1937-1941* (Chicago: Henry Regnery Co., 1950); Harry Elmer Barnes, *Perpetual War for Perpetual Peace* (Caldwall, Idaho: Caxton Press, 1953).

74. Paul W. Schroeder, *The Axis Alliance and Japanese-American Relations, 1941* (Ithaca: Cornell University Press, 1958).

75. Bruce M. Russett, *No Clear and Present Danger: A Skeptical View of the United States Entry into World War II* (New York: Harper & Row, 1972).

76. Williams, *The Tragedy of American Diplomacy*, p. 148.

77. Robert Freeman Smith, "American Foreign Relations, 1920-1942," in Barton J. Bernstein, ed., *Towards a New Past: Dissenting Essays in American History* (New York: Random House, 1967), pp. 252-54; Lloyd C. Gardner, *Economic Aspects of New Deal Diplomacy* (Madison: University of Wisconsin Press, 1964), pp. 133-51.

78. Borg and Okamoto, eds., *Pearl Harbor as History*.

79. Pelz, *Race to Pearl Harbor*.

80. James H. Herzog, *Closing the Open Door: American-Japanese Diplomatic Negotiations, 1936-1941* (Annapolis: Naval Institute Press, 1973); Jonathan G. Utley, "Upstairs, Downstairs at Foggy Bottom: Oil Exports and Japan, 1940-1941," *Prologue* 8 (Spring 1976): 17-28; John M. Haight, Jr., "Franklin D. Roosevelt and a Naval Quarantine of Japan," *Pacific Historical Review* 40 (May 1971): 203-26.

81. Robert J. C. Butow, *The John Doe Associates: Backdoor Diplomacy for Peace, 1941* (Stanford: Stanford University Press, 1974); Irvine H. Anderson, Jr., *The Standard-Vacuum Oil Company and United States East Asian Policy, 1933-1941* (Princeton: Princeton University Press, 1975).

82. Herbert Feis, *Churchill, Roosevelt, Stalin: The War They Waged and the Peace They Sought* (Princeton: Princeton University Press, 1957); William H. McNeill, *America, Britain and Russia: Their Cooperation and Conflict, 1941-46* (London: Oxford University Press, 1953); John L. Snell, *Illusion and Necessity: The Diplomacy of Global War, 1939-1945* (Boston: Houghton Mifflin Co., 1963); Gaddis Smith, *American Diplomacy During the Second World War, 1941-1945* (New York: John Wiley & Sons, 1965).

83. Gabriel Kolko, *The Politics of War: The World and United States Foreign Policy, 1943-1945* (New York: Random House, 1968).

84. Christopher Thorne, *Allies of a Kind*; William Roger Louis, *Imperialism at Bay*.

85. Michael Schaller, *The U.S. Crusade in China, 1938-1945* (New York: Columbia University Press, 1979).

86. Ibid., pp. xi-xii.

87. Peter Mellish Reed, "Standard Oil in Indonesia, 1898-1928," *Business History Review* 32 (Autumn 1958): 329-37.

88. Joan Hoff Wilson, *American Business and Foreign Policy, 1920-1933* (Lex-

ington: University of Kentucky Press, 1971); Gardner, *Economic Aspects of New Deal Diplomacy.*

89. May, Foreword, in May and Thomson, eds., *American-East Asian Relations,* pp. xiii-xiv.

90. Gary R. Hess, *American Encounters India, 1941-1947* (Baltimore: Johns Hopkins Press, 1970); A. Guy Hope, *American and Swaraj: The U.S. Role in Indian Independence* (Washington: Public Affairs Press, 1968); Alan Raucher, "American Imperialists and the Pro-India Movement, 1900-1932," *Pacific Historical Review* 43 (February 1974): 83-110.

91. Russell H. Fifield, *Americans in Southeast Asia: The Roots of Commitment* (New York: Thomas Y. Crowell Co., 1973).

92. Peter W. Stanley, "The Forgotten Philippines," in May and Thomson, eds., *American-East Asian Relations.*

93. May, Foreword, in May and Thomson, eds., *American-East Asian Relations,* p. xiii.

94. Peter W. Stanley, *A Nation in the Making: The Philippines and the United States, 1899-1921* (Cambridge, Mass.: Harvard University Press, 1974).

95. Ibid., p. 277.

96. Theodore Friend, *Between Two Empires: The Ordeal of the Philippines, 1929-1946* (New Haven: Yale University Press, 1965); Gerald E. Wheeler, "Republican Philippine Policy, 1921-1933," *Pacific Historical Review* 28 (1959): 377-90.

97. George E. Taylor, *The Philippines and the United States: Problems of Partnership* (New York: Frederick A. Praeger, 1964); William J. Pomeroy, "The Philippines: A Case History of Neocolonialism," in Selden, ed., *Remaking Asia.*

98. For a sampling of this traditional view, *see* John W. Spanier, *American Foreign Policy Since World War II* (New York: Frederick A. Praeger, 1968); Herbert Feis, *China Tangle: The American Effort in China from Pearl Harbor to the Marshall Mission* (Princeton: Princeton University Press, 1953); Neumann, *America Encounters Japan*; Frank N. Traeger, "American Foreign Policy in Southeast Asia," *Studies on Asia* (1965): 17-54.

99. *See*, for example, Walter LaFeber, *America, Russia, and the Cold War, 1945-1975,* rev. ed. (New York: John Wiley & Sons, 1976); Thomas G. Paterson, *Soviet-American Confrontation: Postwar Reconstruction and the Origins of the Cold War* (Baltimore: Johns Hopkins Press, 1973); Stephen E. Ambrose, *Rise to Globalism: American Foreign Policy, 1938-1970* (Baltimore: Penguin Books, 1971).

100. Akira Iriye, *The Cold War in Asia: An Historical Introduction* (Englewood Cliffs, N.J.: Prentice-Hall, 1974).

101. Joyce and Gabriel Kolko, *The Limits of Power: The World and United States Foreign Policy, 1945-1954* (New York: Harper & Row, 1972).

102. Lisle A. Rose, *Roots of Tragedy: The United States and the Struggle for Asia, 1945-1953* (Westport, Conn.: Greenwood Press, 1976).

103. Ibid., p. 248.

104. U.S. Department of State, *United States Relations with China: With Special Reference to the Period 1944-1949* (Washington, D.C.: Government Printing Office, 1949).

105. Ibid., p. xvi.

106. Anthony Kubek, *How the Far East Was Lost: American Policy and the Creation of Communist China* (Chicago: Henry Regnery Co., 1963). *See also* Freda Utley, *Last Chance in China* (Indianapolis: Bobbs-Merrill Co., 1952).

107. Tang Tsou, *America's Failure in China, 1941-1950* (Chicago: University of Chicago Press, 1963).

108. Ibid., p. 591.

109. Joyce and Gabriel Kolko, *Limits of Power*, pp. 246-47.

110. Louis McCarroll Purifoy, *Harry Truman's China Policy: McCarthyism and the Diplomacy of Hysteria, 1947-1951* (New York: New Viewpoints, 1976).

111. Ernest R. May, *The Truman Administration and China, 1945-1949* (Philadelphia: J. B. Lippincott Co., 1975).

112. Robert M. Blum, "The Peiping Cable: A Drama of 1949," *New York Times Magazine* (13 August 1978): 8-10.

113. Department of State, *Foreign Relations of the United States, 1949*, vol. 8, *The Far East: China* (Washington, D.C.: Government Printing Office, 1978).

114. Warren W. Tozer, "Last Bridge to China: The Shanghai Power Company, the Truman Administration and the Chinese Communists," *Diplomatic History* 1 (Winter 1977): 64-78.

115. Lawrence S. Wittner, "MacArthur and the Missionaries: God and Man in Occupied Japan," *Pacific Historical Review* 40 (February 1971): 77-98; Howard Schoenberger, "The Japan Lobby in American Diplomacy, 1947-1952," *Pacific Historical Review* 46 (August 1977): 327-59.

116. Akira Iriye, "Continuities in U.S.-Japanese Relations, 1941-1949," in Yonosuke Nagai and Akira Iriye, eds., *The Origins of the Cold War in Asia* (New York: Columbia University Press, 1977).

117. William Manchester, *American Caesar: Douglas MacArthur, 1880-1964* (Boston: Little, Brown & Co., 1978).

118. Robert T. Oliver, *Syngman Rhee: The Man Behind the Myth* (New York: Dodd, Mead, 1955); Glenn D. Paige, *The Korean Decision: June 24-30, 1950* (New York: Free Press, 1968); Gregory Henderson, *Korea: Politics of the Vortex* (Cambridge, Mass.: Harvard University Press, 1968); Soon Sung Cho, *Korea in World Politics, 1940-1950: An Evaluation of American Responsibility* (Berkeley: University of California Press, 1967).

119. LaFeber, *America, Russia, and the Cold War*, pp. 101-37; Ambrose, *Rise to Globalism*, pp. 192-216.

120. Ernest R. May, *"Lessons" of the Past: The Use and Misuse of History in American Foreign Policy* (New York: Oxford University Press, 1973).

121. John Lewis Gaddis, "Korea in American Politics, Strategy, and Diplomacy, 1945-1950," in Nagai and Iriye, eds., *The Origins of the Cold War in Asia*; Russell D. Buhite, " 'Major Interests': American Policy Toward China, Taiwan, and Korea, 1945-1950," *Pacific Historical Review* 47 (August 1978): 425-51; Stephen E. Pelz, "When the Kitchen Gets Hot, Pass the Buck: Truman and Korea in 1950," *Reviews in American History* 5 (December 1978): 548-55.

122. Buhite, " 'Major Interests,' " p. 449. *See also* the original essays in Francis H. Keller, ed., *The Korean War: A 25-Year Perspective* (Lawrence: Regents Press of Kansas, 1977).

123. Hess, *The United States Encounters India. See also* Evelyn Colbert, "The

Road Not Taken: Decolonization and Independence in Indonesia and Indochina," *Foreign Affairs* 51 (April 1973): 608-28; George McT. Kahin, "The United States and the Anticolonial Revolutions in Southeast Asia, 1945-50," in Nagai and Iriye, eds., *The Origins of the Cold War in Asia*; Robert J. McMahon, "Anglo-American Diplomacy and the Reoccupation of the Netherlands East Indies," *Diplomatic History* 2 (Winter 1978): 1-23.

124. Edward R. Drachman, *United States Policy Toward Vietnam, 1940-1945* (Rutherford, N.J.: Fairleigh Dickinson University Press, 1970); Gary R. Hess, "Franklin Roosevelt and Indochina," *Journal of American History* 59 (September 1972): 353-68 and "The First American Commitment in Indochina: The Acceptance of the 'Bao Dai Solution,' 1950," *Diplomatic History* 2 (Fall 1978): 331-50; Walter LaFeber, "Roosevelt, Churchill, and Indochina: 1942-1945," *American Historical Review* 80 (December 1975): 1277-95; Christopher Thorne, "Indochina and Anglo-American Relations, 1942-1945," *Pacific Historical Review* 45 (February 1976): 73-96; George C. Herring, "The Truman Administration and the Restoration of French Sovereignty in Indochina," *Diplomatic History* 1 (Spring 1977): 97-117.

125. Fifield, *Americans in Southeast Asia*; Evelyn Colbert, *International Politics in Southeast Asia, 1941-1945* (Ithaca: Cornell University Press, 1977).

13 ______ "'Non-Benign Neglect": The United States and Black Africa in the Twentieth Century

THOMAS J. NOER

Recently a prominent historian argued that the section on American imperialism is "the worst chapter" in any book on American diplomacy.[1] An essay on United States' relations with black Africa might well be titled "the invisible chapter" in any book. The section on Africa is not the "worst chapter": it usually does not exist. Despite the contemporary interest in and controversy over American policy toward Africa, diplomatic historians have relegated United States-African relations to a position subservient to every continent except Antarctica.

This neglect has known no methodological bias. Regardless of their philosophical persuasion or research strategy, historians of American foreign relations have had little to say about Africa. Whether new left, old left, nationalist, traditionalist, realist, or eclectic, they agree on one thing: Africa should be left to political scientists, sociologists, and anthropologists. While one can easily trace the historiographical quarrels over the Open Door, the origins of the cold war, the role of public opinion, the pelagic seal hunting controversy, or myriad other issues, it is nearly impossible to find much debate over America's African policy. The area south of the Sahara is usually dismissed by diplomatic historians with a few words about the founding of Liberia and the mandate system after World War I. They occasionally rediscover Africa in the 1960s to mention America's role in the Congo crisis and to illustrate the problems of United States adjustment to Third World independence.

There are a number of reasons for this disinterest. Historians emphasize geographic areas they deem most crucial to American economic and strategic interests. Africa has generally been judged to have been of little importance to either. Africa has lacked the proximity of Latin America and the assumed economic potential of Asia. No monumental event like the Panama Canal intrigue or the Pearl Harbor attack looms to attract the scholar.

The writings of diplomatic historians have reflected the evidence they have examined. Consequently, they have mirrored the prevailing view of State Department records that Africa was largely a European concern. As recently as 1958, for example, the United States had more diplomats in West Germany than in all of Africa. Until 1962 all economic and military aid to Africa was channeled through the European desks of the former colonial ruler. Historians working solely within State Department records will thus find ample support for the assumption that Africa was of little importance.

The paucity of material on Africa reflects problems other than source selection. Research on Africa in the United States is almost as uninviting as exploration of the continent was in the nineteenth century. While most historians working on foreign affairs have a solid background in either Europe, Asia, or Latin America, few have much knowledge of the languages, geography, or cultures of Africa. Sources within the United States on Africa are scarce and scattered. For much of the twentieth century Africa served as a dumping ground for inexperienced or inept American diplomats. Thus few historians have undertaken biographical studies of United States envoys.

An additional explanation for the lack of material on America and black Africa rests on the assumption that the only period of Africa's history of any importance to America has been the two postcolonial decades. Many scholars dismiss this period as "current events" since official records are closed. Writing from incomplete evidence with little time for objective reflection is repugnant to many steeped in the tradition of older, more "historical" topics.[2] This type of "instant" history has been at best tolerated and at worst discredited by many involved in diplomatic history. Because of this disdain, the work on the independence period has been dominated by active participants in the formation or implementation of American policy or by partisans eager to condemn American anticolonialism and cooperation with white regimes. Thus the majority of studies of United States-African relations that are familiar to diplomatic historians have been marked by passion rather than research, impression more than reflection, and ideology over substance. This, in turn, has further alienated professional historians and caused them to abandon the area to journalists, advocates, and former governmental officials.

These limitations may make the lack of interest in black Africa understandable, but they do not make it justifiable. Many of the crucial questions of American diplomatic history might profitably be asked about Africa. Interpretations of the goals, tactics, and influences on American policy developed in studies of United States relations with Europe, Asia, and Latin America can be tested by using the African experience. A number of significant issues in the twentieth century that examination of United States involvement with black Africa could clarify include: American-European relations in the age of imperialism and colonialism; the importance of economic interests to American policy; the influence of racial considerations on American diplomacy; the impact of ideology on foreign relations; and the decision-making process within the State Department and the White House.

European relations have been the dominant area of study by historians of twentieth-century American foreign policy. Few use the African area to support their interpretations. The "great rapprochement" or "Anglo-American understanding" could well be tested by examination of the American response to British imperialism and colonialism in black Africa. Similar studies of American reaction to French, Spanish, Portuguese, and German colonialism would sharpen interpretations of United States policy toward these nations. While studies of American and European imperialism in Asia and Latin America abound, there are few on United States policy in Africa where imperialism was far more successful and the number of European actors greater.

An important element in American adjustment to European imperialism is the question of the influence of economics on policy. All diplomatic historians are familiar with the emergence and wide acceptance of the "Open Door" framework for explaining American diplomacy. Neither advocates nor critics of this interpretation have devoted attention to American-African relations. If, as its supporters contend, the Open Door was global and resistance to restrictions on American trade and investment universal, Africa would offer a prime area to test this hypothesis. Those convinced that the role of economics has been greatly overestimated might well use the African example to show the limits of this thesis. Unfortunately, both sides have been content to fight out their theories as applied to Latin America and Asia rather than to venture into Africa.

Aside from rediscovering economics, diplomatic historians writing in the 1960s emphasized the impact of racial considerations on United States policy. Again the most important example has largely been neglected. If social Darwinism, "Anglo-Saxonism," and other theories of racial inequality were an important consideration in American policy, what of

Africa? While we have heard much of America's Asian "little brown brothers," historians have written little on the "black brothers" of Africa.

While historians have condemned America for the persistent influence of idealism and morality on foreign policy or have argued that antirevolutionary objectives have controlled United States actions, nearly all have ignored America's reaction to black nationalism and independence movements in Africa. The ideological element in American diplomacy has not been tested in Africa. Even the most radical critics of American actions have been content with a few sentences labeling American policies as racist or reactionary. While such generalizations may be correct, they are generally assumed rather than proven and analyzed.

Finally, diplomatic historians of all persuasions have ample opportunity to find evidence on who makes foreign policy and through what process by studying American-African relations. The role of pressure groups and public opinion is an important topic for all historians. The impact of missionaries, business leaders, and other groups is well-documented and the subject of great historiographical debate but, again, the African example is usually ignored. The significance of various ethnic groups' impact on foreign policy has been a major theme in diplomatic histories. Little has been produced on the role of black Americans in shaping African diplomacy. Africa also offers an excellent opportunity for those interested in the decision-making process within the government. The competition between "hard" interests such as economics and military considerations and "soft" concerns such as commitments to human rights and the equality of races allow for any number of case studies of diplomatic decisions.

The existing literature on United States-African relations has explored, at different levels of sophistication and with varying success, all of the topics mentioned above. However, most of the work on America's African policy has been devoted to the independence period and particularly to United States involvement in southern Africa. Works on other geographic areas in Africa and on earlier time periods are still rare.

Most scholars interested in American diplomacy within a particular geographic area begin with broad, general accounts. While many books on the United States and Africa contain brief background sections, there are only two real surveys of American policy. Journalist Russell Warren Howe's *Along the Afric Shore: A Historic Review of Two Centuries of U.S.-African Relations* is a brief and breezy sweep through the material.[3] Howe relies on fewer than two dozen secondary sources, on interviews with unnamed United States diplomats, and on scattered consular reports. There is an abundance of incidents and anecdotes. Balance and perspective are sacrificed for color and drama. The murder of an American consul in Madagascar receives more space than American policy in the period 1919-1939. Howe is far more analytical on the post-1945 period. He describes the split within the State Department between 'Europeanists'' and ''Africanists'' that limited United States response to African independence. His book is useful largely because there are so few studies of American-African relations that extend beyond a short time period or an individual country.

More satisfactory for diplomatic historians is Edward Chester's *Clash of Titans: Africa and U.S. Foreign Policy*.[4] Chester has researched widely in published sources and in the State Department's *Foreign Relations* series. The book is the best single source on the development of American relations with Africa. It is largely descriptive with little analysis of the influence of domestic groups on policy or of persistent themes in American diplomacy. Chester argues that the United States generally opposed European imperialism in Africa but did not feel its concern worthy of a major diplomatic incident. There is a brief survey of American reaction to the colonial administration of Africa in the 1920s and 1930s. The book is weakest on the period since 1945. Chester has little feel for African politics and particularly the dynamics of independence. As the *Foreign Relations* series is unavailable for the most recent years, he was forced to rely on some dubious secondary accounts. His conclusion is that American policy was a mixture of humanitarian and economic interests tempered by ''a number of colorful but essentially inconsequential episodes.'' While *Clash of Titans* is flawed in its analysis, it remains the only scholarly account of United States policy toward all of Africa in the entire twentieth century.

While a few historians have tentatively sketched the roots of American awareness of black Africa in the late nineteenth century, there is very little on United States response to the advancement of European control.[5] Studies of American interest and the consolidation of European hegemony have concentrated on United States involvement in the Congo and in South Africa.

Works on the Congo have stressed the hostile reaction of American diplomats, missionaries, and journalists to the harsh rule of Belgium's Leopold II. While America did participate in the Berlin conference that sanctioned Belgian control of the Congo, Americans were generally appalled by the blatant exploitation of the black African. Active lobbying by American agents of Leopold avoided any direct United States action, but the Congo experience confirmed America's generally unfavorable impressions of European expansion.[6]

The conflict between Britain and the Afrikaners in South Africa that culminated in the Boer War (1899-1902) led to more direct American involvement and thus has received more historical attention. John H. Ferguson's *American Diplomacy and the Boer War* is a model of traditional diplomatic method.[7] Ferguson argues that United States leaders sympathized with England in its conflict with the Boers but America maintained neutrality in the struggle. The book is highly legalistic and largely devoted to the technical aspects of American neutrality. It is based almost exclusively on official State Department records for the period of the war. There is little on the origins of American policy, the influence of domestic pressure groups, or American expectations for a British South Africa.

In a more recent study of American policy toward South Africa in the period 1870-1914, Thomas Noer contends that United States support of British control was the logical and nearly inevitable result of racial, economic, and humanitarian considerations.[8] America identified Britain as the agent of "progress" as business, religious, and political leaders assumed British political control would be advantageous for United States trade, the expansion of Christianity, and the "elevation" of the black African. Thus America actively encouraged British dominance before and during the Boer War. Americans were greatly disillusioned with the results of the British victory and the failure of London to achieve either economic or racial progress. By the outbreak of World War I the United States had abandoned active interest in the area.

Most work on America and South Africa in the period after the Boer War has been devoted to the influence of black Americans. The triumph of Britain led to attempts to formulate racial policies that would insure a stable, educated, black labor force without threats to white supremacy. South Africa turned to the American South and particularly to Booker T. Washington's Tuskegee Institute as a possible model. Several articles have examined the impact of Washington, Tuskegee, and black American missionaries on South Africa.[9]

Ultimately the attempt to export American racial programs to South Africa failed. White South Africans attributed black rebellions to the meddling influence of Afro-Americans.[10] When South Africa formulated the racial laws for their new nation in 1910, they cited the American South as an example to be avoided. Rather than declare racial equality and then be forced to use violence and legal gimmicks to preserve white control, South Africans argued it would be wiser to expressly state the inequality of the races and avoid impossible black expectations.[11] A few historians have attempted, with limited success, to examine the reciprocal relationship between Africa and black Americans in other regions of Africa.[12]

One topic diplomatic historians have explored that had a dramatic impact on black Africa is the Versailles peace conference. While few studies have considered the stimulus President Wilson's statements on self-determination had on the emerging Pan-Africanist movement, many discuss the mandate system developed for the former German colonies in Africa. Debate has centered on the origins of the mandate system and its importance for an understanding of Wilson and the peace settlement.

Some writers argue that the concept of League of Nations mandates developed from leaders in the British dominions (particularly South African leader Jan Smuts), while others contend it was basically Wilson's attempt to make workable a tenet of the Fourteen Points.[13] More significant is the debate over the intent of the mandate system. The idea of giving control of Germany's possessions to Britain, France, Belgium, and South Africa under league supervision has been hailed as "a significant if incomplete victory for Wilsonian principles,"[14] attacked as "thinly disguised imperialism,"[15] or presented as part of a shrewd plan "by which the advanced capitalist powers could expand economically into the underdeveloped world."[16] Such generalizations remain unconfirmed because there is no satisfactory study of the implementation and consolidation of the mandate system in the post-1919 period.[17]

There are two studies that are crucial to an understanding of the role of African issues at Versailles. George L. Beer, chief of the colonial division of the American peace delegation, wrote a series of reports and suggestions on African questions during and immediately after the war. Published in 1923, Beer's papers offer support for either those critical of Wilson for misguided idealism or those who portray the president as a sophisticated advocate of American world economic supremacy.[18] Beer was an outspoken liberal who felt America had a moral obligation to stamp out the evils of the slave and liquor trades, a duty to export Christianity, and a mission to better the life of the black African. Despite such humanitarian concerns, Beer also devoted large sections of his reports to plans for American economic penetration of black Africa and the "problem of the open door in Africa." Beer's analysis and suggestions were written before the peace settlement and no historian has evaluated their impact on American actions during or after Versailles.

Seth Tillman's acclaimed work on Anglo-American relations at Versailles remains the best study of the entire mandate question.[19] Tillman not only presents a solid analysis of the origins of the concept, but shows the difficulties both Wilson and the British prime minister, David Lloyd George, encountered in gaining the support of the British dominions for self-determination. His work suggests the African experience showed the problems of translating "self-determination" and "impartial adjustment of colonial claims" from rhetoric to policy.

The disposal of the German colonies in 1919 left Africa firmly under colonial rule. The period from 1919 to 1945 witnessed tremendous upheavals in Africa as the colonial powers developed, refined, and discarded a variety of approaches to colonial administration and blacks gradually mobilized for independence. There has been virtually no work on American diplomatic involvement with Africa in this period. There are two studies of the image of Africa in the minds of Americans, but both lack a complete narrative of American policies and actions. Clifford Haley Scott's dissertation on "American Images of Sub-Sahara Africa, 1900-1939" illustrates sporadic economic and continual missionary interest in Africa but is inadequate on diplomatic activity.[20]

More significant is Edward McKinley's innovative and engaging study, *The Lure of Africa: American Interests in Tropical Africa, 1919-1939.*[21] McKinley draws on sources ranging from pulp fiction to official trade statistics to Tarzan movies in describing the impact of Africa on the American imagination. The book blends traditional diplomatic history, popular culture, and sociology to show how Africa was portrayed in the press, movies, fiction, and travel accounts. He argues that Americans perceived Africa as "more of a land of animals and scenery than a land of peoples." Stereotypes of Africa and the African made Americans unable to think seriously about the region and thus left them virtually unprepared for the postwar surge toward independence. Suggestive and imaginative as McKinley's account is, it does not carry its narrative beyond 1939 to test the validity of its assertion that the public's image of Africa limited American response to the end of colonialism.

Material on the two nations that escaped European control, Liberia and Ethiopia, is somewhat more abundant than on colonial Africa. The two major works on American-Liberian relations emphasize internal Liberian politics and the dominance of the Firestone Rubber Company on the politics and economy of the nation.[22] Brice Harris's examination of United States policy in the Italo-Ethiopian crisis is largely concerned with relations with Italy but does contain some important material on direct American contacts with Ethiopia as well.[23]

World War II was the catalyst that activated African nationalism into the drive for independence. The war not only financially and emotionally drained the colonial powers but wartime propaganda and experiences encouraged African leaders. Despite the vast number of studies of American diplomacy during the war, little has been written on the impact of the Atlantic Charter and Franklin Roosevelt's anticolonialism on black Africa.[24]

Racial solidarity and a shared militancy among blacks in Africa and the United States have been important elements in American involvement with the continent since 1945. While traditional diplomatic historians have not explored the interaction between blacks and black protest in the Old World and the New, other scholars have. Rupert Emerson and Martin Kilson, for example, have traced the relationship between the American civil rights movement and United States adjustment to the move toward African independence.[25] They argue that the United States early developed a policy of a middle road between active encouragement of black liberation and support of continued European control. This policy rapidly became outmoded in the late 1950s as America's dedication to peaceful, gradual change became obsolete in the turmoil of independence movements. As American blacks became more militant, United States policymakers became increasingly defensive and their diplomacy contradictory and unsuccessful. Others have also examined the emerging issue of race and the linkage between American and African blacks.[26]

The global cold war in the late 1940s and 1950s posed a dilemma for American policymakers involved with Africa. The United States was verbally dedicated to the end of colonial rule. Roosevelt's statements during World War II had fired the imagination and anticipation of black Africans. As the cold war intensified, however, American leaders feared a rush to independence would lead to weak nations that would be easy prey to international communism. John Foster Dulles's distrust of neutralism and hatred of the indigenous socialism proclaimed by African leaders moved America away from even verbal support of African freedom. State Department officials in the 1950s warned of "premature independence" and the United States became, in the words of one observer, "more royalist than the Queen."

Two studies document the shift of American policy in the 1950s toward active support of continued European control. Harin Shah's perceptive book, *The Great Abdication: American Foreign Policy in Asia and Africa*, is an excellent example of Third World impatience with continued American support of its NATO allies and disgust with the prevailing anticommunist conception of international politics.[27] Ronald Walters's analysis of the period 1958-1963 argues that there was a softening of United States opposition to African independence only when it became obvious that colonialism was doomed.[28]

Studies of United States African policy since 1955 have been dominated by political scientists and journalists highly critical of America's procolonial diplomacy. Based largely on United Nations documents, press releases, speeches, and other published sources, they offer an incomplete but passionate critique of American actions. Nearly all conclude with a plea for a more active and African-oriented policy.

Writing in 1963, Vernon McKay attacked the Eisenhower administration for its insensitivity to Africa and Africans and emphasized the impact of the cold war perspective on American policy.[29] Rupert Emerson was even harsher in his appraisals of American actions. Emerson concludes that "American fascination with the menace of Communism impaired the ability to understand what moved the African political leaders and to establish sympathetic and mutually satisfactory relations with them."[30] Unlike more recent scholars, he argues that the Kennedy administration did have a sincere commitment to Africa and "lent a freshness and new vitality to the American approach to Africa."

While liberal critics such as McKay and Emerson set the tone for most of the writing about America's postwar policy, not all were convinced of the detrimental effects of anticommunism on American diplomacy in Africa. Others argued that far from overestimating the threat of communism to the continent, America had not been sufficiently aroused to its dangers. The most obvious example of this approach is *Africa and the Communist World*, edited by Zbigniew Brzezinski.[31] Brzezinski presents a covey of cold warriors who saw a grand design for domination of independent Africa by Russia, China, and eastern Europe that demanded a more militant American response.

The best existing summary of American policy in the entire postwar period is Waldemar Nielsen's *The Great Powers and Africa.*[32] Like McKay and Emerson, he is unsympathetic to American policies in the 1950s. Nielsen contends that the anticolonial rhetoric of Roosevelt quickly gave way to a cold war American commitment to its NATO allies and their African empires. America not only feared that independence might lead to communist takeovers in Africa, but that African independence movements themselves were directed by Moscow. He sees a slight shift in American rhetoric and policies following the rupture with Britain and France after the Suez crisis, but concludes the United States soon returned to a rigid anticolonialism. Nielsen argues that Eisenhower's style, inaction on civil rights at home, and disinterest in visiting African leaders managed to "make the policy seem worse than it was."

Like most who have studied America and Africa, Nielsen contends there was a brief flourishing of official interest in the area under John F. Kennedy. He cites Kennedy's appointments of individuals sympathetic to Africa, his rhetoric, and personal courting of African leaders as signs of a new commitment to the continent. However, to Nielsen these gestures were mostly cosmetic. Kennedy's need for Southern congressional support, his desire for continued good relations with Europe, and the chaotic results of "premature independence" in the Congo limited any major adjustments of America's African policy.

The debate over Kennedy's African diplomacy is one of the few areas of United States-African relations where there is substantial literature and historiographic debate. Kennedy's supporters, led by Arthur M. Schlesinger, Jr., contend that the New Frontier altered the passive policies of Eisenhower and shifted America from support of colonialism to an African-oriented policy empathetic with the aspirations of African leaders. Critics downplay Kennedy's innovations and accuse the president of failing to break from the cold war perspective of his predecessors. Changes by Kennedy were stylistic rather than substantive.

Schlesinger's *A Thousand Days: John F. Kennedy in the White House* strongly emphasizes Kennedy's interest in and commitment to an independent Africa.[33] Schlesinger devotes a sizable portion of a chapter on "New Directions in the Third World" to Africa and includes another chapter devoted exclusively to "Africa: The New Adventure." He argues that Kennedy's concern for African freedom dates to "childhood tales of Ireland's long struggle for independence." When he assumed office Kennedy rapidly revamped American policy by ordering support of United Nations resolutions condemning Portuguese repression in Angola, instituting an arms embargo toward South Africa, and appointing a group of young, aggressive, American envoys to the new African states. Kennedy's selection of Adlai Stevenson as American ambassador to the United Nations and liberal G. Mennen Williams as Assistant Secretary of State for African Affairs are cited by Schlesinger as additional signs of his concern for Africa.

Schlesinger does admit that Kennedy's support of African aspirations caused problems within NATO and among "Europeanists" in the State Department. As a result, Kennedy refused to allow Stevenson to support stronger United Nations resolutions on Angola, South Africa, and South-West Africa (Namibia). Schlesinger, however, still contends that Kennedy totally reoriented United States policy: "In no part of the third world did Kennedy pioneer more effectively than in Africa."[34]

Those who helped formulate or implement Kennedy's African policy share Schlesinger's favorable assessment. Journalist William Attwood, Kennedy's ambassador to Guinea, stresses the president's personal charm with individual Africans and his willingness to tolerate economic and political diversity among the new African nations. Under Secretaries of State Harlan Cleveland, Chester Bowles, and Mennen Williams agree that Kennedy revamped both the goals and the methods of America's African diplomacy.[35]

In contrast, another Kennedy appointee, George Ball, gives a good statement of the "Europeanist" perspective. Ball contends that American policy was too sympathetic toward Africa, too idealistic, too concerned with world opinion, and preoccupied with domestic concerns generated by the civil rights movement.[36]

The revisionist assault on Kennedy's foreign policy has not yet produced a full rejoinder to the Schlesinger interpretation. Even Richard J. Walton, one of Kennedy's earliest and most severe critics, concedes that Kennedy had "a genuine affection for Africa and its peoples [and an] understanding of nonalignment."[37] Walton praises Kennedy for his appointments and personal attention to African leaders. He is especially impressed with his handling of the complex Congo situation. Despite strong domestic and European opposition, Kennedy supported the central government against the secession of Katanga province under Belgian puppet Moise Tshombe. American support was crucial in preserving the Congo's unity, argues Walton, and "was one of [Kennedy's] most substantial achievements."[38]

A stronger critique of Kennedy is offered by Bruce Miroff in his work *Pragmatic Illusions*.[39] Miroff has few specifics on Kennedy's African diplomacy, but his analysis of Kennedy's overall foreign policy discounts the president's commitment to neutralism and diversity. Miroff offers a portrait of Kennedy as a rigid cold warrior locked into a bipolar world view. Far from being supportive of diversity, he was a counterrevolutionary convinced that only the American political and economic model was appropriate for the Third World. The Kennedy rhetoric and engaging personality masked a deep commitment to the preservation of American economic and political control of the underdeveloped world.

A more impressive revisionist analysis of the Kennedy administration is offered by Melvin Gurtov.[40] In an extended discussion of Kennedy and Africa, Gurtov offers an interpretation similar to that of Miroff but with more substance and illustration. The decolonization of Africa forced America to make a "choice between self-determination and the oft-proclaimed need for North Atlantic unity against international communism." Pressure from domestic liberals forced Kennedy to publicly proclaim concern for Africa, but there were no major differences between his actions and the procolonial policies of Eisenhower. The United States refused to vote for binding sanctions against South Africa and rejected Third World pleas for strong action against the continued Portuguese presence in Angola and Mozambique. America intervened in the Congo not because of disinterested desires to maintain Congolese unity, but for economic gain and to block any communist influence in a divided nation.

A balanced interpretation of Kennedy's African policy is Ibezim Chukwumerije, "The New Frontier and Africa, 1961-1963."[41] Chukwumerije agrees that Kennedy had a strong personal interest in Africa and Africans. His personality, youth, and appointments led to a sincere affection for Kennedy among African leaders. However, Kennedy's United Nations policies, his refusal to commit the United States to ending colonialism and white supremacy, and his failure to substantially increase economic aid for Africa revealed a lack of real change from his predecessor. Kennedy's major innovations were stylistic. This in itself was important given African sensitivity to treatment by white leaders, but did not constitute a major alteration of foreign policy.

The most direct American involvement in Africa in the cold war period was the Congo crisis of the early and mid-1960s. In a rare embarrassment of riches in the historiography of United States-African relations, there are two excellent studies of America's Congo policy. Ernest Lefever asserts that there was a basic continuity in American actions from Eisenhower to Kennedy to Johnson. All were dedicated to a unified Congo under a central government able to maintain stability and economic viability, and to block Russian or Chinese encroachment.[42] The United States chose to work through the United Nations rather than by more direct intervention to prevent Soviet countermoves in the area. This strategy also channeled Third

World criticism of non-African intervention toward the United Nations rather than directly at Washington. The United States successfully served as a balance wheel between militant Afro-Asian leaders and more conservative European diplomats. Far from being a mask for imperialism, as some have argued, Lefever concludes that American policy was restrained and effective. The United States attained its goal of a unified Congo favorable to the West without direct military involvement.

Far more critical of American actions is Stephen Weissman.[43] The fundamental force in American policy, argues Weissman, was an overriding fear of Russian or Chinese influence in Africa. The horror of a communist nation in central Africa, following shortly after Castro's proclamation of Cuba as a socialist state, led to American overreaction and ultimately to failure. While the United States succeeded in its goals, "if measured by the sole criterion of power to get one's way," it failed to create a truly united Congo with a democratic political structure. Far from being successful or conservative, as Lefever concludes, Weissman sees United States actions as self-serving, heavy-handed, and totally insensitive to the desires of African leaders.

The Congo episode was a rare incident that led to direct American involvement in African affairs. Research on American policy since the Congo crisis has been largely devoted to the American response to the struggle for black liberation from white control. These studies have concentrated on three areas: America and the violent liberation of the Portuguese colonies; United States reaction to the unilateral declaration of independence of Rhodesia in 1965; and the enduring question of American diplomacy and South Africa. Each of these topics has provoked a number of studies. Diplomatic historians will find that most are highly polemical, based largely on published sources or interviews, and often written in haste to capitalize on a "hot" topic.

John Marcum has produced the best study of American policy toward the decolonization of Angola, Mozambique, and Guinea-Bissau.[44] Marcum argues that Kennedy made a tentative move toward support of independence but pressures from military leaders for continued American use of bases in the Portuguese Azores and the influence of "Europeanists" in the State Department led to a return to the policy of giving verbal encouragement to independence but continued economic and diplomatic assistance to Portugal. Fearful of violent reform and revolution, and ever mindful of the Cuban experience, America adopted a position of trying to force Portugal to accept the idea of self-determination for its African possessions while pressuring Africans to abandon violence. This policy succeeded only in angering both sides in the struggle.[45]

In a recent article, Allen Issacman and Jennifer Davis summarize American policy toward Portuguese Africa in the 1970s and the attempt of

Washington to adjust to the overthrow of the Portuguese dictatorship in 1974.[46] They are extremely censorious of American policy in the entire post-World War II period and argue that American military and economic aid was crucial in helping Portugal maintain its empire in Africa. America desperately wanted to preserve a Portuguese presence in Africa to allow American economic penetration, to prevent revolutionary governments, and to provide security for the white regime in South Africa.

While these works are helpful in outlining the basics of America's approach to Portugal's colonies, they share a strident, partisan tone. They see little complexity or diversity in American policy. They tend to find little competition among various interests in influencing American actions. All are valuable, however, in illustrating how the cold war and the fear of violent change permeated American thinking and blocked a real understanding of the dynamics of the liberation struggles.

The decolonization of the Portuguese territories was the most dramatic and successful of the liberation movements in Africa in the recent past. The contemporary struggle for majority rule in Rhodesia has also provoked American diplomatic action. There is one excellent study of America and the Rhodesian question: Anthony Lake, *The "Tar Baby" Option: American Policy toward Southern Rhodesia*.[47] Lake, a former foreign service officer and special assistant to the president's national security adviser, draws on interviews with United States officials, published reports and documents, and his own governmental experience. His book is a case study of American policy from 1965 to 1975. Lake argues that from 1965 to 1969 America strongly supported Britain in its conflict with its renegade colony. The Nixon administration abandoned this cautious policy in support of the "tar baby" option. This stressed "communication" with all white minority governments through renewed economic, political, and cultural ties. "Tar baby" resulted in crucial economic and diplomatic support for the embattled Southern Rhodesian regime.[48]

The area of Africa that has produced the most intense debate over American actions has been South Africa. South Africa's commitment to apartheid has raised questions about the basic objectives of United States foreign policy. South Africa personifies the clash between tangible economic and strategic considerations and more abstract humanitarian ideals. Given the concern of blacks, liberals, religious groups, and others over American policy, it is not surprising that there is an abundance of material on this area. Unfortunately, like so many of the works on recent American policy toward Africa, most are underresearched and overwritten. They deplore American policy rather than explain it and, with few exceptions, fail to integrate actions into the traditions of American diplomacy.

Fortunately for historians interested in American diplomacy and southern Africa there is an excellent reference tool. Mohamed El-Khawas and Francis Kornegay have edited a collection of bibliographic essays on American-southern African relations that summarize existing material.[49] Although they vary widely in quality, the essays provide at least a minimal listing of existing works. Topics covered are United States involvement with Angola and Mozambique, America and Southern Rhodesia, the persistent question of Namibia, United States investment policy, and the impact of black Americans on United States policy.

El-Khawas's opening essay on America, Angola, and Mozambique is a model of completeness and analysis. Not only does he give a thorough and annotated list of books, articles, and pamphlets but also offers a useful summary of American policy since 1945. Equally helpful is Kornegay's summary of black Americans and southern Africa. He argues that the cold war decisively limited the intensity and impact of black criticism of America's African policies. He also explores the relationship between black protest within the United States and black liberation in southern Africa.[50] Less useful are the essays on the United States and Rhodesia by Sulayman Nyand, on America and Namibia by Barbara Rogers, and on American investments by Tami Hultman and Reed Kramer. The first two are excellent on internal changes in Rhodesia and Namibia, but contain little on United States diplomacy. The essay on investments cites a great number of studies but offers little analysis.

Despite the current debate over America and South Africa, there is no single satisfactory historical study of American diplomacy in the area. A number of critiques of United States policy have brief historical sections, but they are more concerned with influencing present actions than with illustrating past decisions.[51] Several studies of South Africa's foreign policy contain sections on American diplomacy.[52] Works dealing with inter-African relations have material on African pressures on the United States for a stronger stance against apartheid.[53] The sole lengthy historical study of American policy covers only the period 1960-1967, is based on published sources, and is useful only for analysis of several specific policy decisions.[54] A recently declassified National Security Council review of American options in southern Africa provides a fascinating, if incomplete, look at the policy choices facing America in the early Nixon years and documents the Kissinger "tilt" toward the white regimes.[55]

There are a number of suggestive studies of specific interest groups and recent African policy. Arnold Beichman argues that American representatives at the United Nations have often worked against official State Department policies to place America in a more sympathetic position on African issues.[56] There is a brief study of Congress and Africa which is useful for gauging the varying importance of African questions.[57] Of great value to those interested in the development of organized opposition to apartheid is a fine volume by George Shepherd.[58] A recent study of lobbyists and American foreign policy has several sections on Africa.[59]

Two essays provide analytical frameworks for study of America's foreign policy and Africa. Immanuel Wallerstein's brief essay "Africa, the United States, and the World Economy" supports the new left emphasis on economic interests as the prime agent in American diplomacy.[60] Wallerstein contends that the United States has used direct and indirect involvement in black Africa "to bring about the dual U.S. objective: an expansion of African involvement in the world economy, and a relative open door for U.S. investment and trade." Just as the crisis of overproduction drove America to a frantic search for new markets in the 1890s, a similar "crisis in effective demand" in the 1960s led to a surge of American interest in Africa as a possible market and source of raw materials.

A far different explanation for American actions is offered by the former United States ambassador to Zambia, Robert Good.[61] In Good's interpretation it is lack of communication and cultural differences that have shaped America's response to independent Africa. Western nations, particularly the United States, have been and remain, unable to understand the process of state-making in Africa. Ethnocentric notions of politics and economics have blinded America to the realities of black Africa. Americans have misunderstood the legacy of colonialism and the need for constant assertions by Africans of their independence. Ignorance of the African experience has affected American diplomacy more than have the drive for markets or cold war anticommunism.

Generalizations such as those offered by Wallerstein or Good are intriguing but untenable without supporting evidence. The historiography of United States-African relations abounds in generalizations and suffers from a poverty of particulars. African policy is one of the few areas of American diplomatic history lacking an outline of *what* happened, which is so necessary to know before the historian can ask *why*. The most obvious need is more studies based on in-depth research and historical objectivity, and related to the major themes of American diplomacy. Advocacy has played an important part in the literature of the United States and Africa. This is understandable and even commendable given the tragedies of colonialism and minority rule. However, mere advocacy does little to give an accurate picture of the past. The plague of present-mindedness that dominates so much of the material can be cured by the historical techniques and imagination so apparent in diplomatic histories of American relations with other areas of the world.

If diplomatic historians are to take seriously American relations with Africa they must begin at the undergraduate and graduate levels. The cursory concessions made to Africa in the textbooks and in classrooms must be replaced by the incorporation of the findings of those who have delved into African policy. Graduate students looking for a research area uncrowded by established scholars and standard interpretations will find an abundance of topics on United States-African diplomacy. This, however, will require that they gain competencies in African history, economics, geography, politics, and languages.

Africa can be used as a testing area for existing interpretations of American diplomacy and as a region for comparison with American actions in Asia and Latin America. However, scholars of America's African policy must do more than merely confirm or challenge prevailing theories of American foreign relations. If Africa is to become a legitimate area of interest, they must attempt to break, at least temporarily, from standard interpretations. The grafting on to Africa of approaches and findings from other geographic areas may be convenient but is likely erroneous. Africa, as explorers, diplomats, and historians have found out, is unique.

If Africa is studied as a distinct area of American foreign relations, there are any number of subjects demanding attention. One approach, virtually ignored, has been country studies. A narrative of American relations with an individual nation would reveal United States response to imperialism, colonial administration, and independence. No single African nation has been examined in this fashion. This method would require intensive research in American sources, in the records of the European colonial power, and in material from the African nation. While not a simple task, this would seem to be the type of international, multiarchival approach diplomatic historians so often demand but so rarely produce.

A more specific need is an historical analysis of American United Nations policy. While there have been some studies of this topic, they tend to be computations of votes rather than discussions of the policies and negotiations behind the tallies.[62] The United Nations has been crucial to Africans as a source of agitation for independence, as a vehicle for economic and technical aid, and recently as a forum for the campaign against white rule. A solid study of the politics of United States involvement in the United Nations and Africa would be an invaluable source for understanding America's approach to the continent.

The impact of pressure groups on United States policy also contains a variety of neglected topics. The role of missionaries, business leaders, explorers, and scientists in shaping America's perception of colonial Africa has not been fully developed for any area or period. The influence of the civil rights and black power movements on American policy is mentioned in nearly every study of United States relations with Africa but has never been fully analyzed. There is a similar need for interpretations of the impact of white liberal lobbying organizations such as church and labor groups supportive of African independence.

The public's image of black Africa also needs to be examined more deeply. If, as some have contended, American racism limited the capacity of the United States to take seriously black leadership in Africa, this should be documented and analyzed. The American perception of Africa as primitive, violent, and homogeneous has influenced the nation's foreign policy, but few have explored the origins or importance of these stereotypes.

There remains a strong need for further study of America's vacillating commitment to African independence in the cold war years. The race to independence of black Africa in the late 1950s and 1960s has dominated literature on African history but there are few corresponding studies of America's preparation for and adaptation to this movement. Materials in the Truman, Eisenhower, Kennedy, and Johnson presidential libraries offer a number of insights into this issue. As the records of the State Department become available historians will have a sizable amount of documentary evidence on America and African independence.

With the declassification of materials in Washington, scholars will also be able to examine the structural elements in America's African policy. Nearly all who have studied American-African relations in the post-World War II period have noted the split within the government between "Europeanists" and "Africanists." This is often cited as reason for the caution and occasional confusion of American actions. Yet this split has been asserted more than illustrated and its impact assumed rather than proven.

The attention paid to Africa by the media in recent years will likely stimulate a surge of scholarly interest in black Africa. The debate over American policy in Rhodesia, South Africa, and Angola has created an as-yet-unfilled demand for knowledge of the origins of United States diplomacy in that area. Just as Castro's takeover in Cuba led to a rush to examine American relations with Latin America and the war in Vietnam inspired diplomatic studies of Asian policy, the present turmoils in Africa might tempt historians of American foreign relations to turn toward a new geographic area. When this happens we can enjoy the pleasures of fresh debates, scathing reviews, revisions, and footnote feuds. For the present, however, Africa remains the "dark continent" for historians of American foreign policy.

Notes

1. James A. Field, Jr., "American Imperialism: The 'Worst' Chapter in Almost Any Book," *American Historical Review* 83 (June 1978): 644-68.

2. Curiously this has not stopped the avalanche of books on the cold war despite the lack of archival evidence.

3. Russell Warren Howe, *Along the Afric Shore: An Historic Review of Two Centuries of U.S.-African Relations* (New York: Barnes & Noble, 1975).

4. Edward Chester, *Clash of Titans: Africa and U.S. Foreign Policy* (Maryknoll, N.Y.: Orbis Books, 1974).

5. *See* Harold Hammond, "American Interest in the Exploration of the Dark Continent," *The Historian* 18 (Spring 1956): 202-29; Clarence Clendenen, Peter

Duigan, and Robert Collins, *Americans in Africa, 1865-1900* (Stanford: Hoover Institute, 1966) and Allan R. Booth, *Americans in South Africa, 1784-1870* (Capetown: Balkema, 1978).

6. Paul McStallworth, "The United States and the Congo Question, 1884-1914" (Ph.D. diss., Ohio State University, 1954) and Leslie Meyer, "Henry S. Sanford and the Congo: A Re-Assessment, *African Studies* 7 (1969): 441-55.

7. John H. Ferguson, *American Diplomacy and the Boer War* (Philadelphia: (University of Pennsylvania Press, 1939).

8. Thomas J. Noer, *Briton, Boer, and Yankee: The United States and South Africa, 1870-1914* (Kent: Kent State University Press, 1978). Other works on America and South Africa in this period include Myra Goldstein, "The Genesis of Modern American Relations with South Africa, 1895-1914" (Ph.D. diss., State University of New York at Buffalo, 1972); Alfred Dennis, *Adventures in American Diplomacy, 1896-1906* (New York: E. P. Dutton, 1928) and Stuart Anderson, "Racial Anglo-Saxonism and the American Response to the Boer War," *Diplomatic History* 2 (Summer 1978): 219-36.

9. Louis Harlan, "Booker T. Washington and the 'White Man's Burden,'" *American Historical Review* 71 (January 1966): 441-67; Kenneth J. King, "African Students in Negro American Colleges: Notes on the 'Good African,'" *Phylon* 31 (Spring 1970): 16-30 and Edwin S. Redkey, "The Meaning of Africa to Afro-Americans, 1890-1914," *Black Academy Review* 3 (Spring-Summer 1972): 5-38.

10. Shula Marks, "The Ambiguities of Dependence: John L. Dube of Natal," *Journal of South African Studies* 1 (April 1975): 162-80; George Shepperson, "Notes on Negro Influence on the Emergence of African Nationalism," *Journal of African History* 1 (1960): 299-312.

11. Noer, *Briton, Boer, and Yankee*, pp. 111-34.

12. Clarence Contee, "The Emergence of DuBois as an African Nationalist," *Journal of Negro History* 54 (January 1969): 48-63; William C. Harr, "The Negro as Protestant Missionary to Africa" (Ph.D. diss., University of Chicago Divinity School, 1946); St. Clair Drake, "Negro Americans and 'The African Interest,'" in John P. Davis, ed., *The American Negro Reference Book* (Englewood Cliffs, N.J.: Prentice-Hall, 1966).

13. George Curry, "Woodrow Wilson, Jan Smuts, and the Versailles Settlement," *American Historical Review* 66 (July 1961): 983-85.

14. Daniel Smith, *The Great Departure: The United States and World War I* (New York: John Wiley & Sons, 1965).

15. Thomas Bailey, *A Diplomatic History of the American People*, 7th ed. (New York: Appleton-Century-Crofts, 1964), p. 605.

16. N. Gordon Levin, *Woodrow Wilson and World Politics: America's Response to War and Revolution* (New York: Oxford University Press, 1968).

17. Rayford Logan made a very tentative attempt to look at this question in his *The African Mandates in World Politics* (Washington, D.C.: Public Affairs Press, 1948).

18. George L. Beer, *African Questions at the Paris Peace Conference* (New York: Macmillan Co., 1923). For an analysis of Beer and his ideas *see* William Louis, "The United States and the African Peace Settlement of 1919: The Pilgrimage of George Louis Beer," *Journal of African History* 4 (1963): 413-33.

19. Seth Tillman, *Anglo-American Relations at the Paris Peace Conference of 1919* (Princeton: Princeton University Press, 1961).

20. Clifford Haley Scott, "American Images of Sub-Sahara Africa, 1900-1939" (Ph.D. diss., University of Iowa, 1968).

21. Edward McKinley, *The Lure of Africa: American Interests in Tropical Africa, 1919-1939* (Indianapolis: Bobbs-Merrill Co., 1974).

22. Earle Anderson, *Liberia: America's Friend* (Chapel Hill: University of North Carolina Press, 1952) and Raymond W. Bixler, *The Foreign Policy of the United States and Liberia* (New York: Pageant Press, 1957).

23. Brice Harris, *The United States and the Italo-Ethiopian Crisis* (Palo Alto: Stanford University Press, 1964).

24. Although it does not often deal directly with Africa, useful on this topic is William Roger Louis, *Imperialism at Bay: The United States and the Decolonization of the British Empire, 1941-1945* (New York: Oxford University Press, 1978). Jean-Donald Miller is completing a dissertation at the University of Connecticut on "The United States and Sub-Saharan Africa, 1939-1950: The Roots of American Policy towards Decolonization" that should be helpful.

25. Rupert Emerson and Martin Kilson, "The American Dilemma in a Changing World: The Rise of Africa and the Negro American," *Daedalus* 94 (Fall 1965): 1055-84.

26. Rubin Weston, *Racism and United States Imperialism: The Influence of Racial Assumptions on American Foreign Policy, 1893-1946* (Columbia: University of South Carolina Press, 1972) is mostly concerned with the Philippines, displays an alarming ignorance of Africa, and has little documentation. Far more successful on the "African connection" of American blacks are Robert G. Weisbord, *Ebony Kinship: Africa, Africans, and the Afro-American* (Westport, Conn.: Greenwood Press, 1973) and William B. Helmreich, *Afro-Americans and Africa: Black Nationalism at the Crossroads* (Westport, Conn.: Greenwood Press, 1977). *See also* James Roark, "American Black Leaders: The Response to Colonialism and the Cold War, 1943-1953," *African Historical Studies* 4 (1971): 253-70.

27. Harin Shah, *The Great Abdication: American Foreign Policy in Asia and Africa* (New Delhi: Arma Ram, 1957).

28. Ronald Walters, "The Formulation of United States' Policy Toward Africa, 1958-1963" (Ph.D. diss., American University, 1971).

29. Vernon McKay, *Africa in World Politics* (New York: Harper & Row, 1963).

30. Rupert Emerson, *Africa and United States Policy* (Englewood Cliffs, N.J.: Prentice-Hall, 1967). Similar liberal critiques of American policy in this period are Walter Goldschmidt, ed., *The United States and Africa* (New York: Frederick A. Praeger, 1963) and Chester Bowles, *Africa: Challenge to America* (Berkeley: University of California Press, 1956).

31. Zbigniew Brzezinski, ed., *Africa and the Communist World* (Stanford: Hoover Institute, 1963).

32. Waldemar Nielsen, *The Great Powers and Africa* (New York: Frederick A. Praeger, 1969).

33. Arthur M. Schlesinger, Jr., *A Thousand Days: John F. Kennedy in the White House* (Boston: Houghton Mifflin Co., 1965).

34. Ibid., p. 551. Others who share Schlesinger's favorable interpretation of Ken-

nedy are Theodore Sorenson, *Kennedy* (New York: Harper & Row, 1965); Lewis Paper, *The Promise and the Performance: The Leadership of John F. Kennedy* (New York: Crown Publishers, 1975); Donald Lord, *John F. Kennedy: The Politics of Confrontation and Conciliation* (Woodbury, N.Y.: Barrons, 1977); and Carl Brauer, *John F. Kennedy and the Second Reconstruction* (New York: Columbia University Press, 1977). Although Brauer is concerned with the domestic civil rights issue, he argues that Kennedy's commitment to racial equality at home strongly influenced his policy toward Africa.

35. William Attwood, *The Reds and Blacks: A Personal Adventure* (New York: Harper & Row, 1967); Harlan Cleveland, *The Obligations of Power* (New York: Harper & Row, 1971); G. Mennen Williams, *Africa for the Africans* (Grand Rapids: William B. Eerdmans Publishing Co., 1969). Although he was an important symbol of the "liberal" approach to Africa, Williams has produced a disappointing book. There is little beyond his official speeches and statements.

36. George Ball, *The Discipline of Power: Essentials of a Modern World Structure* (Boston: Little, Brown, & Co., 1968).

37. Richard J. Walton, *Cold War and Counterrevolution: The Foreign Policy of John F. Kennedy* (New York: Viking Press, 1972).

38. Ibid., pp. 204-05.

39. Bruce Miroff, *Pragmatic Illusions: The Presidential Politics of John Kennedy* (New York: David McKay, 1976).

40. Melvin Gurtov, *The United States Against the Third World* (New York: Frederick A. Praeger, 1974).

41. Ibezim Chukwumerije, "The New Frontier and Africa, 1961-63" (Ph.D. diss., State University of New York at Stony Brook, 1976).

42. Ernest Lefever, *Uncertain Mandate: The Politics of the UN Congo Operation* (Baltimore: Johns Hopkins Press, 1967) and "U.S. Policy, the UN, and the Congo," *Orbis* 11 (Summer 1967): 394-413.

43. Stephen Weissman, *American Foreign Policy in the Congo, 1960-1964* (Ithaca: Cornell University Press, 1974).

44. John Marcum, *The Politics of Influence: Portugal and Africa—A Case Study in American Foreign Policy* (Syracuse: Syracuse University Press, 1972).

45. For a similar interpretation *see* William Minter, *Portuguese Africa and the West* (New York: Monthly Review Press, 1972). Minter's work is especially useful in tracing shifts in America's UN policy in the early and mid-1960s.

46. Allen Issacman and Jennifer Davis, "United States' Policy toward Mozambique Since 1945: The Defense of Colonialism and Regional Stability," *Africa Today* 25 (January-March 1978): 29-55.

47. Anthony Lake, *The 'Tar Baby' Option: American Policy toward Southern Rhodesia* (New York: Columbia University Press, 1973).

48. *See also* Robert Good, *UDI: The International Politics of the Rhodesian Rebellion* (New York: Faber and Faber, 1973).

49. Mohamed A. El-Khawas and Francis A. Kornegay, eds., *American-Southern African Relations: Bibliographic Essays* (Westport, Conn.: Greenwood Press, 1975).

50. *See also* Milton Morris, "Black Americans and the Foreign Policy Process: The Case of Africa," *Western Political Quarterly* 25 (September 1972): 451-63.

51. Among the best are Waldemar Nielsen, *African Battleline: American Policy*

Choices in Southern Africa (New York: Harper & Row, 1965) and William Hance, ed., *Southern Africa and the United States* (New York: Columbia University Press, 1968). A conservative attack on American policy as being too supportive of black liberation and not appreciative of the strategic and economic importance of South Africa is William Yarborough, *Trial in Africa: The Failure of U.S. Policy* (Washington, D.C.: Heritage Foundation, 1976).

52. James Barber, *South Africa's Foreign Policy, 1945-1970* (New York: Oxford University Press, 1973) and Amry Vandenbosch, *South Africa and the World: The Foreign Policy of Apartheid* (Lexington: University of Kentucky Press, 1970).

53. *See* Christopher Stevens, *The Soviet Union and Black Africa* (New York: Macmillan Co., 1976) and W. Scott Thompson, *Ghana's Foreign Policy, 1957-1966: Diplomacy, Ideology, and the New State* (Princeton: Princeton University Press, 1969).

54. Jonathan Wouk, "U.S. Policy Toward South Africa, 1960-1967: Foreign Policy in a Relatively Permissive Environment" (Ph.D. diss., University of Pittsburgh, 1972).

55. *The Kissinger Study of Southern Africa: National Security Study Memorandum* 39 (Westport, Conn.: Lawrence Hill & Co., 1976).

56. Arnold Beichman, *The 'Other' State Department: The United States' Mission to the United Nations* (New York: Basic Books, 1968).

57. Washington Task Force on African Affairs, *Congress and Africa* (Washington, D.C.: African Bibliographic Center, 1973).

58. George Shepherd, *Anti-Apartheid: Transnational Conflict and Western Policy in the Liberation of South Africa* (Westport, Conn.: Greenwood Press, 1977).

59. Russell Warren Howe and Sarah Hays Trott, *The Power Peddlers: How Lobbyists Mold American Foreign Policy* (Garden City, N.Y.: Doubleday Co., 1977).

60. Immanuel Wallerstein, "Africa, the United States, and the World Economy," in Frederick S. Arkhurst, ed., *U.S. Policy Toward Africa* (New York: Frederick A. Praeger, 1975).

61. Robert Good, "Colonial Legacies to the Postcolonial States," in Roger Hilsman and Robert Good, eds., *Foreign Policy in the Sixties: The Issues and the Instruments* (Baltimore: Johns Hopkins Press, 1965).

62. *See*, for example, Arvin Rubinstein and George Ginsberg, eds., *Soviet and American Policies in the United Nations: A Twenty-Five Year Perspective* (New York: New York University Press, 1971).

14 ____ United States Relations with the Middle East in the Twentieth Century: A Developing Area in Historical Literature

ROGER R. TRASK

Only since the end of World War II has the Middle East become a major concern in United States foreign policy.[1] The region was little known to Americans before 1945, even though the United States established diplomatic relations with the Ottoman Empire, which at the time controlled much of the modern Middle East, as early as 1830. Until the twentieth century, steadily developing American contacts in that part of the world were seldom newsworthy and rarely controversial. The emergence of the Middle East as a major arena of cold war conflict, the critical importance of its oil resources, and the Arab-Israeli dispute have forced the region into the headlines and to a certain degree into the nation's historical consciousness. Two historiographical studies by John A. DeNovo of American relations with the Middle East surveyed the work of American historians, first through the 1950s and then through the 1960s.[2] This essay builds on DeNovo's foundations and brings the assessment through the 1970s.

The fact that historians often respond to contemporary concerns in their selection of research topics helps to explain both the low level of scholarly interest in the American role in the Middle East before World War II and the recently increasing volume of writing on the region. Although pre-World War II American diplomatic historians wrote substantial works about Europe, Latin America, and East Asia, they virtually ignored the Middle East. A notable exception was the economist Leland J. Gordon, who, in 1932, published a still useful study of the first century of Turkish-American contacts, emphasizing economic relations.[3] But most of the important historical literature has appeared since the war.

John DeNovo lamented that no broad survey of United States-Middle East relations had been written. Thomas A. Bryson's recent work, spanning the years from 1784 to 1975, partially fills the gap. His coverage of the period up to 1945, during which, he argues, the United States followed its national interest in avoiding political partisanship, is brief and episodic. In a longer section for the post-World War II era, Bryson asserts that the United States violated the national interest by establishing a special relationship with Israel. His narrative covers the basic details, but the need for a complete, analytical survey, based to a higher degree on original research, still exists.[4]

A common theme among those few scholars who have studied the pre-World War II period is that United States relations with the Middle East, although usually low-key, were substantial and significant. Important foundations for later, more extensive ties had developed by 1939. DeNovo pursues these themes in *American Interests and Policies in the Middle East*. He describes American cultural, economic, and diplomatic activities in Turkey, Iran, and the Arab nations between 1900 and 1939. The United States adapted well to rising Middle Eastern nationalism; to the extent that the United States was imperialistic, it was cultural and economic imperialism. Political noninvolvement was central to American policy, but by 1939 oil and Zionism began to erode this traditional policy in the Arab world. Unless other scholars can gain access to new sources, such as the presently closed records of Middle East nations, DeNovo's comprehensive book will remain the standard for a long time.[5]

Two recent studies about American missionaries and other philanthropists by Robert L. Daniel and Joseph L. Grabill are important contributions. Daniel shows that the philanthropic activities of Americans in the Middle East have been a main influence for a century and a half. The strength of Grabill's book lies in his coverage of the World War I period, where he emphasizes the importance of missionary lobbying on behalf of self-determination for Armenians, a Christian minority in Turkey, and other national groups. Grabill makes clear that missionaries were the dominant American influence in the Middle East until after World War I.[6] The Turkish persecutions of the Armenians beginning in the 1890s and the Armenian efforts to establish an independent nation during and after World War I have attracted the attention of several historians. Richard G.

Hovannisian's two well-documented volumes on Armenia's struggle for independence in 1918 and 1919 provide information on sympathy in the United States for the Armenians and the proposal for an American-held Armenian mandate. James B. Gidney has written a solid monograph on the Armenian independence movement and the mandate plan. Ultimately, the United States Senate rejected the mandate and Turkey and the Soviet Union divided the Armenian area.[7]

Diplomatic historians have examined the American response to the collapse of the Ottoman Empire in detail. Laurence Evans has written an in-depth study, based mainly on American sources, of the decade beginning in 1914. Concentrating on policy formulation, Evans argues that between 1918 and 1920 the United States moved from a policy of involvement to one of withdrawal in the Middle East. He also stresses the concept of the Open Door as a basis for American policy, especially for the 1920-1923 period.[8] Harry N. Howard, a diplomat and scholarly pioneer in Middle East studies in the United States, published in 1931 a detailed treatment of the breakup of the Ottoman Empire. His later books include a study of the King-Crane Commission (1919), which recommended United States mandates in Syria and Armenia, and *Turkey, the Straits and U.S. Policy*, which gathers together his research on a critical strategic question. More than half of this book discusses the pre-World War II period; it is informative on the Straits conventions of Lausanne (1923) and Montreux (1936) and United States interest in those settlements. Its most important contribution is the section dealing with the years after 1939.[9]

Other than the substantial section in DeNovo's *American Interests and Policies*, there is no major account of United States relations with the Middle East as a whole in the interwar period. Phillip J. Baram's *The Department of State in the Middle East, 1919-1945*, documented from American sources, only partially fills the gap. Baram, excluding Turkey from his study, emphasizes the World War II period. He argues that the key Middle East policymakers in the State Department, in order to expand general American interests and to promote the Open Door for American businessmen, supported moderate rather than radical Arab nationalists. They also opposed Zionist hopes for a national home in Palestine, a stand which Baram criticizes.[10]

As for studies of United States relations with individual Middle East countries during the interwar period, much remains to be done. Peter M. Buzanski's study of Admiral Mark L. Bristol, United States High Commissioner in Turkey from 1919 to 1927, examines Bristol's diplomatic role and the United States Navy's involvement in diplomacy. Thomas Bryson's article on Bristol as an Open Door diplomat adds to the story, but a full-scale biography of Bristol, utilizing his voluminous papers in the Library of Congress, is still needed.[11] My own work constitutes the most detailed view of bilateral problems and trends in Turkish-American relations during the interwar period. In *The United States Response to Turkish Nationalism and Reform, 1914-1939* and a series of articles, I have examined the work in Turkey of American diplomats, businessmen, missionaries, educators, archaeologists, philanthropists, and others during the era of Kemal Atatürk. The United States response to the virulently nationalistic Turkish revolution, which profoundly affected the work of Americans in Turkey, was to accept the revolution and accommodate to it. It was a model response, which might well have been emulated by the United States in its relations with other nations at the time and since.[12]

On other nations, there has not been enough scholarly work. Abraham Yeselson's book on United States-Persian relations carries the story only through World War I. George Lenczowski's history of Iran's foreign relations from 1918 to 1948 can be read in conjunction with Yeselson, but Lenczowski discusses only briefly the American role prior to World War II. New and detailed research is needed on United States-Iranian relations before 1940. The same is true for Egypt. Lenoir C. Wright published a study of the limited political, economic, and cultural contacts between the United States and Egypt up to 1914 but nothing exists for the ensuing period before World War II. Laurence Evans's discussion of United States policy on the Syrian mandate during the World War I years is the only other noteworthy work on this period.[13] With the exception of the Turkish republic and the Armenian question, American diplomatic historians have not been drawn to extensive research on bilateral relationships between the United States and Middle Eastern nations (or nations-to-be) during the interwar period.

The involvement of the United States in World War II and the cold war forced a rapid and seemingly permanent expansion of the American presence in the Middle East. Before the war, American interests were essentially nonpolitical, but the wartime strategic and economic importance of the Middle East, the emergence of the region as a center of cold war tension, Israel's creation in 1948, and the dependence of many Western countries on Middle East oil quickly ended the era of political disinterest. Both statesmen and historians responded to these changes, the historians by beginning a detailed examination of American relations with the Middle East since 1939.

For the World War II period there is still no comprehensive history of United States interests and involvement, although John DeNovo has a major volume in preparation. His well-documented article on the economic mission of William S. Culbertson to the Middle East during the last year of the war, and Martin W. Wilmington's study of the wartime Middle East supply center stress the area's economic importance and Anglo-American tensions over economic questions. The Culbertson group's work, DeNovo concludes, "revealed a vision of expanded official American participation in the affairs of the Middle East. Integrated into their vision of the United States as a major power in that region were elements of hardheaded commercial self-interest, political and strategic goals that reflected the urge to national power, and messianic idealism—the desire to 'help' the peoples of the Middle East."[14] Also significant was Arthur C. Millspaugh's work in Iran from 1943 to 1945. Hired by the Iranian government to reorganize its financial system, Millspaugh's reform efforts conflicted with vested interests and led to his ultimate failure. Both James A. Thorpe and Hassan Mojdehi have told the story of the Millspaugh mission.[15]

Iran provided the setting for an early cold war confrontation. The Soviets' quest for Iranian oil concessions and their refusal to honor their promise to withdraw occupation troops within six months of the end of World War II caused serious controversy. Several scholars who have studied these events do not agree in placing responsibility for the conflict. An excellently documented recent book by Bruce R. Kuniholm is certain to attract attention. Kuniholm examines events in Turkey, Greece, and especially Iran from the war period to 1947 and the United States response to Soviet involvement in these areas. He argues that the Truman administration's response to a serious Soviet threat was rational and justified, representing the president's rejection of the Munich appeasement model. The American-Soviet confrontation along the northern tier, Kuniholm makes clear, was an important factor in the development of the cold war. This book will help historians to more explicitly recognize the importance of the Middle East as they study the origins of the cold war.[16]

Richard A. Pfau also has examined the problems in Iran. In an account of the 1944 Iranian oil crisis, he states that the United States objective was to avoid letting opposition to the proposed Soviet oil concession harm the cooperative war effort. Justus D. Doenecke has published two articles examining the revisionist interpretations of United States policy in Iran, especially those of Lloyd C. Gardner, Denna F. Fleming, and Joyce and Gabriel Kolko. According to Doenecke, these historians see the conflict between the United States and the Soviet Union in Iran between 1944 and 1947 and later, as stemming from State Department support for efforts by American companies to control Iran's petroleum resources. Richard W. Cottam has argued that American oil interests did not determine United States policy in Iran in the 1940s; rather, that policy was primarily a defensive reaction against aggressive Soviet moves. Eduard M. Mark's revisionist essay asserts that the Soviet attempt to establish a permanent presence in northern Iran was to counter an earlier American push for similar concessions.[17] Rouhollah K. Ramazani's account of Iran's foreign policy from 1941 to 1973 deals extensively with the United States role and maintains that the Iranian government saw the United States as a counterweight to less desirable British and Russian pressures. In his synthesis of Iranian-

American relations from 1941 to 1954 Michael K. Sheehan traces the growth of United States influence in Iran, although he does not critically analyze American political and economic motives.[18]

Like Iran, Turkey became an early cold war hot spot and later played an important role in the North Atlantic defense system. Although officially neutral until late in World War II, Turkey's economic resources and geographical location made it critically important to the United Nations allies. Edward Weisband stresses Anglo-American-Turkish relationships in his impressively documented study of Turkish foreign policy between 1943 and 1945. Weisband demonstrates that Turkey feared Russian expansionism during the war and anticipated the Soviet pressures in the Balkan area that later helped bring on the cold war. David J. Alvarez's well-documented article on Laurence A. Steinhardt, the United States ambassador in Turkey between 1942 and 1945, stresses his understanding of and moderate response to Turkey's determination to remain neutral until late in the war. Alvarez's dissertation on Turkish-American relations, 1945-1946, examines the role of the State Department's Office of Near Eastern and African Affairs in the formulation of United States policy.[19]

Any book on the early cold war or the origins of the Truman Doctrine must discuss the Soviet Union's effort in 1945-1946 to extend its influence in the Turkish Straits. Harry Howard follows the traditional interpretation by blaming the Soviet Union for the start of the cold war. The pronouncement of the Truman Doctrine in 1947, Howard argues, illustrated America's commitment to resisting Soviet pressures in Turkey and elsewhere. Stephen G. Xydis and Jonathan Knight also have examined the Truman administration's response to Soviet pressure on Turkey. Xydis sees the president's firm stand as a major step toward the Truman Doctrine; Knight rejects a monolithic anti-Soviet interpretation, viewing Truman's effort as one which supported Turkey while avoiding a direct confrontation with the Soviet Union. Bruce Kuniholm's book deals extensively with Turkish-Soviet problems and the United States' response.[20] George S. Harris considers all major aspects of American relations with Turkey in a book covering the years 1945 to 1971. The "troubled alliance" between the two countries, determined in part by Turkey's desire for economic and military aid, according to Harris, was endangered by the early 1970s. Harris's book, an authoritative study, is based on extensive research, including Turkish sources and his personal observations while assigned to the United States embassy in Ankara. Ferenc A. Vali's study of Turkey's post-Ottoman foreign policy also provides information on relations with the United States, the general nature of which he approves.[21] For the more recent period, Laurence Stern discusses critically the Greek-Turkish struggle over Cyprus and its effects on United States policy; he indicts the United States for letting questions about NATO's effectiveness overrule humanitarian concern for the people of Greece and Cyprus.[22]

Important works on United States relations with the Arab states generally emphasize the post-World War II period. Robert W. Stookey's *America and the Arab States: An Uneasy Encounter*, is perceptive and informative. A former United States foreign service officer, Stookey combines personal experience and thorough research in a survey that is somewhat critical of what he believes was an excessive American commitment to political Zionism. Stookey's well-done synthesis offers an excellent bibliographical essay. Earlier surveys by John S. Badeau, William R. Polk, and George Antonius, describing the development of Arab nationalism, are helpful. A number of recent doctoral dissertations on the Arab states testify to increasing interest in this important facet of American foreign relations.[23]

Bilateral studies of post-World War II relations with other countries of the Middle East, except for Israel, are conspicuously absent. Little has been written about Iraq, Syria, Lebanon, Jordan, Egypt, Saudi Arabia, and the other states of the Arabian peninsula. These nations have not been ignored, of course, in broad studies of the Middle Eastern policy of the United States or of the Arab-Israeli conflict. But because of the inaccessibility of sources, the lack of perspective, and the commercial attractiveness of more popular topics, it is perhaps too early to expect bilateral studies. Such works will provide important fields of research for future students of United States-Middle East relations.

A few general studies of American policy in the Middle East, usually emphasizing Soviet-United States cold war rivalry, do exist. Because they stress recent events they usually become dated rapidly. Still useful for an understanding of the early postwar period are J. C. Hurewitz's *Middle East Dilemmas*, strong on historical background, and John C. Campbell's *Defense of the Middle East*. Campbell analyzes the military, political, diplomatic, and economic aspects of the Middle East and argues that the United States should prevent Soviet subversion in the area. Collections edited in the 1960s by Hurewitz, Georgiana Stevens, and George Lenczowski provide a variety of views on the American role in the Middle East.[24] As State Department and other documentary records become available for more of the postwar period, there will surely be many scholarly studies of United States-Middle East relations. Several recent dissertations illustrate this trend. The value of these studies lies in the detail they provide, based on extensive work in documentary sources.[25]

Understandably, the emergence of Israel and the Arab-Israeli conflict has interested recent American scholars more than any other Middle East topic. These controversial and often emotionally laden events have provided the basis for historiographical disagreements. As Robert Stookey remarks, "completely dispassionate works on the Palestine problem are written only in heaven." Howard M. Sachar's recent comprehensive history of Israel deals extensively with that nation's relationship with the United States. Sachar contends that Israel's existence and its future security depend on continued good relations with the United States. These close relationships, in turn, depend on the nature of Soviet-American relations. A more recent but similar book is Nadav Safran's *Israel: The Embattled Ally*. Safran argues, in an undocumented work with a pro-Israeli slant, that the long-standing United States-Israel connection should be formalized in an alliance which would serve the interests of both parties and contribute to world peace. Another recent survey covering the 1967-1976 period by Bernard Reich has less depth but is helpful in understanding the special relationship between the United States and Israel.[26]

Zionism and its influence on United States policy toward Israel has been studied extensively. Several historians have disagreed about the bases for Woodrow Wilson's decision in October 1917 to approve England's Balfour Declaration expressing support for the Zionist aspirations for a Jewish nation in Palestine. Selig Adler argues that American Zionist leaders, especially Louis Brandeis, were instrumental in influencing Wilson. Leonard Stein believes that Wilson's adviser, Colonel House, under Brandeis's influence, persuaded Wilson to support the Balfour Declaration. Richard N. Lewbow, in a well-documented essay, suggests that House really did not sympathize with the Zionists and that Wilson's decision reflected his strong personal feelings on the matter. Barbara W. Tuchman has told the story of her grandfather, Henry Morgenthau, who while United States ambassador to Turkey in 1914 arranged for financial support for the Jews then in Palestine but later became an "assimilationist," favoring the integration of Jews into various nations rather than in a separate state.[27] Yonathan Shapiro, Ben Halpern, Samuel Halperin, Melvin I. Urofsky, and Naomi W. Cohen have published broad surveys of the history of American Zionism. Both Shapiro and Urofsky stress the period from 1897 (the birth of political Zionism) to 1930. Shapiro argues that Brandeis's political ambitions explain his leadership of the Zionist movement and that by 1930 American Zionists were committed to Palestine as a Jewish national home. Urofsky asserts that American Zionists pledged themselves politically to the movement in reaction to the Holocaust. Halperin's impressively documented book centers on the years after 1930 and provides information on various Zionist organizations, fund-raising activities, and the like. Cohen's account examines the impact on the American Zionist movement after 1917 of leaders such as Brandeis.[28]

Many scholars have studied the relationship between American Zionism and the United States government as the agitation to establish a Jewish national home increased during and immediately after World War II. One of the earliest books was Frank E. Manuel's *The Realities of American-Palestine Relations*. Even with its pronounced Zionist bias, it is useful because of the information it provides. Both J. C. Hurewitz and Richard P. Stevens in books on the Palestine question conclude that President

Roosevelt made conflicting pledges to Arab and Jewish leaders about a Jewish national home. Howard Sachar also discusses the American interest in the Palestine question in *Europe Leaves the Middle East, 1936-1954.*[29]

There are substantial differences of opinion about the United States role and President Truman's motives in the period from 1945 to 1948, which culminated in his diplomatic recognition of Israel immediately after it declared independence. Many writers, among them Zvi Ganin, John Snetsinger and Margaret Arakie, stress the Zionist influence on Truman. Snetsinger argues that while Truman had no strong personal commitment to the Zionist program, the need to attract the Jewish vote in 1948 determined his decision. Alfred M. Lilienthal severely criticizes Truman and other American officials for allowing the Zionists to play an influential role in policy development.[30] Truman's course, described as one of balance between the extremes advocated by Zionists on the one hand and State Department advisers who opposed recognition on the other, is effectively defended in an article by Ian J. Bickerton. Both George T. Mazuzan and Shlomo Moskovits discuss the Palestine policy of the United States within the broad context of the cold war. Mazuzan views United States recognition as part of the effort to prevent the expansion of Soviet influence in the Middle East.[31] Several dissertations discuss Zionist influence on United States policy toward Israel, both in the late 1940s and more recently.[32] Although the need can be questioned because of the existing volume of literature, it is likely that there will be a continuing flow of writings on the subject. They will be useful to the extent that they utilize new sources and add to the analysis of existing works.

Writing on the Arab-Israeli conflict for the period after 1948 has been extensive, although it is somewhat early for historical accounts having the benefit of both thorough documentary research and the perspective of time. Herman Finer's *Dulles Over Suez*, dealing with the 1956 crisis, is critical of United States policy which Finer views as inconsistent with the nation's best interests. Chester L. Cooper, who served in London in 1956 as liaison between the American and British intelligence groups, has recently published an intriguing account of the Suez crisis, stressing the decision-making process within the British government.[33] Joseph Churba, at one time in United States Air Force intelligence, strongly criticizes United States policy for appeasing the Arab nations and the Soviet Union and discounting the strategic importance of Israel. William B. Quandt, who served as a Middle East expert for the National Security Council during the 1970s, analyzes recent events in the Middle East from the third Arab-Israeli war in 1967 through Henry Kissinger's 1976 shuttle diplomacy. He proposes a continuing role for the United States in achieving a Middle East settlement.[34] Kissinger's efforts in the Middle East have been the subject of much analysis, albeit more journalistic than scholarly, as illustrated by the books of

Edward R. F. Sheehan, who is favorable to Kissinger, and Gil C. Alroy, who is critical of him. A collection of essays edited by Eugene V. Rostow, advocating continuing United States support for Israel against Arab-Soviet pressures, reflects the opinions of an influential group of private American foreign-policy experts.[35]

Finally, American historians and other scholars have devoted much attention to the critical question of Middle East oil. For the pre-World War II period, John A. DeNovo's dissertation covering the years 1908-1928 and his article describing the efforts of the United States government before World War I to develop a national oil policy are useful.[36] General studies of Middle East oil development and its involvement in the diplomacy of the area have been published by Benjamin Shwadran, Stephen H. Longrigg, George W. Stocking, George Lenczowski, and David H. Finnie.[37] Michael B. Stoff's *Scarcity and Order* examines the continuing efforts by the United States to formulate a national oil policy in the 1940s. Aaron D. Miller's well-documented book discusses the impact of Saudi Arabian oil on the Middle East policy of the United States in the 1940s and the development of a "special relationship" between the United States and Saudi Arabia. Irvine H. Anderson is preparing a book on United States policy and ARAMCO, the Arabian-American oil company, in the 1940s. Based on United States and British government documents, corporate records, and interviews, Anderson's work traces United States strategic interest in Saudi Arabia's oil from 1943 to 1950. He discusses the support from the Departments of State and of Defense for the building of the trans-Arabian pipeline in the late 1940s and the Department of State's encouragement of the fifty-fifty profit-sharing agreement between ARAMCO and Saudi Arabia, arranged in 1950. Anderson argues that a de facto oil policy resulted from interaction between private and governmental groups, which reached a full consensus with the fifty-fifty agreement. Burton I. Kaufman in a recent article and a book stresses the use by the United States government of multinational corporations operating in the 1950s in the Middle East as instruments of American foreign policy. He rejects the idea that private interests determined the oil policy of the United States.[38]

American scholars during the 1970s have become much more interested in United States relations with the Middle East. The number of persons working in the field and the volume of literature is impressive compared to what existed a decade or two ago. The fact that many doctoral candidates are choosing Middle East topics for their dissertations is especially encouraging. In his new bibliography of United States relations with the Middle East, Thomas Bryson lists more than two hundred and fifty dissertations which discuss aspects of United States-Middle East relations or the foreign policy of one or more Middle East countries. The most popular research subject has been Israel and the Arab-Israeli dispute, amounting to about twenty percent of the dissertations listed. United States relations with Turkey, in both the Ottoman and Republican periods, is the next most appealing topic, about fifteen percent of the total. Other attractive subjects are oil and Egypt, although few of the latter deal directly with United States-Egyptian relations. At the other end of the scale are nations like Syria, Lebanon, and Jordan, which have received comparatively little attention for either the pre- or post-World War II eras.

As for gaps in the literature and needs for future research, John DeNovo's suggestions remain pertinent. For example, scholars have not responded well to his 1970 plea for cross-cultural studies. This research area is still, as DeNovo described it, "the least developed and most demanding." While there has been more activity in the two other topic areas he identified—American interest groups and "international interplay, especially among the powers"—the opportunities for productive research are still great.

There is a place for additional bilateral studies of relations between the United States and individual Middle East nations: for Iran (especially the pre-1939 period), Egypt, Syria, Iraq, Lebanon, Jordan, and Saudi Arabia. Turkey, Israel, the Arab-Israeli conflict, and oil have been adequately studied, although as additional sources become available and as time provides perspective, further research on these topics will be warranted. Hopefully in the near future another American historian will undertake the task of writing a comprehensive survey of the Middle East policy of the United States from the eighteenth century to the present.

While scholars writing specialized studies on United States-Middle East relations have disagreed on some issues, the sharp disputes between traditionalists and revisionists that have occurred in the writings on other areas, such as Latin America and East Asia, have not developed. Some scholars have noted the pursuit by Americans of the Open Door in the Middle East before World War II, but they have generally not indicted the United States as intensely imperialistic. Cold war revisionists, on the other hand, see the United States operating in the Middle East since 1939 with the same objectionable methods and goals that they believe the country pursued after World War II on a global basis. The sharpest disputes, and the most divergent interpretations, come in studies of the post-World War II Arab-Israeli conflict. Questions about Truman's motives for support for Israel and about the longer range pro-Israeli policy of the United States, only recently muted, have divided these writers.

John DeNovo, concluding his 1970 essay, described the state of research on United States-Middle East relations "as developing, but still immature." This description remains appropriate, although the field is less immature than it was a decade ago. No longer can it be said that the Middle East is being neglected by American diplomatic historians; but there are still rich opportunities for research in the field for both the pre-World War II years and more recent times.

Notes

1. For purposes of this essay, the Middle East includes Turkey, Iran, Iraq, Syria, Lebanon, Jordan, Israel, Egypt, Saudi Arabia, and the other states of the Arabian peninsula.

2. John A. DeNovo, "American Relations with the Middle East: Some Unfinished Business" in George L. Anderson, ed., *Issues and Conflicts: Studies in Twentieth Century American Diplomacy* (Lawrence: University Press of Kansas, 1959) and "Researching American Relations with the Middle East: The State of the Art, 1970" in Milton O. Gustafson, ed., *The National Archives and Foreign Relations Research* (Athens: Ohio University Press, 1974).

3. Leland James Gordon, *American Relations with Turkey, 1830-1930: An Economic Interpretation* (Philadelphia: University of Pennsylvania Press, 1932).

4. Thomas A. Bryson, *American Diplomatic Relations with the Middle East, 1784-1975: A Survey* (Metuchen, N.J.: Scarecrow Press, 1977). A useful survey is William A. Helseth, "The United States and Turkey: Their Relations from 1784 to 1962" (Ph.D. diss., Fletcher School of Law and Diplomacy, 1962). Bryson has recently published *United States/Middle East Diplomatic Relations, 1784-1978: An Annotated Bibliography* (Metuchen, N.J.: Scarecrow Press, 1979). I am indebted to Professor Bryson for letting me examine a copy of his manuscript before its publication.

5. John A. DeNovo, *American Interests and Policies in the Middle East, 1900-1939* (Minneapolis: University of Minnesota Press, 1963). DeNovo plans subsequent volumes for the 1939-1945 and 1945-1950 periods. If one reads his book along with James A. Field, Jr., *America and the Mediterranean World, 1776-1882* (Princeton: Princeton University Press, 1969) and David H. Finnie, *Pioneers East: The Early American Experience in the Middle East* (Cambridge, Mass.: Harvard University Press, 1967), the only serious gap will be for the 1880s and 1890s. For information on access to records of Middle Eastern nations, *see* U.S. Department of State, Historical Office, *Public Availability of Diplomatic Archives* (Washington, D.C.: Government Printing Office, 1976). Most of the Middle East countries do not permit public access to their records. Israel makes available materials on political and foreign affairs after thirty years, and after fifty years (therefore, none so far) on defense matters. Turkey allows access to foreign relations materials only through 1918.

6. Robert L. Daniel, *American Philanthropy in the Near East, 1820-1960* (Athens: Ohio University Press, 1970); Joseph L. Grabill, *Protestant Diplomacy and the Near East: Missionary Influence on American Policy, 1810-1927* (Minneapolis: University of Minnesota Press, 1971).

7. Richard G. Hovannisian, *Armenia on the Road to Independence, 1918* (Berkeley: University of California Press, 1969) and *The Republic of Armenia: The First Year, 1918-1919* (Berkeley: University of California Press, 1971); James B. Gidney, *A Mandate for Armenia* (Kent: Kent State University Press, 1967). *See also* two articles by Robert L. Daniel, "The Friendship of Woodrow Wilson and Cleveland Dodge," *Mid-America* 43 (July 1961): 182-96 and "The Armenian Question and American-Turkish Relations, 1914-1927," *Mississippi Valley Historical Review* 46 (September 1959): 252-75. Several articles on the Armenian problem by

Thomas A. Bryson appeared in: *Armenian Review* 21 (Winter 1968): 3-22; ibid., 21 (Summer 1968): 23-41; ibid., 21 (Autumn 1968): 10-28; *Records of the American Catholic Historical Society* 81 (March 1970): 3-26; *Muslim World* 61 (1971): 202-09; *Armenian Review* 26 (1973): 23-42; and in Robert W. Thomson, ed., *Recent Studies in Modern Armenian History* (Cambridge, Mass.: Armenian Heritage Press, 1972). Bryson's publications on Armenia grew out of his Ph.D. dissertation, "Woodrow Wilson, the Senate, Public Opinion, and the Armenian Mandate, 1919-1920" (University of Georgia, 1965). *See also* his *Walter George Smith* (Washington, D.C.: Catholic University Press, 1977), about a prominent American Armenophile.

8. Laurence Evans, *United States Policy and the Partition of Turkey, 1914-1924* (Baltimore: Johns Hopkins Press, 1965). Two useful articles on U.S. economic interests in Turkey before World War I are: Naomi W. Cohen, "Ambassador Strauss in Turkey, 1909-1910: A Note on Dollar Diplomacy," *Mississippi Valley Historical Review* 45 (March 1959): 632-42, and John A. DeNovo, "A Railroad for Turkey: The Chester Project, 1908-1913," *Business History Review* 33 (Autumn 1959): 300-29.

9. Harry N. Howard, *The Partition of Turkey: A Diplomatic History, 1913-1923* (Norman: University of Oklahoma Press, 1931); *The King-Crane Commission: An American Inquiry in the Middle East* (Beirut: Khayats, 1963); "The United States and the Problem of the Turkish Straits: A Reference Article," *Middle East Journal* 1 (January 1947): 57-72; and *Turkey, the Straits and U.S. Policy* (Baltimore: Johns Hopkins Press, 1974).

10. Phillip J. Baram, *The Department of State in the Middle East, 1919-1945* (Philadelphia: University of Pennsylvania Press, 1978).

11. Peter M. Buzanski, "Admiral Mark L. Bristol and Turkish-American Relations, 1919-1922" (Ph.D. diss., University of California, Berkeley, 1960); Thomas A. Bryson, "Admiral Mark Lambert Bristol: An Open Door Diplomat in Turkey," *International Journal of Middle Eastern Studies* 5 (1974): 45-67. *See also* Buzanski's "The Interallied Investigation of the Greek Invasion of Smyrna, 1919," *Historian* 25 (May 1963): 325-43. Thomas Bryson is preparing a book on the role of the United States Navy in the Middle East.

12. Roger R. Trask, *The United States Response to Turkish Nationalism and Reform, 1914-1939* (Minneapolis: University of Minnesota Press, 1971). The articles are: "The United States and Turkish Nationalism: Investments and Technical Aid During the Atatürk Era," *Business History Review* 38 (Spring 1964): 58-77; "The Odyssey of Samuel Insull," *Mid-America* 46 (July 1964): 204-15; " 'Unnamed Christianity' in Turkey During the Atatürk Era," *Muslim World* 55 (January 1965): 66-76 (part 1), ibid. (April 1965): 101-11 (part 2); "Joseph C. Grew and Turco-American Rapprochement, 1927-1932," in Sidney D. Brown, ed., *Studies on Asia, 1967* (Lincoln: University of Nebraska Press, 1967); and "The 'Terrible Turk' and Turkish-American Relations in the Interwar Period," *Historian* 33 (November 1970): 40-53. *See also* Robert L. Daniel, "The United States and the Turkish Republic before World War II: The Cultural Dimension," *Middle East Journal* 21 (Winter 1967): 52-63, and Hugh S. Johnson, "The American Schools in the Republic of Turkey, 1923-1933: A Case Study of Missionary Problems in International Relations" (Ph.D. diss., American University, 1975).

13. Abraham Yeselson, *United States-Persian Diplomatic Relations, 1883-1921*

(New Brunswick, N.J.: Rutgers University Press, 1950); George Lenczowski, *Russia and the West in Iran, 1918-1948: A Study of Big Power Rivalry* (Ithaca: Cornell University Press, 1949); Lenoir C. Wright, *United States Policy Toward Egypt, 1830-1914* (New York: Exposition-University Press, 1969); Laurence B. Evans, "The United States Policy in the Syrian Mandate, 1917-1922" (Ph.D. diss., Johns Hopkins University, 1957).

14. John A. DeNovo, "The Culbertson Economic Mission and Anglo-American Tensions in the Middle East, 1944-1945," *Journal of American History* 63 (March 1977): 913-36; Martin W. Wilmington, *The Middle East Supply Center*, ed. Laurence Evans (Albany: State University of New York Press, 1971).

15. James A. Thorpe, "The Mission of Arthur C. Millspaugh to Iran, 1943-1945" (Ph.D. diss., University of Wisconsin, 1973); Hassan Mojdehi, "Arthur C. Millspaugh's Two Missions to Iran and their Impact on American-Iranian Relations" (Ph.D. diss., Ball State University, 1975). *See also* Douglas L. Smith, "The Millspaugh Mission and American Corporate Diplomacy in Persia, 1922-1927," *Southern Quarterly* 14 (January 1976): 151-72, about Millspaugh's earlier work in Iran.

16. Bruce R. Kuniholm, *The Origins of the Cold War in the Near East: Great Power Conflict and Diplomacy in Iran, Turkey, and Greece* (Princeton: Princeton University Press, 1980).

17. Richard A. Pfau, "The United States and Iran, 1941-1947: Origins of Partnership" (Ph.D. diss., University of Virginia, 1975); Pfau, "Avoiding the Cold War: the United States and the Iranian Oil Crisis, 1944," *Essays in History* 18 (1974): 104-14 and "Containment in Iran, 1946: The Shift to an Active Policy," *Diplomatic History* 1 (Fall 1977): 359-72; Justus D. Doenecke, "Revisionists, Oil and Cold War Diplomacy," *Journal of Iranian Studies* 3 (Winter 1970): 23-33; and "Iran's Role in Cold War Revisionism," *Journal of Iranian Studies* 5 (Spring-Summer, 1972): 96-111; Richard W. Cottam, "The United States, Iran, and the Cold War," *Journal of Iranian Studies* 3 (Winter 1970): 2-22; Eduard M. Mark, "Allied Relations in Iran, 1941-1947: The Origins of a Cold War Crisis," *Wisconsin Magazine of History* 59 (Autumn 1975): 51-63.

18. Rouhollah K. Ramazani, *Iran's Foreign Policy, 1941-1973: A Study of Foreign Policy in Modernizing Nations* (Charlottesville: University Press of Virginia, 1975) and "Iran and the United States: An Experiment in Enduring Friendship," *Middle East Journal* 30 (Summer 1976): 322-34; Michael K. Sheehan, *Iran: The Impact of United States Interests and Policies, 1941-1954* (Brooklyn: Theo Gaus's Sons, 1968).

19. Edward Weisband, *Turkish Foreign Policy, 1943-1945* (Princeton: Princeton University Press, 1973); David J. Alvarez, "The United States and Turkey, 1945-1946: The Bureaucratic Determinants of Cold War Diplomacy" (Ph.D. diss., University of Connecticut, 1975) and "The Embassy of Laurence A. Steinhardt: Aspects of Allied-Turkish Relations, 1942-1945," *East European Quarterly* 9 (March 1975): 39-52.

20. Howard, *Turkey, the Straits, and U.S. Policy*; Jonathan Knight, "American Statecraft and the 1946 Black Sea Straits Controversy," *Political Science Quarterly* 90 (Fall 1975): 451-75; Stephen G. Xydis, "New Light on the Big Three Crisis Over Turkey in 1945," *Middle East Journal* 14 (Autumn 1960): 416-32; Kuniholm, *Origins of the Cold War in the Near East.*

21. George S. Harris, *Troubled Alliance: Turkish-American Problems in Historical Perspective, 1945-1971* (Washington, D.C.: American Enterprise Institute; Stanford, Calif.: Hoover Institution, 1972); Ferenc A. Vali, *Bridge Across the Bosphorus: The Foreign Policy of Turkey* (Baltimore: Johns Hopkins Press, 1971). For further background on the Truman Doctrine, *see* Stephen B. Xydis, *Greece and the Great Powers, 1944-1947: Prelude to the Truman Doctrine* (Thessaloniki: Institute for Balkan Studies, 1963).

22. Laurence Stern, *The Wrong Horse: The Politics of Intervention and the Failure of American Diplomacy* (New York: Times Books, 1977). The "wrong horse" was the U.S.-backed military junta which came to power in Greece in 1967. Two recent dissertations are: Mary P. Burke, "United States Aid to Turkey: Foreign Aid and Foreign Policy" (Ph.D. diss., University of Connecticut, 1977) and Nurham Ince, "Problems and Politics in Turkish Foreign Policy, 1960-1966: With Emphasis on Turkish-United States Relations, the Cyprus Question, and the Leftist Movement" (Ph.D. diss., University of Kentucky, 1974).

23. Robert W. Stookey, *America and the Arab States: An Uneasy Encounter* (New York: John Wiley & Sons, 1975); John S. Badeau, *The American Approach to the Arab World* (New York: Harper & Row, 1968); William R. Polk, *The United States and the Arab World*, 3d ed. (Cambridge, Mass.: Harvard University Press, 1975); George Antonius, *The Arab Awakening: The Story of the Arab National Movement* (New York: G. P. Putnam's Sons, 1946); Malcolm C. Peck, "Saudi Arabia in United States Foreign Policy to 1958: A Study in the Sources and Determinants of American Policy" (Ph.D. diss., Fletcher School of Law and Diplomacy, 1970); Edward A. Raleigh, "An Inquiry into the Influences of American Democracy on the Arab Middle East, 1819-1958" (Ph.D. diss., Pacific University, 1960). *See also* Joseph J. Malone, "America and the Arabian Peninsula: The First Two Hundred Years," *Middle East Journal* 30 (Summer 1976): 406-24, a useful survey.

24. John C. Campbell, *Defense of the Middle East: Problems of American Policy* (New York: Harper & Row, 1960); J. C. Hurewitz, *Middle East Dilemmas: The Background of United States Policy* (New York: Harper & Brothers, 1953); Hurewitz, ed., *Soviet-American Rivalry in the Middle East* (New York: Frederick A. Praeger, 1969); Georgiana G. Stevens, ed., *The United States and the Middle East* (Englewood Cliffs, N.J.: Prentice-Hall, 1964); George Lenczowski, ed., *United States Interests in the Middle East* (Washington, D.C.: American Enterprise Institute, 1968). *See also* John A. DeNovo, "The Eisenhower Doctrine," in Alexander DeConde, ed., *Encyclopedia of American Foreign Policy: Studies of the Principal Movements and Ideas*, 3 vols. (New York: Charles Scribner's Sons, 1978): 1:292-301.

25. Examples of recent dissertations are: Harvey J. Fields, "Pawn of Empires: A Study of United States Middle Eastern Policy, 1945-1953" (Ph.D. diss., Rutgers University, 1975); Donald J. Decker, "U.S. Policy Regarding the Baghdad Pact" (Ph.D. diss., American University, 1975); Stephen B. L. Penrose, "From Suez to Lebanon: Soviet-American Interaction in the Middle East, 1956-1958" (Ph.D. diss., Fletcher School of Law and Diplomacy, 1973).

26. Stookey, *America and the Arab States*; Howard M. Sachar, *A History of Israel: From the Rise of Zionism to Our Time* (New York: Alfred A. Knopf, 1976); Nadav Safran, *Israel: The Embattled Ally* (Cambridge, Mass.: Harvard University Press, 1978); Bernard Reich, *Quest for Peace: United States-Israeli Relations and the*

Arab-Israeli Conflict (New Brunswick, N.J.: Transaction Books, 1977). An earlier volume by Safran, *The United States and Israel* (Cambridge, Mass.: Harvard University Press, 1963) is still useful.

27. Selig Adler, "The Palestine Question in the Wilson Era," *Journal of Jewish Social Studies* 10 (1948): 304-44; Leonard Stein, *The Balfour Declaration* (New York: Simon and Schuster, 1961); Richard N. Lewbow, "Woodrow Wilson and the Balfour Declaration," *Journal of Modern History* 40 (December 1968): 500-23; Barbara W. Tuchman, "The Assimilationist Dilemma: Ambassador Morgenthau's Story [Palestine, 1914]," *Commentary* 63 (May 1977): 58-62. For further information, *see* Milton Plesur, "The Relations Between the United States and Palestine," *Judaism: A Quarterly Journal of Jewish Life* 3 (1954): 469-79 and Stuart E. Knee, "The King-Crane Commission of 1919: The Articulation of Political Anti-Zionism," *American Jewish Archives* 29 (April 1977): 22-52.

28. Yonathan Shapiro, *Leadership of the American Zionist Organization, 1897-1930* (Urbana: University of Illinois Press, 1970); Ben Halpern, *The Idea of the Jewish State* (Cambridge, Mass.: Harvard University Press, 1961); Samuel Halperin, *The Political World of American Zionism* (Detroit: Wayne State University Press, 1961); Melvin I. Urofsky, *American Zionism from Herzl to the Holocaust* (Garden City, N.Y.: Anchor/Doubleday, 1975); Naomi W. Cohen, *American Jews and the Zionist Idea* (New York: KTAV, 1975). *See also* Selig Adler, "The United States and the Holocaust," *American Jewish Historical Quarterly* 64 (September 1974): 14-23.

29. Frank E. Manuel, *The Realities of American-Palestine Relations* (Washington, D.C.: Public Affairs Press, 1949); J. C. Hurewitz, *The Struggle for Palestine* (1950; reprint ed., New York: Schocken Books, 1976); Richard P. Stevens, *American Zionism and United States Foreign Policy* (New York: Pageant Press, 1962); Howard M. Sachar, *Europe Leaves the Middle East, 1936-1954* (New York: Alfred A. Knopf, 1972).

30. Zvi Ganin, *Truman, American Jewry, and Israel, 1945-1948* (New York: Holmes and Meier, 1978); John Snetsinger, *Truman, the Jewish Vote and the Creation of Israel* (Stanford: Hoover Institution Press, 1974); Margaret Arakie, *The Broken Sword of Justice: America, Israel, and the Palestine Tragedy* (London: Quartet Books, 1973); Alfred M. Lilienthal, *The Other Side of the Coin: An American Perspective of the Arab-Israeli Conflict* (New York: Devin-Adair, 1965).

31. Ian J. Bickerton, "President Truman's Recognition of Israel," *American Jewish Historical Quarterly* 58 (December 1968): 173-239; George T. Mazuzan, "United States Policy toward Palestine at the United Nations, 1947-1948: An Essay," *Prologue* 7 (Fall 1975): 163-76; Shlomo Moskovits, "The United States Recognition of Israel in the Context of the Cold War, 1945-1948" (Ph.D. diss., Kent State University, 1976). As a follow-up to Mazuzan's essay, *see* Zuhair Hamdau, "A Study of the Arab-Israeli Conflict in the United Nations during the Period between 1947 and 1957" (Ph.D. diss., Union Graduate School, 1976).

32. Alan R. Balboni, "A Study of the Efforts of the American Zionists to Influence the Formulation and Conduct of United States Policy during the Roosevelt, Truman, and Eisenhower Administrations" (Ph.D. diss., Brown University, 1973); Earl D. Huff, "Zionist Influences upon U.S. Foreign Policy: A Study of American Policy toward the Middle East from the Time of the Struggle for Israel to the Sinai

Conflict" (Ph.D. diss., University of Idaho, 1971); Steven F. Windmueller, "American Jewish Interest Groups: Their Roles in Shaping United States Foreign Policy in the Middle East. A Study of Two Time Periods: 1945-1948, 1955-1958" (Ph.D. diss., University of Pennsylvania, 1973).

33. Herman Finer, *Dulles Over Suez: The Theory and Practice of His Diplomacy* (Chicago: Quadrangle Books, 1964); Chester L. Cooper, *The Lion's Last Roar: Suez, 1956* (New York: Harper & Row, 1978). *See also* Howard J. Dooley, "The Suez Crisis, 1956: A Case Study in Contemporary History" (Ph.D. diss., University of Notre Dame, 1976); Marwan H. El-Qazzaz, "A Comparative Analysis of United States Policy in the 1956 Suez War and the 1967 Arab-Israeli War" (Ph.D. diss., Southern Illinois University, 1976).

34. Joseph Churba, *The Politics of Defeat: America's Decline in the Middle East* (New York: Cyrco Press, 1977); William B. Quandt, *Decade of Decisions: American Policy toward the Arab-Israeli Conflict, 1967-1976* (Berkeley: University of California Press, 1977).

35. Edward R. F. Sheehan, *The Arabs, Israelis, and Kissinger: A Secret History of American Diplomacy in the Middle East* (New York: Reader's Digest Press, 1976); Gil C. Alroy, *The Kissinger Experience: American Policy in the Middle East* (New York: Horizon Press, 1975); Eugene V. Rostow, ed., *The Middle East: Critical Choices for the United States* (Boulder, Colo.: Westview Press, 1977).

36. John A. DeNovo, "Petroleum and American Diplomacy in the Near East, 1908-1928" (Ph.D. diss., Yale University, 1948) and "Petroleum and the United States Navy Before World War I," *Mississippi Valley Historical Review* 41 (March 1955): 641-56.

37. Benjamin Shwadran, *The Middle East, Oil and the Great Powers*, 3d rev. ed. (New York: Halsted, 1973); Stephen H. Longrigg, *Oil in the Middle East, Its Discovery and Development,* 3d ed. (New York: Oxford University Press, 1968); George W. Stocking, *Middle East Oil: A Study in Political and Economic Controversy* (Nashville: Vanderbilt University Press, 1970); George Lenczowski, *Oil and State in the Middle East* (Ithaca: Cornell University Press, 1960); David H. Finnie, *Desert Enterprise: The Middle East Oil Industry in Its Local Environment* (Cambridge, Mass.: Harvard University Press, 1958).

38. Michael B. Stoff, *Scarcity and Order: The Development of National Policy for Foreign Oil, 1941-1947* (New Haven: Yale University Press, 1979); Aaron David Miller, *Saudi Arabian Oil and American Foreign Policy, 1941-1949* (Chapel Hill: University of North Carolina Press, 1980); Burton I. Kaufman, "Mideast Multinational Oil, U.S. Foreign Policy, and Antitrust: the 1950s," *Journal of American History* 63 (March 1977): 937-59 and *The Oil Cartel Case: A Documentary Study of Antitrust Activity in the Cold War Era* (Westport, Conn.: Greenwood Press, 1978). Anderson's working title is *ARAMCO, Saudi Arabia, and the United States, 1943-1950: A Study in the Dynamics of Foreign Oil Policy*. He anticipates possible publication in 1981.

15 Good Neighbors? The United States and Latin America in the Twentieth Century

RICHARD V. SALISBURY

An assessment, through a review of recent scholarly publications, of the relationship between the United States and Latin America during the first half of the twentieth century shows that American policy ranged from imperialism to neighborliness.[1] By 1900 the United States had unquestionably embarked upon an imperial course in Latin America and in the next fifty years inter-American relationships varied from outright military intervention, with all the hostility that it engendered, to the overt disavowal of such intervention in both the Good Neighbor policy and the spirit of hemispheric cooperation during World War II. During the past several decades some scholars have challenged the assumptions held and the methodologies used by previous generations of diplomatic historians in their analyses of inter-American affairs.[2] This activity has led to new interpretations, perspectives, and schools of thought.[3]

Samuel Flagg Bemis and Frank Tannenbaum are acknowledged spokesmen for an earlier generation of scholars who took the traditional approach in studying the Latin American policy of the United States. Indeed, Bemis's influential book, *The Latin American Policy of the United States*, has been compared with A. Whitney Griswold's landmark study of the Far Eastern policy of the United States.[4] Although Bemis states that national security was the dominant factor in the formulation of the government's Latin American policy, he insists that this policy was tempered by the inherent "idealism of the American people." The official policy of the United

States, in the estimation of Bemis, actually served the interests of the Latin American nations during the early twentieth-century era of intervention by shielding the Americas against pernicious extracontinental intervention. This was "imperialism against imperialism," which "did not last long and . . . was not really bad." When the immediate external threats diminished, the United States liquidated its interventionist policy and, building upon the hemisphere's shared idealistic, legalistic, and republican tradition, proceeded to implement the Good Neighbor policy which in turn led to the development of hemispheric solidarity during World War II.[5] Mutuality of interests juxtaposed against the image of an all-powerful, yet benevolent, colossus are not necessarily inconsistent elements in the work of Samuel Flagg Bemis. It should come as no great surprise that the Bemis paean to hemispheric harmony, described elsewhere as Fourth of July rhetoric, appeared during World War II.[6]

Writing a dozen years later, Frank Tannenbaum, in *The American Tradition in Foreign Policy*, vigorously reasserted the traditional interpretations elaborated by Bemis. Tannenbaum, a distinguished Latin American historian, viewed the mid-1950s drift in United States domestic and foreign policy as a function of the "distorted doctrines" of economic determinism and power politics, doctrines which neither described "our behavior" nor reflected the "American experience." The behavior of the United States, according to Tannenbaum, contradicted such theories, for on those occasions when the executive branch of the government operated as if it were guided by these doctrines public opinion forcefully rejected them and demanded "a return to the traditional, though inadequately formulated American belief that the little nations of the world have the same right to live their lives as the powerful."[7] Specifically repudiating the *realpolitik* pronouncements of Hans J. Morgenthau and George F. Kennan, Tannenbaum stressed the doctrine of coordinate states—the existence of a community of nations believing in one another's political equality and moral integrity—and applied this concept to the Latin American policy of the United States. The Big Stick policy of Theodore Roosevelt and subsequent United States intervention in the Caribbean area thus appeared as temporary aberrations which were ultimately viewed by the general public as morally wrong. When such realization occurred, as it did during the 1920s, popular pressure served to bring about the restoration of the nation's traditional or coordinate state policy. This process, according to Tannenbaum, explained both the Good Neighbor policy and the high degree of hemispheric cooperation during World War II.[8]

George F. Kennan formulated a realist's response to the traditional interpretations. Writing in 1951, Kennan characterized the traditional legalistic-moralistic approach as "the most serious fault of our past policy formulation." This approach ran "like a red skein through our foreign policy of the past fifty years."[9] It was difficult for Kennan to conceive of an international system which assumed the existence of "a world composed exclusively of sovereign national states with a full equality of status." Such a system was a fundamental departure from the realities of national power.[10] In so far as Latin America was concerned, Kennan had some specific policy recommendations for the United States government. In his capacity as counselor to the Department of State, Kennan prepared an official report in which he analyzed the hemispheric policy of the United States. Kennan lamented the fact that the United States was enmeshed in a web of multilateral hemispheric commitments. He bluntly described such multilateralism as "agreeable and easy escapism from the real problems of foreign policy." Kennan went on to say that "success in the conduct of foreign policy, particularly in the Latin American area, rests ultimately . . . with the power and will to discriminate . . . in the application of our national power." He thereupon urged extreme caution on the part of the United States government in future hemispheric negotiations and conferences, emphasizing the fact that the vital interests of the United States in the Americas might in the future come under pressures that could only be effectively dealt with "by the full and concentrated diplomatic strength of this country."[11]

Gordon Connell-Smith, a British scholar, presents in *The United States and Latin America* a self-styled realistic approach to hemispheric international affairs. Connell-Smith emphasizes what he calls the self-image of the United States, an image that presents inter-American relations as being basically different "from those normally obtaining between great powers and weak ones." He ascribes this phenomenon to the assumption on the part of traditionalists like Bemis that United States policy regarding Latin America has been characterized by benevolence and mutuality of interests within the hemispheric community. Such a policy has been easy to justify for, in Connell-Smith's estimation, the United States has had little difficulty in equating morality with power. He suggests that North American historians have not, by and large, been able to rid themselves of this national self-image and remain resolute in their belief "that, in spite of many—even serious—mistakes, their country's intentions have been good."[12]

Although the traditionalist-realist dialogue persists, it has been overshadowed during the 1960s and 1970s by the emergence of revisionist interpretations of United States foreign policy. In the broadest terms, the revisionists view this foreign policy as being the handmaiden of the capitalistic system. In his highly influential book, *The Tragedy of American Diplomacy*, William Appleman Williams argued that North American policymakers in the first half of the twentieth century operated on the assumption that the nation's domestic well-being depended upon overseas economic expansion.[13] The mechanism for the maintenance of such well-being was the extension of the Open Door policy throughout the world.[14] Such a strategy, in the opinion of Williams, led to the rise of a twentieth-century North American empire. Yet this empire, based as it was upon the Open Door principle, differed in several important respects from other imperial structures. The Open Door policy was not dependent for its success on military strategy or on the balance-of-power concept for "it was conceived and designed to win the victories without the wars." The policy was predicated on the assumption that the preponderant economic power of the United States would transform the economic and political structures of the underdeveloped world into "a pro-American mold." Williams emphasized that the Open Door policy as originally conceived was highly pragmatic and owed little to legalistic and moralistic precepts. Such a policy, however, containing as it did an obvious bias against the forces of economic and political nationalism, was not flexible enough to survive crises brought about by the phenomenon of twentieth-century revolutionary nationalism. The obvious case in point, according to Williams, was the tragic failure of the twentieth-century Cuban policy of the United States.[15]

Within the ranks of the revisionists are those who advocate the dependency theory. Relying heavily on Marxian models and analyses, dependency theorists emphasize "the dependence of Latin America, economically, politically, militarily, and culturally on the United States."[16] Latin American scholars, stressing economic factors, have produced most of the recent literature on dependency, but an increasing number of North American academicians has begun to address the topic as well. Stanley J. and Barbara H. Stein, for example, have traced the origins of twentieth-century neocolonialism in their assessment of Latin America's colonial past. They conclude that contemporary Latin America, underdeveloped in terms of both economy and society, has little prospect of becoming "fully independent . . . in its decisions on vital areas of domestic policy because enduring neocolonial structures since independence . . . have profoundly permeated the process of change and impede full-scale breakthrough to modernization."[17] Because dependency theorists link North American "development" with Latin American "underdevelopment," policymakers in the United States and corresponding elites in Latin America perceive their mutual interests in terms of maintaining the phenomenon of Latin American dependence.[18]

Terming such revisionist interpretations "inadequate," Abraham Lowenthal suggests consideration of the bureaucratic politics model. Such an approach "treats United States policy not as the choice of a single, rational actor, but rather as the product of a series of overlapping and interlocking bargaining processes within the North American system, involving both intragovernmental and extragovernmental actors." Although admitting that such processes are definitely "affected by extrabureaucratic constraints," Lowenthal emphasizes that they are still "very much influenced by events and procedures internal to governmental organizations." Such a model, in Lowenthal's estimation, has been either ignored or downplayed by analysts of inter-American affairs.[19] Those studies which do utilize this model generally deal with events of the last several decades. Ernest R. May and John W. Sloan, however, have applied the bureaucratic politics model to earlier episodes of twentieth-century inter-American affairs.[20]

Another approach to the study of United States-Latin American relations is the systemic or structural model. Scholars who adhere to this approach view the phenomenon of hemispheric international affairs as being part of a greater international system. Inter-American relationships, therefore, must be studied in a global context with emphasis being placed on a multi-archival and multidimensional methodological approach. Historians should not only consult North American archival sources, but should also utilize, if possible, Latin American, European, and even Asian primary material. Such a comprehensive research base is difficult to develop and control; yet, within recent years a number of scholars have, with reasonable success, brought such a multiarchival dimension to their research. Thomas D. Schoonover has pioneered this approach in his quantification-based studies of nineteenth-century trade relationships involving Central America, the United States, and Europe.[21] He is now in the process of extending his research into the early twentieth century. Friedrich Katz and Berta Ulloa have mined the archives of Europe, Mexico, and the United States in an effort to provide a new focus on foreign influence during Mexico's early twentieth-century revolutionary process.[22] Richard V. Salisbury has emphasized in his work the role of Costa Rican policymakers and their efforts to pursue a viable foreign policy for their nation against a backdrop of external—Mexican, North American, and European—economic, political, and cultural penetration.[23] Kenneth J. Grieb's persistent and ultimately successful efforts to gain access to the Guatemalan Foreign Ministry archives are revealed in several of his recent studies.[24] Frederick B. Pike's heavy reliance on Chilean archival sources adds significantly to his account of United States relations with Chile.[25] Both Stanley E. Hilton and Frank D. McCann bring a multiarchival perspective to their research on Brazil's relationships with the United States and the European powers.[26] These and other scholars are in the process of producing monographs that will ultimately serve as the basis for a structuralist synthesis of inter-American affairs.[27]

Thus, historians have pursued a variety of approaches in their efforts to describe and explain the Latin American policy of the United States. Some of the individuals currently working in the field fall within one of the interpretive frameworks already mentioned. Others reject such categorization and have developed their own research perspectives. Scholarship pertaining to United States-Latin American relations published during the past two decades presents a rich assortment of approaches, perspectives, and methodologies.

Before reviewing a selection of this literature a caveat is in order: no attempt will be made to deal comprehensively with the bilateral relations of the United States and each individual Latin American nation. Up to World War II, the Latin American policy of the United States, for the most part, focused on the Caribbean region. Indeed, the ability of the United States government to implement its policy through armed intervention, political manipulation, and economic penetration tended to diminish proportionately the farther south one went in the hemisphere. Accordingly, the impact of North American strategic, economic, and altruistic policy imperatives on Mexico, the Central American states, and the island republics of the Caribbean will receive primary attention.

It is precisely this region, the Caribbean, that Dana G. Munro covers in his volumes, *Intervention and Dollar Diplomacy in the Caribbean, 1900-1921* and *The United States and the Caribbean Republics, 1921-1933.* Munro brings both diplomatic and scholarly credentials to his work. As a University of Pennsylvania graduate student he spent the period from 1914 to 1916 in Central America doing research for his doctoral dissertation. Published in 1918 under the title *The Five Republics of Central America*, the study remains a standard work.[28] During the 1920s Munro served as a Central American desk and field officer in the Department of State and was minister to Haiti prior to his retirement from the foreign service and entrance into academia in 1932.

Unlike Samuel Flagg Bemis, Munro does not attempt to whitewash United States policy during the era of intervention. Indeed, he specifically states that "many of the American government's actions were ill-judged and unfortunate in their results." The main thrust of Munro's argument relates instead to policy motivation, and the former diplomat takes great pains to point out that this motivation was "basically political rather than economic." In Munro's view, North American policy was directed at eliminating conditions in the Caribbean that endangered the independence of the nations in the area. The primary objective of United States policy, accordingly, was to discourage revolutions because revolutionary activity and the interstate conflict which often followed jeopardized foreign lives and property. Under these circumstances European intervention, with its attendant threat to United States security, was a distinct concern. The improvement of economic conditions in the Caribbean region was a second objective of North American policy, for sound economies would provide an appropriate climate for the development of political stability. Given the limited financial resources of the Caribbean states, it was obvious that a significant percentage of such economic development would have to come from external sources. Accordingly, "officials in the State Department sometimes held out the hope of increased trade and new fields for American investment as a third objective." After introducing this point, however, Munro immediately minimizes the influence that private investment might have had on the development of United States policy. He indicates that there is little evidence to substantiate the claim that the United States government made a sustained effort to foster trade and concludes that, in any event, the Caribbean states, Cuba excepted, "were too small and too poor in natural resources to offer attractive opportunities for foreign enterprise." Although Munro acknowledges that the methods used by the United States government were sometimes questionable, he insists that the objectives themselves were "neither sinister nor sordid" and categorically rejects the revisionist thesis proclaiming an alliance between the United States government on one hand and "the selfish interests of American businessmen and bankers" on the other.[29]

Lloyd C. Gardner and Robert Freeman Smith have analyzed the same chronological period that Munro covers. Although utilizing, like Munro, North American archival sources, these revisionist scholars differ significantly in their assessment of the United States government's policy motivation. Gardner's "American Foreign Policy, 1900-1921," describes how North American industrial expansion permeated the policymaker's world. "American diplomacy was not simply a quest to bring law and order into international relations, but also a desire to put American banks into underdeveloped areas of the world; not only an optimistic idealization of American political experience, but a drive to expand trade and cultural influence into world marketplaces." Gardner equates the underdeveloped Caribbean region with what he calls "neo-frontier wastelands—wasted in the sense that their resources were not being developed and used by the industrial nations for the benefit of the whole world economy." The North American role, therefore, in world politics was to provide these areas with "political democracy . . . and stability." This mission despite being coated with a heavy overlay of the "rhetoric of morality," was "the foreign policy reflection of the Gospel of Efficiency," a gospel which North American policymakers persistently spread throughout the hemisphere during the first two decades of the twentieth century.[30]

Robert Freeman Smith, in "American Foreign Relations, 1920-1942," sees as a basic objective of North American policymakers "the establishment and maintenance of a world order which would be conducive to the prosperity and power of the United States." The year 1920 saw leaders in the United States confident of their ability to guarantee what Smith calls an Open Door world. Such a system called for "a stable world order in which the United States could enjoy the fruits of an imperial position without the military, financial, and administrative burdens of a colonial empire." The tactics that policymakers employed to establish this system included "Dollar Diplomacy, protectorates, intervention, and the extension of the political and value system of the industrial United States." During the decade of the 1920s the United States tended to rely less upon blatant military intervention and instead, by emphasizing different methods, managed to maintain safe, stable conditions throughout the hemisphere. Specific elements in this strategy included the formation of a Central American treaty system, North American adjudication of various boundary controversies, and the promotion of private loans. By 1929, in Smith's estimation, the United States had attained its avowed objective of an Open Door world order. With the exception of the Soviet Union, "the international legal-economic-ideological system of the industrial-creditor nations was predominant, and the United States had been generally successful in molding this along the lines of a Pax Americana." Conditions in the Caribbean region appeared so good that Herbert Hoover was able to contemplate the withdrawal of the North American military presence in such client states as Nicaragua and Haiti. A new North American empire had been established "without a large military establishment or the acquisition of a major colonial empire."[31] Thus the economic determinism that Munro so forcefully rejects is obviously the key determinant, in so far as Gardner and Smith are concerned, in the elaboration of North American policy in the Western Hemisphere.

In their assessments of the Latin American policy of the United States, Munro as well as his revisionist critics rely almost exclusively on North American sources. The utilization of such a one-dimensional approach tends to sustain the belief that the Latin American nations, either singly or collectively, accepted a passive role in their relationships with the United States. The area within Latin America where such a view would seem especially applicable is Central America, where, during the first third of the twentieth century, a group of small and impotent states was forced to live with intermittent military and continual economic and political pressures from the United States. Although North American influence and interference in Central American affairs cannot be denied, it is both unfair and unrealistic to assume that such intervention precluded the development of any independent Central American initiatives or responses to isthmian internal and international problems.

Richard V. Salisbury's "Domestic Politics and Foreign Policy: Costa Rica's Stand on Recognition, 1923-1934," suggests that Costa Rica's experience with the United States and the other Central American nations reveals the evolution of a remarkably independent Costa Rican isthmian policy. Utilizing both Department of State and Costa Rican Foreign Ministry records, Salisbury has established that it was a Costa Rican and not a North American diplomatic initiative which led to the introduction of more stringent recognition provisions to the Central American treaties elaborated at the 1922-1923 Washington conference. The new recognition policy made it virtually impossible for a de facto isthmian revolutionary government to receive diplomatic recognition from either the United States or the other Central American states. The United States government enthusiastically supported the new policy because North American officials believed that it would discourage revolutionary activity and thus provide a stabilizing influence on the isthmus. In late 1924, Costa Rica, through timely ratification of the Washington treaties, made the agreements a formal part of isthmian international law and then acted in concert with the United States and the other Central American nations to frustrate the revolutionary-tainted presidential aspirations of General Tibúrcio Carías Andino of Honduras. Much to the displeasure of North American policymakers, however, Costa Rica refused to sustain this recognition policy during the 1926 Nicaraguan recognition crisis and proceeded to denounce the Washington treaties in the wake of the 1932 Salvadorean recognition crisis. Thus, despite the fact that Washington wanted to retain the recognition policy, the contrary actions of Costa Rica effectively paved the way for its removal from the isthmian scene. The Costa Rican government demonstrated that at least on some occasions North American policy was not necessarily a fiat to the isthmus.[32]

When Dana G. Munro indicated that the United States government's primary policy objective was to discourage revolutions, he was referring specifically to Central America and the Caribbean and not to Mexico. This was not an oversight, for Munro's analysis did not encompass United States-Mexican relations. The revolutionary activity that plagued the Caribbean region differed greatly from that which afflicted Mexico in the early twentieth century. The barracks revolution or coup d'etat involving short-term and high-level political change was a problem that North American policymakers contended with in the Caribbean area. The Mexican Revolution, however, comprising socioeconomic as well as political change and extending over several decades, posed perhaps the greatest challenge to the Latin American policy of the United States during the first half of the twentieth century. The nature of this challenge and the responses that it elicited from the United States government are major themes in Cole Blasier's study, *The Hovering Giant: United States Responses to Revolutionary Change in Latin America.*

Blasier establishes at the outset that his approach to the subject "was not facilitated or burdened by explicit doctrinaire predispositions." Although recognizing that scholars of the liberal and radical persuasions had developed impressive arguments, Blasier, characterizing these terms as "vague labels," chose not to associate himself with any particular school. Instead, through the utilization of both North American and German archival sources Blasier develops his own multidimensional perspective of foreign currents and influences in the Mexican revolutionary process.[33] According to Blasier, the Mexican Revolution threatened North American interests in two ways: the damage done to United States investors and the diminution of North American political influence. Revolutionary leaders in Mexico, as they endeavored to change traditional economic, social, and political structures, proceeded to develop "more independent domestic and foreign policies and were less likely to conform to U.S. policies." Blasier establishes three distinct stages in the North American reaction to the Mexican Revolution. During the first stage, the rebel movement of 1910-1911, United States policymakers adopted a flexible response. Francisco Madero, for example, was allowed to mount his revolutionary movement against the Díaz regime from bases in the United States. The apparent weakness of the Díaz government, Madero's popular support in both the United States and Mexico, and the fact that the revolution was not originally perceived as a danger to North American economic or political interests were factors in the United States government's adoption of a benign attitude regarding the Madero movement. The second or reformist stage of the revolution (1911-1913) saw Madero in power as Mexico's elected president. During this stage the United States was at best indifferent and, at worst, in the person of the ambassador, Henry Lane Wilson, hostile to Madero's regime. Blasier attributes this phenomenon to the growing hostility of United States business interests to Madero, for the president's brand of nationalism called for a redefinition of Mexican priorities in terms of national and not of foreign interests. Madero's efforts to establish a more equitable relationship with United States interests were perceived not as a strengthening of Mexican society but "as blows to U.S. private interests, restrictions on U.S. prerogatives, and evidence of . . . presumed hostility toward the United States." The third or overt revolutionary stage (1915-1941) posed "a clear threat" to North American private and political interests in Mexico. With the escalation of the revolutionary process, United States officials had two basic options: accommodation with or destruction of the revolutionary movement. North American policymakers chose the former. This was the preferred policy because, as Blasier points out, North American leaders became convinced that outstanding points of conflict, both private and public, could be resolved and this would in turn "preclude the interference of a hostile Great Power in the hemisphere."[34]

North American accommodation with revolutionary Mexico involved economic and strategic considerations. As early as 1915, Venustiano Carranza "agreed . . . to entertain foreign claims against Mexico, maintained representatives in Washington, and established a record of being able to give and take in negotiations thereafter." During the 1930s when President Lazaro Cárdenas injected a high degree of socioeconomic content into the revolutionary process through the nationalization of foreign oil holdings and agricultural property, the executive proclaimed that Mexico would provide compensation for such expropriations. Blasier acknowledges that economic considerations were definitely secondary to strategic considerations as United States policymakers shaped their responses to the third stage of the Mexican Revolution.

> In Mexico . . . U.S. private interests were extremely incensed by provisions in the new constitution which asserted national ownership of the subsoil (including oil) as well as other revolutionary innovations in that document. Those interests failed to persuade President Wilson to make recognition of the Carranza government conditional on Mexican commitments with respect to foreign investments. Wilson feared that such pressures would force Mexico to turn toward imperial Germany, the introduction of whose influence in the Caribbean and Mexico would endanger the United States during World War I. Similarly, President Roosevelt accepted Cárdenas' expropriation of U.S. oil properties in Mexico. His administration reached a global settlement of outstanding issues with Mexico in 1941 over the oil companies' express objections in order to discourage Mexico from turning to Nazi Germany.[35]

Blasier reinforces his assessment of the primacy of strategic over economic interests through the application of the bureaucratic politics model to United States-Mexican relations. He carefully separates the responses developed on the part of high-echelon officials (the president and secretary of state, for example), and the responses generated at lower intragovernmental and extragovernmental levels. High-level officials actively took part in all policy matters related to the strategic considerations which surfaced during the crucial third stage of the Mexican Revolution. Accordingly, Presidents Wilson and Roosevelt made the vital national security decisions described above on the eve of both world wars. Nonstrategic decisions, on the other hand, were formulated by lower level policymakers during the rebel and reformist stages of the revolution. Such decisions were generally "in accord with U.S. private interests or at least not blatantly opposed to them." Although agreeing with revisionist assertions regarding the United States government's efforts to maintain dominance within the hemisphere, Blasier points out that "such efforts are hardly unique to the capitalist world." He concludes that the United States response to the Mexican Revolution derived essentially from a desire "to maintain . . . political primacy within its sphere of influence."[36]

Blasier is not the only scholar to apply the bureaucratic politics model to United States relations with revolutionary Mexico. John W. Sloan tests the claims of revisionist theorists regarding the linkages between United States policymakers and private investors. According to Sloan, the revisionists disagree with the bureaucratic politics model's assumptions that differing personal and organizational perspectives were held by United States policymakers. The revisionists insist that the elemental policy objective of the United States government in Latin America was to protect and promote the interests of the North American investor community. Sloan therefore proceeds to "review United States policy attempts to protect United States private investors in Mexico" during the Mexican Revolution. The basic question confronting Sloan is whether or not North American officials showed "a common concern about the goal and the means of protecting United States investors." An affirmative answer would support the assertions of the revisionists; a negative response would uphold the proponents of the bureaucratic politics model.[37]

After reviewing the pattern of relationships between the United States and Mexico from 1911 to 1941, Sloan concludes that the "diplomatic record . . . tends to support the assumption of the BPM." Although United States policymakers did evince a "common concern" for the safeguarding of private investment, these officials "advocated a wide variety of policies toward Mexico." President Taft, for example, steadfastly resisted armed intervention while the ambassador, Henry Lane Wilson, pursued a contrary policy. Woodrow Wilson intervened in Veracruz in 1914 for political and not for economic reasons. The North American business community in Mexico was actively opposed to this intervention. On the other hand, when the oil companies clamored for intervention in 1919, Wilson refused to accede to their demands. In 1920 and again in 1927 American ambassadors resigned in protest over a policy that they perceived was not supportive enough of United States business interests in Mexico. Ambassador Dwight Morrow, on the other hand, helped to implement a softer policy vis-à-vis Mexico despite resistance from the oil companies. Ambassador Josephus Daniels overcame opposition from aggrieved North American investors and high-level officials in the Department of State to help "the United States accept the legitimacy of Mexico's nationalization of the oil industry and the land distribution program." Sloan concludes that given the significant amount of divergence of opinion within the North American policymaking structure, "the full power of the United States was never brought to bear against the revolution in a much weaker and isolated country." The result of these differing United States policy perspectives was the nationalization of foreign oil interests by President Cárdenas. In Sloan's view, revisionist theory cannot explain this phenomenon whereas the bureaucratic politics model provides a logical explanation for the Mexican government's policy.[38]

The case for the revisionists, however, receives strong support in Robert Freeman Smith's study, *The United States and Revolutionary Nationalism in Mexico, 1916-1932*. Smith characterizes the Mexican Revolution as the "first important challenge to the world order of the industrial-creditor and capitalistic nations made by an underdeveloped nation trying to assert control over its economy and reform its internal system." The role played by the United States was counterrevolutionary in that Washington acted "as the self-anointed enforcer for the Western Hemisphere of the legal-economic order of the industrial-creditor nations." North American business and political leaders rejected Mexico's efforts to impose national restraints over the foreign business community. Although there was considerable disagreement regarding the tactics to be employed, the end result was nonetheless "some kind of interference in the internal affairs of Mexico." Despite the efforts of Mexican nationalistic leaders, the questions regarding the pivotal oil industry from 1916 to 1932 were invariably resolved for, rather than against, the interests of the foreign oil producers.[39] By the late 1920s Smith notes the coalescence of interests between Mexican and North American policymakers. President Calles, for example, readily acquiesced in Morrow's diplomacy because the Mexican executive had already decided to place the consolidation of political power in the hands of the revolutionary elite above the economic nationalism envisioned in the 1917 Constitution. Calles thus orchestrated Mexico's return to the ranks of "well behaved underdeveloped countries within the international system of the industrial-creditor nations," and accordingly allowed the basic objective of United States policy ("the curtailment of the revolution before the process fundamentally altered the status of foreign holdings") to become reality.[40]

Mark T. Gilderhus, in *Diplomacy and Revolution: U.S.-Mexican Relations under Wilson and Carranza*, presents a different theoretical model to explain United States-Mexican relations. According to Gilderhus, both the traditional and revisionist interpretations of Wilsonian diplomacy present historians "with a conceptual dilemma." The essence of this dilemma is that the traditionalist, in emphasizing the importance of ideology in explaining Wilson's actions, is unable to provide a rationale "for more tangible influences." The revisionist, on the other hand, explains Wilson's ideology "as justification and rationalization for self-interested behavior." Such extremes make "unwarranted claims" and present "a false and artificial duality." In an effort to resolve this conceptual dilemma, Gilderhus utilizes N. Gordon Levin's interpretive model of Wilson as a liberal capitalist. Liberalism and capitalism, values that Wilson respected, suggest a linkage between the "ideal and material components" in Wilson's thought and action.[41]

Liberal capitalism provided the basic framework for the fulfillment of Wilson's foreign as well as domestic objectives. This meant that Wilson was comfortable within "a system of sociopolitical values and institutions characterized by political liberty, social mobility, constitutional government, and the capitalist mode of production and distribution."[42] Given Wilson's penchant for proclaiming the universal validity of his own assumptions, this meant that the rest of the world should also operate within this framework. As exemplified by the United States, political liberalism, in Wilson's view, represented the highest form of political society that man could aspire to. By the same token, Wilson considered economic capitalism as a "legitimate foundation to sustain political liberalism." Wilson went one step further, however, and called upon entrepreneurs to "eschew the pursuit of special advantage and behave with appropriate regard for the principles of fair play and equal opportunity." In other words, Wilson expected and demanded that conditions of absolute freedom would prevail within the marketplace. It was at this point that Wilson encountered difficulty in implementing his policy, for freedom within the marketplace was predicated upon Wilson's commitment to respect the right of self-determination for all people. Private economic interests responded negatively to Wilson's dicta. These interests were joined by foreigners who resented Wilson's assumptions regarding what was right for their societies. The body of Gilderhus's work depicts the difficulties that Wilson encountered in attempting to apply this seemingly self-contradictory policy to Mexico. "For eight years Wilson tried to reconcile the affirmations of the Mexican Revolution with his vision of international order. In the end he never found a way."[43]

A constant source of frustration for Wilson's Mexican policy involved border relations between the two countries. Throughout his two terms, but particularly from 1915 to 1917, military and paramilitary activity along the border brought the United States and Mexico to the brink of war and sorely tested Wilson's self-deterministic approach to international affairs.[44] Friedrich Katz, in "Pancho Villa and the Attack on Columbus, New Mexico," provides an excellent example of the application of new methodology to a seemingly well-covered topic. Supported by evidence uncovered in United States, British, French, and German archives, Katz calls into question previous interpretations of the Columbus raid. His study focuses on reassessing Villa's motives for the attack and in so doing presents an entirely new perspective on the Columbus incident and the international crisis it provoked. According to Katz, most historians have interpreted Villa's raid as an irrational and irresponsible act of revenge. The discovery of new evidence, however, has convinced Katz that the primary motivation which induced Villa to attack Columbus was his "firm belief that Woodrow Wilson had concluded an agreement with Carranza that would virtually convert Mexico into a U.S. protectorate." Although acknowledging that such a plan did not materialize, Katz suggests that "Villa had reasonable grounds for supposing that it did." He therefore concludes that Villa's raid can no longer be characterized "as the blind revenge of an unprincipled bandit" but instead "as a calculated effort to safeguard . . . Mexico's independence."[45]

The literal intrusion, in the form of the Villa raid, of the Mexican Revolution into North American territory caused a major crisis between the two nations. The purported extension of the Mexican Revolution into Central America during the mid-1920s created another international controversy. Scholars who have studied this period generally agree that the second United States intervention in Nicaragua (1926-1933) was precipitated by a belief on the part of North American policymakers that a dangerously leftward-leaning Mexico was busily engaged in attempting to extend influence throughout the isthmus. The prospect of a series of Mexican client states in Central America was objectionable to the United States government, and reports of Mexican material assistance to the dissident Nicaraguan liberals provided all the justification that Washington needed to send in the marines to prop up the shaky foundations of the conservative regime headed by Adolfo Díaz. These scholars also conclude that the United States government overreacted to what in reality was a marginal or perhaps even a nonexistent Mexican threat.[46]

Richard V. Salisbury, however, in "United States Intervention in Nicaragua: The Costa Rican Role," points out that North American policymakers were not alone in their perception of a Mexican threat on the isthmus. President Ricardo Jiménez of Costa Rica, for example, emphatically brought the fact of Mexican intervention in Costa Rica's internal affairs to the attention of the United States government. The Costa Rican leader outlined the efforts of the Mexican minister to cultivate radical elements throughout the country and to promote the passage of radical legislation in the Costa Rican Congress. Jiménez, therefore, in October 1926, gave the United States carte blanche to intervene in Nicaragua and thus stop Mexican efforts to radicalize the isthmus. The president's action was all the more significant given his widespread reputation as a champion of Central American nationalism and as a vigorous opponent of North American imperialism. The attitudes held and the evidence presented by Ricardo Jiménez served to reinforce North American policymakers in their resolve to establish a Pax Americana on the isthmus.[47]

The 1960s and 1970s brought a new perspective to scholars who investigated United States intervention in Nicaragua. Unilateral intervention in the Dominican Republic in April 1965, followed later in that year by a major escalation of United States military efforts in Vietnam, provided this new dimension. William Kamman, in *A Search for Stability: United States Diplomacy Toward Nicaragua, 1925-1933*, stresses the importance of strategic considerations in the United States government's decision to intervene in Nicaragua and considers economic factors to be, at best, of secondary importance. In weighing alternatives to intervention, North American policymakers rejected nonintervention on the one hand and multilateral intervention on the other. According to these officials, nonintervention would lead to chaos on the isthmus while multilateral intervention would bring about "complications which could obstruct what the United States was trying to do." Kamman believes, nonetheless, that the United States erred when it failed to cooperate with other Latin American nations in attempting to resolve the Nicaraguan crisis. Difficult as it might have been, such a cooperative venture would have spared the United States government the intensely hostile charges of imperialism that constituted, for the most part, the Latin American response to the second intervention in Nicaragua. Kamman concludes that any lessons that might have been learned from the Nicaraguan experience were apparently lost on Lyndon B. Johnson during the 1960s.[48]

Neill Macaulay's *The Sandino Affair* makes basically the same assessment of United States policy in Nicaragua. The maintenance of North American political hegemony on the isthmus was, in Macaulay's view, the primary policy determinant for the second intervention. Private economic interests had little impact on United States policy in Nicaragua.[49] Indeed, as United States Marines continued their fruitless pursuit of the liberal guerrilla leader, Augusto César Sandino, the North American government, despite repeated objections from North American entrepreneurs, withdrew its official protection of business interests in Nicaragua.[50] In addition to his excellent analysis of the Sandino insurgency, Macaulay also assesses the dynamics of guerrilla warfare in Nicaragua and the lessons that this experience would furnish protagonists of future insurgencies in Cuba, the Dominican Republic, and Vietnam.[51]

Richard Millett's *Guardians of the Dynasty* presents another view of the motivating factors for the Nicaraguan intervention. Millett reveals a remarkable Department of State memorandum prepared by Undersecretary of State Robert Olds. Mexican influence, according to Olds, had to be turned aside in Central America because the isthmus was the strategic sphere of influence of the United States. The Mexican challenge in Nicaragua, however, affected more than the strategic interests of the United States for, Olds went on to say, the credibility of the nation was also at stake. The Díaz government had received United States recognition and "until now Central America has always understood that governments which we recognize and support stay in power, while those which we do not recognize and support fall. Nicaragua has become a test case. It is difficult to see how we can afford to be defeated." It is easy to see why Millett equates such phraseology with that "advanced in later years to justify American intervention in Vietnam."[52] Millett describes the gradual development and ultimate adoption of a "Nicaraguanization" policy. This involved the training, by the United States Marine force, of a Nicaraguan National Guard which would ultimately be able to maintain internal order without having to rely on a continued North American military presence. The irony of this policy was that the National Guard did not become "guardians of the Nicaraguan people, but rather the crucial and effective guardians of the dynasty."[53] Given the Somoza dynasty's 1979 overthrow by a latter-day Sandinista revolutionary force, such a legacy could very well haunt United States-Nicaraguan relations during the 1980s.

Fidel Castro's successful revolutionary struggle against the Batista dictatorship and the subsequent leftward orientation of the Cuban revolutionary process helped to create a revival of interest among academicians in United States-Cuban relations. Those seeking explanations for the Cuban Revolution had little difficulty in finding them in the prerevolutionary relationship between the two countries. Robert Freeman Smith, for example, whose revisionist work has been described above, continues in the same vein in *The United States and Cuba: Business and Diplomacy, 1917-1960.*[54] Lester D. Langley's *The Cuban Policy of the United States* suggests that North American hostility toward Castro's revolution resulted from the Cuban leader's rejection of "a fundamental American assumption about Cuba." The basic problem for Cuba was, in Castro's estimation, the maldistribution of wealth and not "the lack of democracy or unrestricted investment." Langley indicates that Castro's repudiation of "the Jacksonian credos of democracy, capitalism, and progress" inevitably led to the open clash between the United States and Cuba. Both nineteenth- and twentieth-century United States policymakers assumed that Cuba would benefit from the "Jacksonian equation of democracy and capitalism." Cuba's twentieth-century experience, however, belied this assumption, for unrestricted North American investment in combination with a continued dependence on sugar produced a neocolonial economic order. North American political paternalism, an outgrowth of early twentieth-century intervention, was unsuccessful in fostering the development of "Anglo-Saxon political principles." Cuban politicians, up to the Batista era, were thus "geared to the prospect of American intervention."[55] Batista's post-1934 rule provided continuity for North American policy because the dictator continued to keep Cuban markets open to United States industry and maintained a proper degree of peace and order. "The emphasis was on productivity and stability even though Cuba was still a sugar economy and was ruled by a dictator."[56] Thus the pre-1959 Cuban system, predicated as it was on North American economic and political values, proved to be highly vulnerable to attack from a charismatic revolutionary nationalist such as Fidel Castro.

If there was one element in the Latin American policy of the United States that scholars of the immediate post-World War II era tended to agree upon, it was the Good Neighbor policy. Any disagreement, if indeed it could be described as such, involved the origins rather than the substance of the policy.[57] Traditionalists monopolized the historiography of the era and competed with one another in extolling a policy characterized by such salutary features as the mutuality of hemispheric interests and the formal renunciation of North American domination. The most authoritative statement of the traditionalist perspective is found in Bryce Wood's study, *The Making of the Good Neighbor Policy*.[58] David Green, on the other hand, suggests in *The Containment of Latin America* that the Good Neighbor policy represented not a mutuality but a clash of fundamental hemispheric interests. North American policymakers had to develop strategies to contain the growth of revolutionary nationalism in Latin America. Eschewing the interventionist tactics of the preceding generation, these policymakers endeavored to preserve North American economic control throughout the hemisphere. "Partly through fortuitous wartime circumstances, and partly by design," Green writes, "the Roosevelt administration ultimately strengthened the power and influence of the United States over many Latin American national economies."[59] Dick Steward's *Trade and Hemisphere: The Good Neighbor Policy and Reciprocal Trade* lends support to this thesis by noting that the reciprocity treaties of the 1930s placed Latin America "squarely within the orbit of America's Open Door Empire."[60] Robert Freeman Smith emphasizes that the Good Neighbor policy was simply an extension of previous policies. Despite the fact that "new tactics . . . were introduced . . . the economic and political hegemony of the United States was still the basic objective."[61] The onset of World War II and the concomitant surge of hemispheric solidarity simply submerged, for a period of time, the basic antagonisms between the United States and Latin America. The clash between North American economic and political imperatives and the forces of Latin American revolutionary nationalism, in the estimation of these revisionists, had been only postponed.

Scholars in the 1960s and 1970s have been unable to agree upon either an interpretive framework or a common explanation for the Latin American policy of the United States. There are some unreconstructed traditionalists and realists who maintain the emphases of their post-World War II predecessors. Although the revisionists seem to dominate the field numerically their influence seems to have peaked as scholars now begin to question the dogmatic inflexibility of revisionist theory. Adherents of the bureaucratic politics model have challenged the assumptions held by various revisionist scholars. The application of the bureaucratic politics model to more case studies in the Latin American policy of the United States would be a welcome addition. More work by adherents of the structuralist approach would also have a salutary effect. As more and more Latin American, European, and Asian archives open up, the next generation of structuralist scholars should continue the work begun by the current pioneering generation. Some scholars reject rigid interpretive and methodological criteria and labor instead to produce the basic monographs needed to reduce the extensive lacunae in the field. Perhaps it is to this segment of the academic community that most encouragement should be given. Theoretical assumptions have little validity unless they are firmly anchored to a broad empirical base.

Much work remains to be done even though a great deal of good diplomatic history has been written. Given the breadth of this past and present scholarly activity, it appears that the lack of consensus among diplomatic historians is a positive sign. If inter-American historiography during the last two decades of this century is as innovative and substantive as it has been for the past twenty years, the discipline will be very well served.

Notes

1. For additional historiographical articles *see* Richard M. Abrams, "United States Intervention Abroad: The First Quarter Century," *American Historical Review* 79 (February 1974): 72-102; Gordon Connell-Smith, "Latin America in the Foreign Relations of the United States," *Journal of Latin American Studies* 8 (May 1976): 137-50; Jorge I. Domínguez, "Consensus and Divergence: The State of the Literature on Inter-American Relations in the 1970s," *Latin American Research Review* 13:1 (1978): 87-127; David M. Pletcher, "United States Relations with Latin America: Neighborliness and Exploitation," *American Historical Review* 82 (February 1977): 39-59; David Green, "Language, Values, and Policy Perspectives in Inter-American Research," *Latin American Research Review* 10 (1975): 177-88; Roger R. Trask, "Inter-American Relations," in Roberto Esquenazi-Mayo and Michael C. Meyer, eds., *Latin American Scholarship Since World War II* (Lincoln, Neb.: University of Nebraska Press, 1971); David F. Trask, "Gunboats in the Caribbean Danger Zone," *Latin American Research Review* 13:3 (1978): 246-49.

2. The term "North American" is used as a synonym for "United States." Although somewhat imprecise this term is common throughout the Western Hemisphere.

3. The vast extent of inter-American historiography can best be appreciated by consulting David F. Trask, Michael C. Meyer, and Roger R. Trask, eds., and comps., *A Bibliography of United States-Latin American Relations since 1810: A Selected List of Eleven Thousand Published References* (Lincoln: University of Nebraska Press, 1968); Michael C. Meyer, ed. and comp., *Supplement to A Bibliography of United States-Latin American Relations Since 1810* (Lincoln: University of Nebraska Press, 1979); Charles C. Griffin and J. Benedict Warren, eds., *Latin America: A Guide to the Historical Literature* (Austin: University of Texas Press, 1971). Useful topical articles and biographical sketches appear in Helen Delpar, ed., *The Encyclopedia of Latin America* (New York: McGraw-Hill, 1974).

4. Lester D. Langley, "The Diplomatic Historians: Bailey and Bemis," *The History Teacher* 6 (November 1972): 65.

5. Samuel Flagg Bemis, *The Latin American Policy of the United States* (New York: W. W. Norton & Co., 1967), 384-93.

6. Green, "Language, Values, and Policy Perspectives," p. 178.

7. Frank Tannenbaum, *The American Tradition in Foreign Policy* (Norman, Okla.: University of Oklahoma Press, 1955), p. 5.

8. Ibid., pp. xiii, 86.

9. George F. Kennan, *American Diplomacy, 1900-1950* (Chicago: University of Chicago Press, 1951), p. 82.

10. Ibid., p. 84.

11. U.S. Department of State, *Foreign Relations of the United States, 1950, 2: The United Nations; The Western Hemisphere*, "Memorandum by the Counselor of the Department [Kennan] to the Secretary of State," 29 March 1950 (Washington, D.C.: Government Printing Office, 1976), pp. 620-21. For an assessment of the Kennan memorandum *see* Roger R. Trask, "George F. Kennan's Report on Latin America (1950)," *Diplomatic History* 2 (Summer 1978): 307-11. For additional studies of inter-American affairs in the post-World War II period *see* Roger R. Trask, "The Impact of the Cold War on United States-Latin American Relations, 1945-1949," *Diplomatic History* 1 (Summer 1977); Stephen G. Rabe, "The Elusive Conference: United States Economic Relations with Latin America, 1945-1952," *Diplomatic History* 2 (Summer 1978): 279-94.

12. Gordon Connell-Smith, *The United States and Latin America: An Historical Analysis of Inter-American Relations* (London: Heinemann Educational Books, 1974).

13. William Appleman Williams, *The Tragedy of American Diplomacy* (New York: Dell Publishing Co., 1962), p. 11.

14. Ibid., p. 48.

15. Ibid., pp. 1-8.

16. Domínguez, "Consensus and Divergence," p. 101.

17. Stanley J. and Barbara H. Stein, *The Colonial Heritage of Latin America: Essays on Economic Dependence in Perspective* (New York: Oxford University Press, 1970).

18. Abraham F. Lowenthal, "United States Policy Toward Latin America: 'Liberal,' 'Radical,' and 'Bureaucratic' Perspectives," *Latin American Research Review* 7 (Fall 1973): 11. Relationships between Latin American elites and United States diplomats are explored in Fredrick B. Pike, *The United States and the Andean Republics: Peru, Bolivia, and Ecuador* (Cambridge, Mass.: Harvard University Press, 1977); Walter LaFeber, *The Panama Canal: The Crisis in Historical Perspective* (New York: Oxford University Press, 1978) and Frank Gerome, "United States Involvement in Panamanian Politics during Taft's Administration," in Robert H. Claxton, ed., *Dependency Unbends: Case Studies in Inter-American Relations* (Carrollton, Ga.: Thomasson Printing Co., 1978): 61-72. For some different views on dependency theory *see* Robert R. Kaufman, Daniel S. Geller, and Harry I. Chernotsky, "A Preliminary Test of the Theory of Dependency," *Comparative Politics* 7 (April 1975): 303-30; David Ray, "The Dependency Model of Latin American Underdevelopment: Three Basic Fallacies," *Journal of Inter-American Studies and World Affairs* 15 (February 1973): 3-21.

19. Lowenthal, "United States Policy Toward Latin America," p. 14.

20. Ernest R. May, "The 'Bureaucratic Politics' Approach: U.S.-Argentine Relations, 1942-1947," in Julio Cotler and Richard R. Fagen, eds., *Latin America and*

the United States: The Changing Political Realities (Stanford: Stanford University Press, 1974); John W. Sloan, "United States Policy Responses to the Mexican Revolution: A Partial Application of the Bureaucratic Politics Model," *Journal of Latin American Studies* 10 (November 1978): 283-308.

21. For an assessment of the application of quantification techniques to U.S. diplomatic history *see* Thomas O. Schoonover, "How Have State Department Officials (or Diplomatic Historians) Behaved? A View from the Computer," *Society for Historians of American Foreign Relations Newsletter* 7 (September 1976): 12-17.

22. Friedrich Katz, *Deutschland, Díaz und die mexikanische Revolution: Die deutsche Politik im Mexiko 1870-1920* (Berlin: VEB Deutscher Verlag der Wissenschaften. Schriftenreihe des Institutes fur allgemeine Geschichte an der Humboldt-Universitat Berlin, 1964); Berta Ulloa, *La Revolución intervenida: Relaciones diplomáticas entre México y Estados Unidos, 1910-1914* (México: El Colegio de México. Centro de Estudios Históricos, Nueva Serie, 12, 1971).

23. Richard V. Salisbury, "The Anti-Imperialist Career of Alejandro Alvarado Quirós," *Hispanic American Historical Review* 57 (November 1977): 587-612 and "Costa Rica and the 1920-1921 Union Movement: A Reassessment," *Journal of Inter-American Studies and World Affairs* 19 (August 1977): 393-418.

24. Kenneth J. Grieb, *Guatemalan Caudillo: The Regime of Jorge Ubico, Guatemala 1931-1944* (Athens: Ohio University Press, 1979); "The Myth of a Central American Dictator's League," *Journal of Latin American Studies* 10 (November 1978): 329-45.

25. Frederick B. Pike, *Chile and the United States, 1880-1962: The Emergence of Chile's Social Crisis and the Challenge to United States Diplomacy* (Notre Dame: University of Notre Dame Press, 1963).

26. Stanley E. Hilton, *Brazil and the Great Powers, 1930-1939: The Politics of Trade Rivalry* (Austin: University of Texas Press, 1975); Frank D. McCann, Jr., *The Brazilian-American Alliance, 1937-1945* (Princeton: Princeton University Press, 1973).

27. The multidimensional approach that the structuralists utilize has begun to find its way into survey texts of inter-American affairs. Examples are: Federico G. Gil, *Latin American-United States Relations* (New York: Harcourt Brace Jovanovich, 1971), and Harold Eugene Davis, John J. Finan, and F. Taylor Peck, *Latin American Diplomatic History: An Introduction* (Baton Rouge: Louisiana State University Press, 1977).

28. Dana G. Munro, *The Five Republics of Central America* (New York: Oxford University Press, 1918).

29. Dana G. Munro, *Intervention and Dollar Diplomacy in the Caribbean, 1900-1921* (Princeton: Princeton University Press, 1964) and *The United States and the Caribbean Republics, 1921-1933* (Princeton: Princeton University Press, 1974).

30. Lloyd C. Gardner, "American Foreign Policy, 1900-1921: A Second Look at the Realist Critique of American Diplomacy," in Barton J. Bernstein, ed., *Towards a New Past: Dissenting Essays in American History* (New York: Random House, 1968), pp. 210-15.

31. Robert Freeman Smith, "American Foreign Relations, 1920-1942," in Bernstein, ed., *Towards a New Past*, pp. 237-45. For another assessment of United States policy in Latin America in the post-World War I era *see* Joseph S. Tulchin, *The*

Aftermath of War: World War I and U.S. Policy toward Latin America (New York: New York University Press, 1971).

32. Richard V. Salisbury, "Domestic Politics and Foreign Policy: Costa Rica's Stand on Recognition, 1923-1934," *Hispanic American Historical Review* 54 (August 1974): 453-78; "Costa Rica y la crisis Hondureña de 1924," *Revista de Historia* 3 (January-July 1978): 43-68; "Costa Rica y la crisis Nicaraguense de 1925-1926," *Revista del Pensamiento Centroamericano* 30 (April-June 1975): 9-18.

33. Cole Blasier, *The Hovering Giant: U.S. Responses to Revolutionary Change in Latin America* (Pittsburgh: University of Pittsburgh Press, 1976), pp. xv-xix.

34. Ibid., pp. 211-16.

35. Ibid., pp. 217-20.

36. Ibid., pp. 225-26.

37. Sloan, "United States Policy Responses to the Mexican Revolution," p. 284.

38. Ibid., pp. 306-7.

39. Robert Freeman Smith, *The United States and Revolutionary Nationalism in Mexico, 1916-1932* (Chicago: University of Chicago Press, 1972), pp. x-xi.

40. Ibid., pp. 255-59.

41. Mark T. Gilderhus, *Diplomacy and Revolution: U.S.-Mexican Relations under Wilson and Carranza* (Tucson: University of Arizona Press, 1977).

42. N. Gordon Levin, *Woodrow Wilson and World Politics: America's Response to War and Revolution* (New York: Oxford University Press, 1968) as quoted in Gilderhus, *Diplomacy and Revolution*, p. xi.

43. Gilderhus, *Diplomacy and Revolution*, pp. xi-xii. For an analysis of the Carranza-Wilson diplomacy waged by special agents *see* Larry D. Hill, *Emissaries to a Revolution: Woodrow Wilson's Executive Agents in Mexico* (Baton Rouge: Louisiana State University Press, 1973), and Kendrick A. Clements, "Emissary From a Revolution: Luis Cabrera and Woodrow Wilson," *The Americas* 35 (January 1979): 353-71.

44. For different interpretations of the Villa raid *see* Clarence C. Clendenen, *The United States and Pancho Villa: A Study in Unconventional Diplomacy* (Ithaca: Cornell University Press, 1961); Charles Harris III and Louis R. Sadler, "Pancho Villa and the Columbus Raid: The Missing Documents," *New Mexico Historical Review* 50 (October 1975): 335-47; James A. Sandos, "German Involvement in Northern Mexico, 1915-1916: A New Look at the Columbus Raid," *Hispanic American Historical Review* 50 (February 1970): 70-88.

45. Friedrich Katz, "Pancho Villa and the Attack on Columbus, New Mexico," *American Historical Review* 83 (February 1978): 102.

46. Neill Macaulay, *The Sandino Affair* (Chicago: Quadrangle Books, 1967); William Kamman, *A Search for Stability: United States Diplomacy Toward Nicaragua, 1925-1933* (Notre Dame: University of Notre Dame Press, 1968); Richard Millett, *Guardians of the Dynasty: A History of the U.S. Created Guardia Nacional de Nicaragua and the Somoza Family* (Maryknoll, N.Y.: Orbis Books, 1977).

47. Richard V. Salisbury, "United States Intervention in Nicaragua: The Costa Rican Role," *Prologue* 9 (Winter 1977): 209-17.

48. Kamman, *A Search for Stability*, pp. 233-35.

49. Macaulay, *The Sandino Affair*, pp. 25-26.

50. Ibid., pp. 198-200.

51. Ibid., pp. 7-13, 257-73.

52. Millett, *Guardians of the Dynasty*, p. 52. For another comparison of the North American experience in Nicaragua and Vietnam *see* John J. Tierney, Jr., "U.S. Intervention in Nicaragua, 1927-1933: Lessons for Today," *Orbis* 14 (Winter 1971): 1012-28.

53. Millett, *Guardians of the Dynasty*, p. 261. For other "occupation" studies *see* Hans Schmidt, *The United States Occupation of Haiti, 1915-1934* (New Brunswick, N.J.: Rutgers University Press, 1971); David Healy, *The United States in Cuba, 1898-1902: Generals, Politicians and the Search for a Policy* (Madison: University of Wisconsin Press, 1963) and *Gunboat Diplomacy in the Wilson Era: The U.S. Navy in Haiti, 1915-1916* (Madison: University of Wisconsin Press, 1976); G. A. Mellander, *The United States in Panamanian Politics: The Intriguing Formative Years* (Danville, Ill.: Interstate Printers & Publishers, 1971).

54. Robert Freeman Smith, *The United States and Cuba: Business and Diplomacy, 1917-1960* (New York: Bookman Associates, 1961).

55. Lester D. Langley, *The Cuban Policy of the United States: A Brief History* (New York: John Wiley & Sons, 1968). For additional analyses of Cuban political dependence in the pre-Batista era *see* Jules Robert Benjamin, *The United States and Cuba: Hegemony and Dependent Development, 1880-1934* (Pittsburgh: University of Pittsburgh Press, 1977) and Louis A. Perez, Jr., "The Platt Amendment and Dysfunctional Politics in Cuba: The Electoral Crises of 1916-1917," in Claxton, ed., *Dependency Unbends*, pp. 49-59.

56. Langley, *The Cuban Policy of the United States*, p. 187. The Batista regime's relationship with the United States is also explored in Irwin F. Gellman, *Roosevelt and Batista: Good Neighbor Diplomacy in Cuba, 1933-1945* (Albuquerque: University of New Mexico Press, 1973).

57. David Green, *The Containment of Latin America: A History of the Myths and Realities of the Good Neighbor Policy* (Chicago: Quadrangle Books, 1971). For a broad revisionist perspective on Roosevelt's foreign policy *see* Lloyd C. Gardner, *Economic Aspects of New Deal Diplomacy* (Madison: University of Wisconsin Press, 1964).

58. Bryce Wood, *The Making of the Good Neighbor Policy* (New York: Columbia University Press, 1961).

59. Green, *The Containment of Latin America*, p. ix.

60. Dick Steward, *Trade and Hemisphere: The Good Neighbor Policy and Reciprocal Trade* (Columbia: University of Missouri Press, 1975), p. viii.

61. Robert Freeman Smith, "American Foreign Relations, 1920-1942," p. 246.

16 ______ Some Sources and Problems for Diplomatic Historians in the Next Two Decades

GERALD K. HAINES and
J. SAMUEL WALKER

Much like post-Modern art which has exploded into countless factions and is moving in numerous directions all at once, diplomatic history has broken out of its classical confines and is pushing into areas never before considered within the realm of diplomatic historians. There is no prominent direction, no one clearly discernible trend which dominates the writing of diplomatic history today. Instead, there is a quest for new means of understanding, a search for new ways of bringing sense to the complex and often confusing area of foreign affairs. Accordingly, diplomatic historians have explored new theories and adopted new tools and methods in their approach to the subject. Some have moved into interdisciplinary studies, stressing political science models, psychoanalytical methods, sociological factors, and quantitative techniques. Despite this explosion in concepts and methods, there remains an ultimate reliance on traditional sources and source materials. The diplomatic historian is still dependent on archival records and manuscript collections for primary data. This chapter discusses what primary sources will be available for research during the next two decades and examines some of the problems historians will encounter in attempting to gain access to these sources.

Diplomatic historians working in the modern era face an almost overwhelming task of sifting and winnowing an enormous amount of documentation. Unlike scholars working on earlier periods who examine a limited amount of collected data and project trends and ideas from fragments of the record, the twentieth-century scholar is faced with a mountain of paper. He must select pertinent documentation from this voluminous pile. It is an increasingly difficult and time-consuming task. The problem becomes even more acute for research on topics during and following World War II as the diplomatic process and record-keeping techniques become more complex and more complete.

Department of State Records

The most logical place to begin a discussion of source material is with the records of the Department of State. These records have constituted the backbone for international relations research for years and they remain today a major source of primary information. Yet many historians do not understand the basic organization of these records or how to use them effectively. Presently, the records of the department are open for research through the year 1949 and are deposited at the National Archives in Washington, D.C. There are no restrictions on their use, although some material remains classified and has been withdrawn from the files. The material deposited at the National Archives consists of the central files of the department (Record Group 59), the records of United States foreign service posts (Record Group 84), and various "Lot Files." The central files include all dispatches, telegrams, and communications sent to the department, department responses, internal memoranda, notes, and correspondence from private citizens, corporations, and other federal agencies. Most diplomatic historians are acquainted with the Department of State's decimal filing system. A subject-oriented system, the department used it with little change from 1910 to 1949. It consisted of nine primary classes designated by the numbers 0 through 8. The major class number 0 through 8 represented the major functions or interests of the department as follows:

CLASS	SUBJECT AREA COVERAGE
0	General Miscellaneous
1	Administration U.S. Government
2	Extradition
3	Protection of Interests
4	Claims
5	Congresses and Conferences
6	Commerce Customs Administration
7	Political Relations of States
8	Internal Affairs of States[1]

Each of these classes was further subdivided according to the decimal system allowing every subject to have a distinctive file number. For example, 8**.00 related to political affairs in a country (**).[2] 8**.00B concerned communism and communistic activities. In every class except class 5 the correspondence was arranged in some degree according to the country concerned. All independent countries and some smaller political divisions had distinct numbers consisting of two digits or two digits and a letter. For example, the United States was assigned 11, Great Britain 41, Russia 62, and the Bahamas 44E. Thus, information relating to political affairs in Great Britain is filed under 841.00. Records pertaining to relations between Great Britain and the United States are found under 711.41. It is quite simple to follow a particular subject through a rather long period of time. For instance, records relating to communist activities in Great Britain could be followed from 1910 to 1949 with relative ease since the basic filing number (841.00B) stayed the same.

The department adopted a new decimal classification scheme for its central files on 1 January 1950. Designed to modernize the subjects under which the department's correspondence was filed, it provided greater range for the expansion of certain subjects, especially under the headings of international relations and the internal affairs of states. To give more range for the internal affairs of states the class 9 was introduced.

Since the next block of records that will be turned over to the National Archives for research is the 1950-1954 central files, it is essential to gain a grasp of this new organization. The classification scheme in major outline form is:

CLASS	SUBJECT MATTER
0	Miscellaneous
1	Administration of U.S. Government
2	Protection of Interests (Persons and Property)
3	International Conferences, Congresses, Meetings and Organizations, United Nations, Organization of American States, Multilateral Treaties
4	International Trade and Commerce, Trade Relations, Treaties
5	International Informational and Educational Relations, Cultural Affairs and Programs
6	International Political Relations, Other International Relations

CLASS	SUBJECT MATTER
7	Internal Political and National Defense Affairs
8	Internal Economic, Industrial, and Social Affairs
9	Other Internal Affairs, Communications, Transportation, Science[3]

To maintain some continuity with the old filing system the two-digit country numbers were retained—the United States was still 11, Great Britain 41, Japan 94. Germany, however, which had been 62, became East Germany 62b and West Germany 62a.

The difficulty for researchers comes in attempting to switch to the new system while following a particular subject forward from the 1940s. A few comparisons with the old filing system may help clarify the changes. The old class 7 Political Relations of States, for example, became class 6 International Political Relations; the old class 8 Internal Affairs of States became classes 7, 8, and 9. Under the old system, material relating to economic affairs of Great Britain would have been filed under 841.50. Under the new system they were filed under 841.000. Using the earlier example, communist activities in Great Britain would now be found under 741.001. The system also made allowances for new subjects, such as television 9**.44. Unfortunately, the classification manual for this filing system is difficult to obtain. The Department of State retains copies and the Diplomatic Branch of the National Archives has several copies. But the manual has not been microfilmed and is unavailable in most major libraries.

The historian of contemporary foreign relations will no sooner become acquainted with these changes than he will have to deal with an entirely new system. In March 1963 the department adopted a subject-numeric filing system for its records throughout the department and overseas posts. A menmonic symbol was selected for 55 primary subjects. These symbols ranged from 1 to 4 letters and were chosen because of their meaning or obvious relationship to the subject matter for which they stood (e.g., AGR for agriculture). A brief outline of this breakdown follows:

PRIMARY SUBJECT	CODE SYMBOL
Administration	
Accounting and Disbursing	ACC
Buildings and Grounds	BG
Budget	BUD

PRIMARY SUBJECT	CODE SYMBOL
Consular	
Consular Affairs (general)	CON
Passports and Citizenship	PPT
Protective Services	PS
Visas	V
Culture and Information	
Education and Culture	EDU
Education and Cultural Exchange	EDX
Information Activities (general)	INF
United States Information Service (USIS)	
Cultural Activities	CUL
Motion Pictures	MP
Press, Publications, Visuals	PPV
Radio	RAD
Television	TV
Economic	
Agriculture (general)	AGR
Aid for International Development	AID
Aviation (Civil)	AV
Economic Affairs (general)	E
Economic Integration	ECIN
Finance	FN
Fuels and Energy	FSE
Foreign Trade	FT
Industries and Commodities (general)	INCO
Petroleum	PET
Political and Defense	
Communism	CSM
Defense	DEF
Intelligence	INT
Political Affairs and Relations	POL
Science	
Atomic Energy (general)	AE
Science and Technology	SCI
Space and Astronautics	SP
Social	
Health and Medical Care	HLTH
Refugees and Migration	REF
Social Conditions	SOC[4]

Simple serial numbers were assigned to subject breakdowns at lower levels. For example, a paper relating to human rights in general would be classified SOC 14; a memorandum dealing with the status of women would be given the classification SOC 14-2. The most detailed subdivision contains no more than four digits. The same number was also assigned to similar lower levels (e.g., Communist bloc activities were assigned number 6. Thus, if the department received information relating to communist activities in such areas as aid, trade, education, and cultural fields, the subdivision number remained the same, AID 6, FT 6, EDU 6). Abandoning the two-digit number for country designations, the new system simply used country abbreviations—U.S., USSR, E. GER., W. GER., G.B. Using our example once again, communist political activities in Great Britain would be classified GB-CSM 6. The indexes and finding aids for this system are also difficult to obtain. One has to consult either the Office of the Historian of the Department of State or the Diplomatic Branch of the National Archives for copies.

Again in 1973 the department changed its central filing system. This time it replaced the alpha-numeric system with an automated document system (ADS) for its enormous central file. Under the ADS, reliable high-speed search and retrieval of information is possible because the information is stored in a computer and on microfilm rather than on paper.

The texts of telegrams are filed by electronic means and converted to microfilm. About one-half of them are indexed automatically using TAGS (traffic analysis by geography and subject codes). The rest are reviewed in detail and indexed by analysts in the Foreign Affairs Information Management Center. Access to the system is gained through terminals which are connected to a central computer. At each terminal there is a typewriter keyboard on which requests are typed. Typing the request triggers the computer for a search of the data stored in it. By simply typing out the reference number of a telegram, for instance, the text of the telegram is displayed. If a paper copy is needed, a teletypewriter prints the text on command. When the reference number is not known, other index terms may be used. For example, if London, economic matters, Brazil, July 1974 were typed, the computer would display all references to documents containing information to or from the United States embassy in London during July 1974 concerning British investments in Brazil. The search may be further narrowed by requesting only classified documents or those that mention a particular person's name.[5]

The onset of the computer age for records will present new problems to diplomatic historians working with materials of the 1970s. They will have to familiarize themselves with computer technology and microform materials in order to use the records effectively. A computer-created index offers the capability of retrieving information more quickly and in greater quantity than the current systems. Yet, access to information on microfilm will be a problem. A roll of film may contain classified documents which cannot be made available to researchers or it may contain matters relating to privacy. These documents cannot simply be spliced from the film. This problem will be formidable for archivists and historians alike in the future.

Researchers will also find that the chits or notations on documents which in the past provided them with valuable information as to the history of a memorandum or a despatch, how it was evaluated, and who saw it, will not appear on the clean copy of the microfilm. This problem may entail retaining office and bureau paper files and may compound difficulties in obtaining useful information.

Supplementing the central files of the department are the records maintained at the various foreign service posts throughout the world and the various "Special Files" or "Lot Files." At the outbreak of World War II the United States maintained approximately 60 diplomatic and 300 consular posts; on 1 January 1967 it had 123 diplomatic posts, 164 consular posts, and 9 missions. Most of the records from these posts through 1949 have been retired to the National Archives. It is anticipated that the records relating to the decade of the 1950s will be sent to the National Archives within the next five years. These post records include material not sent to the department but retained at the individual post. While much of it is simply duplicate copies of despatches sent to the department there is valuable material not found elsewhere, especially concerning economic matters. The records consist chiefly of correspondence with the department, with the governments to which diplomatic representatives were accredited, and with other diplomatic and consular representatives, individuals, business firms, and social and professional organizations.

From 1912 to 1948 the foreign service followed a classification scheme similar to the department's decimal system and it was relatively easy to trace a topic or subject in the post records and in the central files.[6] However, in November 1948 the foreign service adopted a new classification system which remained in effect until the alpha-numeric system of 1963.[7] The historian dealing with the decade of the 1950s, therefore, is forced to learn two separate systems—the central decimal file and the foreign service post decimal system. For example, under the old system, correspondence relating to internal affairs of states could be found in both the central file and the post files under the 800 category. Under the old system, information concerning military affairs would be under the same number 8**.20 in the central file and 820 in the post file. Under the new systems, however, the military affairs of a particular nation would be found under class 7 for the central files and under class 4 for the post files. The following is a summary of the classification system adopted for foreign service post correspondence in the 1950s:

CLASS	SUBJECT
0	Miscellaneous
1	Administration
2	Citizenship, Immigration Protective and Legal Services
3	Political and Governmental Affairs
4	National Defense Affairs
5	Economic, Industrial, and Social Affairs
6	Informational, Cultural, and Scientific Affairs[8]

In addition to examining the central files and the foreign service post files, the researcher must also often pore through numerous Special Files or Lot Files. These Lot Files were maintained by various offices, bureaus, or individuals in the department and relate to a variety of subjects. They are sometimes overrated by historians as a primary source since many of the records are duplicates of documents found in the central file. Nevertheless, the Lot Files often contain unique information and cannot be overlooked. For example, the records of the Office of European Affairs (Matthews-Hickerson files, Lot 5) are a collection of topical files for the years 1941-1947 maintained by H. Freeman Matthews and John D. Hickerson, directors of the Office of European Affairs. These files represent only the residue of a much larger set of files, most of which was integrated into the central file.

The volume of Lot Files increased enormously with World War II and the growing work load of the department. Lot Files have been utilized extensively recently in the compilation of the *Foreign Relations* series and in the years to come will be essential in researching certain topics. A few of the most valuable files of this type include the records maintained by the Secretariat, the files of the Policy Planning Staff, the files maintained on Atomic Energy and Disarmament, the National Security Council files, and special politico-military collections. Many of these files have already been transferred to the National Archives while others remain in the custody of the Department of State. Unfortunately, there is no published list of these files or their location. Both the Diplomatic Branch of the National Archives and the Office of the Historian of the Department of State maintain special in-house lists of these files, their locations, and the amount of material involved.[9]

A valuable aid in using the Lot Files as well as the central files of the department is and will continue to be the published *Foreign Relations* series. The Office of the Historian, which compiles the series, is determined to approach a twenty-year line for publication—that is, the publication of selected documentation approximately twenty years after the origination of the material. The series now faces a time lag of twenty-seven to twenty-eight years. In order to reduce this time gap the Office of the Historian has revised the series into triennial sets beginning with the year 1952. Henceforth, documents on a given subject will be published in volumes covering three years rather than one year. The compilers hope in this way to achieve a twenty-year line in compilation by the end of 1983. With the tremendous increase in the volume of Department of State documents during the postwar years and the need to extend the coverage of the series well beyond department documents in order to present a thorough picture of United States foreign policy, the Office of the Historian is proposing to supplement the published volumes with a microfilm addition, thus increasing the total number of documents available to researchers.[10] Hopefully, the series will not simply concentrate on the classical relations between states but will provide coverage of cultural, ideological, and socioeconomic problems as well. By printing the file designation or the source of the documents, in the case of department records the decimal number or Lot File number, the series acts as a valuable index to the records and expedites a researcher's quest for pertinent information.

Other Agency Records

Scholars interested in international relations are faced not only with a vast amount of material generated by the Department of State but must delve into an array of other agency records as well. While Department of State records continue to provide a wealth of material concerning events and occurrences in foreign nations, the researcher examining United States policy and its origins must not ignore the input of other agencies on the decision-making process. With the emergence of the Central Intelligence Agency, the Department of Defense, and the National Security Council since World War II, the decision-making process has become far more complex and the relative importance of the Department of State has declined. There is now an integrated interplay of political, military, economic, and intelligence considerations.[11] Thus the diplomatic historian must deal not only with Department of State materials but with vast quantities of military, intelligence, and presidential data as well. This has not proven to be an easy task. The Central Intelligence Agency has not as yet turned over any of its major files to the National Archives and its own archives are virtually closed to the public. Only some Office of Strategic Services material, CIA's predecessor, has been accessioned by the National Archives, although the agency has declared its intent to make its numbered policy papers available in the near future.[12]

The National Security Council maintains that its internal working memoranda are not record material and retains all of the minutes of its meetings. Recently, however, sanitized copies of some of its summary minutes have been declassified under Freedom of Information requests and the council has agreed to send the National Archives a list of all its declassified documents.

The council keeps a file of its own staff papers, known as institutional files. Those no longer needed for current use are transferred for storage at the Central Intelligence Agency. As of this writing the National Archives has accessioned no records of the National Security Council. The National Security Council also maintains presidential files. They include copies of all policy papers of the National Security Council in addition to files kept for the president. By custom, these files have been retained by a president for deposit in a presidential library.

The Department of Defense has been more liberal in opening its records, despite some major problems. Unlike the Department of State records which are maintained in a central filing system, military records since World War II are divided into various office, division, and bureau files. Many of these offices continued to use the War Department Central Decimal File System, however, through the 1960s. This system is similar in many respects to the Department of State classification system. It is subject-oriented with the numbering and arranging of subjects based upon the Dewey Decimal System of library classification. Surprisingly, the key subject files for international relations research are under class 300, Administration. This class covers all matters pertaining to war and peace.[13]

Of major interest to historians studying national security affairs are the records of the Office of the Secretary of Defense, the Joint Chiefs of Staff, and the International Security Affairs Office. Currently, the records of the Office of the Secretary of Defense are accessioned into the National Archives through 1954 and are available for research through 1949.

While the Joint Chiefs of Staff files are presently open through 1957, the Joint Chiefs maintain that no formal or informal minutes of their meetings were kept after World War II. Thus, no records pertaining to these meetings are available. It is a serious drawback to research on the decision-making process. The Joint Chiefs have, however, recently begun to declassify their general national security studies which were originally prepared as briefings. They have released four volumes to date: 1945-1947, 1947-1949, the Korean War, and 1950-1952. These studies relate to all facets of national security policy including such topics as Berlin, NATO, China, and Soviet development of the atomic bomb. They are an excellent starting place for research into the period from the military perspective.[14]

The records of the International Security Affairs Office, although a key office in the formulation of national defense policies, are not available for research. Similarly, the National Security Agency, which deals with cryptography and is becoming increasingly important in this scientific age, has released very little information. The National Security Agency only recently declassified materials relating to operation "Magic" and Pearl Harbor and has provided no information on its current activities. Hopefully, in the near future we will see a loosening of restrictions from these relatively new national security agencies, but for now the scholar working in this period is faced with numerous barriers.

Presidential Libraries

Increasingly, scholars of contemporary history have made use of the presidential library system for source materials. These libraries, eight at present—Herbert Hoover, Franklin D. Roosevelt, Harry S. Truman, Dwight D. Eisenhower, John F. Kennedy, Lyndon B. Johnson, Richard M. Nixon, and Gerald R. Ford—offer the scholar a unique blend of public records and private papers. Not only are the files of the president and his commissions, committees, councils, and staff available, but many of the papers of his aides and administrative officials are deposited there as well.

As scholars begin to do in-depth research on such topics as the wars in Korea and Indochina, the crisis in the Middle East, the turmoil in Latin America, the U-2 incident and Russian-American relations, and countless other controversial subjects during the 1950s and 1960s, the papers in presidential libraries loom increasingly important.

How does one begin to use the materials found in a presidential library? Each library from Hoover to Johnson now has published a list of its holdings. These finding aids provide a list of all the collections in the library, a brief description of their content, and the number of linear feet each contains.[15] The best suggestion for beginning research, however, is to write the libraries directly concerning more detailed descriptions of their collections. While the library collections vary greatly in content and accessibility, the earlier presidential libraries have far more of their collections open for research than the collections at libraries of later administrations. This is simply a factor of time and declassification procedures. At the Truman Library scholars interested in foreign policy have found the President's Secretary's File and the papers of Dean Acheson particularly helpful.[16] At the Eisenhower Library the Ann Whitman File and the papers and diaries of John Foster Dulles, Christian A. Herter, and James C. Hagerty have been conducive to the study of foreign affairs.[17] In general, when combined with the presidential National Security Council files at these libraries, these records provide a remarkably detailed record of the formulation of United States policy at the presidential level for the 1940s.

Beginning with the Kennedy administration, presidents made extensive use of the White House Central Files for nonclassified correspondence and memoranda and maintained their records in basically the same filing system. It consisted of a Subject File, a Name File, and a Chronological File. A separate Confidential File was maintained for security-classified or otherwise sensitive materials.[18] It was arranged in the same manner as the Central Files. President Johnson made a particular effort to have all his correspondence and staff papers channeled through the White House Central Files system so the files at the Johnson Library are fairly complete.[19] The Central Files, of course, need to be supplemented by other important collections. In the Kennedy Library the President's Office Files, which were the working files maintained by Kennedy's secretary, Evelyn Lincoln, and the National Security Files, which were the working files of the Special Assistant to the President for National Security Affairs, McGeorge Bundy, are major sources.

The national security staff under Bundy was a markedly different operation from that under Robert Cutler and James Lay during the Eisenhower administration. The previously sharp distinction between planning and staff personnel and functions was deliberately blurred to gain integration of purpose. The National Security Council itself came to be regarded as a more specialized forum for the discussion of critical issues rather than a routine meeting for ratifying decisions. This change has been carried forward until today the National Security Council is perhaps the most important foreign policy decision-making body.[20]

Administrations following Kennedy's have maintained the filing system instituted for NSC material. In the Johnson Library the National Security Files were the working files of President Johnson and his two successive Special Assistants for National Security Affairs, McGeorge Bundy and Walt W. Rostow. The National Security Council also undertook narratives and documentary histories of crises and incidents during the Johnson administration. These range from a twenty-one-volume work on the Pueblo crisis of 1968 to a three-volume work on the Gulf of Tonkin attack to a one-volume work on the Congo C-130 crisis of July 1967.[21] There are also tapes of most of Johnson's telephone calls and some transcripts of these calls. However, there is a fifty-year restriction on this material and it is unavailable for research.[22]

In the Nixon Library, the President's Office Files, which are summaries of all types of meetings held in the Oval Office, the President's Personal File maintained by Rosemary Woods, and the Special Files which contain all sensitive materials collected by the president's top aides such as H. R. Haldeman, John Ehrlichman, John Dean, and Henry Kissinger are important. However, the hundreds of reels of White House tapes made in the Oval Office, the Cabinet Room, and at Camp David may prove to be the most valuable material yet for studying foreign policy decision-making on the presidential level. For example, discussions between Nixon and Henry Kissinger in his capacity as National Security Adviser and later as Secretary of State are frequently recorded. Unfortunately, the poor quality of the recordings makes it difficult to transcribe the material, so there may be considerable delay before this information is available.[23]

The Presidential Records Act of 1978 will have an important impact on scholars seeking access to presidential documents. The act provides that presidential records created on or after 20 January 1981 are to be owned and controlled by the United States government. Presidential records will include all documentary materials of the president and his staff relating to his duties but will exclude materials relating solely to his private political associations or to purely personal matters.

The Archivist of the United States will take custody of presidential records when the president leaves office. He will make the records available to the public and place them in a presidential library or other federal depository. However, the president may restrict access to certain categories of records for as long as twelve years after he leaves office.[24]

In addition to the presidential files and records of the administrative staff, each of the presidential libraries has solicited the private papers and manuscript collections of public figures who were prominent during the period.[25] These papers present special problems for researchers. They are not subject to the Freedom of Information Act and are donated to the presidential library system by a deed of gift. This deed outlines donor restriction guidelines which close or restrict material relating to proposed appointments to office, personnel matters, confidential business affairs, and information or statements that might be used to embarrass, damage, injure, or harass any living person. The libraries contend that such restrictions increase the chances for receiving collections intact and that without such restrictions, a "chilling effect" on the creation of papers by public officials would be more likely.[26] Donor restrictions also apply to most presidential papers now deposited in libraries, though the Presidential Records Act will alter this situation in the future.

Congressional Materials

In addition to materials in presidential libraries, the scholar interested in contemporary international affairs must search other manuscript collections and sources. Most scholars are familiar with the *National Union Catalog of Manuscript Collections*, which guides them to the location of the papers of various individuals. Many scholars, however, are unaware that the United States Senate Historical Office is another important source for tracking down manuscript collections. The Senate Historical Office is now in the process of providing a comprehensive catalog of locations of all former senators' papers. In addition, the Historical Office is editing the Executive Sessions of the Senate Foreign Relations Committee. After 1947 the Senate required transcripts for all closed-door committee hearings. Prior to 1947 a transcript of such meetings was not always made. The series presently runs through 1957 and is chronological in its approach. There are also several subject volumes. They range from the *Legislative Origins of the Truman Doctrine* to *Economic Assistance to China and Korea.*[27]

Selected executive session hearings of the House Committee on International Relations have also been published. But the House has no historical office and no systematic program for publishing these hearings.[28] The records of the hearings themselves from both the House and the Senate are at the National Archives, but legal title remains vested in the House and Senate. Senate committee records may not be used except by permission of the committee or its chairman and House of Representative records cannot be seen without an order of the Clerk of the House. Persons interested in using these records should consult the National Archives or the Senate Historical Office.[29]

Freedom of Information Act

It is not just the volume of records the scholar of contemporary foreign relations must contend with but the whole question of access as well. Once the scholar has identified records which might be of interest, he must attempt to actually see them. This is often a difficult task. Fortunately, in dealing with federal records the researcher has a fairly effective tool to help pry open some of this material—the Freedom of Information Act. First passed in 1966, it was strengthened significantly in the disclosure-conscious Watergate year of 1974.[30] There are a number of important features of the act of which scholars should be aware. First, the act applies only to the records of agencies of the executive branch of the government. The records of Congress and its committees and of the courts are not covered by the act. Likewise, the papers and records of the president and his immediate White House staff, traditionally considered the president's property, were excluded from the act. However, the Presidential Records Act of 1978 permits access to records of presidents from 1981 onward. Five years after the president leaves office, the Freedom of Information Act will apply to those records not subject to restrictions specified by the president. The FOIA will apply to the remaining records after the presidentially imposed restrictions have expired. Presidential records prior to 1981 remain outside the reach of the act.[31] Second, the act establishes several exemption categories including security-classified materials, personnel rules and practices, trade secrets, medical files, and investigatory records. More importantly, however, the act assumes that records are to be made available in compliance with the current trend of openness in government; this means that the burden of proving that a document should be withheld is on the government. The act also requires that "any reasonably segregable portion of a record" must be released. This means, for example, if a document has a paragraph that, in the judgment of the agency, must remain closed, the agency must nevertheless provide a copy of the document to the requester with the restricted paragraph excised. The process is called "sanitization" and the agency must tell the requester that a portion of the document has been deleted and the reason for the deletion. A third feature of the act is that it allows "any person" to make a request. A researcher need not be an American citizen. All one must do is be able to reasonably describe the records desired. Finally, the act assists the researcher by setting time limits within which the agency must respond to a request. An agency must respond within ten working days to an initial request; if the request is denied in whole or in part, the agency must provide the name of the agency official to whom appeals should be addressed, and the agency must respond to an appeal within twenty working days.[32]

The procedure for filing an FOIA request is quite simple. The researcher should describe the records sought as fully as possible, label the letter and the envelope "FOIA Request," and mail it to the agency responsible for the records. The researcher should note in the letter that he should be informed in advance of any search fees involved since a number of agencies charge for record searches.[33]

This seems at first glance to be a simple process. However, it presents certain problems, especially for the researcher or graduate student who is working under a strict time limitation. At either the initial or the appeal level an agency can extend the deadline for responding to a request because "records must be collected from various geographical locations, a voluminous amount of separate and distinct records are involved, or there is a need to consult with other agencies before making a final determination on access." This clause has resulted in long delays in gaining access to material. Some requests for Central Intelligence Agency or National Security Council documents, for example, have languished in those agencies for over two years before any final action was taken.[34]

Freedom of Information requests also bring to the forefront the entire question of "privileged access." When a request is granted, let us say, for Department of Defense documents in the 1960s concerning the sending of troops to the Dominican Republic, other scholars have no way of knowing which material has been released without repeating the same FOI procedures. There is no agency-wide "clearinghouse" or master list of declassified material. The researcher is forced to turn to the private Carrolton Press reference system for declassified documents information. While this is a useful service, it is incomplete.[35] There is no systematic approach to the problem. What is needed is a master list to coordinate the opening of documents from the various agencies. One further example will illuminate this problem. There is no coordination between presidential libraries and the National Archives as to what has been declassified and opened to the public. A researcher may find a National Security Council document withdrawn from the Department of the Army files in the National Archives only to discover the same document available at the Truman Library.

Nevertheless, the Freedom of Information Act is an important tool for researchers seeking to obtain documents. While historians have used the FOIA successfully on many occasions, they have been reluctant to pursue denials. In the National Archives, for instance, only ten percent of initial denials were appealed in 1978. Thirty-five percent of those who appealed the initial decision, however, received additional portions of the records. It is worth the effort.[36]

Executive Order 12065

Closely related to the FOIA is President Jimmy Carter's Executive Order 12065 of 29 June 1978. While the order is, in general, intended to increase openness in government by limiting classification and accelerating declassification of records, it could have some far-reaching and rather adverse effects on scholars working in the international relations field. Attempting to balance the public's interest in access to information with the need to protect certain national security information from disclosure, the order provides, with few exceptions, that documents be declassified after no more than twenty years. This appears to be a major breakthrough for historians studying contemporary American affairs, and in many areas it will be. However, the order also provides that foreign government information "shall be exempt from automatic declassification and twenty-year systematic review." Only after thirty years will such information be subject to review.[37] The Information Security Oversight Office (ISOO) directive which clarified the executive order defined foreign government information quite broadly as any information presented to the United States with "the expectation expressed or implied" that it be kept in confidence automatically.[38] By the addition of the word "implied" (not in the Executive Order 12065 definition) the ISOO extended the definition of foreign government information to almost any information received in a foreign country or from a foreign official in the United States. The key issue here will be how reviewers interpret the documents. If they interpret this clause broadly, which the ISOO seems to imply, the executive order will have the effect of closing most foreign affairs materials for thirty years or more instead of opening more records sooner.[39]

Department of State guidelines for implementing the executive order are also vague. They call for the continued restriction of information which, if disclosed, could be expected to "cause identifiable damage to current United States policy interest."[40] What this means is uncertain. Will all information about contingency plans, base negotiations, plans for covert political or military operations and United States positions on border disputes and unresolved territorial issues remain classified? Hopefully, the Department of State as well as other agencies will adopt a liberal approach to their declassification review programs, but there are no guarantees.[41]

Mandatory Review

Unfortunately, the Freedom of Information Act does not apply to presidential materials, at least for the records created prior to 1981. The researcher has an alternative means of seeking access to these files, however, with the use of mandatory review. Mandatory review procedures are spelled out in Executive Order 12065.[42] Under these guidelines a researcher may request a review of classified materials that are at least ten years old from any agency. Mandatory review differs from FOI in that it applies only to classified information. The time span allowed for a response from an agency is also greater—sixty days. Mandatory review does have one distinct advantage over FOI. Since it applies solely to classified materials, an agency may be forced to release a document under mandatory review it might otherwise restrict under FOI.[43]

The Freedom of Information Act, the new executive order, and mandatory review have undeniably enlarged the scope of access and accountability of the federal government. The once radical idea of allowing access to documents of every kind is now widely accepted. A recent Harris poll found eighty-five percent in favor of people having the right to see their government's records. Because of the Freedom of Information Act it is possible, for example, to test the record of Henry Kissinger in the light of documents that might otherwise be sealed for a generation or two.[44] This is a procedure that other countries are only beginning to consider. Great Britain's Official Secrets Act effectively shields the government bureaucracy from close and timely scrutiny. The records of other nations are not as available as the records of the United States government and this in itself presents difficulties for anyone attempting to deal with international relations. Hopefully, the trend toward openness in government will continue during the coming decades not only in the United States but in other nations as well.[45] Despite the problems, diplomatic historians interested in contemporary international affairs and policy decisions should have a vast array of sources available to them in the next two decades and the tools for using them efficiently and effectively.

Notes

1. U.S., Department of State, *Department of State Classification Manual*, 4th ed. (Washington, D.C.: Government Printing Office, 1939). The manual is also available as National Archives Microfilm Publication M600.

2. The asterisks represent the location of the country designation.

3. U.S., Department of State, Division of Communication, *Records Codification Manual* (Washington, D.C.: Government Printing Office, 1950).

4. U.S., Department of State, *Records Classification Handbook* (Washington, D.C.: Government Printing Office, 1963).

5. Milton O. Gustafson, "Archival Implications of State Department Recordkeeping," *Prologue* 5 (Spring 1975): 36-38.

6. U.S., Department of State, Bureau of Indexes and Archives, *Classification of Correspondence* (Washington, D.C.: Government Printing Office, 1912).

7. U.S., Department of State, *Foreign Service Handbook, Records Classification* (Washington, D.C.: Government Printing Office, 1948).

8. Ibid.

9. "Internal finding aid for Lot Files," Diplomatic Branch, National Archives, Washington, D.C. *See also* Department of State List, "Lot Files in the National Archives and Department of State," National Archives, Washington, D.C.

10. David Trask and William Slany, "What Lies Ahead for the Foreign Relations Series?" *Society for Historians of American Foreign Relations Newsletter* 9 (March 1978): 26-29.

11. Interview with David Trask, Office of the Historian, Department of State, 1 August 1979. *See also* the remarks of William Slany, lecture delivered at the National Archives, 26 June 1979.

12. Interview with Edwin Alan Thompson, Director, Declassification Division, National Archives, 26 July 1979.

13. The basic outline of the War Department Decimal File System is:

CLASS	SUBJECT
000	General
100	Finance and accounting
200	Personnel
300	Administration
400	Supplies, services, and equipment
500	Transportation
600	Buildings and grounds
700	Medicine, hygiene, and sanitation
800	Rivers, harbors, waterways

See U.S., Department of War, Adjutant General of the Army, *War Department Decimal File System*, rev. ed. (Washington, D.C.: Government Printing Office, 1943).

14. Interview with William Cunliffe, Assistant Branch Chief, Modern Military Records, National Archives, 18 July 1979. The series is entitled *The History of the Joint Chiefs of Staff: The Joint Chiefs of Staff and National Policy.* It is available on microfilm from the Modern Military Branch of the National Archives.

15. *Historical Materials in the Herbert Hoover Presidential Library* (General Services Administration, 1977) (hereafter cited as GSA); *Historical Materials in the Franklin D. Roosevelt Library* (GSA, 1977); *Historical Materials in the Harry S. Truman Library* (GSA, 1979); *Historical Materials in the Dwight D. Eisenhower Library* (GSA, 1977); *Historical Materials in the John F. Kennedy Library* (GSA, 1978); and *Historical Materials in the Lyndon B. Johnson Library* (GSA, 1979).

16. Neal Peterson, Office of the Historian, Department of State, lecture delivered at the National Archives, 20 February 1979.

17. Ibid. See also David Haight, "The Dwight D. Eisenhower Library as a Research Center for the Study of International Affairs: Opportunities and Projects," *Society for Historians of American Foreign Relations Newsletter* 10 (June 1979): 11-20.

18. "National Security Files: A Register of the Working Files of the Special Assistant for National Security Affairs 1961-1963," (finding aid), 18 July 1979, John Fitzgerald Kennedy Library, Boston, Mass.

19. Interview with Sharon Fawcett, former staff archivist, Lyndon Baines Johnson Library, Austin, Tex., 18 July 1979.

20. "National Security Files," JFK Library.

21. "List of National Security Studies," *Historical Materials in the Johnson Library*, p. 6.

22. Interview with Sharon Fawcett, 18 July 1979.

23. Interview with Joan Howard and David Van Tassel, staff, Richard Milhous Nixon Library, Washington, D.C., 17 July 1979.

24. Presidential Records Act of 1978, PL 95-591, 19 January 1978.

25. The Nixon Library because of the legal questions still pending has not as yet solicited any private collections.

26. *See* Alonzo L. Hamby and Edward Weldon, eds., *Access to the Papers of Recent Public Figures: The New Harmony Conference* (Bloomington, Ind.: Organization of American Historians, 1977).

27. Interview with Donald A. Ritchie, Associate Historian, U.S. Senate Historical Office, 23 July 1979.

28. Ibid.

29. Interview with David R. Kepley, staff, Natural Resources and Legislative Branch, National Archives, 10 August 1979. *See also* Richard A. Baker, ed., *Conference on the Research Use and Disposition of Senators' Papers, Proceedings, Washington, D.C., September 14-15, 1978* (Washington, D.C.: U.S. Senate, 1979).

30. Freedom of Information Act, PL 89-487, 4 July 1966, 80 *United States Statutes at Large*: 250-51. *See also* PL 93-502, 21 November 1974, 88 *United States Statutes at Large*: 1561-64.

31. Presidential Records Act, PL 95-591.

32. Interview with Trudy Peterson, Chief, Natural Resources and Legislative Branch, National Archives, 11 July 1979. *See also* Trudy Peterson, "Archives, Access and the Federal Freedom of Information Act," *Law Library Journal* 72 (Fall 1979): 659-62.

33. Sample request letter:

(Name and address of government agency
Washington, D.C.)

Dear Sir or Madam:

Pursuant to the Freedom of Information Act, 5 U.S.C. 552, I hereby request access to (or a copy of) [describe the documents containing the information that you want in as great detail as possible].

If this request is denied either in whole or in part, please inform me as to your agency's appeal procedures. If any expenses in excess of $________ are incurred in connection with this request, please inform me of all such charges prior to their being incurred for my approval. If you do not grant my request within ten working days, I will deem my request denied.

Thank you for your prompt attention to this matter.

Sincerely,

34. Interview with Trudy Peterson, 11 July 1979; interview with James E. O'Neill, Deputy Archivist of the United States, 2 August 1979.

35. Annadel Wile, ed., *Declassified Documents Reference System* (Washington, D.C.: Carrolton Press, 1974-).

36. Interview with Trudy Peterson, 11 July 1979.

37. Executive Order 12065, *Federal Register* (3 July 1978): 28949-63.

38. ISOO Directive #1, *Federal Register* (5 October 1978): 46280-85.

39. Interview with Milton O. Gustafson, Chief, Diplomatic Branch, National Archives, 12 July 1979.

40. U.S., Department of State, *Department of State Guidelines for Systematic Review of Department of State Records Under EO 12065*, 8 July 1979.

41. Interview with Milton O. Gustafson, 12 July 1979, and interview with David F. Trask, 1 August 1979.

42. *Federal Code of Regulations*, Title 3, The President, pp. 28956-57.

43. Interview with Judy Koucky, Mandatory Review Office, National Archives, 1 August 1979.

44. Editorial, *New York Times*, 29 June 1979, p. A26.

45. For a listing of the policies and practices in most countries of the world concerning access to unpublished diplomatic papers, *see* Arthur G. Kogan, *Public Availability of Diplomatic Archives* (Washington, D.C.: Department of State, Historical Office, Bureau of Public Affairs, 1976).

About the Contributors

ERNEST C. BOLT, JR., is professor of history at the University of Richmond. He received his Ph.D. from the University of Georgia, where he studied with J. Chal Vinson. He is the author of *Ballots before Bullets: The War Referendum Approach to Peace in America, 1914-1941* (University Press of Virginia, 1977) and is presently preparing a biography of Louis Ludlow.

PAOLO E. COLETTA, professor of history at the United States Naval Academy, received his Ph.D. from the University of Missouri, where he studied with Charles F. Mullett. He has written extensively on the Progressive era and on United States naval history. His books include a three-volume biography of William Jennings Bryan (University of Nebraska Press, 1964-1969) and *The Presidency of William Howard Taft* (University Press of Kansas, 1973). Dr. Coletta is currently researching a biography of Cyrus Vance.

HUGH DE SANTIS received his Ph.D. from the University of Chicago, where he studied with Akira Iriye. He is the author of *The Diplomacy of Silence: The American Foreign Service, the Soviet Union, and the Cold War, 1933-1946* (University of Chicago Press, 1980) and articles in the *Political Science Quarterly, Chicago History*, and the *Journal of American Culture*. He is the research analyst for the regional political and security affairs of Western Europe at the Department of State.

JONATHAN R. DULL received his Ph.D. from the University of California, Berkeley, where he studied with Gerald Cavanaugh. His book, *The French Navy and American Independence: A Study of Arms and Diplomacy, 1774-1787* (Princeton University Press, 1975), was corecipient of the Gilbert Chinard prize for 1976. He has published several articles on eighteenth-century diplomatic and military history and is presently writing a collection of essays on Benjamin Franklin as a diplomat. Dr. Dull is assistant editor of the Papers of Benjamin Franklin at Yale University.

GERALD K. HAINES is an archivist in the Diplomatic Branch of the National Archives. He received his Ph.D. from the University of Wisconsin, Madison, where he studied with John A. DeNovo. He has written articles for *Diplomatic History, Prologue*, the *Australian Journal of Politics and History*, and the *Society for Historians of American Foreign Relations Newsletter*. Dr. Haines is currently working on a comparative study of United States and Japanese regionalism and on a reference guide to Department of State Lot Files for Greenwood Press.

RONALD L. HATZENBUEHLER is associate professor and former chairman of the Department of History at Idaho State University. A student of Lawrence S. Kaplan, he received his Ph.D. from Kent State University. His articles have appeared in the *Pacific Historical Review*, the *William and Mary Quarterly*, and *Rendezvous*. He is currently working on a study of war justification.

EDITH JAMES is director of the Motion Picture Archives, Defense Audio-visual Agency, Department of Defense. She was formerly assistant editor of the Papers of Woodrow Wilson at Princeton University. She received her Ph.D. from the University of Maryland, where she studied with Winthrop R. Wright. She has published several articles on Edith Bolling Wilson, on the history of Princeton University, and on archival administration.

LESTER D. LANGLEY received his Ph.D. from the University of Kansas and has taught at the University of Georgia since 1970. He has published widely on nineteenth-century American diplomacy and on United States relations with Latin America. His books include *The Cuban Policy of the United States: A Brief History* (John Wiley & Sons, 1968), *Struggle for the American Mediterranean: United States-European Rivalry in the Gulf-Caribbean, 1776-1904* (University of Georgia Press, 1975), and *The United States and the Caribbean, 1900-1970* (University of Georgia Press, 1980). Dr. Langley is presently working on a study of Andrew Jackson's diplomacy.

ROBERT J. McMAHON is a historian in the Department of State, Office of the Historian. He received his Ph.D. from the University of Connecticut, where he studied with Thomas G. Paterson. He has written articles for *Diplomatic History* and the *Proceedings of the Citadel Conference on War and Diplomacy*. He is currently revising his dissertation, "The United States and Decolonization in Southeast Asia: The Case of Indonesia, 1945-1949," for publication by Cornell University Press.

ANNA KASTEN NELSON is adjunct associate professor of history at George Washington University. She received her Ph.D. from George Washington University, where she studied with Howard Merriman. She has edited *The Records of Federal Officials* (Garland Publishing Co., 1978) and published several articles on the Mexican War, government historical offices, and foreign policy records.

THOMAS J. NOER is associate professor of history at Carthage College, Kenosha, Wisconsin. He received his Ph.D. from the University of Minnesota, where he studied with Kinley Brauer. His publications include *Briton, Boer, and Yankee: The United States and South Africa, 1870-1914* (Kent State University Press, 1978) and articles in the *South Atlantic Quarterly, American Neptune, Phylon*, and the *Journal of Ethnic Studies*. Dr. Noer is presently researching a book on "The United States and 'White' Africa, 1948-1968."

RICHARD V. SALISBURY is associate professor of history at Western Kentucky University. He received his Ph.D. from the University of Kansas, where he studied with Charles L. Stansifer. He has published articles on Latin American affairs in a variety of journals, including the *Hispanic-American Historical Review*, the *Journal of Inter-American Studies and World Affairs*, and *Prologue*. He is currently working on a study of the anti-imperialist movement in Latin America in the early twentieth century.

MARK A. STOLER is associate professor of history at the University of Vermont. He received his Ph.D. from the University of Wisconsin, Madison, where he studied with John A. DeNovo. He is the author of *The Politics of the Second Front: American Military Planning and Diplomacy in Coalition Warfare, 1941-1943* (Greenwood Press, 1977) and several articles on recent diplomatic and military history and on teaching methods. Among his current projects is a study of George D. Aiken and American foreign policy.

ROGER R. TRASK is deputy historian of the Historical Office, Office of the Secretary, Department of Defense. A student of John A. DeNovo, he received his Ph.D. from Pennsylvania State University. His publications include *The United States Response to Turkish Nationalism and Reform, 1914-1939* (University of Minnesota Press, 1971) and articles in *Business History Review*, *Mid-America*, *Muslim World*, the *Historian*, and *Diplomatic History*. He is currently preparing a survey of United States relations with Latin America.

J. SAMUEL WALKER is associate historian of the United States Nuclear Regulatory Commission. He received his Ph.D. from the University of Maryland, where he studied with Wayne S. Cole. He is the author of *Henry A. Wallace and American Foreign Policy* (Greenwood Press, 1976) and has written articles for *Agricultural History*, the *History Teacher*, the *New Mexico Historical Review*, and *American Heritage*.

Author Index